D1583175

003084

For the world of tomorrow

The question of which came first, the chicken or the egg, has now been answered by the study of evolution. The egg came first, for birds are the descendant of egg-laying scaly reptiles.

The question of which will succumb first, the bird or its egg, remains open. Will the Oystercatcher die from the effects of oil pollution before or after its eggs have been finally sterilized by poisonous chemicals tipped into the oceans?

In the course of their evolution, birds have developed strategies to protect their eggs from predators and extremes of weather. They have no strategy that can protect them against DDT.

'If you can't beat them, join them' is an old maxim which applies to birds just as it does to man himself. For those birds flexible enough, survival may depend on an ability to adapt to man and his ways.

The Collared Dove takes shelter under our eaves and feeds in our gardens. Its advantage over many other birds is its willingness to adapt to our artificial landscapes and our concrete jungles.

Is it possible that man is now becoming a causative factor in the evolutionary process – forcing more adaptable species to change, just as the great Ice Ages did thousands of years ago?

Can there ever be beauty in death? The sad beauty of this wild goose belies its terrible fate — its body twisted into the pose of the 'dying swan' by the effects of lead poisoning.

In the face of such an image it is vital that we should not simply accept these things as inevitable but that we should mobilize our energies in defence of the living.

If we can manage to shorten the 'Rec Lists' of species in danger, then there will be hope for the future – for us, as well as for the wild creatures with which we share this planet.

Foreword

Nature should be a source of endless delight. Some of us have the great good fortune to be actively involved as professional conservationists. For others, a wealth of books, television programmes and films provides a magic carpet from which to enjoy the spectacular variety of the world's wildlife. Within this realm, birds are the object of a special wonder. From the bizarre species of remote islands and jungles to the familiar birds of our hedgerows and gardens, they all belong to a natural world that enriches our lives in countless ways.

But can their survival be taken for granted? Literally hundreds of species are in serious danger of extinction. Each one is unique; the product of millions of years of evolution. But today, as many as one in ten of the world's birds could be under sentence of death. We are their executioners, sometimes with gun and trap, but mostly by our destruction of their habitats and degradation of the environment. We possess the power and the knowledge to halt the accelerating rate of extinctions. We must do so. We cannot bring back what is already gone; that is a loss that will impoverish the lives of our children and all future generations.

When we were invited to take part in the SAVE THE BIRDS campaign, we accepted gladly. SAVE THE BIRDS is an exciting book that pulls no punches. It is beautiful, but its message is tough and uncompromising. We need to save the birds if, in the end, we are to save ourselves.

Too often we allow ourselves to believe that because a problem is large there is nothing we, as individuals, can do about it. Nothing could be further from the truth. The SAVE THE BIRDS campaign is based on the premise, 'Think globally – act locally'. It is a challenge we accept wholeheartedly, and one in which we invite you to join us.

Sir David Attenborough CBE, FRS

Ian Prestt CBE

Save the Birds

Anthony W. Diamond
Rudolf L. Schreiber
David Attenborough
Ian Prestt

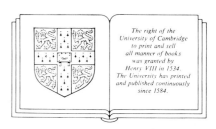

The right of the
University of Cambridge
to print and sell
all manner of books
was granted by
Henry VIII in 1534.
The University has printed
and published continuously
since 1584.

A PRO NATUR book
Published by Cambridge University Press

CAMBRIDGE   LONDON   NEW YORK
NEW ROCHELLE   MELBOURNE   SYDNEY

The project team

With the publication of this book, the International Council for Bird Preservation is launching a major worldwide campaign:

Save the Birds

The SAVE THE BIRDS project was conceived by PRO NATUR GmbH, Geleitsstrasse 14, D-6000 Frankfurt/Main, West Germany, and was implemented in close association with ICBP, 219c Huntingdon Road, Cambridge CB3 0DL.

From every book sold, a contribution will be made to ICBP's SAVE THE BIRDS account, to finance international projects for the conservation of threatened habitats and the preservation of endangered species.

Initiator and creative director	Rudolf L. Schreiber
Principal author	Anthony W. Diamond
Authors: Saving Britain's Birdlife	David Attenborough, Ian Prestt
Chief scientific consultant	Christoph Imboden, ICBP
Editor and project manager	Martyn J. Bramwell
Project assistants	Nikolaus Dahl, Helga Schaer, Elly Schierbeek, Mary Pennell
Scientific advisers	Nigel Collar, Timothy Dee, Jane Fenton, Paul Goriup, Chris Harbard, Nick Smart, Thomas Urquhart
Design director	Gerd A. Müller
Designers	Stefan Werner, Ben White
Photographic acquisitions	Michael Alexander, Doris Paulini/GEO, Helga Schaer/PRO NATUR
Bird portraits	Alistair Robertson, Robert Gillmor
Technical illustrations	Trevor Boyer, Mick Loates, Maurice Pledger, John Rignall, Mike Saunders
Cartography	Eugene Fleury
Typesetting	Paston Press, Loddon, Norfolk
Proof reading	Fred Gill
Production	Mohndruck Graphische Betriebe GmbH, Gütersloh, West Germany

PRO NATUR GmbH
Geleitsstrasse 14
D-6000 Frankfurt/
Main 70
West Germany

ICBP
International Council for
Bird Preservation
219c Huntingdon Road
Cambridge CB3 0DL
England

First published in Great Britain and Australia in 1987 by the Press Syndicate of the University of Cambridge, The Pitt Building, Trumpington Street, Cambridge CB2 1RP, and at 10 Stamford Road, Oakleigh, Melbourne 3166.

World maps throughout are based on the Peters projection by kind permission of the originator Dr Arno Peters, and of the copyright holders Kümmerly + Frey AG, Berne, Switzerland.

British Library Cataloguing in Publication Data

Save the birds. — (A Pro Natur book).
1. Birds, Protection of
I. Diamond, Anthony W. II. Series
639.9'78   QL676.5

ISBN 0 521 34367 4

This book is printed on 'Gardagloss' acid-free paper supplied by Cartiere del Garda, Riva, Italy.

© PRO NATUR GmbH 1987

Contents

For the World of Tomorrow

RUDOLF L. SCHREIBER

A world book about bird conservation should, by rights, begin with a world record. Miniature wonders like the feather of a sparrow no longer amaze us, satiated as we are with sensational news of every kind.

The world record for long-distance bird migration is held by the Arctic Tern (*Sterna paradisaea*). This slender white bird, with its black cap and deeply forked tail, spends the greater part of its year on the wing, commuting between the Arctic and Antarctic regions in an annual round trip of almost 40,000 kilometres. It symbolizes perfectly the global scale of the conservation idea — and at the same time puts human endeavour into perspective. Every year we burn up vast quantities of fossil fuel — organic reserves that took millions of years to accumulate — simply to carry ourselves through the air in rigid aluminium containers. Admittedly, the dream of emulating the birds inspired us to invent marvels of technology, yet compared with the free flight of a bird our best efforts remain mere mechanical contraptions.

Birds fly naturally, and the air they need beneath their wings, and whose oxygen

Roads link our towns and cities and give us our freedom of movement, but their disruptive impact on the landscape has long been overlooked.

fuels these highly efficient flying machines, is the very air that we exploit and pollute with hardly a second thought. We burn huge quantities of kerosene and petrol to get from one side of the world to the other: but what are the consequences?

The estimated number of automobiles in the world today is about 500 million. If we assume that one-tenth of these are in use at any given time, then every second some 50 million engines are polluting the air with their exhaust fumes. Even this may not seem too frightening to some people, but it must be remembered that the biosphere — the thin, life-sustaining layer surrounding our planet — is of finite thickness. It is, quite literally, an 'enclosed space'. To continue pouring poisonous gases into the atmosphere at this rate is the global equivalent of driving a car into a garage, then finding that the door has slammed shut and locked — and that the vehicle's engine cannot be switched off.

The Arctic Tern is one of the world's most graceful and distinctive migrants — a bird whose range encompasses every major ocean and continent.

Breakfast in Paris; lunch in New York: *Concorde* makes it all possible. But the milk in the French coffee contains caesium from Chernobyl, and the fruit of the lunchtime fruit salad is contaminated with pesticides. There is no escape from these realities — not ever at twice the speed of sound.

This example may seem contrived, but how much time remains for us to realize the full impact of air pollution on the life of our planet? The knowledge we now have of the extent of atmospheric contamination and of the damage being done to the protective ozone layer high above the earth should be a cause for great concern, and should provoke in us a determination to fight this threat just as we would fight to escape from a fume-filled garage. The long-term effects of damage to the ozone layer are potentially disastrous since they will include ever-increasing levels of exposure to harmful radiation from the sun. We can foresee this calamity. We can research and describe it. Yet we do nothing. The idea of millions of people dying or being incapacitated by radiation effects seems so far-fetched that we simply dismiss the idea from our minds.

Let us then turn to something closer to everyday experience. We have all seen pictures of the blackened bodies of oiled sea-birds washed up on our shores. What exactly do they represent? Just a few dead birds? Nothing more? All those who recognize the warning lights in our environment – the acid lakes, polluted rivers, dying forests and spreading deserts – will see in these birds a token of the deadly threat that *Homo sapiens* now presents to all life on earth – including, in the long term, himself.

But we must be fair to ourselves. To most people the oily death of an Arctic Tern is totally insignificant. And is this attitude not, perhaps, quite justified when up to 40,000 children die every day from starvation and malnutrition? Are a few dead birds the price of progress? This indeed might be the opinion of those who still measure progress in

kilowatt-hours, dollars and yen, or the price of crude oil. Price has become the yardstick. We know the price of everything, but we appreciate the value of very few things. We must learn all over again that many things have no price, yet their value may still be beyond measure.

We know that tropical rainforests are irreplaceable regulators of our climate, and that these vast jungles harbour more genetic resources than most other habitats combined. But we also know the price that tropical hardwoods command. And that counts.

We know that the poorer countries of the world need simple, low-technology economies if they are to become self-sufficient. But we also know their value as export markets for agro-chemicals and 'high-tech' machinery. And that counts.

We know that every day 2.5 billion dollars are spent on armaments, and that money on that scale could ease many of the world's most pressing problems. But we also know the high profits to be made from this worldwide trade in fear and mistrust. And that counts.

A power station in Siberia. Electricity should help us make earth's wildernesses habitable, but such dreams will be doomed to fail if 'development' is not accompanied by far better environmental planning than we have shown to date.

Our forests are under enormous pressure – from air pollution in the northern hemisphere; from ruthless exploitation in the south. Scientists now forecast serious consequences – not least for world climates.

We have surrendered a large part of our common sense and moral sense to economists who would have us believe that by manipulating prices and commodities the world – or at least world markets – can be saved. But if we continue on our present course there will be very little left to save. To save ourselves we must begin by saving the Arctic Tern. And if we wish to eliminate the accumulation of DDT and other poisons from the fish on which the Arctic Tern feeds, we must start by weaning our agriculture away from the agro-chemicals on which it now depends so heavily.

About one million tonnes of pesticides and herbicides, 200 grams for every human being, are spread on the world's soils each year. These poisons are far more efficient than any farmer could hope for, or need. He expects them to protect his crops from insects, fungi and weeds, and of course they do; but they also kill many innocent and useful creatures at the same time. Birds living in cultivated areas are often the first and most obvious victims.

The old principle of medicine, that the remedy must never do more harm than the disease itself, has been perverted by modern agricultural practices. Many soils have been treated so heavily and frequently with nitrogen fertilizers that they have lost their natural ability to recover after intensive cropping. Such force feeding may be effective in the short term, but the fields will be left sterile and exhausted the moment that chemical fertilizers become too expensive to use. For as long as it can produce, a soil will be pushed to its limits. The inevitable result: more monocultures, greater use of chemicals, and increased wind and water erosion over large areas of the land.

The dilemma of an agricultural system geared solely to high profit has been recognized for some time. Economists know that nature, too, has its price, and that in the future a large proportion of national budgets will have to be spent on natural assets that used to be free. Water, the most fundamental of all natural resources, is today a costly commodity. As the water requirements of our towns and cities grow, more and more of that water will have to be purified and recycled; and the more our water reserves are contaminated by chemicals from agriculture and industry, the more costly the purification process will become. In many heavily populated areas the water supply has long since lost its capacity to purify and replenish itself naturally.

'The straight line is ungodly,' said the Viennese artist Friedensreich Hundertwasser, and indeed fields like these may well be an ecological hell. Unhindered by hedges and trees, wind and water will soon erode the soil, while the monoculture system itself can be sustained only by the constant application of agro-chemicals. The ecological and economic cost–benefit equation has broken down.

In the richer parts of the world we call our urban developments cities, conurbations and metropolitan areas – impressive names for vast areas of brick and concrete. In the poorer regions they are represented by sprawling slums and shanty towns. Both are equally sterile and unattractive to the majority of wild creatures. Among birds, only the most adaptable – the pigeons, sparrows, gulls and a few others – see any advantage or opportunity in them. But is a bird's point of view of any interest to us? What importance can a bird's reaction have when we consider the scale of the struggle for survival taking place all over the world today?

The value of a human life is clearly defined in most civilizations. The value of an animal's life is rarely even considered. But in our search for survival strategies in the future we will have to balance our worship for one and our disregard for the other. Conservationists and political leaders alike will have to realize that there can be no conservation of animal life without provision also for the needs of human populations. Nor can humanitarian aid and development programmes hope to succeed if they fail to include the needs of plant and animal life. This interdependence has become very clear in the drought-stricken regions of Africa in recent years. Where survival is at stake, no tree or shrub is safe from a human population desperate for fuelwood, and fodder for its livestock. Any attempt to preserve the flora of such an area that does not take into account the plight of the people who live there would be quite absurd – and doomed to failure. In an overexploited world, man cannot continue to thrive at the expense of nature. Nature conservation must become an integral part of our efforts to resolve the world's problems – human, environmental and economic.

But does the conservationist who gives up his free time to clean oiled Arctic Terns, Oystercatchers and Teal really have to concern himself with global economics? Does not the sheer scale of the problem make any such small contribution seem futile? The answer must surely be that there must be a starting point; an essential first step. Taking that first step can often leave individuals and institutions open to criticism, sometimes even ridicule, yet how often have important first steps been delayed, or never even attempted, because we have lacked the will?

The grim legacy of an industrial society. What we 'bury safely, and forever', future generations are all too likely to find contaminating their drinking water.

The irony of a food and agriculture policy out of control: these oranges are being destroyed so that the excess supply does not undermine prices. Production is first fuelled by incentives and by creating demand: we then spend millions on storing or destroying the surplus. Is this what we call good management?

Many scientists today believe that the human population explosion is the most fundamental of all problems and the root cause of many of the world's ills. More than five billion people live on the earth, of which half a billion are hungry and more than a billion barely eke out a living. While you have been reading this chapter nearly 2,500 children have been born into the world. And while it took the human population 150 years, from 1750 to 1900, to double in size, it now threatens to double every 40 years. The population of the Third World requires even less time. It is doubling every 25 years.

Even the most fervent optimists cannot be sure of how we can achieve a lasting and tolerable balance on this planet. Already we are unable to feed our growing populations, and increasing exploitation is threatening the earth's few remaining stable biomes. In poor countries a large family is the only available insurance against the difficulties of old age. Yet in order to convince people to produce fewer children we must offer a realistic and practical alternative. And more important even than the question of who will feed the poor is the question of just how long an over-exploited earth can go on feeding any of us.

Roughly eleven per cent of the ice-free surface of the earth is under some sort of cultivation, and the more pressure we place on this land the more it suffers from degradation and soil loss. Every year some eleven million hectares of agricultural land are lost to erosion, desertification, contamination or building development. There is a clear trend: more and more people are having to share less and less productive land, and as the pressure mounts, the survival chances of many wild animals steadily diminish.

But who cares? Our first concern is for ourselves, and in the mistaken belief that the survival of birds is purely a matter of culture or ethics we afford their conservation a pitifully low priority.

The images reflected in the glass walls of high-rise prestige buildings are seldom attractive. Mostly they reflect themselves. The sight of a bird is a stroke of luck.

The concrete city. How many of these soul-less developments would be built around the world if the planners and architects themselves had to live in them?

The Arctic Tern takes the whole world as its habitat. As it sweeps over the oceans, the industrially polluted North Sea coast is only a few dozen hours' flying time from the burning shanty towns of southern Africa. We are only just beginning to understand these global connections, yet if we are serious about tackling world environmental problems we must start by recognizing the far-reaching consequences of the decisions we make in everyday life.

If we want to reduce the huge amounts of pesticide used on the land in Bangladesh, we must start by refusing to buy imported frogs' legs. These natural regulators of insect pests, whose legs are torn from their bodies while they are still alive, are sorely missed in the humid subtropical flood plains of their native land. As more and more frogs are taken for export, more and more chemical pesticide must be applied to the land to compensate. And if we want to prevent the destruction of the Amazon rainforest, the earth's most important producer of oxygen, we should avoid buying luxury furniture made from tropical South American hardwoods. The cash-registers and supermarket tills of the industrialized world are polling stations at which we decide the fate of habitats and species thousands of kilometres away at the farthest corners of the earth. We must adopt the motto, 'Think globally – act locally', for our planet is much smaller, and infinitely more vulnerable, than we ever thought.

A novel package tour for divers in the Bahamas. Tourism can offer many benefits if properly controlled, but too many operators are using up their 'working capital' – nature – by over-exploiting it. If this continues unchecked, the 'last paradise' advertised in the operator's brochure may indeed be the last.

Peace, solitude – and the inevitable signs of man's presence. Even at 3000m there is no escaping the litter with which we desecrate the landscape.

We find it hard to think of the earth as being vulnerable. Surely extinctions have been occurring for millions of years, yet hasn't nature always proved resilient? In our guilt we desperately look for excuses and alibis; but they do not come cheaply. While in ages past one animal or plant species became extinct every 190 or so years, today it is one every 20 minutes. How long can the 'blue planet' continue to sustain such heavy losses? If every threatened species is a flashing warning light, then the whole world must be ablaze with the lights of impending plant and animal extinctions.

But are we looking? Has the rapid succession of grim news stories about acid rain and oil pollution blunted our perceptions, made us turn our backs on these stark realities? Already there are those who do not want to hear another word. 'Enough,' they say, 'I have my own life to lead: my own problems to solve.'

Simply being aware of the facts does not make them disappear. But perhaps the worldwide scale of these problems, and the pressures they now create, can still shift the balance in favour of action. The problems themselves know no borders or frontiers: they demand international co-operation — the replacement of old-style foreign policies by a new, global, domestic policy embraced by all nations. The nuclear accident at Chernobyl and the chemical disaster at Basle have clearly demonstrated the urgency of such international co-operation. Could this be the time for us to start afresh?

The conditions for such a new start have surely never been better. We have total, global, communication. News travels round the world in seconds. Yet even this technology is misused. The great and the small, the vital and the trivial, are all intermixed; words that determine war or peace sharing news space with gossip about the private lives of people whose prominence itself stems solely from the unlimited ease of communications. At times we are bombarded with an unending stream of grim and frightening news, and at those times we often react — and act — with concern and real generosity and compassion. But while our emotions are at first painfully bruised, we soon grow a thicker skin. And memories are short.

Who issues and directs this news? Some ninety per cent of all foreign news is issued by four western news agencies, while over eighty per cent of all data processing and dissemination is done in Japan, the United States and Western Europe. It is easy to see that the Third World never gets a chance to raise its voice on the news networks of the world.

And something else never gets a chance. Nature. We have data banks for virtually every sort of information, yet to this day there is no comprehensive global data base concerned with the state of the world environment. Is it not worth the investment? Is there no demand for it? Is our interest limited to nature films and beautiful scenery, leaving serious matters like the future of our world to a few specialized agencies?

To seek to stem the invasion of the micro-chip would be as futile as it would have been to oppose the worldwide spread of printing. Technical progress, however, can no longer be measured simply by what is possible and what can be marketed. It must be subject to morality too. Microchips guide nuclear missiles. They also run the computers that co-ordinate worldwide efforts to promote peace and the relief of suffering. The chip itself knows no morality: that responsibility is ours alone.

From high above the surface the earth is a vulnerable blue pearl in the black infinity of space. Those who can see our planet in this way are not taken in by the glib fallacy that nature can heal every wound we inflict upon it.

We must not sit back and accept this situation. There is far more at stake than the majestic flight of the eagle, or the graceful power of the cheetah. What is at stake is the future. What is required is a totally new outlook. The media must learn to see the state of the environment as a challenge to which they can respond – by disseminating ideas, by promoting research and investigation, and by discussing options and potential solutions. We, the public, must be better informed about the global relationships that link our actions with those of people in distant lands, and with the habitats, plants and animals of those far-off places. Appeals can be dramatically effective – but they are only effective when people understand the underlying causes of the problem, and can see that practical solutions are possible.

The opportunities for worldwide co-operation are better now than at any time in the past. We have learned a great deal from past mistakes. We have more scientists and technologists, economists and agronomists alive and working today than existed in the whole of the last 100 years. We have instantaneous worldwide communications, and we have the computing power to process the most complex statistics and provide us with models and predictions. In short, we have the means. All we need is the will.

Save the birds: save the world. It has become as simple as that, because lasting conservation of the world's birds can only be achieved if we take action to protect and conserve the ecological health of the whole planet. So simple, yet so hard.

Perhaps we can start by taking a lesson from the birds themselves. They acknowledge no borders. It is a principle we should make our own.

Birds are the earth's global ambassadors. They recognize no man-made boundaries; only those of the natural world. We should learn from them, for planet earth is our common living space, and our future depends on it.

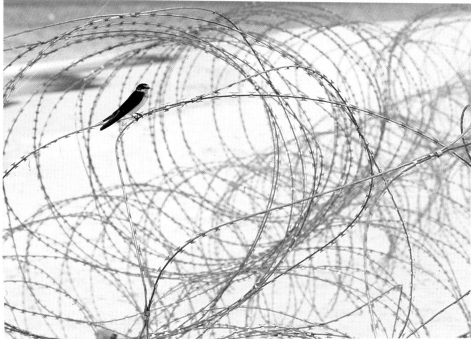

When we modestly place mankind at the top of the evolutionary tree we tend to forget not only that birds evolved much more recently than mammals but also that they outnumber them by two to one, having about 9000 species compared with the mammals' 4000.

In terms of evolutionary diversity the birds are one of the most successful of all animal groups, and the key to their conquest of so many different habitats and lifestyles lies in their remarkable versatility. Although specialized for flight they can, with varying degrees of accomplishment, walk, run, perch, climb, swim and dive as well.

Man, by contrast, is a walking animal. He cannot fly, and his ability to swim is pathetically limited. Yet in the space of just a few thousand years he has risen to total dominance of the natural world. His technological development has made his mastery of air and water almost as complete as his mastery of land. Today his influence is global. And as that influence continues to grow, the world's birds are threatened by pressures that are testing their versatility and adaptability to the limits.

The World of Birds

ANTHONY W. DIAMOND

Adaptation and survival

The nitrate deserts of Chile and Peru are not where you might expect to find gulls. These are the most barren deserts on earth; in many areas rain has never been recorded. The soil is dry and powdery, the ground littered with rocks and pebbles. There are no plants, no resident animals, no shade, and only a regular afternoon wind to give any respite from the relentless heat. By day, ground temperatures reach over 50°C; at night the air temperature drops to within a few degrees of freezing. And yet at nightfall in the early southern summer, Grey Gulls leave the coast 30km away and head inland to start a new breeding cycle in the desert. Once the eggs are laid one bird must remain on the nest, warming the eggs through the chill night and early morning and then standing up to shade them in the heat of the day.

Panting and fluffing out its feathers, the parent bird endures the heat until soon after noon, when a cool wind brings relief. Its mate spends the day feeding at the coast, then flies inland at night to take the next day's gruelling spell. Even when the eggs hatch there is no respite for the adult birds. They must continue to shade the vulnerable young from the fierce heat of the desert sun, and the persistent chicks will seek shelter beneath the body of any available adult, whether or not it is the chick's natural parent. Ten thousand pairs of Grey Gulls breed in one desert colony each year, commuting daily between the desert and the deep blue sea in an incongruous demonstration of the hardihood of birds.

Just as Grey Gulls perversely choose to breed in a desert at the hottest time of year, so Emperor Penguins lay their eggs in the freezing darkness of the Antarctic winter. After laying her egg on the ice, the female waddles back to sea, where she feeds and fattens up for two months, leaving her mate to incubate the egg continuously in temperatures that frequently drop below −60°C. He makes no nest, but holds the egg between the top of his feet and a fold of skin on his belly, and by huddling as close as he can to his colleagues he saves up to 80 per cent of the heat he would lose if he stood alone. Emperors are big penguins, nearly a metre tall and weighing 30kg. They need the whole Antarctic summer to raise a chick, and by laying the egg in the bitter winter blizzards they ensure that the chick hatches right at the start of the summer flush of food.

Penguins are protected from intense cold by very dense feathers and a thick layer of blubber under their skin. Grey Gulls use the full range of feather movement to alter the insulating properties of their plumage to protect them from heat. Both demonstrate the remarkable versatility of feathers in enabling birds to live in conditions far beyond the limits of human endurance.

Emperor Penguins (*Aptenodytes forsteri*) lay their eggs in May or June, just as the Antarctic winter is beginning. Two months later the chicks are born into a world of bitter cold and darkness. Temperatures drop to −40°C and lower, and hurricane-force winds are commonplace. The birds respond by huddling close together to conserve body heat – a level of communal behaviour found in no other penguin species.

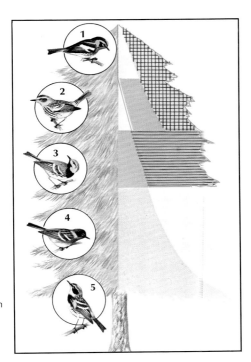

The feeding zones of a single American spruce
As many as five species of American warbler may share the feeding niches offered by just one tree.

1. Blackburnian
2. Cape May
3. Black-throated Green
4. Bay-breasted
5. Myrtle

Sharing living space

Grey Gulls and Emperor Penguins have little company but their own at the extremes of the avian world. Most species live in kinder habitats, sharing them with many other species, and to assure continued co-existence they must occupy different parts of the habitat and make their livings in a wide variety of different ways.

Sharing a mixed woodland habitat
The mixed aspen and willow groves of North America's temperate woodlands have a rich and varied undergrowth of shrubs and herbs and can support a dozen or more different bird species without excessive competition.

1. American Robin
2. Bluebird
3. White-crowned Sparrow
4. Junco
5. House Wren
6. Common Flicker
7. Calliope Hummingbird
8. American Goldfinch
9. Chipping Sparrow
10. Lincoln Sparrow
11. Black-headed Grosbeak
12. Traill's Flycatcher
13. Song Sparrow

A North American woodland glade may support a dozen species of small bird, each with its own role in the system – its ecological niche. Robins forage for worms and beetles in the soil and leaf-litter. Bluebirds watch from perches, then drop to the ground after larger insects. The various sparrows and the junco share the smaller seeds among them, and feed their nestlings on small insects caught in different parts of the vegetation. House Wrens skulk among the dense underbrush, searching for insects; flickers probe for beetle grubs beneath the bark of trees; hummingbirds buzz from flower to flower feeding on nectar, and flycatchers sally forth after butterflies and other flying insects.

A single spruce tree can hold enough resources for five kinds of wood-warbler to share among them. The Cape May Warbler gleans the tips of the highest branches; the Blackburnian works nearer the trunk and lower down; the Black-throated Green occupies the upper half of the inner canopy; the Bay-breasted holds the very centre of the tree, while the Myrtle Warbler feeds on the ground itself, and in the open spaces around the trunk and the bases of the branches.

So birds divide the world between them. At the very limits of life only the hardiest species can be found, but within more favourable environments the finer features of the habitat determine who lives where, and on what they will feed.

The power of flight

A few birds are flightless, but all are feathered, and the special characteristics of birds are direct consequences of their flight and their feathers.

To fuel their flight muscles for long periods of sustained effort birds require a higher metabolic rate than mammals and therefore a more efficient respiratory system. Birds' lungs are small, but they connect with thin-walled air-sacs that extend throughout the body and even into the larger bones. Air is channelled through them to pass continuously in one direction through the lungs so that oxygen is taken up by the blood while breathing out as well as in. This unique and intricate respiratory system has been adapted brilliantly to serve the ends of courtship and territorial advertisement through the medium of sound. Birds owe the power and diversity of their voices to the remarkable breathing system with which they have mastered flight.

The rapid metabolic rate maintained by birds would be wasted if they could not conserve the heat produced. Feathers are exceptional insulators, and they are strong, waterproof and light. They are coloured both by pigments and, because their structure is so complex, by the scattering and reflection of light within the feather itself. Complementing their brilliantly coloured plumages birds also have colour vision, rarely found in mammals, and over millions of years of evolutionary change this has encouraged plants to colour their flowers and fruits to attract the birds that pollinate them and disperse their seeds.

Birds inspired man's quest for powered flight. Yet it takes a complex multi-million dollar technology to enable a jet fighter to do what a Peregrine Falcon (*Falco peregrinus*) can do with instinctive ease. In its hunting dive, or 'stoop', the Peregrine can reach a speed of 200km/h.

The hovering capability of a helicopter is no match for the aerial agility of a hum-mingbird. These tiny forest birds can hang motionless in the air, their wings a blur, and then dart sideways or backwards to the next bloom as they feed on the nectar of forest flowers. The birds' wings beat at up to 40 beats a second.

The lure of flight

Throughout history man has striven to emulate the flight of birds. From the legendary Daedalus and Icarus flying from captivity with wings of feathers attached to their arms, through Leonardo da Vinci's designs for man-powered flying machines to Otto Lilienthal and his bizarre contraptions of the last century we have struggled to use our own muscles to power artificial wings. None of the real machines worked any better than Icarus' legendary ones, and Daedalus' successful flight on feathered wings remains an impossible dream. But modern engines drive a range of aircraft that imitate the various ways birds fly. Helicopters hover laboriously in deafening and clumsy emulation of a hummingbird, and jet fighters scream in supersonic simulation of a stooping falcon. But whatever our mechanical achievements in the air, we still marvel at the wild perfection of the flight of birds.

The aerodynamics of flight

Aircraft wings and propellers and the wings and flight-feathers of birds share the same cross-section; thicker at the front, tapering smoothly to a point at the rear, with the lower surface flatter, the upper more curved. This shape is known as an aerofoil, and it is universal in flying animals and machines because they all work on the same aerodynamic principle.

When a wing is pushed forward through the air – or when air rushes over the wing – the air moves farther and faster over the bulging upper surface than it does along the flat underside. This lowers the pressure of air above the wing, and so the wing is lifted by the comparatively high pressure underneath. The direction of the resultant force on the wing is always at right-angles to the surface of the wing, so if a bird tilts the plane of its wing forward and downward, it gains both vertical lift and forward propulsion from the same downward beat. Flying is very different from swimming and walking, in which we push backwards against a resistant medium. Air is insubstantial and easily compressed, so flight relies on creating and manipulating the difference in air pressure between the upper and lower wing surfaces.

A bird's wing is a subtle variation on the aerofoil shape in which the lower surface is hollow rather than flat, the down-curved leading edge guiding the airstream smoothly back to the trailing edge. Each flight-feather at the tip of the wing is itself an aerofoil, and twists in the rushing slip-stream to act as a propeller. All the varied wing-shapes found in birds, from the broad stubby wing of a woodland bird to the long, narrow gliding wing of an albatross, retain the same basic aerofoil cross-section.

Nature's aerofoil
Densely packed flow-lines over the upper surface of the wing indicate the increased speed of the air in this region. The result is reduced pressure above the wing and relatively high pressure below, so creating lift.

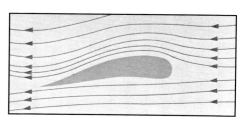

Engineered for flight
The internal structures of the bird are highly adapted to the requirements of flight. Bones honeycombed with air cavities combine lightness and strength, while the flat plates of the sternum and its deep projecting keel provide large attachment areas for the flight muscles.

The massive pectoral muscles that power the downbeat of the wings may, in some species, account for up to half the bird's body weight. (The bird illustrated here is a Whimbrel (*Numenius phaeopus*).

Mastery of the air

Summer skies are crowded with aerial plankton in the form of hordes of insects drifting high above the earth. Through the swarms swoop swifts and swallows, their broad, open mouths straining food from the sky just as a whale sieves krill from the sea. Swifts spend more of their life on the wing than any other bird, and like hummingbirds they are so specialized for flight that their shrunken legs and feet can barely support them on the ground.

Swifts' narrow scythe-shaped wings give them great speed and endurance, but they cannot glide without losing height: they are the sprinters of the sky. Long-distance fliers have broader wings that can use air-currents to provide the energy for gliding for hours at a time. Wandering Albatrosses have straight, narrow wings spanning three and a half metres. They are exactly like those of a man-made glider, and 'ride' the wind deflected off the waves.

The sinister shape of a soaring vulture marks a different kind of gliding — one that requires sustained lift at low speed. Vultures spread their huge, splay-fingered wings to catch the updraughts of thermal air currents generated when the bare plains are heated by the morning sun. The broad, well-separated flight feathers of the wing-tips act like the slots in an aircraft wing, interrupting the eddies of air that would otherwise stall the wing at low speed. They enable the bird to soar for hours, rising in a spiral to the summit of one thermal, then side-slipping down and across to the next. In this way, vultures can patrol thousands of square kilometres without needing to flap their wings from take-off to landing.

Sparrowhawks are smaller and more active relatives of vultures, their kinship reflected in their broad, rounded wings and fiercely hooked bill. But the hawk's wings are proportionally slimmer, and allied with a long, flexible tail they allow the bird to jink and dodge in thick woodland, approaching its prey from behind cover before dashing out for the kill.

The humble sparrow has conquered the world with its generalized, all-purpose wings. Yet the routine daily acts of take-off, level flight, turning, accelerating, slowing down and landing are none the less remarkable for being in the repertoire of this widespread and frequently ignored little bird.

Exceptional manoeuvrability is the trade-mark of the Sparrowhawk (*Accipiter nisus*), which hunts in a dashing pursuit in thick cover.

Albatrosses, like this Black-browed Albatross (*Diomedea melano-phris*) with its 240cm wing-span, are the supreme development of the gliding and soaring seabird

The huge wing area of the African White-backed Vulture (*Pseudogyps africanus*) is a perfect adaptation for sustained soaring.

To reduce its air speed ready for landing, the pigeon beats its wings back and forth rather than up and down. The tail feathers are also spread wide to assist the braking effect.

Touch, hearing and sight

The faster a bird flies, the more acute its eyesight needs to be. Swifts and birds of prey have eyesight three or four times keener than a man's, and some hawks' eyes are bigger than ours even though the bird may be one-fiftieth our weight or less. Most of the space inside a bird's skull is taken up by its eyes and the optic part of the brain, sight being much the dominant sense even in nocturnal species. Birds see colour well, and in terms of acuity and sensitivity their eyes are greatly superior to those of most mammals.

Most nocturnal birds have eyes that are extremely sensitive to dim light but do not distinguish colours well. But they also hear sounds inaudible to man. A Barn Owl, blindfolded, can catch a mouse in total darkness, locating it purely by ear — and accurately enough to seize it at the first attempt. An owl's ears are not symmetrical; the ear chambers in the skull differ in size, and one is set lower than the other to exaggerate the difference in the time at which a sound arrives at each ear. Though very tiny, the difference enables the owl to locate the sound-source very accurately.

An owl's ability to hear the rustle of a mouse in the dark leaf-litter depends as much on the owl's own silence as on the mouse's sound, and however well the owl hears the mouse, it will not catch it if the mouse also hears the owl. This special requirement of the nocturnal hunter is reflected in the unusual specialization of the owl's plumage. Owls' feathers are soft and light, and their wing-feathers are uniquely trimmed with fluffy barbs that deaden the sound of their flight.

Worms that live in mud cannot be seen or heard, and the shorebirds that seek them must use other means to locate them. The curlew's slender, probing bill is sheathed in living tissue, densely packed with microscopic touch-receptors sensitive to the pressure-waves sent through the mud by the worms and molluscs below. The woodcock of Europe is similarly adapted for feeding in leaf-litter and loose forest soil.

Touching
Sensitive tissue, rich in nerve-endings, covers the probing bill of the Curlew (*Numenius arquata*), enabling the bird to 'feel' the vibrations caused by worms and burrowing insects.

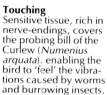

All-round vision
The Woodcock (*Scolopax rusticola*) has a 360° field of view, including a sector of binocular vision to the rear. This provides optimal protection against surprise attacks from predators while the bird is feeding on the ground.

Hearing
An asymmetrical arrangement of the ear cavities is important for the location of sound sources. The Boreal Owl (*Aegolius funereus*) can determine the direction of sounds with remarkable accuracy.

Sharp-focus vision
Like all hunters, including man, the Kestrel (*Falco tinnunculus*) has large eyes, placed right at the front of the head. This creates a large field of three-dimensional vision — essential for the accurate judgement of distance when diving to attack prey.

Birds of the water

Most seabirds must master the air in order to make their living; they can feed and rest on the sea, but they travel by air. But for penguins the sea is their medium of movement as well as their source of food. Their wings and flight muscles are modified exclusively for swimming, and move them through the water as swiftly and skilfully as any seal or dolphin. Underwater they are more like mammals than birds, with streamlined bodies and sleek dense fur-like plumage, plunging through the waves and diving tens of metres deep with a proficiency unmatched by any other bird.

Even though penguins have abandoned the air for the sea, their virtuosity also extends to land. Every year, millions of Adelie Penguins trudge over 300km from the sea across the Antarctic ice to breeding grounds that may be buried under snow, but to which they navigate unerringly on foot.

The countless refinements of legs and feet

Many families of birds are expert swimmers without being as specialized as penguins. Most can fly well too, because they swim not with their wings, as penguins do, but with their feet, leaving their wings free for flight. All swimming birds' feet are modified with webs or flaps of skin, stretched between the toes in ducks, geese, cormorants and pelicans, or set on the sides of the toes and overlapping when the foot thrusts backwards through the water, as in grebes and coots. The legs are set well back on the body to give the greatest thrust, and may be so far back that the bird has difficulty walking. This is why ducks and geese walk with a waddle, and why grebes and divers (loons) shuffle clumsily along with their bellies on the ground. Swimming birds need strong legs to push them through the water and to thrust upwards from the surface into flight, and in some, such as grebes and shearwaters, the legs are flattened laterally to reduce resistance in the water.

Grebes are specialized aquatic birds that never come to land. Their nests of water plants are built up from the bottom in shallow water, or float on the surface, anchored to living plants. They feed underwater on fish, crabs and plants.

A duck's webbed feet are efficient swimming organs, but its strong round-sectioned legs are set much farther forward on its body than those of a grebe. This allows the bird to graze, roost and nest on land, and many geese and ducks feed as much, if not more, on land than in the water.

The Storm Petrel uses its delicate webbed feet to push against the sea as it flutters just above the surface, or to paddle through the plankton when it settles. Its long, slender legs are set well back and can support its body only briefly. On land the birds shuffle awkwardly in and out of their nest-burrows, resting on the long leg-bone rather than standing upright.

The African Jacana takes long legs to a ludicrous extreme. Its elongated toes spread the bird's weight over such a large area that it can walk on the flimsy, floating leaves of water plants, accounting for its more evocative name of 'lily-trotter'.

The long legs of the European Spoonbill have the more conventional function of allowing the bird to wade in water without wetting its belly. Herons, storks and other waterside birds have long legs for the same reason, but few have as specialized a bill as the spoonbill. It is swept from side to side through shallow water, trapping small animals in the sieve-like serrations at the side.

Penguin locomotion
When on land, Adelie Penguins (*Pygoscelis adeliae*) will toboggan down slopes (**1**) or walk with a clumsy waddling gait (**2**). At the ice-edge they scan the water for danger (**3**) then enter with a shallow 'belly flop' (**4**) or steep dive (**5**). To conserve energy the birds 'porpoise' along at the surface (**6**), but when pursuing their prey they dart and dive tens of metres deep (**7**). To regain the ice, the bird accelerates (**8**) then leaps from the water (**9**), often clearing 1.5m vertical ice-edges and leaping 3m horizontally in the process.

The Dabchick or Little Grebe (*Tachybaptus ruficollis*) has lobes along the sides of its toes. In this photograph the lobes on the right foot can be seen spread wide by the water pressure as the foot sweeps backwards.

Wilson's Storm Petrel (*Oceanites oceanicus*) hovers at the surface, 'treading water' as it picks up morsels of food.

The Belted Kingfisher (*Ceryle alcyon*) of North America dives after its prey. When under water the nictitating membrane, or 'third eyelid', is drawn across the eye to protect it from injury.

Recent converts to wetlands life

From its appearance alone, few people would guess that a kingfisher is a waterbird; indeed most members of the kingfisher family are not waterbirds at all, but make their living on land catching insects and small vertebrates. Fishing is a recently acquired habit and the technique used is the same as that used on land. The bird swoops onto its prey from a perch. The feet are small and weak, not webbed, and the two front toes, joined together at the base, are used for digging nest-holes in river banks or termite nests.

Even less like a waterbird, the Dipper looks very much like a member of the thrush family. Yet, like a grebe, it catches its food when wholly underwater, running along the stony bottom of a fast-running stream with its body pressed down by the current, catching insect larvae and crustaceans among the stones of the river bed.

In common with all other ducks, geese and swans, the Mandarin Duck (*Aix galericulata*) has broad webs of skin connecting its three front toes.

Birds of the land

Just as penguins have abandoned flight in order to master the sea, so the finest runners have also relinquished their ability to fly. Ostriches, rheas, emus and cassowaries are all large flightless birds, mostly of open country. To compete with grazing mammals, and escape the predatory ones, they have developed comparable size and speed. The Ostrich of the African plains is as large as most mammals there and can outrun a lion or fell it with a kick. But its best defence is to detect a predator before being seen itself. Its long neck, set above the longest legs of any bird, give it an enormous field of view, which it scans with the largest eyes of any land animal.

Ostriches are vegetarian, and so are most large ground-living birds. Plant food requires a long digestive system, and this adds to the weight of a bird and reduces its powers of flight. Very few bird species are wholly vegetarian, but most of those that are so are large, heavy-bodied, and poor fliers. Great Bustards are about as heavy as the laws of physics will allow a flying bird to be. More typical of ground-living birds is the partridge. Like many others it is a vegetarian that supplements its diet with insects; and it flies readily – if rather clumsily.

The right tools for the job

Although relatively few species eat leaves and stems, other parts of plants are the staple diet of many birds. Seeds provide a rich source of food for many species, most of which have short, deep beaks, worked by strong muscles, to break open the tough outer coating. Fruits support many others, especially in the tropics, where plants can fruit throughout the year. Different types of fruit call for different tools to exploit them, and so are associated with some of the more grotesque bill shapes, ranging from the deep, hooked bill of the parrot to the long, curved bills of toucans and hornbills. Many nectar-eating birds have long, narrow bills to probe the slender flower-tubes. The hummingbirds of the New World, and the sunbirds, sugarbirds and honeyeaters of the Old World, specialize in taking nectar, and in each species the size and shape of the bill is linked directly with that of the flowers it uses most. Many hummingbirds also have a long tongue, sheathed around the top of the skull, with which to probe the deepest recesses of the flowers.

The Red-legged Partridge (*Alectoris rufa*) inhabits dry, steppe-like areas in southwestern Europe. When in danger it first tries to escape by running – using the cover of vegetation and taking to the air only when in imminent danger of being caught.

Standing 2.5m tall and weighing up to 150kg, the Ostrich *Struthio camelus* is a bird of superlatives. It is the biggest bird, has the longest and most powerful legs of any bird, and has by far the biggest eyes – even bigger than those of an elephant.

In general, landbirds and mammals have specialized on different foods. Most birds eat insects. From the ground to the top of the tallest trees small songbirds like warblers and titmice forage busily, sharp-eyed and active, gleaning small insects from leaves and twigs with their slender, pointed bills. Flying insects fall victim to flycatchers and bee-eaters, which sit in wait for passing prey and dart out with deadly precision. Keen eyes are demanded by all these ways of life, and most birds need light to hunt by; but night-flying moths are exploited by nightjars, beautifully camouflaged birds with huge eyes and an enormously wide mouth fringed with long bristles like a night-flying swift.

Each of the 9000 species of bird is master of its own niche in nature. Mankind has not one niche but thousands; he has expanded his exploitation of the earth so that now he overlaps with every other living thing. However far the hummingbird retreats into the forest, or the albatross rides the 'roaring forties', or the swift soars into the sky, none can now escape the influence of man.

Fruits, berries and nuts, and occasionally insects too, form the diet of the impressive One-wattled Cassowary (*Casuarius unappendiculatus*) of the forests and scrub of Papua New Guinea.

The flightless Kiwi of New Zealand (*Apteryx australis*) is nocturnal, and feeds by probing for worms and insect larvae in the leaf litter of the forest floor.

A bill to suit every way of life
Each bird has a bill adapted to suit its way of feeding. The Great Spotted Woodpecker (**1**) hammers decaying wood to extract the grubs; the Double-collared Sunbird (**2**) sips nectar; the Hawfinch (**3**) cracks nuts; the Keel-billed Toucan (**4**) picks up berries and insects; the Swift (**5**) scoops its insect food in mid-air, and the Peregrine Falcon (**6**) needs its sharp, hooked bill to seize and tear its prey.

Models for mankind

For countless generations man has been inspired by the beauty and freedom of birds, and yet despite the pride we take in our skills and technological advances, and our cultural achievements, we often come second best to the avian world. The finest works of human musicians are rivalled by the birdsong of a spring morning, while masterpieces of painting, ceramics and stained glass still fail to match the shimmering iridescence of a hummingbird's plumage. No bird can equal the speed or endurance of a modern aircraft, yet what man-made machine can twist and turn like a hunting swallow, hover and plunge like a sparrowhawk, or ride the air with the effortless grace of an albatross? And even in the ocean realm expensive machines, support vessels and teams of engineers are needed to take a man where penguins dive with ease dozens of times a day.

Man can reach the ocean deeps only with the aid of expensive machines. The Humboldt Penguin (*Spheniscus humboldti*) can dive many tens of metres deep with ease, while the much larger Emperor Penguin is known to dive beyond 250 metres and remain submerged for more than ten minutes at a time.

Perhaps the closest man can come to emulating the flight of a bird is to soar on the air currents in a glider, basing the pattern of its wings on the long, narrow wings typical of many albatrosses, gulls and other large gliding seabirds.

The Ostrich has the largest eye of any land animal – perfect for spotting danger in an open grassland habitat. Man, however, must rely on technology to boost his long-range vision.

A Grasshopper Warbler pours out his song, just one of the countless bird calls and songs that have inspired human musicians throughout history.

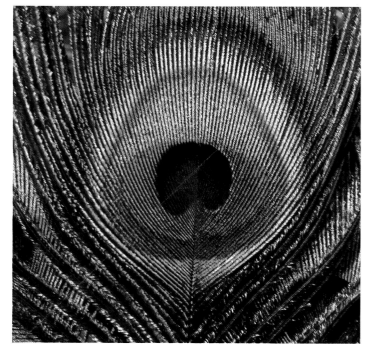

In the world of birds it is the male who almost invariably has the most dazzling and beautiful adornments. In many human societies visual attractiveness is regarded as more the prerogative of the female of the species.

However little we may be aware of birds, we breathe the same air, drink water from the same rain, and feed on the tissues of plants and animals just as they do. The daily life of modern man may shelter us from contact with the natural life of plants and animals, but our need for a healthy planet is no less real simply because we find it so easy to forget.

The ecology of our planet is built up from five main elements — water, earth, plants and animals and the life-giving energy of the sun; and in all earth's environments mankind and birds are forever linked by their shared dependence on the unique chemistry of sunlight on green leaves, a chemistry that sustains all life on earth.

Each of the world's 9000 bird species is biologically tailored to a particular niche in the environment, and in every habitat there is at least one species whose changing fortunes reflect the health of that environment. Birds are the perfect natural 'early warning system'. We must learn to observe them — and to learn from them.

One World for Men and Birds

ANTHONY W. DIAMOND

Solar power and the ecological engine

The natural world could run without sunlight no better than a car without fuel. But birds and other living things are made not of sunlight but of molecules and tissues, of proteins, fats and sugars; and though sunlight floods the earth in exuberant excess, the chemicals that build our bodies are earthbound. They are descendants of the atoms that came together six thousand million years ago to make the planet earth.

This limited stock of chemical nutrients can be rearranged from sugars to fats and proteins, from the leaf of a plant to the body of an insect or the wing of a bird; but though the stock can be refashioned, it cannot be increased. Nutrients are non-renewable resources. Only energy is renewed, daily, from the star we call the sun.

The fundamental chemistry of life on earth: sunlight, water and the miraculous process of photosynthesis by green leaves.

Creating life from light

The vital link between solar power and the living world is the chemical reaction that takes place inside the green leaves of plants. By the chemical magic of photosynthesis — 'building with light' — part of the energy of the sun's light is used to recombine the atoms in water and carbon dioxide into oxygen, sugars and other molecules. Certain other elements are also vital to the process: phosphorus is essential to the chemistry of harnessing sunlight, and nitrogen for building amino-acids and proteins. But carbon is the most important. All organic molecules contain it, and it plays a unique and irreplaceable role in the chemistry of life.

With the chemicals they build from sunlight, air and water, plants make more plants, by growth of their own tissues and by setting fruit and seeds to germinate into new young plants. All parts of the plant in turn are food for some animal. Snails rasp at young stems, aphids suck sap from leaves, wireworms chew at roots and caterpillars bore into fruit, all turning tissue manufactured by the plant into a new kind of tissue performing a new role in the living system.

When a plant makes a sugar molecule it locks up only a fraction of the energy it used to make it. And when that molecule passes from the plant into the aphid or caterpillar that feeds on it, only a fraction of the energy is transferred to the molecule's new host. Plants fix about two per cent of the sun's energy in their own tissues (more when they are growing fast, but no more than eight per cent at best), and each time energy is passed along the chain from one organism to another, no more than ten per cent of it is used to build new tissue. The rest may seem to be wasted, but most of it is used for warming the animal, maintaining its body functions, and for moving it around.

The energy paradox

The sun floods our planet every day with an amount of energy equivalent to the production of about ten million nuclear power stations. Even our modern civilization's profligate waste of energy could be fuelled a thousand times over by this solar energy alone. By 1976 we used more than three times as much energy — and four times as much oil — as we did in 1950. The people on this planet now use as much energy as the plants produce, yet our use of the sun as a source of energy has scarcely advanced in the 2500 years since Romans built the first 'solar' houses.

It is one of the cruellest paradoxes of modern times that although our planet is flooded with abundant free energy, many of the economic and ecological ills of the world arise from a 'shortage' of energy. The economic chaos that has afflicted the world since oil prices soared in the early 1970s is just one of those ills. But most people in the world have no access to oil; neither can they afford to buy it. They get their energy from wood, which they have to cut and carry home, and this desperate demand for fuelwood is one of the major causes of habitat loss in the poorer countries of the world.

Conserving the nutrient stock

The use of energy by living systems seems wasteful; but energy is available in quantities far beyond the capacity of plants to use. By contrast the chemical nutrients – carbon, nitrogen, phosphorus and others – are carefully husbanded, passed along the food chain with the minimum of waste. The chain – from plant to animal to more animals – is made a circle by microscopic organisms in the soil; tiny creatures often visible only under a microscope and composed of a single cell, yet performing a role so vital that without them life would wither overnight. These scavengers of the soil feed on the bodies of the dead, breaking down their tissues into molecules that are absorbed by plant roots and returned to the cycle of life above ground. All animals are part of this ecological cycle. But the nutrient cycle is driven not only by the life within, like running mice driving a treadmill; ultimately it is powered by energy radiated from the sun. Only with that supply of power can the limited resources of the earth be endlessly recirculated through the thin green skin we call the biosphere.

On an even grander scale nutrients are carried along by the geological processes that constantly reshape the earth's surface. Geological movements raise subterranean deposits to the surface and create new land from former ocean basins, while volcanic eruptions pour mineral-rich solutions, gases and lavas onto the surface from the molten interior. New rocks exposed at the surface are soon broken down by the weathering processes of ice, wind and rain, and the mineral nutrients, further modified by plants and soil organisms, are washed into rivers, some to be deposited on lowland plains, most to be carried into the sea, where they remain beyond the reach of living things until some major geological upheaval returns them to the land once more.

Phosphorus is one of the rarest and most important nutrients: its atoms make very high-energy bonds, which all living creatures use in their metabolism. That many plants

could profit from increased supplies of phosphorus than they usually get is demonstrated eloquently by the use by farmers of huge quantities of phosphate as fertilizers. Yet the phosphate we use is mined from geological deposits laid down over millions of years; and most of the phosphate we spread on our fields ends up in the sea. This constant loss from the land to the sea – whence it will return only when the sea floor becomes land – removes one of the most vital of all nutrients from the ecosystems of the land to the sterility of the sea floor.

The world has all the minerals it will ever have, and has had them since the earth was born. For the last 600 million years this stock of chemicals has been recycled around the globe on a geological time-scale of hundreds of millions of years. Plants and animals have used them sparingly and carefully, slowing down their rate of return from land to sea and supporting a wealth of species on a very limited nutrient stock. Now mankind has speeded up their use and the rate at which they are lost from the land; but as yet he has found no way of reclaiming them as fast as they are lost.

Nutrients and energy
Earth's organic resources are constantly recycled (blue arrows). Nutrients produced by photosynthesis (**1**) or stored in plant tissue (**2**) are available to herbi- vores (**3**). When a herbivore dies, its nutrients may pass to a predator (**4**) or to decomposers in the soil (**5**) to be broken down and used again by growing plants (**6**). Energy is not recycled. It is renewed daily by the sun (**7**). At each level of the ecosystem energy is used up and radiated back out of the system (red arrows) by the processes of plant growth (**8**) and by ani- mals maintaining their body-heat and going about their everyday activities (**9**).

The global water-cycle

Water makes up at least 80 per cent of living bodies, and the chemical reactions that sustain life take place in the water held within living tissues. In every way, the movement of water over the face of the earth acts like the bloodstream of the living world, dissolving nutrients from the earth's rocks, transporting them to every part of the biosphere, and at the same time cleansing and refreshing the biosphere by carrying away waste products.

The planet's stock of water was laid down when the earth itself was formed, and this remarkable compound has a number of unique properties which are fundamental to life itself. Water expands when it freezes, instead of contracting, and this expansion makes it less dense — and so it floats. If this were not so the water bodies of the earth would long since have frozen solid as ice, sinking to the bottom, built up year after year, well beyond the reach of the sun's melting warmth. Pond life survives the harshest winter because, while the surface water is frozen, the bottom waters remain at around +4°C.

The endless cycle

Rain clouds are the most familiar source of water. From them water is precipitated into streams and rivers, rushing in torrents from the high ground then slowing on the gentler slopes before meandering across lowland plains to the sea. Some rain is intercepted by plants, even more is held in temporary storage in the soil, and this water joins the ecological water-cycle linking soil, plants and animals.

Vast quantities of water are evaporated from the surface of the oceans. Most returns direct to the oceans as rain, but some, perhaps seven per cent, is carried inland as water vapour and cloud droplets. In polar regions, instead of running into rivers, the water joins glaciers and ice-sheets which, in time, also make their way to the sea.

The three physical states of water — solid ice, free-moving liquid, and gaseous vapour — can exist side by side as no other substance can. Water molecules move from one state to another in an endless cycle that encompasses the entire globe. The molecules are most active and mobile in the gaseous state, each molecule spending about nine days at a time in the atmosphere, and least mobile in the solid state, where a molecule may spend up to 10,000 years frozen in the Antarctic ice-cap. In between, molecules may spend a few weeks in a river; up to a year in the soil; perhaps ten years in a large lake, and several thousand years in the deepest layers of the oceans.

Sea and sky are forever linked by the processes of evaporation, condensation and precipitation of water — the endless life-supporting cycle driven by the energy of the distant sun.

Lakes and marshlands are an integral part of the global water-cycle, acting as natural reservoirs which even out the fluctuations between wet and dry seasons.

Waterfalls play a very important role in maintaining the health of a river system, for as the water falls through the air and crashes into the pool below it becomes enriched with oxygen. The biggest of the Iguaçú Falls on the Brazil/Argentina border is more than 2500m wide and 70m high.

The unique compound

Perhaps the most important property of water is that it is an almost universal solvent. More substances will dissolve in water than in anything else. The two ends of the water molecule carry opposite electrical charges, and so behave rather like miniature magnets, attracting and binding almost any other kind of molecule. Water not only links land, sea and air as it moves constantly between them: in bathing and feeding the cells of every living organism it knits together the very fabric of life on earth.

The global carrier

The very fact that the circulation of water takes place on a worldwide scale should alert us to its inherent vulnerability. Anything that enters the atmosphere, and is soluble in water, will be carried along this endless cycle and will return, somewhere, in time. Rainwater naturally has a high degree of purity, but it is not completely pure: it contains some dissolved gases and chemical compounds, and fine dust particles picked up from the air. But since the beginning of the industrial revolution man has been pumping ever-increasing volumes of smoke, dust and gaseous waste into the atmosphere. A large coal-burning power station, despite its sophisticated dust-extraction systems, still pours thousands of tonnes of gases and fine particles into the atmosphere every year. Much of this effluent is soluble – and toxic – and one of the major environmental hazards facing us today is that of acid rain – polluted rainwater returning to earth with devastating effect tens, hundreds, even thousands of kilometres away.

The global water-cycle
Of the total amount of water entering the atmosphere each year, approximately 84% evaporates from the ocean surface (**1**) while 16% evaporates from bare soil (**2**) or open water (**3**) or enters by transpiration from plants (**4**). About 77% returns to the sea directly as rain and snow (**5**) compared with the 23% that falls on land (**6**). The 7% carried inland by air movements (**7**) is balanced by the return flow of surface run-off (**8**) and ground-water seepage (**9**).

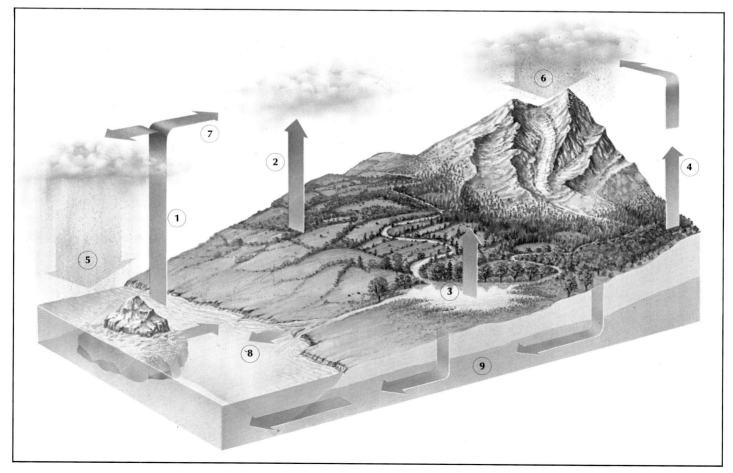

Food webs and the pyramid of numbers

Robins eating worms on a garden lawn have to stay alert not only for worms to eat, but also for other animals that eat robins. On garden lawns the biggest threat is from cats, but wild robins are hunted by small carnivores like stoats and weasels. These in turn must avoid foxes, hawks and owls, which threaten the smaller predators but themselves fall prey only to man.

The energy and nutrients that move successively from the body of the worm through the robin, the animal that eats the robin, and the animal that eats the animal that ate the robin, will one day pass into the soil as the predator's body rots. There they will eventually find their way into the body of another worm, to begin again the endless journey from small mouths to bigger ones. This sequence is called a food chain, and it is a universal feature of the living world.

Even this simple food chain is more complicated than it looks. Like all food chains it is based on plants; in this case the plants that died in the soil where the worm lived, giving up their nutrients to feed the worm. Robins also eat caterpillars and other insects that feed on living leaves, and most food chains are clearly based on living plants. Although called a food 'chain' this progression from one creature to another is of course part of the cycle of nutrients; the two ends of the chain are joined by the microscopic decomposers in the soil.

Food chains, then, can be looked on as the part of a nutrient cycle that takes place above the ground. But they are complicated not only by the meeting of their ends in decomposers, but also by more complex interactions between the individual links of the chain, and between links of different chains. The small carnivores that eat robins also eat worms and insects just as robins do; and so do foxes, which indeed may also turn to fruit at some times of year. An animal may feed at several different levels of a food chain, so acting as competitor as well as predator to others lower down the chain.

The web of life

Robins are not the only animals hunting worms; many other birds eat them too, and so do moles and shrews and snakes and lizards. And robins have more than one enemy; not just stoats and weasels, but hawks too, and by night foxes and owls will seek out their roosts. Each of these animals is in turn a link in its own food chain; and because a plant or animal may act as the link in many chains, those chains are meshed into a many-dimensioned fabric that is called a food web.

A bird — or any other animal — can increase its chances of survival by feeding at several different levels within a food chain, or by occupying the top of several different chains. The more parts of the food web that it can exploit, the better is a species' insurance against scarcity of any one type of food.

Thus many very different species may be related, ecologically, through the links of the food web they share. Just as different ecosystems, and different parts of the planet, are connected through the cycles of water and nutrients on which they depend, so too are many different kinds of animals and plants within an ecosystem woven together in a tight-knit fabric. The loss of a single link in a food web is likely to affect many other links which, at first sight, may seem quite separate and unrelated.

The hidden danger

Another important consequence of food chains lies in the fact that animals higher up the chain are usually bigger, and so need more food, than those lower down. The nutrients that support one worm will satisfy only a fraction of the needs of a robin, so the robin must eat a great many worms. Likewise, the hawk that eats the robin will eat several other birds too, each of which has stored parts of many worms in its own tissues. Any contaminant taken in by the worms is thus concentrated many times over in the bodies of animals higher up the food chain, and will spread sideways and upwards throughout the web of which that chain is but one thread.

The Turkey Vulture (*Cathartes aura*) is on a higher feeding level than the Guanay Cormorants (*Phalacrocorax bougainvillii*), yet even on this crowded island off the coast of Peru the two species are not in conflict. The reason is that the vulture feeds only on carrion and therefore poses no threat.

The Little Bee Eater (*Merops pusillus*) hunts its insect prey on the wing, snatching them in short flights from a favourite perch. The bee eater is at the third level of the food-energy pyramid.

Pyramids of numbers

There is a curious symmetry in wild bird communities. If we spend a day watching birds, in whatever habitat, we expect to see lots of small birds, rather fewer medium-sized ones, and count ourselves lucky to see more than a few large ones. It is as if the birds form a pyramid of numbers.

This symmetry is not confined to the numbers of birds – it extends also to the kinds of food they eat. The smallest birds feed on the smallest food – seeds and insects, pollen grains and nectar. The larger birds eat larger food – fruits or big insects, earthworms, snails, shrews or lizards. The biggest birds at the top of the pyramid are often found to be eating the smaller ones lower down, or mammals like voles, rats and rabbits that are similar in size to the medium-sized birds that share their stratum of the ecological pyramid. It is not surprising that small birds eat smaller food than large

birds do, but why should small birds be so much more abundant than large ones?

The answer lies in the solar-powered ecological cycle, and in a natural law that physicists call the first law of thermodynamics. According to this law, when energy is converted from one form to another the total amount of energy after the change is the same as before. When a bird eats, not all the energy intake is used to build new tissue: some is used to do the work of catching and eating, and some is wasted (although it will be utilized by scavengers of some sort). Thus at each level of the food chain, there is less energy available in edible form than there is at the level below. There must always be more plants than plant-eaters, more plant-eaters than predators, and so on. And so a fundamental law of physics also explains why, in the course of a day, a birdwatcher sees more small gentle birds than large fierce ones.

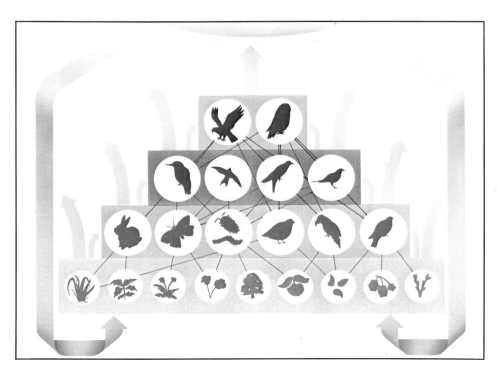

The pyramid of life

The plants and animals in any habitat exist in a complex network of relationships. Dozens of possible food chains interlink to form a food web, shown here in simplified form. In nearly every habitat it is possible to see at least four levels of feeding activity. Above the primary producers, the energy-fixing plants, come the primary consumers, the herbivores. Above them, but fewer in number, are the secondary consumers, or predators. And at the highest level sit the top carnivores – those with no natural enemies but man.

At each level, a small proportion of the food energy consumed is used for growth. Most, however, is used for maintaining body functions, and is eventually lost to the environment (orange arrows). Thus the number of individuals becomes smaller at progressively higher feeding levels.

Lethal links in the food chain

Farmers apply chemical poisons to their land to kill the insects that damage their crops. The pesticides are applied at concentrations that are enough to kill the 'target' insects but not enough to harm vertebrates that may come into contact with them. Yet we all know that untold numbers of birds and other animals have died through being poisoned by pesticides, many of them in lakes and rivers far away from farmers' fields. Why, then, do they die, if the poison is not strong enough to kill them when it is first put on the land?

The first pesticide to be applied widely, and still one of the most useful and effective, was DDT. Like many of its more recently invented relatives, DDT belongs to the chemical family of organochlorines, or chlorinated hydrocarbons. One of the reasons they are so good at their job is that they break down only very slowly: they remain in the environment for many years and so save the farmer the labour of applying them repeatedly. Another of their properties is that they are stored in the fatty tissues of animals that eat them. These two attributes of DDT, allied to a universal ecological feature of animal communities — the food chain — form a truly deadly combination.

The secret of the lethal effect of DDT and its relatives lies in concentration. Although it is applied at very low concentrations, at each step in the food chain DDT is stored within the body of the organism that takes it in. It is either not broken down by the body, or it decomposes into the equally deadly DDE, so the animal that eats the plant or animal that first took it in acquires all the poison its victim ever ate. This process of concentration continues up the food chain until the bird at the very top — such as a grebe eating predatory fish in a freshwater lake — may store DDT at concentrations hundreds of thousands of times greater than that at which the pesticide was first applied. Such concentrations are often enough to kill a bird that would be unaffected by the dose originally applied. It makes no difference whether the poison is applied direct to the water, to control midges for example, or reaches the water only after being washed off the farmland by rain.

Pesticide spraying with tractor-drawn equipment is the most selective method of application, but it still poses a threat to many species of wildlife — and even to man himself.

Crop-spraying from the air is the most radical and dangerous form of pesticide application as the poison is spread over a very wide area.

Concentration is an inevitable consequence of the structure of the food chain; and persistence and toxicity are the qualities that make organochlorines good at their job. Together, these properties threaten the integrity of any ecological community to which pesticides are applied. And it is not only those communities that harbour the target of the farmer's wrath that are at risk. Large sections of the biosphere are connected by the water cycle, and pesticides have now been applied so widely that no part of the planet is free of them. Such is their persistence, and the concentrating power of ecological systems, that they threaten life throughout the earth.

Birds as environmental indicators

In 1962, Rachel Carson's book *Silent Spring* alerted the world to the growing threats to human health posed by the toxic chemicals being added to our environments. Her most striking examples were of birds, especially the tens of thousands of dead bodies that littered the British countryside in 1960 and 1961. Birds continue to provide the most powerful early warning system there is for the misuse of pesticides in agriculture. Because they are so conspicuous and so widely watched by people, changes in their behaviour and numbers are quickly noticed; and because they occupy such a variety of ecological niches they can alert us to contamination of almost any environment. DDE residues in the body tissues of Antarctic penguins provided our first evidence that DDT had penetrated throughout the world's ecosystems and had achieved the notorious status of the first global contaminant.

Peregrine Falcons are among the most widely distributed of all birds. Like other raptors they feed at the top of a food chain, and the toxins they take in when they eat poisoned prey are absorbed and stored in their fat. Many birds lay down reserves of fat before breeding, and as they use it up the poison is released into their bloodstream. High doses have lethal effects on the nervous system; lower doses cause sterility and the death of embryos, and interfere with the chemistry of eggshell formation so that the eggs are so thin-shelled that they break when the adult sits on them. The thickness of the eggshells of many birds has declined over the period that DDT and Dieldrin have been widely used, and so serves as an excellent indicator of the contamination of the environment by pesticides.

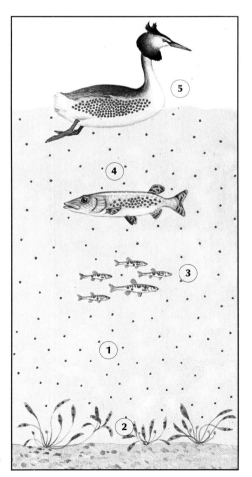

The deadly chain
Poisonous substances can accumulate rapidly as they are passed along a food chain. A large animal feeding on many smaller ones stores more and more poison in its body as time goes on. DDT, which persists in the environment for a very long time, can accumulate at a staggering rate. If an initial concentration of 0.00005 parts per million in the water of a lake (1) is taken to represent one unit, then the likely concentration in water plants and plankton (2) will be up to 800 times greater. Small plant-eating fish (3) may carry 6000 units each. The pike (4) that preys upon them may carry 33,000 units. And at the top of the food chain, the grebe (5) that eventually takes the pike may carry DDT in its body tissue at nearly half a million times the concentration of the chemical in the lake water.

The inevitable result of chemical pest control: a Barn Owl (*Tyto alba*) lies dead, almost certainly as a result of eating poisoned mice.

Soil and climate – templates for a biome

In the biosphere – the thin green skin around the earth where life is found – myriad species of plant and animal are sorted into very definite patterns according to the physical properties of the environment in which they are found. Marshland plants look very similar the world over, and harbour roughly similar kinds of birds. Desert plants are recognizably desert plants whether in Arizona, Namibia or Australia, and the birds that live among them are not found in forests or in wetlands.

The biosphere is not one layer but three. The lowest contains the rocks of the earth's crust, and the soils formed by the breakdown of those rocks. The uppermost is the atmosphere, the gases and water vapour vital to life, circling the globe in a constant swirling motion whose speed and direction fashion the climate. Pressed between the two are the living things, arranged into such recognizable entities as woodland, marsh and desert communities. These characteristic associations of plants and animals are the biomes, the super-habitats found repeatedly around the world wherever similar conditions of soil and climate come together.

The distribution of biomes around the world is clearly influenced by the distribution of the physical properties of the environment. Climate is the most obvious of these, and two particularly important aspects of climate are temperature and rainfall. The average temperature at any part of the earth's surface depends on its altitude above sea level – mountain-tops are colder than coasts – and on its latitude – equatorial coasts are warmer than Arctic ones. Altitude and latitude mimic each other's effects on climate, so that climbing a mountain we pass through zones of climate and vegetation equivalent to those we cross in passing from the equator to the poles.

The atmosphere, the oceans and the uppermost layer of earth's surface rocks together form the biosphere. This photograph, from the space shuttle *Challenger* over the Amazon Basin, shows a small part of this thin, life-supporting zone surrounding our planet.

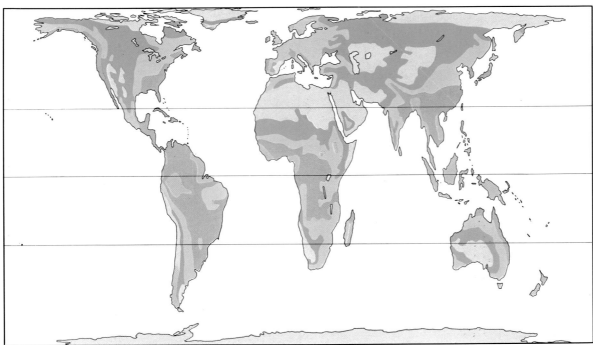

Annual rainfal
The amount of rainfall varies enormously from one part of the world to another.

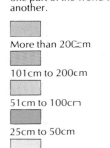

More than 200cm

101cm to 200cm

51cm to 100cm

25cm to 50cm

Less than 25cm

The highest temperatures, and some of the highest rainfall figures, are found in lowlands at the equator. An important property of the tropics, and one which distinguishes them very markedly from the temperate regions, is their relative lack of seasonality. There are differences in climate from month to month within a year, but they are slight compared with the massive swings of the seasonal pendulum in polar regions.

The steep gradient of climate from equator to pole, with its attendant variety of habitats, is a recent phenomenon in the history of the earth. Until a few million years ago, tropical and subtropical climates and their associated plants and animals reached as far north as northern Europe. The assemblages of plants and animals in biomes outside the tropics have therefore arisen much more recently than those living in equatorial latitudes.

The effects of climate on living things are better known than the effects of soil, but there is no doubt that soil and vegetation are intimately related and that both in turn are closely linked with climate. Indeed so closely are all three related that their effects on each other are hard to disentangle. Consider soil. It contains minerals from the disintegration of the rock beneath, and elements from the decomposing plants and animals above. Its upper layers are permeated by the fine hair-like roots of plants, drawing up water and dissolved nutrients. It is washed by rain and baked by sun or frozen by frost as the climate dictates. It is shaped by geology, plants and climate, and in turn affects all three.

If the soil, climate or vegetation of a place is known, the others can be guessed at; if two of the three are known, the third is easily predicted. They form the template that moulds each habitat and the life it supports.

Air, water, soil, plant life and animal life are inextricably linked in the life-processes of the biosphere.

World vegetation

Climate and geology, and hence soil type, determine the ecosystems of the biosphere.

- Tropical forest
- Deciduous woodland
- Temperate forest
- Grassland and scrub
- Montane vegetation
- Desert and semi-desert
- Polar regions

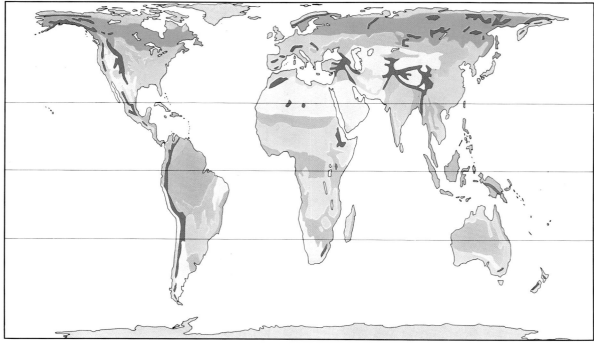

Variations on a forest theme

All biomes obey the same ecological principles. Energy is trapped by plants and passed up the pyramid by animals, while nutrients are cycled between soil, plants and animals. The skeleton of this cycle supports all biomes, though they flesh it out in different ways.

Consider a northern forest of broad-leaved deciduous trees. Winter frosts halt the chemistry of decomposition, allowing leaves that fell in autumn to lie heaped upon the ground. The spring thaw warms this litter and allows microscopic decomposers to release its store of nutrients into the soil. From there they pass into the trees, which burst out in a sudden flush of new growth. Cool rains wash out the iron and aluminium salts, leaching their colour from the upper layers of the soil while staining the lower layers a rich brown with downwashed organic matter. For most of the year, temperatures are so low that the soil's chemistry is slowed and a steady stock of nutrients can be maintained. These soils are rich and fertile, and over much of Europe have been farmed successfully for hundreds or even thousands of years.

Consider now a forest in the lowland tropics, not very different in appearance from a lush temperate woodland in midsummer but retaining that luxuriance all year round. Here the constant warmth and abundant rain support plant growth in a profusion unmatched anywhere else on earth. The chemical reactions of the nutrient cycle are driven at top speed throughout the year, and no sooner is a nutrient released into the soil than it is taken up by the nearest root and incorporated into a tree. The stock of nutrients in the soil is almost nil; everything is stored in the plants. The warm rain dissolves out the silica, leaving behind aluminium and iron salts that give the soil a rich red colour. Stripped of its plants which shaded the ground and stored its nutrients, the earth bakes hard as brick and yields the farmer little profit.

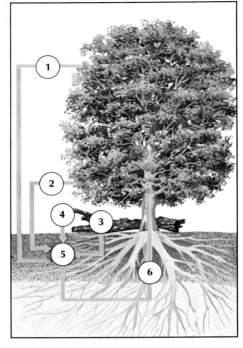

The temperate cycle
Nutrients released into the temperate forest cycle by leaf-fall (**1**), leaf-eaters (**2**), decomposers (**3**) and the waste products of animals (**4**) pass quickly into the soil (**5**). There they are held in storage, readily available to fuel a new season of growth and to smooth the fluctuations in supply from year to year. Temperate forest soils are generally deep and rich in nutrients, and in order to tap this resource the trees have large root systems (**6**) that penetrate deep into the soil layers

Ecological succession
The clothing of the land in vegetation is a dynamic process. As soon as any bare ground is exposed it is colonized by pioneer plants. These in turn are replaced by larger and longer-living species, including shrubs and bushes, until eventually the area reaches its climax flora – in temperate latitudes a mixed deciduous forest. And as the flora goes through its successional changes, so too does the resident avifauna.

Bird species associated with the changing successional stages of a North American forest.

1. Grasshopper Sparrow (*Ammodramus savannarum*)
2. Meadowlark (*Sturnella neglecta*)
3. Field Sparrow (*Spizella pusilla*)
4. Yellowthroat (*Geothlypis trichas*)
5. Yellow-breasted Chat (*Icteria virens*)
6. Cardinal (*Richmondena cardinalis*)
7. Towhee (*Pipilo erythrophthalmus*)
8. Pine Warbler (*Dendroica pinus*)
9. Summer Tanager (*Piranga rubra*)
10. Carolina Wren (*Thryothorus ludovicianus*)
11. Ruby-throated Hummingbird (*Archilochus colubris*)
12. Tufted Titmouse (*Parus bicolor*)
13. Crested Flycatcher (*Myiarchus crinitus*)
14. Wood Pewee (*Contopus sordidulus*)
15. Blue-grey Gnatcatcher (*Polioptila caerulea*)
16. Hooded Warbler (*Wilsonia citrina*)
17. Red-eyed Vireo (*Vireo olivaceus*)
18. Wood Thrush (*Hylocichla mustelina*)

Bare field 1–2 years	Grassland	Grassland-scrub 3–20 years

Succession: a march to the music of time

Habitats are made not by climate and soil alone, but by time as well. The important properties of a bird's habitat are shaped by its plants; but plants, like birds, have birth-rates, death-rates and life-spans, and all these are functions of time.

Any change inflicted on a site changes its suitability for plants. The change may be natural – a lava flow cooling on a mountain side, or a drop in sea level turning a submerged reef into an island – or it may be artificial, for example when a farmer abandons a field. But all such changes alter the conditions and so will benefit some species at the expense of others. New species will then take over, changing the environment and fitting it for others so that over a period of time a succession of different plants provides a succession of different habitats for bird, mammal and insect life.

Succession can be seen most clearly on newly cleared ground. Bare soil is colonized first by the small wind-drifted seeds of the short-lived annual pioneer plants we call weeds. Their seeds are so tiny they can float far and wide, but they hold few food reserves so they must take root and put out leaves at once. Such species are fast-growing and ephemeral; they germinate, seed quickly and abundantly, and die. Their leaves provide shade and cover under which other plants can germinate, and their remains enrich the soil. The plants that follow them grow more slowly but live longer and provide a more stable habitat.

Successions usually proceed to some kind of forest or woodland, but successional changes occur in many kinds of habitat, and each stage, or sere, has its characteristic bird community. Usually the richness of the community increases with time until the final stage, the climax, which may be less diverse than the previous seral stages. Thus habitats are not constant, but single frames in a long-running film whose beginning and end we can guess at but very rarely see.

The tropical cycle
In contrast to those of temperate lands, tropical soils are shallow, physically weak, and poor in nutrients. Those entering the system from leaf-fall (**1**), leaf-eaters (**2**), decomposers (**3**) and forest animals (**4**) are taken up immediately by the dense mat of roots (**5**) in the surface layers of the soil. The bulk of the forest's nutrient stock is stored in the trees themselves (**6**), and if the forest is cleared for agriculture, land once covered with trees 30m tall can easily be exhausted within two or three years.

Pine Forest
25–100 years

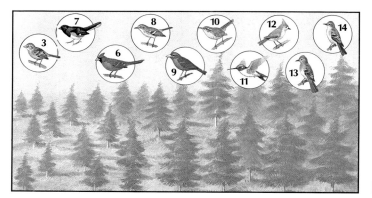

Oak-hickory forest climax
150 years onwards

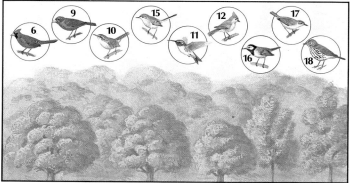

Success through partnership

Birds, plants and insects have been evolving side by side for at least 150 million years, and during that time they have developed intricate relationships with each other — some to their mutual benefit, others rather one-sided but forced upon them by the need to stay alive.

Birds are the most important predators of insects (apart from other insects) and their keen eyes and quick, sharp bills have exerted such strong evolutionary pressures that many insects have developed bizarre and complicated camouflage to escape the birds' attentions. In others, especially some of the spectacular butterflies that must present such tempting targets for a bird, predation by birds has led to the insects' internal chemistry producing toxins whose noxious taste is quickly learnt and avoided ever after.

The evolution of effective camouflage by insects has benefited them at birds' expense. But the plant world abounds with evidence of mutually beneficial relationships with birds. Many flowers are shaped and coloured as if designed with birds in mind, and whole families of plants, especially in the tropics, produce fruits whose colour, chemical composition and even fruiting season are closely fitted to the needs of birds.

Flowers that are pollinated by animals usually offer some attractive reward such as a sugar solution (nectar), which they advertise with signals suited to the sensory equipment of the intended animal 'helper'. Bats and other mammals have poor vision but keen smell, and so pollinate flowers that are large, strong-scented and often white to show up well at night. Insects are of course much smaller, and see blue colours better than red, so the plants they pollinate have small flowers, often sweetly scented and coloured blue. Birds have little sense of smell but very keen vision, especially in the reds and yellows, and they have long beaks and tongues. The flowers they pollinate are often red or yellow, and produce their nectar at the base of the flower and the pollen near the entrance so that the bird's head brushes against the sexual parts as it reaches for the sugar deep inside.

As in most sunbird species, the female Orange-breasted Sunbird (*Nectarinia violacea*) is dull compared with the brilliantly coloured male. The sunbirds of Africa fill the same ecological niche as the hummingbirds of the Americas.

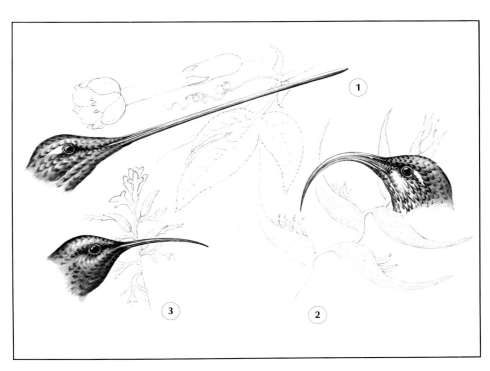

The nectar specialists
The bills of the many different hummingbird species are beautifully adapted to the shapes of the flowers on which they depend for food.

1. Swordbill (*Ensifera ensifera*) with *Passiflora mixta*
2. Sicklebill (*Eutoxeres aquila*) with *Heliconia*
3. Mountain Velvet-breast (*Lafresnaya lafresnayi*) with *Castilleja fissifolia*

Many plants can be pollinated by several different kinds of bird, but others are so shaped that only one kind of bird can pollinate them. Many tropical *Heliconia* flowers can be penetrated only by the bill of a particular species of hummingbird. Here mutual dependence is complete: without that bird to pollinate it the plant will not perpetuate its kind, and without the plant the bird will go short of a rich source of energy. The plant must not only be the right shape, size and colour to attract that species, but must also ensure that some flowers are always available so that the bird does not die or switch to another kind of plant. Such a close relationship can persist only in an environment where plants can flower all year round, which is why plant–pollinator relationships are so highly developed in the tropics.

Birds are important to plants not only for pollinating their flowers but also for dispersing their seeds. Many plants produce fruits that attract birds by their bright colours and reward them with nutritious flesh covering the seeds within. In the tropics this again produces very close relationships, but even in environments where fruit cannot be set all year round, plants may still use birds to disperse their seeds. In Europe the oak trees whose ancestors were used to build the ships that carried European man around the world sprang mostly from acorns carried off, buried and forgotten by European Jays.

Bizarre performer with a unique specialization

Far from the northern forests, in the savanna woodlands and fragmented forest edges of Africa, there exists between a bird, a bee, a badger and mankind a relationship as remarkable as any in the annals of natural history. The bird leads men or badgers to the bees' nest, and shares the spoils of wax, grubs and honey. The bird is the Greater Honeyguide, aptly known to science as *Indicator indicator*; the bee is the African honeybee; the badger is the Ratel or Honey Badger; and mankind is represented by various tribes of pastoral cattleherders and the scattered remnants of the hunter-gatherers of the forest, the Ndorobo and their kin.

Honeyguides are dull-plumaged birds, mostly grey-green with flashes of white on the tail, and yellow on the shoulders of the male. Unless they show themselves they are quite impossible to find; but when they want a man or a ratel to see them they give a distinctive rattling chatter and flit conspicuously ahead until they see they are being followed. They lead on through the bush, chattering and fluttering, until suddenly they fall still and silent. If a honey-hunter was following, he casts around for the bees' nest while his companions gather green sticks to light a fire. Then, when the nest is found, it is plugged with smoking sticks to stupefy the insects while it is hacked open with a hand-axe. (The ratel seems unaffected by the bees' potent sting and will simply tear the nest apart.)

Of all the eighteen or so kinds of honeyguide, only this species regularly guides; but all share the same extraordinary specialization. They eat wax; mostly of bees' nests but also the waxy protective coating of scale insects and the waxy skin of some fruit. Now wax cannot be digested by any other bird or any mammal, yet this entire family of birds is avid for it. Is there another mutually beneficial relationship hidden here, within the intestine of the honeyguide; perhaps between a wax-digesting microbe and its remarkable host? The honeyguide still has secrets to reveal.

A unique partnership
With persistent rattling calls the Greater Honeyguide (*Indicator indicator*) lures the Ratel (*Mellivora capensis*) — and native honey collectors as well — into the vicinity of bees' nests. Once the badger or human raiders have left, the bird feeds on the bees' wax.

The varied demands on living space

Most birds are quite strictly confined to particular habitats, which must provide them with food and shelter and a suitable climate. The most successful birds are able to fulfil these needs in many parts of the world. Mallards, for example, can find suitable places to live throughout most of the northern hemisphere.

An ideal home
The scene below contains everything needed by a breeding pair of Mallard (*Anas platyrhynchos*). **1.** Dense cover for the nest; **2.** Grassy banks and quiet backwaters in which to rest; **3.** All-round views for protection against predators; **4.** Deep water to provide a variety of food; **5.** Reed-bed cover for protection during the moult; **6.** Short succulent grasses for grazing.

A small pond with a patch of reeds, overhanging trees, and rank bushes almost choking the incoming stream may look unpromising to us, but it can provide a Mallard with all it needs to rear a brood of young. A dense patch of brambles, nettles or rushes provides the thick cover the female needs in which to hide her nest; if there is no ground cover she can use a hollow tree. While his mate incubates their eggs, the male can roost on the most open part of the bank – open so that he can see danger coming before it gets too close, and close to the water so that he can make a quick escape.

The shallow water of the pond itself provides a variety of food for the enterprising ducks. They can reach the tasty leaves of water plants at the surface, or up-end for the deeper ones, or dive to the bottom to uproot plants or snatch aquatic snails and insects from the bottom. In midsummer, the female brings her brood of ducklings to the pond to feast on mosquito larvae in the water, new-hatched dragonflies on emergent plant stems, and mayflies or swarms of midges in the air. Short grass on the banks provides good grazing for the adults and for the young as they mature, and prevents predators from approaching unseen.

When the young are fully grown, the adults lose their flight feathers in a heavy moult. At this time they cannot fly and are very vulnerable to predators, so they must be able to retire for most of the time into the protective cover of a dense bed of reeds.

Thus the most unprepossessing little pond can meet all the needs of a discerning duck. Such places, wastelands to many human eyes and all too often used as convenient dumping-grounds for refuse, are vital habitats to many wild birds and the other creatures whose food webs they share.

Neighbours with differing requirements

Most habitats are shared by many birds, with each species making different use of it. Some may spend the whole year – or even their whole life – within the bounds of a single suburban garden, while to others it might simply be a convenient stopping place for an hour or so on a migration route of several thousand kilometres.

Blue Tits commonly nest in small gardens, finding all the food they need to raise a brood of a dozen young in little more than half an acre. In winter they may move into a nearby copse or hedgerow, or even into the reeds around the village pond.

Starlings nest in holes in buildings or trees, foraging for their brood in lawns and pastures over a much wider area than that used by Blue Tits. After their young are grown, Starlings congregate in flocks, feeding in fields by day and travelling farther at night to roost in dense flocks in woods or on town buildings.

Kestrels nest in buildings, often in church towers, or in the disused stick-nests of tree-nesting birds like crows and magpies. They range widely to feed, over several square kilometres while they are feeding young. The short grasses of pastures and roadside verges make good hunting-grounds for the voles, mice and large insects that Kestrels feed on: their distinctive hovering attitude as they hang poised above the ground, waiting to drop swiftly down into the grass, is a characteristic sight in many towns as well as in the country.

White Storks nest on buildings in many European towns and villages, though much less widely than they used to. They leave the built-up areas to feed in surrounding damp fields and meadows. Here they hunt mice, voles, moles, lizards, snakes and frogs, and take them back to the nest to feed their young. The young storks are raised within sight and sound of the Blue Tits, Starlings and Kestrels which share their habitat; but in the autumn the stork families leave the smaller birds behind to set off on a migration of several thousand kilometres to their winter quarters in Africa or the Middle East.

Overlapping ranges
Four widespread European species may nest in close proximity to a single human dwelling, but their living ranges differ enormously. While the Blue Tit (*Parus caeruleus*) (**1**) requires only a small space, the Starling (*Sturnus vulgaris*) (**2**) ranges farther afield and the Kestrel (*Falco tinnunculus*) (**3**) hunts over a still wider area. The White Stork (*Ciconia ciconia*) (**4**) has the greatest requirement on space: it travels to a second home in Africa for the winter months.

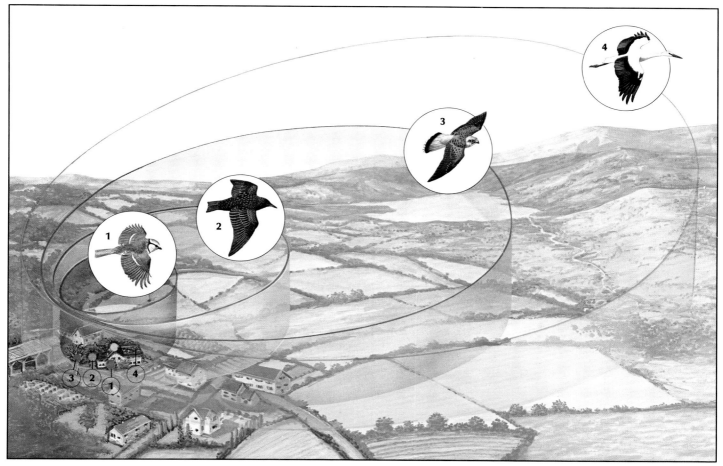

Hazardous journey

White Storks are among the best-loved and best-known birds in Europe. By a happy historical accident they chose the same habitat to nest in as people have chosen to settle in, so for hundreds of years White Storks and people have lived side by side in harmony. From their natural nest sites in tall trees they moved to the tops of tall buildings such as church towers, and to the roofs and chimneys of ordinary dwellings. The legend of storks bringing babies has delighted countless generations of children and helped their embarrassed parents to postpone the truth. So popular were the birds that in many places people put up special platforms for them to nest on — often a cartwheel fixed to the top of a tall post. But for 50 years or more, and in spite of many efforts to encourage them, they have declined steadily in most of Europe, especially in the cooler north and west.

White Storks (*Ciconia ciconia*) used to be common throughout Europe; indeed in some villages their nests adorned nearly every house. Today they are a rarity. Modern roof designs provide few suitable nesting places, but the main reasons for the bird's decline are the disappearance of Europe's wetlands and the reduction of the unpopulated areas that are essential to its way of life.

High-voltage power lines pose a constant threat to migrating storks, especially when weather conditions prevent the birds from soaring high. Losses are particularly high among inexperienced juvenile birds.

Drainage schemes have destroyed many vital feeding grounds, and where the young cannot be properly fed, even the safest nesting site is worthless. The storks have no choice but to abandon the area.

Migration routes of the White Stork
Storks are soaring birds and therefore prefer to fly over land, where they can make full use of rising air currents and 'thermals'. Their sea crossings are as short as possible: the Mediterranean is bypassed via the Straits of Gibraltar in the west and the Dardanelles in the east. The birds' most distant wintering grounds lie 10,000km from their European breeding grounds.

Most White Storks winter in tropical West, South and East Africa and in the Middle East. At stages along their routes the birds rest in large flocks near waterholes and in wetland areas. These 'stepping stones' are of vital importance: without them the birds could not make their annual migrations.

Hunters lie in wait for many migrant birds, especially in the countries bordering the northern shores of the Mediterranean, where hunting is pursued with passionate enthusiasm. For migrating storks, the eastern Mediterranean and North Africa are the most dangerous parts of their journey.

Arid areas and deserts are danger zones for all migrants, especially if they are held up by headwinds and are forced to land with their energy reserves almost gone. The over-exploitation of the land in the Sahel region has led to widespread desertification, which has made this potentially deadly region even wider.

Disappearing habitats

Each species of bird occupies a particular ecological niche – which in some ways is like a person's profession. A bird's niche defines the role it plays in its habitat; as a disperser of mistletoe seeds, say, or as a pollinator of *Heliconia* flowers. But there is no welfare state to support the bird. If it loses its job, it dies. Not many birds are so specialized that they depend on a single species of plant or animal for their survival, but the great majority can survive only within a fairly narrow range of habitat conditions.

Many birds live only near running water, where they need banks lined with vegetation for cover and sites for nests and roosting, and abundant aquatic life to provide them with food. Such waterways are becoming hard to find; modern river management straightens and scours the banks, fells the nearby trees and leaves a channel of surgical cleanliness and sterility. The water itself is a thin soup of pesticides, oil, petrol, industrial waste and detergent. The banks and river bottom are strewn with nylon lines and lead shot, the debris of anglers whose litter threatens the survival of their quarry and its attendant bird-life.

Vast areas of the northern hemisphere were once covered with mixed forest, with deciduous broad-leaved trees and needle-leaved conifers dominating a rich and varied flora. In these woods were huge gnarled trees, half-rotten at the core but thriving at the crown; the perfect home for woodpeckers, with soft wood in which to dig their nest holes, abundant beetles boring under the bark, and hollow limbs to send their drumming calls reverberating through the forest.

For thousands of years, mankind has burnt and chopped and sawn his way through these once endless forests until now only pathetic remnants are left. Most are now farmland or cities, but some were turned into forests of conifers – serried ranks of proud straight trees, their lower branches neatly trimmed, the ground beneath them cleaned of litter and green plants alike. Even in the scattered hardwood forests, old trees are gone, pronounced a danger to the health of the forest. Almost all the woodpeckers too are gone, and the woods are largely still and silent.

Across the temperate regions of the developed world, agriculture has had a major impact on the rivers and streams that feed and drain the land. Riverside cover of reeds and overhanging trees has been ripped out, leaving sterile banks offering little food or cover for animal life. Such modifications also threaten the water regime of the surrounding landscape.

The conversion of natural wetlands into open paddy fields in Southeast Asia leaves little undisturbed habitat for those species like the Chinese Little Bittern (*Ixobrychus sinensis*) that require dense cover in which to nest.

The Middle Spotted Woodpecker (*Dendrocopos medius*) depends on old mixed forests where dead wood offers plentiful supplies of woodboring insects and suitable sites in which nest holes can be excavated. Like all woodpeckers, the bird is sensitive to the changes caused by intensive forestry: it is now in decline throughout Europe as the ancient woodlands are cut down and replaced by conifer plantations.

Mankind's global habitat

Every wild animal and plant occupies its own ecological niche in the environment. Some species use bigger niches than others, and some habitats provide more niches, others fewer; but in general, the species which share a particular place, like actors on a stage, play different parts.

The ancestors of our own species no doubt obeyed this natural law, as other species did and as a few primitive tribes still do in the remoter parts of the world. Our primate ancestors probably lived in African savannas as hunter–gatherers, eating fruit, leaves, eggs, berries and roots, and meat when they could catch it. They lived in families or bigger social groups, finding safety in numbers in an environment that probably carried a much higher population of large predators than the modern African savannas. If biologists could have been there to study them, they would probably have described our ancestors as social, terrestrial omnivores of open, wooded grasslands.

For hundreds of thousands of years, while we spread throughout the earth, we kept more or less to our niche. We were part of our environment, sharing it with a wide variety of other species, some of which we used, some of which used us.

Then we invented tools and weapons. With them we could hunt much more effectively than we had before. We became predators, and began to compete with the larger carnivores, taking prey that they would otherwise have killed. We were also able to defend ourselves against the carnivores much better than we had before. We expanded into the predators' niche, and left less room for them.

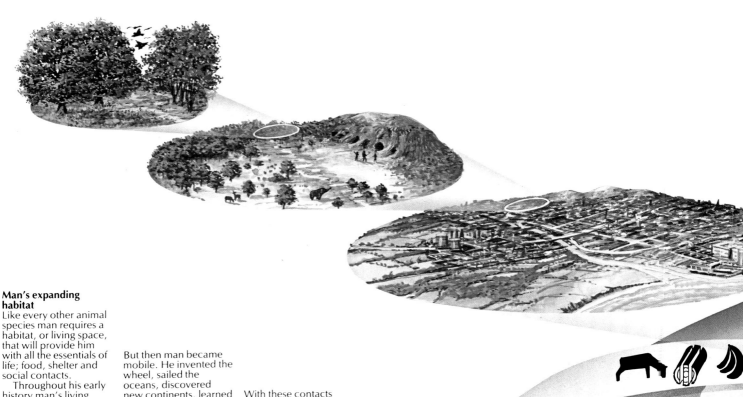

Man's expanding habitat
Like every other animal species man requires a habitat, or living space, that will provide him with all the essentials of life; food, shelter and social contacts.

Throughout his early history man's living space was small. A tribe of cave dwellers could find all it required within an area of a few square kilometres. Apart from occasional nomadic wanderings, man for a long time lived in territories no bigger than those of many of the animals around him.

But then man became mobile. He invented the wheel, sailed the oceans, discovered new continents, learned how to fly – and finally ventured into space. The expansion of his range brought man into contact with others of his own kind; first with neighbouring tribes, then with inhabitants of other regions, and finally with the peoples of distant continents.

With these contacts came the beginnings of trade in goods. At first, food and skins were exchanged. Later, luxury goods for the fortunate few formed the basis of trade. Finally there developed a worldwide trade in food, materials and manufactured goods.

With our tools we could make shelters that we could carry with us into places where there was no shelter. We learnt to make fire, which allowed us to stay alive in places that had been too cold before, to cook food so that it lasted longer and was less likely to give us diseases; and most important of all, allowed us to change our habitat, burning woodland and forest to change it into grassland.

Today our livelihood depends on this international, global trade.

In the ecological sense, every individual's living space now covers a large part of the earth's surface. Every imaginable commodity is traded worldwide, our social contacts are international and the people of the world are linked by a global network of communications.

The world has shrunk to the size of a village again. And even if we cannot visit personally every part of that global habitat, we all share responsibility for its welfare since we benefit equally from its resources and amenities.

Then we learnt to grow crops instead of depending on the wild food plants that we could find. We became farmers, changing natural habitats into the first man-made monocultures. While farmers produced more food than they themselves could eat, others were released to take up other tasks. Cities grew up where no food was grown but people were busy with activities that affected the world far beyond the bounds of where the people actually lived. International trade was born. People in cities in Europe traded with people in India and China, and through the complex network of trade the actions of people began to affect wild species living thousands of miles away. Roman emperors sent emissaries deep into Africa and India to bring back bizarre creatures to entertain them: lions, peacocks, elephants and camels were early victims of the international wildlife trade.

Each of these developments in human history can be seen as a quantum leap in the expansion of our ecological niche. Consider your own 'niche' and how far it extends. The wood that makes the furniture and framework of your house, and the paper for books, magazines, newspapers and carrier bags, was not made from trees from your own back yard nor even, very often, from your own country. The demands for wood in the western world are satisfied to a large extent by the rainforests of the tropics. The hamburgers that are the cheap fast-food staple of North America have fuelled the levelling of forest in Central America to grow beef slightly cheaper than it can be grown farther north. Many developed nations have set up manufacturing plants in tropical countries to build cars and trucks with cheaper labour than can be found at home. The smoke-stacks of Britain fuel the atmosphere with acids to rain down on the lakes of Scandinavia, poisoning their fish and denuding them of birds.

While birds and other animals keep to the ecological rule of 'one species, one niche', mankind has steadily expanded his to include the whole planet.

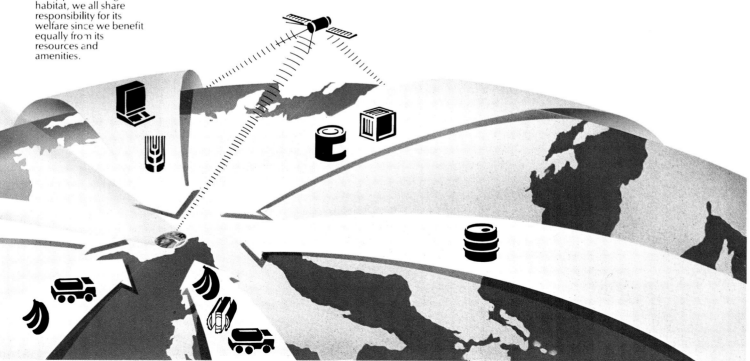

Spaceship *Earth*

We are all passengers on a spaceship from which we cannot disembark. The ship will never land anywhere, and so far as we know it did not take off from anywhere. We are born on it, we will die on it, and generations of the far distant future will depend on its survival as completely as we do.

The ship, of course, is the planet we call earth. We have all been keenly aware of the dangers faced by astronauts travelling in space and of how critically dependent they are on the soundness of the engineering and maintenance of their craft. The pictures they have taken of the earth, poised in the black void of space, have brought home to many of us that our planet, too, is a spaceship, and that our survival depends not only on how well it was put together but also on how well we look after it.

A space capsule is a self-contained ecosystem, built by men. Like the earth it is powered partly by energy from the sun and partly by energy stored inside it: the nuclear and thermal energy of the earth are analogous to the rocket fuel aboard the spaceship. Within the ship there are cycles of water, nutrients, oxygen and other gases, whose efficiency and freedom from contamination are vital to the inhabitants.

Astronauts take aboard all the water they will need for their journey, just as the earth still carries the water it began with hundreds of millions of years ago. Like astronauts, we too must recycle the water we use and take care that it does not become contaminated. The carbon dioxide we breathe out must be restructured into food and oxygen; plants do this for us on earth, and without a healthy carpet of green vegetation there would be no animal life on earth. One of the features of earth that sets it apart from other planets that we know of is the high concentration of oxygen produced by living plants. The composition of our atmosphere, which we often think of as a purely 'physical' property of the planet, is in fact created and maintained by living organisms.

Devotees of science fiction have encouraged us to believe that if we destroy this planet we can always move to another one. This is not just fiction; it is bizarre fantasy. No planet has yet been discovered with conditions suitable for our sort of life — or indeed for any kind of life that we know of — which means that there is none within reach of earth. The physical conditions of our planet are really very special. Earth has a combination of distance from the sun, temperature, gravity and atmospheric composition which is unique in the universe of which we know. It is unrealistic to plan to colonize new planets; instead we must improve our management of this one.

A spiral nebula like this, very similar to our own, consists of billions of stars, many with their own attendant solar systems. Yet even this is only a tiny part of an immeasurable cosmos.
   Whether or not life exists on any of these distant worlds is one of the most intriguing questions facing man.

The natural ecosystems of the earth are like the life-support systems of a spacecraft. They each take part in the cycles of water and nutrients, and the passage of energy through food webs and food chains, according to strict natural laws which apply as much to real ecosystems as to spacecraft.

Natural ecosystems are the life-support systems of Spaceship *Earth*. If they break down, we shall be as helpless as travellers in a crippled spaceship.

Each natural ecosystem depends on the integrated workings of many different living species. Like the circuits of a well-designed spacecraft, ecosystems are robust and designed to suffer the loss or failure of a proportion of their parts without total failure. Throughout the history of life on earth, ecosystems have adjusted to the loss of some species through extinction, and the incursion of others through evolution or immigration. And just as a spacecraft contains many more circuits and rivets than it needs, so most ecosystems can suffer the loss of a number of species without breaking

down irrevocably. But we can no more predict how many species a system can 'safely' lose than an engineer can be sure how many rivets his ship could lose before it would be crippled. But it is certain that we are losing 'rivets' from Spaceship *Earth* at a far faster rate than the ship was designed to withstand, and far faster than they can be replaced by the ecosystems' natural mechanisms of maintenance.

The earth – a giant space capsule
The earth is a closed and limited system. It is powered by the sun, and has been functioning without pause for about 4600 million years.

Each part of the natural world has its parallel in the space capsule of the future. Solar panels capture the energy of the sun, taking the place of earth's vegetation, while waste products are broken down and re-used, and nutrients and oxygen are produced, by an on-board closed-cycle biological processor, perhaps based on algae. Coloured arrows represent the main cyclic processes – oxygen in red, carbon dioxide in buff, water in blue, nutrients in green and waste products in yellow.

'Some wayward stranger in a spacecraft, coming from some other part of the heavens, could look at earth and never know that it was inhabited at all. But that same wayward stranger would certainly know instinctively that if the earth *were* inhabited, then the destinies of all who lived on it must inevitably be interwoven and joined. We are one hunk of ground, water, air, clouds, floating around in space. From out there it really is "one world". . . .'

Frank Borman, Apollo 8, 24 December 1969.

Earth's Great Ecosystems

ANTHONY W. DIAMOND

There are no sharp boundaries in the natural world. Each ecosystem merges into those adjoining it, and each interacts with the others. We can only understand these living habitats if we regard each one as a vital part of the global biosphere.

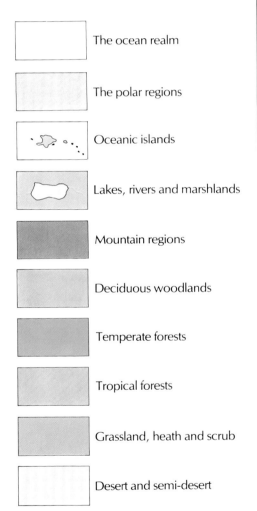

The ocean realm

The polar regions

Oceanic islands

Lakes, rivers and marshlands

Mountain regions

Deciduous woodlands

Temperate forests

Tropical forests

Grassland, heath and scrub

Desert and semi-desert

The map projection
This map and the individual world maps that form part of the introduction to each of the following habitat sections have been drawn using the Peters Projection – a map projection in which the countries of the world are represented according to their surface areas.

While the countries and continents appear distorted by comparison with the more familiar Mercator projection, this map offers a true representation of the size of the world's landmasses while also maintaining their north–south and west–east relationships.

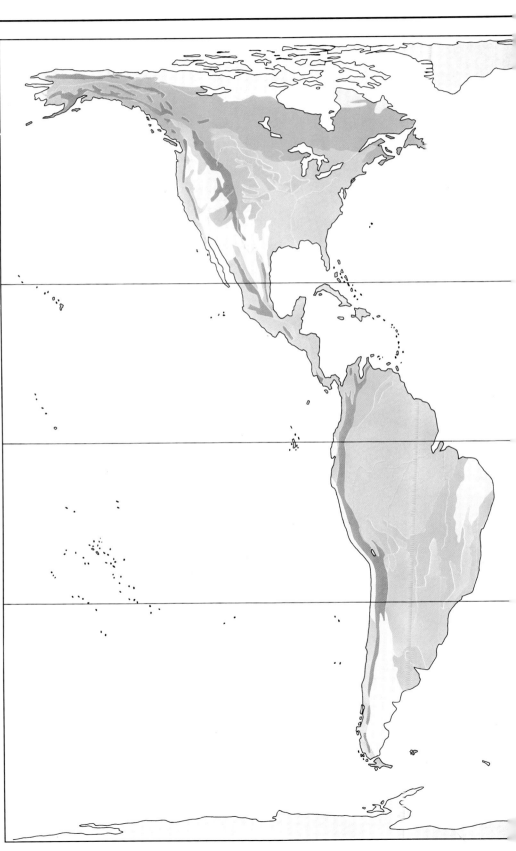

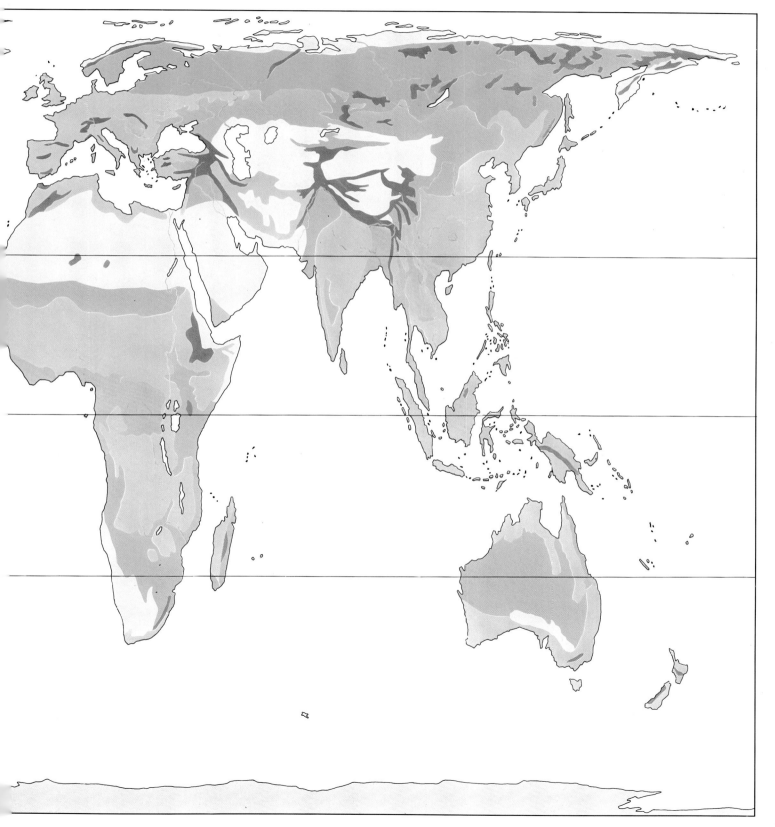

The world's oceans contain more than 97 per cent of the free water present on the face of the globe. They form a vast and constantly moving reservoir, absorbing and redistributing the radiant energy of the sun; controlling the climatic regimes of the continents; mixing, storing and eventually redepositing the minerals washed from the land by rivers and supporting a flora and fauna as rich and varied as that of any ecosystem on land.

Water temperature, current movements, sunlight hours and nutrients combine to determine the distribution of the marine plankton — the teeming communities of microscopic plants and animals that support all life in the oceans. And on that vital food resource hangs the fate of the world's seabirds, from the solitary albatross sweeping effortlessly over the empty expanse of the southern oceans to the millions of cliffnesters crowding the steep, rocky coastlines of North America and Eurasia.

The global ecosystem

The great oceans cover seven-tenths of our planet and are shaped, but not completely separated, by emergent land-masses. Their depth and colour impose strict limitations on the life within them, yet through their unity they link the very ends of the earth in one continuous life-supporting ecosystem.

The sea is predominantly blue. There are green areas near coasts, and brown areas off muddy estuaries and over shallow banks, but the endless expanse of the open ocean is characteristically and unmistakably blue. We are so used to this that it may not strike us as remarkable or significant. The sky, after all, is blue, and water is a transparent medium, so why should it, too, not be blue? But the sky contains no life: there are no plants there to stain it green with their life-sustaining chlorophyll. Yet the sea does support plant and other life-forms, and it receives all the nutrients washed off the land by rivers. Certainly it has life; so why is the ocean never the rich green that land can be?

The answer is that life is very sparse in the open oceans; so sparse that it lends no colour of its own to the sea. There are no marine equivalents of forest or bushland or grassy plains. Rooted in shallow coastal waters there are giant kelps, smaller sea-weeds and 'sea grasses' which mimic land plants, but to grow in the open ocean plants like these would have to anchor their roots up to ten kilometres deep. Truly oceanic plants consist of the tiny one-celled diatoms and algae called plankton, microscopic and evanescent. In sufficient numbers their bodies can stain the sea red, brown or green, but such 'blooms' are shallow-water phenomena.

The food chains of the open ocean start with planktonic plant cells called phyto-plankton. They are too small to build up internal stores of nutrients and so their growth, and thus the productivity of the entire ocean system, is determined by the concentration of nutrients in the sea water itself. And these nutrients, like the plant cells that feed upon them, are very scarce because, although they are fed continuously into the oceans from the land, they are soon lost by sinking to the bottom, out of reach of surface life.

The deepest parts of the sea floor plunge farther below sea level than the highest mountains rise above it, and the interiors of most ocean basins are several kilometres deep. Plant life, and all the animal life that feeds on it, depends on light; but light penetrates only 30 to 120 metres below the surface in most parts of the ocean, so plants can photosynthesize only in that thin surface layer. When they die, if they are not intercepted by some scavenger their bodies slowly sink until they fall out of the lighted zone into the black abyssal depths. The phytoplankton are thus engaged in a frantic race to gather nutrients and cycle them as often as they can before they sink irrevocably out of reach.

Feeding directly on the phytoplankton are the teeming millions of minute floating, drifting and swimming animals that make up the zooplankton. Together, the plant and animal plankton form the basic food resource on which all other marine animal life depends.

This microscope view of animal plankton clearly shows several tiny crustaceans and the larvae of many other marine organisms.

The largest animals on earth feed exclusively on tiny floating marine organisms collectively called plankton.

The huge baleen whales have a comb of baleen (whalebone) plates in the mouth instead of teeth, and with these they filter small crustaceans, the krill, from the water. Krill, at up to 6cm long, are the giants of the plankton world.

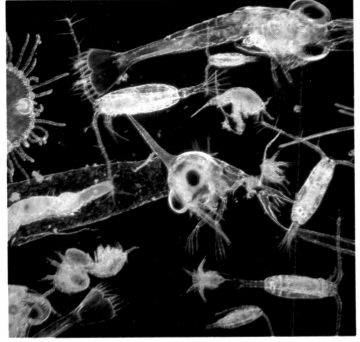

The chemistry of the oceans

The ocean basins act as sinks for all the elements brought down by rivers. Their chemistry is quite different from that of freshwater bodies because while minerals accumulate on the sea floor, water evaporates from the surface, and living things within the sea concentrate some elements more than others.

Phosphorus, so crucial for the chemistry of photosynthesis, is very scarce at sea, but like other elements it becomes more concentrated in certain areas. These are places where deep-sea currents are drawn upward, bringing their rich stores of nutrients from the abyssal ooze to the sunlit surface, where the phytoplankton can use them. These deep waters are cold as well as fertile, and phosphorus, curiously, dissolves more readily in cold water than in warm, so cold upwelling currents are particularly fertile places. They are found most often off the west coasts of continents, where prevailing offshore winds push the surface waters away from the coast and deeper waters rise to replace them. These upwellings are the most productive parts of the oceans, and harbour the world's richest fisheries and most spectacular colonies of seabirds.

The global regulator

The oceans have been aptly likened to a global thermostat. Water has a great capacity to absorb heat — three thousand times the capacity of air — and so the oceans insulate the earth against extremes in temperature. The influence of the seas on climate is profound. We know how climates near coasts are moderate and equable compared with those far inland, with cooler summers and warmer winters; but the oceans' effects extend much farther than the coast. The warm waters of the Gulf Stream, which flow northeast across the North Atlantic from the Caribbean, are at a slightly different temperature each year. The differences are so slight that they have no effect in the warm tropics where the current begins, but they are enough to change the time of the spring thaw in Europe, alter the southern limit of the ice around Iceland, and shift the pack-ice in the Barents Sea.

The changes in air temperature which control the distribution of low and high pressure in the atmosphere are intimately linked with the currents of the ocean, which thus affect the climate of the land as much as that of the sea. These currents not only link events in the depths of the ocean with those in the upper reaches of the atmosphere but they also move between the ocean basins, slowly but inexorably transporting water and the elements within it from one end of the planet to the other. It may take an individual molecule six thousand years to circumnavigate the globe; a trivial feat, perhaps, when set beside a sailor or a seabird speeding round in months, but awesome in its implications for the future of all that enters the oceanic system.

The sheer enormity of the oceans is one of their most important properties. The gases and elements dissolved in their waters are the reserves of the planetary bank, acting as a gigantic shock-absorber against short-term changes in the atmosphere. The sea also gives us rain. Most of the rain that falls on land has been evaporated from the surface of the sea, and the endless cycle from rain to land to river to sea and back again reminds us that oceans and land are inseparable components of a single global system.

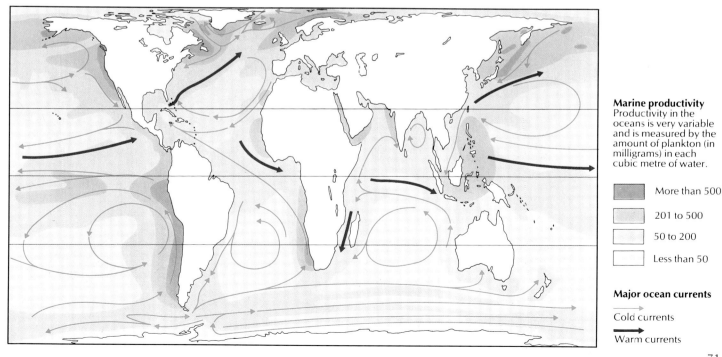

Marine productivity
Productivity in the oceans is very variable and is measured by the amount of plankton (in milligrams) in each cubic metre of water.

More than 500

201 to 500

50 to 200

Less than 50

Major ocean currents

Cold currents

Warm currents

Biology of the ocean realm

Two physical factors — the depth of the oceans and the limited ability of light to penetrate water — restrict the biological productivity of the open sea. Measurements in many oceans show that their primary productivity — the amount of energy produced by their plants — is similar to that of deserts on land. Thus, although the oceans cover seven-tenths of the surface of the globe, they account for less than one-quarter of the total organic production of the planet.

Because oceanic plants are so very small, the plant-eaters at the base of the ecological pyramid must also be very small. The food chain between plants and top carnivores is thus much longer in oceans than it is on land. Since energy is lost at each link in the chain, the resources available to the larger carnivores are scarce. All seabirds are carnivores and so support themselves on a narrower, more sharply pointed pyramid of energy than is the case with landbirds. Add to this the vast distances involved, tempestuous seas and stormy winds, and it is not surprising that so few species have specialized in living at sea.

Seabirds – the marine specialists

Only three per cent of bird species are seabirds, though the sea covers 70 per cent of the earth. Seabirds are specialists in a very demanding environment, and one that seems monotonously uniform — a flat, wet desert of limitless extent. Yet in fact the sea is richly patterned; not only round its edges, where the shallow continental seas and cool upwellings teem with life, but even in the deep oceans, where unseen currents carry cold Antarctic water to the equator, or tropical water from one end of the ocean to the other. Here, subtle oceanographic boundaries cause profound changes in seabird distributions, and impose a pattern on the sea as clear to its birds as the patterns of woods and fields on land appear to man.

The temperature and salt content of the water determine the kinds of plankton that live in a particular area and, through them, the distribution of birds and other larger animals. Temperature is affected by the water's origin; much comes from melting polar ice and is cold and fresh at first, warming and becoming salty as it moves towards the tropics. The boundaries between currents and different water-bodies are the great divides of the sea, as important to seabirds and other oceanic life as the edge of a forest or desert on land. Even in the equatorial zone, where ocean life is at its most sparse and uniform, subtle changes of a few parts per thousand in salt content or a single degree in temperature can cause a dramatic change from one fauna to another.

Seabirds' specialized feeding methods

1. Skua harassing other seabirds, forcing them to disgorge their food.
2. Gannet diving with wings partly folded back.
3. Tern diving from the wheeling flock.
4. Frigatebird diving to snatch food from the surface, but without entering the water.
5. Skimmer scooping food from the surface, with the lower mandible cleaving the water surface.
6. Albatross picking food scraps from the water, its wings half-raised in aggressive posture.
7. Gull swimming around, picking up food morsels.
8. Storm Petrel 'dancing' on the water – a combination of hovering flight and 'treading water'.
9. Phalarope swimming in tight circles to swirl food items into the uppermost water layer.
10. Cormorant in steep streamlined dive, using its feet for propulsion.
11. Auk pursuing fish prey, using its wings for propulsion.
12. Shearwater making a shallow dive from a few metres above the waves.
13. Penguin pursuing fish prey at depth, using its wings for propulsion.

Current boundaries can also be attractive feeding areas for birds. Plankton often accumulates along them, attracting fish and squid to crop the plankton, and birds in turn to hunt the fish and squid. Such oceanic 'fronts' are especially important in the tropics, where the constant high temperature and low solubility of phosphate contribute to seas as sterile as the soil of a tropical forest. Here, seabirds' prey is normally so widely scattered that it can be exploited only when it becomes concentrated. This happens at ocean fronts, and also when a school of predatory fish rounds up smaller fish and squid and drives them to the surface in a shoal. There, for a few hectic minutes, seabirds swoop and plunge among them, twisting and jostling in the air as fish and squid jump briefly from the water to escape the menace below.

Man's use, and abuse, of the oceans

Since mankind first ventured on to the sea he has profited from the skill in exploiting its resources that seabirds have perfected over aeons of evolutionary time. Polynesian seamen still navigate by watching the flight of birds, and fishermen's lore the world over describes which birds to follow in order to find fish. On remote atolls of the tropical Indian Ocean, breeding seabirds are not just cropped for food; some are more subtly used, frightened just enough to bring up their food to be used by fishermen as bait. On windswept islands between Australia and Tasmania, and south of New Zealand, young Sooty and Short-tailed Shearwaters are harvested each year in the traditional 'muttonbird' industry, while in the tropical Seychelles, islanders crowd the jetties to scramble for Sooty Tern eggs collected in crateloads from the outer islands. On remote islands from Chile to South Africa, phosphate-rich deposits of seabird guano are mined for use throughout the world as agricultural fertilizer.

Some of the ways of exploiting seabirds are true harvests, cropping some part of the birds' annual production at a rate that the population can sustain. But others, like the guano industries, are mining the capital resource rather than creaming off the income. In the cold upwelling Humboldt current off Chile and Peru, a traditional guano-mining industry has now been joined by a major industrial fishery taking the anchovies that are the food of the cormorants, boobies and pelicans that make the guano. The result is chaos; a crash in bird numbers, and so in guano production, and an early decline of the fishery too. In the cold Benguela current off Namibia, South African guano miners and fishermen are locked in a similar conflict, with the Jackass Penguin and Cape Gannet caught in the cross-fire.

Those few parts of the oceans where man can harvest fish economically are naturally also those parts where most seabirds live. This fact alone is an eloquent reminder that man shares with all other creatures a dependence on the laws of nature. Few species of seabird are in imminent danger of extinction, but a very great number are declining, and the various causes of decline are instructive indicators of man's far-reaching and profound impact on the ecosystem.

Several female Great Frigatebirds (*Fregata minor*) and a lone Brown Booby (*Sula leucogaster*) wheel and dive over a shoal of fish driven to the surface in panic by an unseen predator below.

Anchovy hunters of the Peruvian coast. This feeding flock consists mainly of Guanay Cormorants (*Phalacrocorax bougainvillii*) along with Brown Pelicans (*Pelecanus occidentalis*) and the endemic Peruvian Booby (*Sula variegata*).

Cahow:
Locking out the competition

On a wild black night in 1603, a Spanish sea captain ran for shelter under the lee of an unknown shore in the western Atlantic. His sailors' terror became a nightmare when howling out of the black night came millions of winged shapes, swirling round the masts and filling the air with unearthly shrieks. That gale was immortalized in Shakespeare's play *The Tempest*, and the sailors took their revenge on the howling shapes; they ate them in their thousands, and within 20 years of the islands being settled the birds were thought to be extinct. They called the islands the Bermudas, and the birds 'cahow' after their fearsome call. For 300 years they remained a folk memory, until scattered specimens cropped up and a systematic search in 1951 revealed the last remnants of the species — about 18 pairs — nesting in shallow burrows and rock crevices on tiny offshore islands and remote sea stacks. Their demise had been hastened by feral pigs and cats introduced by settlers and by rats that came ashore from visiting ships.

Cahows (*Pterodroma cahow*) are petrels; graceful seabirds with long, narrow wings shaped like those of a miniature albatross, and sharing with albatrosses and shearwaters the 'tubenose' family characteristic of large nostrils enclosed in a prominent tube along the top of the hook-tipped beak. Like all their nocturnal tribe their colours are dull shades of black, grey, brown or white. Cahows spend their youth and summers on the open ocean, where they feed mainly on small squid, diving underwater to pursue their prey. They come to land only to prospect or breed, and then only at night.

Breeding birds return to land in October, using the same nest site as the year before but making a new nest of green twigs. Both birds may occupy the burrow night and day until in late December they leave to feed at sea, returning two weeks later to lay and incubate their single large white egg. For over seven weeks they take turns to warm the egg, in spells of up to two weeks, living on the food they stored before it was laid. Once hatched, the tiny chick is left alone, except when being fed, for all but the first few days of its three-month fledging period.

When the chick is two to three weeks old, alone and defenceless in its burrow by day, the White-tailed Tropicbirds (*Phaethon lepturus*) return to Bermuda to breed. They are surely one of the most beautiful and graceful of seabirds, but they too nest in rock-clefts and shallow burrows, and they are robust and fierce birds that make short work of young Cahows. The Cahows were driven from their mainland sites to nest in tropicbird country on the islets; but the contest was unequal, and without inspired human intervention the tropicbird would have sealed the Cahows' fate. Fortunately, tropicbirds are larger than Cahows; not much — precisely three millimetres in chest measurement — but enough to allow a baffle to be built at the Cahow's nest entrance, with a hole just big enough to let a Cahow through but too small to admit a tropicbird. With these baffles in place, and artificial nest burrows made of wire and concrete installed by conservationists, the Cahows tripled their breeding output and raised their population from 17 pairs in 1963 to 32 in 1982.

The secretive Cahow returning to its nest on a small protected island in Bermuda after feeding far out at sea.

This artificial nesting burrow is specially designed to accommodate the Cahow while keeping out predatory tropicbirds.

Heinroth's Shearwater was rediscovered in 1979, 45 years after the last reported sighting. The bird is now believed to breed in the mountains of Bougainville Island in the Solomons, but no details are known of its biology or status.

Cahows were brought to the brink of extinction by predation, destruction of their forested habitat, and erosion of the soil they nested in. But in the 1960s a new threat was poised to wipe them out; a threat all the more serious because nothing could be done on Bermuda to combat it. By 1967 the 22 pairs then on the island managed to rear only six chicks, and the annual decline in productivity over the previous decade reached over three per cent. Had that rate continued, reproduction would have failed entirely by 1978. Eggs that failed to hatch, and chicks that died, contained DDT residues of up to 11 parts per million, more than enough to account for the disastrous decline. The Cahows' summer dispersal over the North Atlantic made them perfect monitors of the contamination of the ocean environment. The Cahows had picked up the residues at sea and given a demonstration of the insidious proliferation of organochlorine insecticides as convincing as it was tragic. Legislation controlling the use of DDT in North America came just in time to halt the Cahows' slide into extinction.

Other petrels and shearwaters around the world are threatened too. At least five species are in urgent need of dedicated conservation work, conservation programmes are in hand for four others, and nearly 20 others are so little known that we do not know their present status. In the last few years, several species known only from ancient museum specimens have come to light — several literally so when fledglings, dazzled by house lights on misty nights, have tumbled, disoriented, into human habitations. The Taiko (*Pterodroma magentae*) in the Chatham Islands, Heinroth's Shearwater (*Puffinus heinrothi*) in New Britain, the Fiji Petrel (*Pterodroma macgillivrayi*) and the Réunion Black Petrel (*Pterodroma aterrima*) in the Indian Ocean have all reappeared very recently, their nesting grounds still unknown but likely to be threatened by the alien animals introduced by man to so many of the world's islands.

Galapagos Flightless Cormorant:
A tourist attraction in danger

Loss of flight imposes obvious limitations on a bird's mobility, but some species cope better than others. Penguins can manage substantial migrations on foot or at sea, but the Flightless Cormorant (*Nannopterum harrisi*) of the Galapagos Islands makes no such attempts and is surely the world's most sedentary seabird. The birds are found on only two islands — Isabela and Fernancina — on the western side of the Galapagos group, where the cool waters of the Humboldt current wash the coasts. They breed along less than 400km of coastline, and have never been seen more than 1km outside their breeding range.

The cormorant is not a pretty sight, especially when it spreads out its wings to dry and reveals the pathetically rudimentary structures bequeathed it by generations of disuse. The dull black plumage is relieved only by the brilliant blue eyes of the adults; the bill is long, strong and hooked; the legs robust, and the feet fully webbed in the manner of all cormorants. They swim low in the water, and though perfectly competent to walk on land, do so as little as possible.

The breeding behaviour of the Flightless Cormorant shows an extraordinary lack of fidelity among mated birds. It is rare for a bird to mate with the same partner in successive seasons; separation and re-pairing is the rule rather than the exception it is in other seabirds. Birds may attempt to breed several times a year – courting, building a nest of seaweed on bare rock, and laying up to four eggs (usually three), though many of the eggs are lost or abandoned and a high proportion are infertile. Nesting is concentrated in the coolest part of the year, from April to November, but frequent failures and re-nestings (with new partners) mean that eggs are laid in most months. The male is larger than the female and feeds the young much longer than his mate, who may pair up with another male and start to breed again even before her previous young are independent.

Flightless Cormorants breed in small groups on boulder beaches, bare rocks and in sheltered lagoons. They seem to nest as close as they can to good feeding grounds in cool, shallow water, where they feed on fish, octopus and eels, rarely venturing farther than 100m from the shore. They often put their nests dangerously close to the water, and one group whose nests were lifted half a metre farther from the sea by a mild earthquake promptly moved them back again by the same amount.

The present population of about 700–800 pairs shows no sign of changing either in range or number, but the reasons for remaining tied to this stretch of coast remain obscure. The sea is cooler here than elsewhere in the Galapagos, but the cormorants enter the water only to feed, and their prey species range much more widely than the cormorants do. Such a tiny population, confined to such a small area, is extremely vulnerable. A small change in oceanographic conditions could take the food source far beyond the reach of a bird reluctant to move more than 100m from land. Genetic defects, too, could build up to dangerous levels, and this danger may well explain the birds' otherwise bizarre breeding behaviour as well as the high failure rate of nesting attempts. Frequent changes of mate must mix the genetic material within the population much more than would be the case in more sexually conventional birds.

Man-made threats also exist, even in this remote archipelago. Crayfish abound in the cormorants' feeding areas, and the traditional fishery by skindivers may soon be replaced by an industrial one using nets, a development certain to cause fatalities. Wild dogs, a menace elsewhere in the islands, have recently been seen close to the nesting grounds and could cause serious damage if they are not controlled in time. Man, too, could become a threat as the increasing numbers of tourists all want to see these fascinating birds. Fortunately the cormorants are very tolerant of people, and a careful watch continues to be kept on their welfare.

Galapagos Cormorants and their young on the rocky coastal breeding ground they share with Fernandina Island's marine iguanas. These huge lizards live on marine plants and, like the birds, feed in the shallow inshore waters.

The Flightless Cormorant's wings are a sorry sight when held out to dry in the sun after swimming.

Audouin's Gull: Europe's rarest seabird

The crowded islands of the Mediterranean are a far cry from the desolate wastes of the Galapagos. The problems faced by seabirds here are posed by people, who have co-existed with the birds for millennia. The species that remain are the resilient ones; the others have long since disappeared.

Most 'seagulls' are not true seabirds. They feed in inshore waters, or even on land, and very rarely out at sea as real seabirds do. Audouin's Gulls (*Larus audouinii*) are more marine than most, but like their relatives they find some of their food on land and close inshore. They breed in loose, scattered colonies on rocky south-facing slopes on islands in the Mediterranean. More than 85 per cent of the population of about 3600 pairs nests in the western Mediterranean, the rest off Cyprus, Lebanon, and in the Aegean Sea. Over 2000 pairs — more than 60 per cent of the total population — breed on the Chafarinas Islands off the northeast coast of Morocco.

Audouin's Gulls lay rather late in the season — not until late April or May. They lay up to three eggs (normally two) and incubate them for four weeks. In early June the rough seas and strong winds of May give way to calmer, sunnier days when the sea is stilled to a glassy calm for days on end. Then the Audouin's Gulls show why they lay so late; only in calm weather can they use their unique and specialized feeding method. Flying very close to the surface, so slowly they seem bound to fall at any moment, they skim their prey from just below the surface — sometimes even dipping their wing-tips briefly in the sea as they do so.

They feed on shoals of small fish, mostly of the herring family, which come to the surface to spawn in the June calms. Such fish are much rarer in the eastern Mediterranean and in this part of their range the birds take much more of their food from land. The gulls stalk bare or grassy fields, leaping up to fly after mice and grasshoppers. Sometimes, in spring, the floods of small migrant birds flying north from their African winter quarters are checked by late storms sweeping in from the Atlantic. After a strenuous flight across the Sahara the birds are often so exhausted they can barely stand, and if they make landfall near a colony of Audouin's Gulls they fall easy prey to the larger birds.

So the gulls will take what food they can, but the timing of their breeding season and the predominance of small fish in their diet shows that they still depend much more on marine resources than the other gulls of the region. Their position at the top of the marine food chain exposes them to contamination of the sea, and the Mediterranean — being almost land-locked — can disperse pollutants even less efficiently than the open ocean.

Adult birds carry significant doses of organochlorines and heavy metals, especially mercury, which reaches 1.2 parts per million in eggs and 15 in nestlings, showing that it is absorbed by the female and passed into her eggs as well as being brought back to the nest in food.

There is as yet no firm evidence that toxins are affecting Audouin's Gulls adversely, though any increase in levels of pollutants must present a serious danger. The most immediate threat to the birds is the disturbance of their breeding colonies by people. South-facing slopes on Mediterranean islands in spring and early summer are attractive for many reasons, and the burgeoning populations of Europe, North Africa and the Levant range more widely every year. Tourists come to sunbathe, or to walk, search for flowers or even look for birds. Fishermen come ashore to rest, repair their gear and search for gulls' eggs to eat. In the main they take the eggs of Herring Gulls (*Larus argentatus*), which are crowded into denser colonies and so are easier to find, but some Audouin's Gull colonies are regularly cropped for eggs, and none are in reserves where they can be properly protected. The most important colonies, on the Chafarinas, are disputed between Spain and Morocco and a Spanish military garrison keeps casual fishermen away. A bigger barracks is due to be built and this must cause concern since bored off-duty soldiers are not noted protectors of wildlife.

Unlike the Flightless Cormorant, whose worst enemy is probably its own biology, Audouin's Gulls have considerable natural advantages. The dispersed and scattered distribution of their nests is probably the most effective, and they seem regularly to change sites from year to year. They are, nonetheless, one of Europe's rarest birds, and it is no good advertisement for the supposedly civilized world that there is not one reserve where such a bird can breed in safety, or that the sea it graces should be so extensively contaminated.

Audouin's Gulls are specialists in the art of picking food morsels from the sea without settling on the water.

The debris of tourism on a beach on the island of Crete – a scene that is repeated again and again round the shores of the Mediterranean.

The largest colony of Audouin's Gulls is on the Chafarinas Islands off the coast of Morocco. Ornithologists regularly check the colony's breeding success and also keep careful watch for signs of poisoning – a common hazard for many kinds of seabirds.

Short-tailed Albatross:
The true cost of bygone fashions

Less than 100 years ago, the Short-tailed or Steller's Albatross (*Diomedea albatrus*) nested in hundreds of thousands on islands in the northwestern Pacific, south of Japan and off the coast of Taiwan. These magnificent seabirds dispersed, after breeding, right across the North Pacific and down the west coast of North America, where bones in Indian kitchen middens attest to their popularity as food. Yet now they are barely numbered in hundreds, breed in no more than two places, and are desperately vulnerable to the human threats of pollution, hunting, disturbance, introduced alien animals and overfishing, as well as natural hazards against which they were formerly protected by their numbers.

Their disastrous decline was caused by the Japanese feather trade, which reached an enormous scale in the nineteenth and early twentieth centuries. In the 17 years to 1903, five million birds were taken: 100,000 a year from the island of Torishima alone. The white breast-feathers were sold as 'swansdown' for filling quilts and pillows, and the black flight-feathers as 'eagle' quills for pens and millinery. Each albatross yielded feathers worth, in those days, about US$1.50.

The only known nesting ground is now on Torishima, the southernmost of the Izu Islands, 520km south of Tokyo. It is naturally hazardous because it is an active volcano. An eruption killed over a hundred people in 1902, and another in 1939 destroyed the village and buried the albatrosses' nesting grounds. Fortunately for the birds they were not breeding then and were safely away at sea. Fear of another eruption in 1965 caused the island to be abandoned.

The albatross population had sunk to 1400 by 1929, and to between 30 and 50 just ten years later. By 1949, after a wartime Japanese garrison had made its presence felt among the birds, none could be found. But a few nests were seen the following year, and effective protection as a National Monument since then has helped to ensure a slow but steady recovery. In 1982 there were 140 adults and 21 chicks on Torishima. In 1980 another 35 birds were counted on Minami-Kojima Island in the southern Ryukyus, but it is not yet known for certain if the birds are breeding there.

Adults return to Torishima in late September, to perform their elaborate courtship rituals. They build their nests among clumps of tall grass growing in patches on the steeper slopes, overlooking the nests of the more widely distributed Black-footed Albatrosses (*Diomedea nigripes*) which nest on the tops of the sea-cliffs below the slopes. The birds' guano enriches the soil and helps establish the grass, which in turn stabilizes the loose soil. Where the soil permits, the nest is a mound of bare earth, concave at the top; elsewhere a scoop in the loose volcanic surface suffices for the single large white egg.

Adult and immature Short-tailed Albatrosses nesting among clumps of coarse grass on the slopes of Torishima. Both parents help in the work of feeding and rearing the young.

Although quiet since 1939, Torishima's still-active volcano poses a constant threat to the albatross breeding grounds.

Both parents incubate, and help to brood and guard the young. The adults feed at sea, chiefly on squid, fish and crustaceans. They share with other tube-nosed seabirds an ability to turn their food into an oil which will keep within their stomach for many days, so enabling the adults to forage farther and longer than they could if they had to bring the food back fresh to the island every day.

Short-tailed Albatrosses take eight or nine years to mature, often do not breed every year, and live for several decades once they reach adulthood. These biological characteristics make them slow to recover from decline but good at surviving short-lived disasters. They were brought to the edge of extinction simply through being slaughtered by hunters. Now they face more subtle hazards. The sovereignty of their newly discovered refuge in the Ryukyus is disputed between the two Chinas, Russia and Japan — and the welfare of a few dozen albatrosses is not those nations' most urgent concern. The waters around the Izus are heavily fished, and like all oceans carry their share of oil and pesticides, so however successfully Torishima may be managed in the birds' interest, it is unlikely that they will ever reach a fraction of their former numbers.

Fishing boats working the waters off Kozu Island in the Izu group represent just one of the modern pressures now faced by the Short-tailed Albatross.

Jackass Penguin:
No safety in numbers

The southern tip of Africa is a region of wild winds, strong currents, tempestuous seas and dense fog. It is one of the world's most dangerous waterways, always busy with oil tankers westbound from the Gulf. Major oil spills are inevitable here, and in the late 1960s and 1970s they killed many thousands of seabirds. Chief among them was the Jackass Penguin (*Spheniscus demersus*), whose flightlessness makes it particularly vulnerable to floating oil.

Jackass Penguins are not the rarest of seabirds; there are probably over 170,000 alive today. But a species' numbers are no guide to its status. Passenger Pigeons (*Ectopistes migratorius*) darkened the skies in their millions in America only 30 years before becoming extinct.

It is the rate at which a species declines that foretells its fate, and this statistic is a gloomy one for the Jackass Penguin. Between 1930 and 1963 the breeding population on Dassen Island, the birds' main stronghold, crashed from 1.5 million to 145,500. Ninety per cent of the total world population has been lost since the beginning of this century.

The species occurs only in the Benguela and Agulhas currents off the southern tip of Africa. Here, cold upwelling water rich in nutrients, and the turbulent mixing of cold and warm water-bodies sustain a profusion of marine life including several commercial fish species. Penguins share these resources with two other abundant seabirds, the Cape Gannet (*Sula capensis*) and Cape Cormorant (*Phalacrocorax capensis*), both of which occur mainly off Namibia, where the stocks of fish — especially anchovy — are most abundant. The penguins are concentrated farther south, where there is a smaller but more reliable stock consisting of several different kinds of fish.

Jackass Penguins breed on 25 islands off the coasts of Namibia and South Africa. In most colonies there are two laying seasons, one in September timed so that the eggs hatch when pilchards and anchovies are spawning, the other in February, when the young fish have grown big enough to eat. The birds nest in dense colonies, and prefer to burrow into the soil or shelter under boulders or in rock crevices. The normal clutch consists of two chalky-white eggs, which both birds incubate for nearly six weeks. The young are fed by both parents for about twelve weeks before going to sea. If food is plentiful one parent guards the chick by day and both by night, but if it is scarce the chick may be left alone by day at the mercy of marauding Kelp Gulls (*Larus dominicanus*).

Like all penguins, Jackasses are flightless. This limits the distance they can travel to feed to about 25km from their breeding grounds, so they are dependent on a food supply that is not only abundant but also predictable. This, no doubt, is why the penguins concentrate in the less rich but more stable mixed-species fishery while the more mobile gannets and cormorants exploit the richer but less stable single-species stocks.

Adult and almost-fledged young Jackass Penguins at their nesting burrows. Both parents share the duties of rearing their 1–2 chicks.

Where guano exploitation has stripped the soil down to bedrock, the birds are forced to nest on the surface in conditions totally unsuited to their biology.

Highly efficient modern sea fisheries are adding to the pressures on the dwindling populations of Jackass Penguins.

As in all countries, the work of volunteer groups is invaluable when swift action is required. Here, young people assist conservationists in the task of cleaning penguins caught in an oil spill.

Jackass Penguins have been hunted at least since 1497, when Vasco da Gama discovered them on Seal Island. But the main influence on their numbers has been the collecting of eggs for food. Over half a million eggs a year were taken up until 1937. This declined to 97,000 in 1949, but collecting continued well into the 1960s. Many islands held huge guano deposits, which supported another major industry, and this too reduced the penguins' numbers by removing the soil in which they burrowed. Penguins are essentially Antarctic birds, ill-fitted for the daytime temperatures of the subtropics. They avoid the heat by spending the day at sea, returning to land at night to nest underground or in shade. Birds forced to nest above ground suffer much higher nest-losses than burrow-nesters do, partly from heat stress and partly from exposure to the predatory Kelp Gulls.

More recently, a major fishing industry has developed, with disastrous effects on the penguins' food supply, and yet another new threat, of harbour development, now threatens at least a quarter of the penguin population.

Erect and immaculate in the avian equivalent of evening dress, penguins remind us irresistibly of ourselves. The Jackass Penguin's fate also reminds us of the consequences of abusing its ecosystem. Oil pollution first raised fears for this bird's survival, but although oil can kill a great many birds it is not likely to endanger the species in the long term. Threats that strike at the survival of the ecosystem are much more serious. The eventual fate of this noisy, comical bird will reflect mankind's ability to manage that system for his own benefit as well as that of the birds.

Abbott's Booby:
A head-on conflict of interests

Boobies are the tropical counterparts of the gannets more familiar in cooler waters. They owe their unlovely name to their extreme tameness: generations of life on remote tropical islands have given them no defence against a terrestrial predator as ruthless and efficient as man, and they remain confiding to a fault.

The history of Abbott's Booby (*Sula abbotti*) is uncertain in detail but tragically clear in outline. The birds once nested on several islands north and east of Madagascar, but succumbed quickly to the early settlers. In the 1930s or possibly 1940s they were finally exterminated on Assumption Island by guano mining. The only population known now is on Christmas Island in the tropical eastern Indian Ocean, 290km south of Java Head.

Abbott's Booby is a large and handsome seabird. Its most distinctive feature is its bill, a sharply pointed dagger with saw-toothed edges, heavier than that of other boobies and more boldly coloured (pink in females, grey in males) with a black tip and a black patch at the base, around each eye.

Most boobies and all gannets nest on the ground, but Abbott's breeds exclusively in tall trees, up to 45m high. Breeding birds have a more restricted repertoire of displays than their ground-nesting relatives, but as if to compensate for this shortcoming the vocal range of Abbott's Booby is much greater and its raucous bull-like bellowing reverberates around the Christmas Island forest like some arboreal cattle fair.

The bulky nest is made of twigs, in which the one chalky egg is laid between May and July. The breeding season is extremely protracted: the chick grows very slowly, taking its first flight when about six months old and returning to the nesting tree for a further seven or eight months to be fed by its parents before finally dispersing out to sea. A successful breeding attempt thus takes more than 12 months, so those birds that raise a chick can normally breed only in alternate years. The adults' lifespan and the age at which they start to breed are not known, but from what is known of their biology (and by analogy with related seabirds) they are likely to live 25–30 years at least and start to breed at 4–7 years. Their potential for increase is thus extremely low, and is further reduced by frequent massive breeding failures.

The obvious and immediate threat to the birds' survival lies in the rich deposits of phosphate in the soil beneath the forest. To reach the guano the forest must be cleared, and vast areas have already been reduced to bare rock by industrial mining. The lunar landscape of barren limestone that remains will take centuries to re-establish a mature forest cover.

To help conserve the boobies, forest is now cleared in patches — leaving trees with booby nests until the young have fledged. Unfortunately the birds are just as good as the miners at choosing the patches of forest overlying rich phosphate, and it remains unclear whether they will breed successfully in the trees that are left after the phosphate has been extracted. It is also doubtful whether those patches of trees will themselves persist as a viable habitat once the protective buffer of surrounding trees has been removed.

The tall virgin rainforest of Christmas Island is the nesting habitat of Abbott's Booby and many other resident species.

Perhaps the best hope for the booby lies in the 1600ha National Park created in 1980. Proposals to extend the Park by 770ha would increase the protected area to 18 per cent of the island, but the birds' breeding success will remain dependent on the limited number of surviving tall trees.

The boobies are not the only endemic birds in the Christmas Island forest. Two other seabirds — Andrew's Frigatebird (*Fregata andrewsi*) and the spectacular Golden Tropicbird (*Phaethon lepturus fulvus*) — are also unique to this very special island, as are several kinds of landbird.

On Christmas Island there is a clear and head-on conflict between an industry and the conservation of an island ecosystem. The cost of conservation here can be calculated with unusual precision — in terms of the price of phosphate.

The greatest threat to Abbott's Booby comes from the mining companies, who strip away the forest cover in order to work the rich phosphate deposits below.
Even when the forest is cleared in patches the results are devastating. With the soil gone, and only sterile rock left, it will take centuries for vegetation to fully recolonize the mined areas and develop into mature forest.

Most of the Christmas Island population of the Golden Tropicbird or Bosunbird nests in tall trees, but some also use crevices among the rocks. This beautiful bird is the endemic Christmas Island subspecies of the White-tailed Tropicbird.

Status report – Oceans: International resource or global dump?

The open oceans are the common resource of all humanity. Put another way, nobody owns them; they are there for the taking and that is the way they are seen by many of those who exploit them. Yet we have seen how events in one part of the ocean, or at one level of the ecosystem, can have consequences throughout the system.

Mismanagement of a priceless asset

Much of mankind's attitude to the sea can be traced to a misplaced faith in its apparently limitless resources. The shallow muddy water over continental shelves and the cool offshore and mid-ocean upwellings are indeed rich in biological resources; but we are already exploiting almost all the fish, oil and minerals they have to offer. Almost every major fishery has been over-fished already, and there is no reason to expect that others will fare any better. Neither will the fisheries of the future add significantly to our food resources. We now obtain about six per cent of our total protein and one-sixth of our animal protein from the sea, and we cannot increase that proportion very much by fishing farther out to sea. We have already seen how simply but completely the depth of the open ocean limits its biological productivity.

We could get more food from the sea if we used its resources more sensibly. A high proportion of the fish we catch we do not eat. We feed it to pigs, or we put it on fields to feed plants which we then feed to cattle and *then* eat. Each time we feed fish to something lower down the food chain than ourselves we lose 90 per cent of its nutritional value through the 'rules' governing the transfer of energy. When we eat meat raised on plants fertilized with fish meal we get barely one-tenth of one per cent of the energy stored in the fish.

Fishing is a stone-age technique conducted with space-age technology. Yet we are now making the same mistakes at sea as we have made on land. We are killing too many animals for the stock to sustain. We are mining the resource instead of harvesting it; eating into capital instead of living off income. But the stakes are even higher now. Not only do we threaten our marine resources by pollution as well as over-exploitation but there are now many more people to be fed, and probably no major new resources to be tapped.

The over-exploitation of fish stocks by highly mechanized fishing methods depletes not only the food reserves of the seabirds but also, in the long term, one of man's most valuable resources.

The industrialized nations are still using the sea as a dumping ground for toxic waste.

Even without spectacular oil spills, the steady seepage of oil pollution into the seas along the world's major shipping lanes claims the lives of hundreds of thousands of seabirds every year.

Our abuse of the sea is also conducted at long range, particularly through the way we obtain energy by burning fossil fuels high in carbon. Oceans are by far the largest reservoir in the planet's carbon cycle; they contain 50 times as much carbon as the atmosphere, and as the atmosphere reaches the limit of its capacity to store carbon, more and more of the excess will end up in the oceans. Atmospheric concentrations of carbon dioxide are increasing year by year and will probably double before equilibrium is reached, but it is now clear that the oceans will not be able to soak up the extra load as fast as we produce it. We are embarked on a colossal ecological, oceanographic and climatological experiment – with little idea of the likely consequences. Our faith in the speed with which the ocean shock-absorber could absorb carbon dioxide has, like our faith in the infinity of its food resource, been badly misplaced.

We treat the oceans as a passive and limitless sink for other wastes as well. Solid, liquid and radioactive waste is tipped over the edge of the land as if we believe the earth is flat and that it will all drop into a bottomless pit of space. And yet we know that these waste products are accumulating year by year, and that somewhere, some day, they will be swept to the surface and on to our shores by the constant circulation of the ocean waters. Already there is abundant evidence of pesticides reaching the highest levels of marine food chains, and we know the same to be true of many heavy minerals. In some cases, human food resources are already implicated. Oysters, for example, can accumulate lead at concentrations 5000 times higher than the mineral's concentration in sea water, while pigs fed on whalemeal have been found to contain lead at levels that would never be tolerated in fish offered for human consumption. Such examples are extreme; yet to ignore them, or dismiss them as insignificant local anomalies, would be irresponsible. They are the direct, measurable consequences of practices and attitudes that must be changed – and changed quickly.

The danger signs we often ignore

Birds first revealed the ocean-wide dispersal of agricultural pesticides. Then the blackened, sticky bodies of seabirds washed ashore in thousands alerted us to the dangers of oil pollution. Now we find that the Audouin's Gulls of the Mediterranean carry levels of mercury that raise the spectre of yet another potential human and ecological disaster. Seabirds provide an early warning system for the marine ecosystem if only we have the wit to watch them and interpret the signs. Before a fishery crashes, young seabirds starve and adults desert their colonies, signalling unmistakably the approaching catastrophe. A fishery that cannot support its seabirds will not long support fishermen.

Some of the immediate threats faced by the rarest seabirds come directly from their nesting grounds – malfunctions of a terrestrial ecosystem rather than the marine. Others are threatened by nets set for fish. But in the longer term, seabirds are more gravely endangered by mankind's continuing misuse of the seas themselves.

Brown Pelicans (*Pelecanus occidentalis*) have proved to be very sensitive indicators of inshore DDT pollution around the coasts of North America over the past 20 years.

In some parts of Norway colonies of Puffins (*Fratercula arctica*) and other seabirds have been unable to raise young for several years because of overfishing of the herring stocks on which they depend.

For most of the year the polar regions are as dry and unproductive as any desert in temperate or tropical latitudes, yet the brief polar summer sees a remarkable burst of biological activity as countless different forms of life try to pack into a few months all the activities of a whole year at more leisured latitudes.

The Arctic is a frozen ocean encircled by land, where terrestrial life has adapted to a harsh world of ice and rock and permanently frozen soil. The Antarctic, by contrast, is a continent — buried under ice several kilometres thick in places and surrounded by an unbroken expanse of wild and stormy ocean. Life here is almost entirely in the sea: the continent itself is virtually empty.

Until about 12,000 years ago, habitats like these extended very much farther from the poles. The space available to polar species today is only a fraction of that available to them during the great Ice Ages.

The intense cold, months-long winter darkness, and restricted resources make these regions the harshest habitats on earth. That birds can live there at all is possible only through miracles of adaptation.

Polar Regions

Deserts of ice and snow

The polar regions are truly deserts: less snow falls there than rain in the Sahara, for much of the snow blown about in blizzards is simply being moved from one place to another. Daylight changes more here than anywhere else on earth, from the perpetual night of winter to the endless days of summer. The bitter cold of winter may reach −80°C, with howling winds to drive effective temperatures lower still.

The opposite poles of the earth have little else but cold in common. The Arctic is an ice-covered ocean, surrounded by the northern fringes of North America, Eurasia and Greenland. The Antarctic is an ice-covered continent, surrounded by seas dotted with isolated windswept islands. Beyond the polar circles at 66½° north and south latitude there is virtually no life in winter, and even in high summer life can flourish only to about 75° latitude.

Pumps that power the system

Both regions play important roles in the climatic and oceanic circulations of the planet. Heavy, cold air over each polar zone maintains permanently high pressure cells that control the climate of the neighbouring temperate regions. Summer meltwater from the Antarctic ice-cap cools the surrounding seas and generates deep, cold currents that travel north as far as the equator. Both ice-caps are vast reservoirs of fresh water; the Antarctic ice-cap is four kilometres thick, and if it melted would raise the level of the sea by 80 metres around the world. A change in summer temperature of just one or two degrees could ruin crops throughout the developed world, and a ten-metre rise in sea level would drown most of the world's big cities. Life in polar regions is sparse and specialized, but those regions are a major dynamic force in determining earth's climatic regimes.

Kittiwakes, Fulmars and Arctic Terns wheel in a mixed flock, feeding on the rich marine fauna associated with the ice and meltwater at the snout of a glacier in West Greenland.

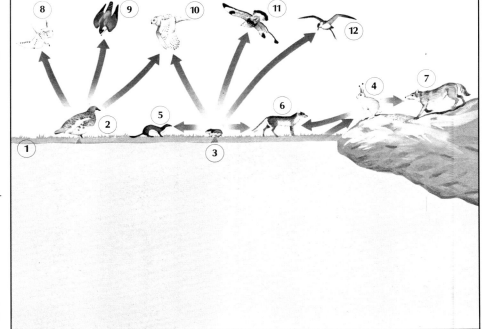

Energy flow in the Arctic
In Arctic regions, the transfer of energy up the food chain takes place almost entirely on land. The summer months produce a rich growth of low herbaceous vegetation which supports large populations of hares and lemmings in addition to the large migratory herbivores such as caribou and reindeer. These small mammals, and ground-feeding birds like ptarmigan, provide food for numerous predators, both terrestrial and airborne. Hunters and hunted alike show adaptations to the polar climate: ptarmigans, foxes, hares and stoats all changing their colours from the warm brown tones of summer to glistening white in the winter months.

1. Ground vegetation
2. Ptarmigan
3. Lemming
4. Arctic Hare
5. Stoat
6. Arctic Fox
7. Wolf
8. Gyrfalcon
9. Peregrine Falcon
10. Snowy Owl
11. Rough-legged Buzzard
12. Long-tailed Skua

Contrasting patterns of life

Average summer temperatures in the polar regions are below 10°C, but between this isotherm and the perpetually frozen deserts round the poles, highly specialized life can survive. In the north these regions are occupied mostly by land; in the Antarctic by sea with scattered islands. The Arctic has been colonized mainly by terrestrial creatures from the surrounding continents, and so has a richer and more continental fauna than the Antarctic, which has been colonized chiefly by marine forms from the cold, nutrient-rich seas around.

Both regions are structurally simple. There are no trees, and the plants are short, hugging the ground to shelter from the bitter winds and striving to survive on the limited nutrients present in the shallow soils. Both were covered by a more extensive ice-cap until the end of the last Ice Age, and have had only a few thousand years for soil to form and life to colonize. Scarcity of nutrients, and the very short growing season (as little as two months at the extremes), limits production to levels as low as those found in many deserts.

Predatory Polar Bears, Arctic Foxes and wolves force Arctic birds to take strict precautions, and the region's seabirds nest on steep inaccessible cliffs or on isolated islands, just as they do farther south. But the Antarctic continent is a vast island that for millions of years has been cut off by sea and ice from colonization by terrestrial mammals. It has no bears or wolves or foxes. Here, the birds' enemies are in the sea – the Leopard Seals and Killer Whales – or in the air, where skuas dive to prey on the eggs and chicks of other birds. Thus Antarctic seabirds nest on flat beaches, and penguins can afford to be flightless.

Antarctic food chains start with algae underneath the ice and end with whales, seals and seabirds. In between comes krill, a small pelagic shrimp that swarms in untold numbers and almost alone supports over twelve million tonnes of warm-blooded predators. In the Arctic, krill are replaced by a fish – the Arctic Cod – as the main link in the food chain between algae and marine birds and mammals. The polar ecosystems are perilously dependent on these two food species for their continued survival.

Seals and penguins are replacing the lost whales of the Antarctic. The Elephant Seal (*Mirounga leonina*) is the largest member of the seal family. Its world population is estimated at 750,000. The King Penguin (*Aptenodytes patagonicus*) stands about 80cm tall.

Energy flow in the Antarctic
The southern continent has no true terrestrial life: its shores are used in summer by breeding seals and penguins, but the main food chain is that of the marine environment. Primary production in the phytoplankton layer is first utilized by the zooplankton, including the large shrimp-like krill, and is then passed up the chain from fish and squid to penguins and higher predators. Another chain is based on the rain of animal detritus falling to the sea bed, where it forms a food resource for worms, shellfish and crabs, some of which in turn are preyed upon by seals and fishes.

1. Phytoplankton
2. Zooplankton
3. Krill
4. Diving Petrel
5. Antarctic Blenny
6. Squid
7. Gentoo Penguin
8. Emperor Penguin
9. Leopard Seal
10. Killer Whale
11. Detritus
12. Detritus feeders

Ruddy-headed Goose: The goose with a price on its head

This endangered waterfowl is considered a pest in two of the countries in which it occurs, and is still shot in considerable numbers in spite of its threatened status.

The Ruddy-headed Goose (*Chloephaga rubidiceps*) belongs to a small but distinctive group of five species of South American wildfowl known as sheldgeese. They are large robust birds that feed by grazing on grass. The Ruddy-headed Goose shares parts of its range with three of the other species, all of which are essentially grassland birds.

There are two distinct populations of the Ruddy-headed Goose. One breeds in northern Tierra del Fuego, migrating north to winter in the grasslands of southern Buenos Aires province; the other is resident all year round in the Falkland Islands. There they nest from late September to early November, laying five to eight buff-coloured eggs in a nest of grass lined with their own down. The nest is hidden away in long grass, under a rock overhang, or sometimes in an old penguin burrow. The female incubates alone for 29 or 30 days while the male waits nearby. In December and January many of the geese moult all their feathers and become flightless, and this is the time when farmers round them up and kill them for the bounty on their heads. The migratory South American birds avoid the vulnerable period of total flightlessness by renewing some of their flight-feathers before migrating and the rest afterwards.

Like any grass-eating animals, Ruddy-headed Geese are not welcome where men make their living raising other grass-eating animals. Believing that a blade of grass that is eaten by a goose could better have been eaten by a sheep, the farmers of the Falklands, Argentina and Chile are united in regarding the bird as a pest. In the windswept grasslands of Tierra del Fuego off the very southern tip of the continent, the Ruddy-headed Goose population increased early this century as introduced sheep turned brushwood into grasslands. By 1950 it was one of the commonest geese there. But then the farmers took action. By 1961 it made up only 10 per cent of the goose population, and 12 years later only one goose in a thousand was a Ruddy-headed, though the other species – the Upland and Ashy-headed – held their numbers. Populations on the wintering grounds declined in parallel until less than one thousand birds could be found in 1976.

The geese have come under attack from three directions. People take their eggs, and are encouraged to do so by bounties placed on them, and they hunt them – both on the breeding grounds and in their winter quarters. But bounties are a notoriously inefficient way of getting rid of pests, creating instead a sustained-yield industry based on the source of the bounty. Few species have declined seriously just through being hunted, and the Falklands population remains high despite egg-collecting and a bounty on beaks.

More serious for the geese was the introduction to Tierra del Fuego in the 1940s of the Patagonian Grey Fox to control rabbits. Like so many predators introduced to islands, the foxes took what they could most easily catch rather than what they were intended to take, and Ruddy-headed Geese proved more vulnerable than rabbits. Tierra del Fuego is uneasily partitioned between Argentina and Chile, who differ in their views on foxes: the Chileans protect them, but the Argentinians trap and poison them on the eastern side of the border. On the wintering grounds in mainland Argentina the geese are still considered pests despite their scarcity, and their eradication there is still a grim possibility.

The Falklands population is much healthier. The early sealers and settlers quickly found the 'Mountain Geese', as they called them, to be the tastiest of the three species in the islands, and between 1905 and 1912 over half a million Upland and Ruddy-headed geese were killed. Many are still killed, and there is still a bounty on their beaks, but the population remains at several tens of thousands. Falkland Island farmers have introduced succulent European grasses to improve the grasslands for their sheep, but these have proved just as attractive to the geese, which now concentrate on the reseeded pastures as well as on the 'greens' of short-growing grass.

In the aftermath of the Falkland Islands conflict in 1982 a new threat faced the goose population. Goose-shooting soon became a favourite sport for bored troops stationed on the islands. The geese are attracted to settled areas because that is where the best grass is to be found, and they move around so much that heavy mortalities in just one or two locations could make serious inroads into the population.

The Patagonian Grey Fox (*Dusicyon griseus*), whose introduction into Tierra del Fuego – like so many other alien introductions – had anything but the desired effect.

A single white-headed male Upland Goose (*Chloephaga picta*) grazes with a group of Ashy-headed Geese (*C. poliocephala*) in the Falkland Islands. Both are members of the South American shel-duck family.

Siberian White Crane:
A success for the super-powers

In the desolate wastes of the Siberian tundra there survives a pathetic remnant stock of a magnificent bird. Each spring, scattered pairs of elegant Siberian White Cranes (*Grus leucogeranus*) glide gracefully in from the south, their trumpeting cries signalling the renewed hope of another spring.

The cranes arrive in late May with the mass flights of returning geese. They may use the same nest for several years, and almost at once they begin to build or repair the bulky structure with grass and sedge leaves. The snow is still lying on the tundra when they start, but as it thaws it surrounds the nest with meltwater 25–50cm deep. The two eggs are incubated by both birds, lying prone on the nest with the long white secondary feathers curving over the black wing-tips and hiding them from view so that the huge white bird is lost in a vast landscape of icy pools and white patches of unmelted snow.

Adults eat the roots and tubers of tundra plants, but the young cranes need to grow fast in order to fledge and they feed more on small rodents, frogs and insects. One young alone survives from the two eggs laid. In early September the family takes flight and heads for the wintering grounds. There they feed and rest with other cranes, intermittently indulging in the curious leaping dances peculiar to their kind, the adult birds calling to each other in a haunting musical duet.

White Cranes once nested over much of the Siberian tundra and probably farther south into the wooded taiga country, but now there are only two breeding areas.

Most birds nest between the Yana and Kolyma rivers in northeastern Siberia, the remaining 50 or so nest 3000km to the west on the lower reaches of the River Ob. They seem to like to nest out of sight of other cranes, but this antisocial tendency alone does not account for the huge distances that separate breeding pairs. Individual territories are about 25km apart, and each 1000km^2 within the breeding range holds only one or two pairs of cranes.

The cranes' winter quarters are widely scattered. A site at Bharatpur in India was reoccupied in the 1960s after 80 years' disuse, and birds have been seen on the Iranian shore of the Caspian; but the winter quarters of the larger breeding population, long rumoured to be along the Yangtze River in central China, were discovered only recently. Late in 1983, the world's known population was more than doubled when over 800 birds were discovered wintering at Lake Poyang, the largest freshwater lake in China. In January 1985 the Yangtze wintering population was estimated to have increased to around 1350 birds. Like other cranes, they depend on wetlands in winter, and their decline is most probably linked with a reduction of this habitat. Hunting, both on the breeding grounds and on migration through Afghanistan and Pakistan, is also a major problem.

The White Cranes' nests are very hard to find, and the birds are desperately shy. If they are disturbed they often desert entirely, or leave the nest for so long that predators have time to move in and take the eggs. Stocks of domestic reindeer are rising, and the disturbance from the reindeer and their attendant herdsmen and their dogs is undoubtedly increasing. The short Arctic summer does not allow the birds a second chance if the first attempt at nesting fails.

The cause of crane conservation has broken ideological barriers. In a dramatic rescue operation eggs have been flown to Moscow airport and from there to the International Crane Foundation in the USA to be hatched and raised by hand. Now a major Soviet programme also hatches eggs in incubators, raising the breeding rate well above the average of less than one young per wild pair. Eventually American and Russian biologists plan to place White Crane eggs, laid in captivity, in the nests of wild Common Cranes (*Grus grus*) in Asia to further boost the stock of wild Siberian Cranes.

Mature Siberian White Cranes feeding in the wetland wintering grounds of Bharatpur in northern India. The famous Keoladeo Ghana Reserve used to be a private game reserve of the Maharajas of Bharatpur.

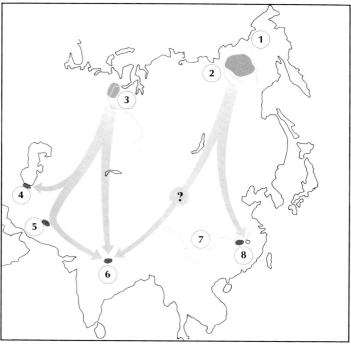

White Crane migrations
The Siberian White Crane is under severe threat of extinction. Enormous distances separate its wintering areas from its Arctic breeding grounds.

● Breeding grounds

● Wintering grounds

➙ Migration routes

1. Kolyma
2. Yana
3. Ob
4. Iran
5. Ab-i-Istada
6. Bharatpur
7. Yangtse
8. Lake Poyang

Auckland Island Flightless Teal: Relict ducks of the Southern Ocean

The Auckland Island Flightless Teal (*Anas aucklandica aucklandica*) is a descendant of the Brown Teal (*Anas anas chlorotis*) of New Zealand, 550km to the north. The Flightless Teal used to be common throughout the main Auckland island, but when pigs and cats were introduced there the birds were very quickly wiped out. The survivors, numbering no more than 600 birds, are now confined to six small offshore islands. Formerly they shared the main island with two other ducks – the Grey Duck (*A. superciliosa*), which was probably never common, and the endemic Auckland Island Merganser (*Mergus australis*), a graceful duck specialized for catching fish in the fast-flowing freshwater streams. The Merganser was last seen in 1902, and is surely now extinct, but the teal thrives on its offshore refuges, where it has become adapted to a most un-duck-like existence.

Ducks are typically freshwater birds, but the Auckland landscape is dominated by its rugged shoreline, dense maritime scrub and forest, and inland mountain peaks. The peat-stained streams have remained little used by ducks since the Mergansers became extinct. The few freshwater pools, beloved of teal elsewhere, would not support the hundreds that populate the islands. Instead, the birds forage along the shore, grubbing for invertebrates in the kelp stacked high above the tide-line. At low tide they venture out into the rock-pools and dabble among the algae exposed by the tide, or dive in shallow water; but most of their time is spent on land, where they feed on invertebrates in the soft soil and on carrion washed ashore.

An even rarer relative lives on Dent Island, off Campbell Island, 250km southeast of Auckland Island. Very few of the Campbell Island Flightless Teal (*Anas aucklandica nesiotis*) have been seen in recent years. The last count suggested a population of no more than 30 birds, and the species may even now have slipped into extinction. The remote impoverished islands that dot the southern oceans are desperately vulnerable to terrestrial predators introduced by man. The invaders represent a threat quite outside the experience of native Antarctic species, which can rarely adapt in time to avoid catastrophe.

The coast of Campbell Island, 500km south of New Zealand, is typical habitat of the Auckland Island Flightless Teal.

Status report – Polar regions: An international challenge

Polar habitats are even more hostile to human life than they are to birds, but the discovery of rich food and mineral resources in polar regions has led man to find ways of living there and exploiting them.

The Arctic offers abundant oil, largely free from political problems but posing a grave threat to the environment and its bird-life. Oil leaks from drilling sites or from damaged tankers or pipelines could pollute both the sea and the coastline. On land, the tundra owes its special characteristics to its permanently frozen subsoil, and this is vulnerable to damage by heat from overland pipelines, and from the wheels and tracks of the gigantic vehicles used to service the far-flung oil installations. Polar life is fragile: the habitat supports only a very few highly specialized species, and the environment is so physically rigorous that the few decomposers cannot cope with the mounting debris of human habitation. In some areas man's occupation of the Arctic threatens to turn it into a frozen garbage heap.

Arctic and subarctic seas support fisheries that are now being over-exploited. Already, thousands of seabirds drown every year in the gill-nets of the salmon fishery off western Greenland. In the Antarctic, the immense stocks of krill that once supported vast schools of whales now support fewer whales but increasing populations of the penguins and seals that are taking their places. New plans to harvest the krill itself could cause even more widespread harm than centuries of whaling ever did.

The Antarctic continent, for centuries free from human interference, has survived the modern age remarkably well. So far. The Antarctic Treaty, ratified in 1961, called a halt to exploitation and reserved the continent for scientific research alone. But the treaty has two shortcomings; it refers only to the landmass and not to the seas surrounding it, and it expires in 1991. An enormous effort will be required on the part of all interested nations to ensure that the treaty is renewed. And renewed it must be, for this is a truly unique situation. Antarctica is a whole continent virtually untouched by civilization; it is a natural laboratory for scientific research, the like of which occurs nowhere else on earth; and it is the world's last great untouched wilderness. It is a priceless asset, and one that plays an essential if little-understood part in the ecological balance of our planet.

Thick-billed Murres or Brunnich's Guillemots (*Uria lomvia*) breed in huge colonies of tens or even hundreds of thousands of pairs in the High Arctic. Yet they are vulnerable to oil spills, entanglement in fishing nets, and potentially to overfishing of their food species (especially the Capelin, *Mallotus villosus*) in their Atlantic winter quarters.

The massive marine oil terminal at Valdez on the coast of the Gulf of Alaska receives more than 1.5 million barrels of crude oil every day from the Prudhoe Bay fields on the edge of the Beaufort Sea.

In relation to their area, oceanic islands hold far more bird species — and a much greater number of rare and endangered birds — than any other habitat. The ocean around them acts as a barrier, filtering out most mainland species and discouraging the few successful colonists from moving on.

In a new environment, free from the hazards of the mainland, island colonists have often evolved very rapidly — creating new species, occupying newly available habitat niches and producing some of the world's most bizarre and highly specialized birds. Islands are true crucibles of evolution, fashioning new species much faster than any other environment.

Nearly all oceanic islands have now been colonized by people who, with their camp-following cats, rats, dogs, mongooses and domestic stock, have wrought havoc on the pristine island ecosystems. Most of the species that have become extinct in historic times were island-dwellers. Today, half the birds listed as endangered cling to their precarious existence in those same vulnerable island worlds.

Oceanic Islands

Planets in an ocean universe

Islands occupy only five per cent of the land area of the earth, but were home to 90 per cent of the birds that have become extinct since 1600. They now harbour half those species currently endangered, and perhaps one-fifth of all the bird species in the world. A bird is ten times more likely to be endangered if it lives on an island than if it lives on a continent.

Not only do islands hold a large share of the world's birds but they also play a special part in planning modern nature reserves. An island is an area of land surrounded by water, and a reserve is an area of one habitat in a sea of others. An understanding of islands is vital to an understanding of the biology of reserves, and this recently recognized parallel has emphasized the critical role that islands have to play in conservation.

Most oceanic islands are small and remote; they harbour relatively few species, and their animal and plant communities are much simpler than those of continents. They are microcosms of the earth, and the history of each island, as it is colonized by man, repeats in some respect mankind's effects on the planet as a whole.

Cradles of evolution

Some islands are fragments of land detached from the nearest continent. Often they became islands when the intervening land was drowned by rising sea level after the last Ice Age, and so have been isolated for only 12,000 years or so. These 'continental' islands normally host a limited selection of the birds of the nearby mainland, but none peculiar to themselves. The islands which have their own endemic species, found nowhere else, are the truly oceanic islands. These are formed by volcanic eruptions beneath the sea, and when they emerge above the surface they are devoid of life. All the animals and plants that come to live there must reach them over water. It is on these remote volcanic islands that the most dramatic evolution and specialization of birds has taken place.

In contrast to low, flat, coral islands, these volcanic islands in Baja California rise steeply from the sea. Their rocks are much more durable, and once the island is colonized and forested, complex communities of animal life may develop.

Worlds apart

1. Hawaiian Islands
2. Cook Islands
3. Marquesas Islands
4. Galapagos Islands
5. Greater Antilles
6. Lesser Antilles
7. Azores
8. Canary Islands
9. Cape Verde Islands
10. Ascension Island
11. St Helena
12. Tristan da Cunha
13. Gough Island
14. South Georgia
15. Aldabra Island
16. Seychelles
17. Mascarene Islands
18. Kerguelen Islands
19. Andaman Islands
20. Christmas Island
21. Ryukyu Islands
22. Mariana Islands
23. Laysan Island
24. Solomon Islands
25. Fiji
26. New Caledonia
27. Lord Howe Island
28. Chatham Island

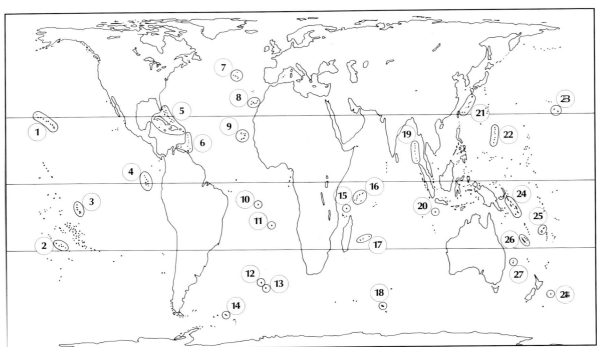

Thrust from the sea – to return to the sea

The undersea eruptions that give rise to islands do not occur haphazardly around the ocean floor. They are concentrated on the mid-ocean ridges, great underwater mountain chains that form where molten rock is forced up through the earth's crust to spill out at either side of the ridge, constantly adding new material to the ocean floor. The eruptions that reach the surface and form islands are exceptional; ocean basins are studded with underwater mountains too short to break the surface. Those that do make islands, do so only for a short time, for the molten rock emerging from the ridge moves the ocean floor like an undersea conveyor-belt, carrying its islands with it down the slope and away from the crest of the ridge. Each island's life above the sea is limited in most cases to a few million years; to take advantage of their brief existence, living things must find them and adapt to them very quickly.

Volcanic islands are often steep and rugged, offering a wide variety of habitats to colonizing creatures. Islands in the tropics soon develop a barrier of coral reefs around them, and as the volcanic core slowly sinks beneath the sea, so the island becomes lower and lower until eventually it is composed entirely of coral. Coral atolls are formed this way and are the commonest kind of 'low' island. Their flat, low landscape, more uniform vegetation and frequent lack of fresh water offer far less opportunity to an invading bird and they are often very poor in bird life. Similarly, islands near the poles have often suffered the extra vicissitudes of glaciation, or cold so extreme as to extinguish life. The faunas of these islands have developed in the course of the last 12,000 years or so, and are consequently also impoverished.

The violent birth and early death of islands, and their constantly changing shape and size and even structure, are a naturally hazardous backdrop to the stage on which island birds act out their evolutionary dramas. Mankind's abrupt invasions have added new dimensions to these natural hazards and made island birds the most critically threatened in the world.

The life of an island
Recently formed islands tend to be large, with steep slopes and incomplete vegetation cover. As time passes, weathering creates rich soils which are soon colonized by plant-life to provide a range of habitats for birds, insects and mammals. But continued erosion combined with slow sinking over many millions of years reduces the island's land area. And as the number of habitat niches dwindles, so too does the number of bird species the island can support.

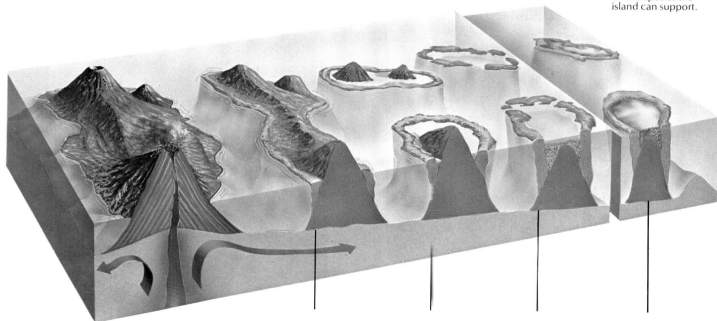

New island, rich in bird-life; for example, Hawaii, with 32 species.

5 million years old. A mature island with varied vegetation and fringing reefs; for example, Oahu, with 40 resident species.

10 million years old. An old island, heavily eroded and ringed by broad barrier reefs; for example, Kauai, with 31 bird species.

20 million years old. A sunken island with coral cays and heavily eroded atoll; for example, Laysan Island, with only 5 species.

A 'raised atoll' is formed when an old sunken island is exposed once more by a drop in sea level. No breeding bird population.

The island environment

The sea around an island is a barrier, filtering out the poor dispersers and letting through only those forms of life that travel well. Living communities on islands are therefore quite different from those on the mainland for the very powerful reason that many mainland species cannot get there.

But islands are not just bits of mainland out at sea. The island environment itself is special. A much higher proportion of its land is taken up by coast than is the case on continents, so all but the very largest islands have a preponderance of coastal habitats. On high islands the mountain peaks are close to the coasts, so the ecological gradients from sea level to summit are extremely steep. The small size of islands and the steepness of their ecological gradients also mean that many habitats occupy only a very tiny area, often too small to support their own specialized faunas. Island birds accordingly occupy more different kinds of habitat than mainland birds — they have broader, more generalized ecological niches. They also often have smaller populations, whose very size makes them more vulnerable to extinction.

Building an island community

Birds, like any other kind of animal including man, are an inseparable part of the ecosystem in which they live. We have seen how the origins and geography of islands make their geology and climate rather special, but what about the living parts of the island environment? These are, of course, affected by the climate and the soils, but first they have to reach the island, and in getting there the most important factor is not the environment of the island but that of the intervening sea, and in particular how much of it has to be crossed.

Plants that are dispersed by sea reach islands most easily of all, but such plants normally live only on the coast and so rarely colonize the interior of an island. Plants with light, wind-drifted seeds can reach remote islands and also penetrate inland, and families like the daisies which specialize in wind-dispersal are characteristic plants of islands. But the best way for a plant to reach an island is to hitch a lift with a bird. Many seeds and fruits are sticky, or have tiny hooks on their surface which catch in birds' feathers and allow the seeds to be carried long distances. Others are swallowed by birds and may remain in the gut for several days before being passed out, by which time a migrant bird may have flown a

Galapagos Hawks (*Buteo galapagoensis*) perched in trees festooned with 'Old Man's Beard'. Like many island birds, the hawks are unaccustomed to predatory man and are therefore very tame and confiding.

Many tropical islands owe their stands of *Pisonia grandis* trees to the Red-footed Booby (*Sula sula*). The birds like to roost in the trees, and the sticky seeds cling to their feet and feathers. A special soil type – 'jemo' soil – common on tropical coral islands, is formed by a chemical interaction between the boobies' droppings and the *Pisonia* leaf-litter.

thousand kilometres or more. Nearly two-thirds of all the plant species on oceanic islands were brought there by birds, either in their intestines or stuck to their feathers or the mud on their feet. So birds have played a dominant role in the establishment of plants on islands, and have had more opportunity than other colonists to bring with them the means to establish the very habitat they left behind.

Birds find it easier to reach oceanic islands than do many other animals. Frogs and toads reach islands very rarely as their thin permeable skins cannot protect them on a long journey through salt water. Lizards often float in on rafts of vegetation, and frequently abound on islands. So the range of food available for meat-eating birds is subtly different on islands: eaters of amphibians will go hungry while lizard-eaters usually thrive. Mammals — even bats — are poor colonizers; most of the motley crowd of rats, mice, cats, dogs and pigs so widespread now on islands have been taken there, on purpose or by accident, by people. On continents, the big predators are mammals; no bird or reptile can compete for killing power with a lion or tiger. Islands are rarely colonized by mammals, and consequently lack large predators. Predatory birds are as common on islands as elsewhere, but cannot fully replace the missing mammals. So island creatures generally enjoy an environment much freer of predators than any continent. Over countless generations of adapting to their island environments they have lost the need to cope with predators and so have no defence against them when they arrive as alien immigrants brought by man. They have had to compete, as all life does, with the species around them, but island birds have fewer neighbours than continental ones because the isolation and peculiar ecology of oceanic islands are barriers that few species are equipped to cross. So island birds may be as ineffective at coping with introduced competitors as they are with introduced predators.

Earth's living laboratories

New species can originate only in isolation from the parent stock, and because islands are the ultimate in isolation they have staged some of the most spectacular bursts of speciation known. In addition to harbouring nearly one-quarter of the known species of bird, the isolation of one island from another has led to a disproportionate concentration of endemic species on islands.

The Dodo and other bizarre flightless birds of the Mascarene Islands showed one kind of speciation, to a degree and of a kind that led to whole new families evolving. Each of the Mascarenes is a solitary, large and, by island standards, relatively ancient island. The first birds to reach there had tens of millions of years in which to produce new species.

An altogether different kind of speciation has produced a greater number of species, though more similar to each other and less different from their ancestors, on other kinds of islands. Where many islands cluster together in an archipelago sufficiently remote for immigrants to be rare, a founding stock can spread throughout the group and develop different characteristics according to the conditions on each island. This process, of radiation of a single stock into separate niches on nearby islands, has produced the famous Darwin's Finches of the Galapagos Islands and the spectacularly varied honeycreepers of Hawaii. Such a process, producing many small populations of different species in a small area, creates a biological paradise but also a potential nightmare of conservation crises.

Island birds have evolved in isolation from their ancestors and their primeval habitat, from most predators, and from many of the competitive pressures that would sharpen the wits of a continental bird. Some kinds — especially the rails, but some pigeons and parrots too — have lost the power of flight in adapting to the special conditions of island life.

Island birds are disastrously tame. They are often catholic in their choice of food, but sometimes specialized on a particular island resource, and they usually occur in small populations, limited by the carrying capacity of a small island. This syndrome of characteristics predisposes island birds to suffer at the hands of mankind and his attendant aliens whenever they invade an island.

The Cactus Finch of the Galapagos Islands (*Geospiza scandens*) is one of the few birds known to use a tool. A sharp cactus spine is snapped off and used to probe for grubs in decaying wood.

Seychelles Black Paradise Flycatcher: The widow-bird of La Digue

The long, black tail of the Seychelles Flycatcher, trailing behind it like a widow's weeds, accounts for its local name of 'La Veuve' – the widow. But in fact only the male is dressed in mourning; the female is white beneath and rufous above, with a glossy black head, bright blue bill and legs, and a blue ring around the eye.

The veuves (*Terpsiphone corvina*) once lived in the shady lowland forests of many of the Seychelle Islands. Man came late to Seychelles – it was 1770 before the islands were settled – but he soon destroyed the lowland forests. He brought rats ashore, and then cats to catch them, and killed the most confiding of the birds for sport and food. Flycatchers now nest mainly on the island of La Digue, though tiny relict groups remain on one or two neighbouring islands. The total population is static at around 70–80 birds.

La Digue is a delightful, peaceful island, where ox-carts take visitors from the jetty to the nearby woodland to see the birds. On the flat land near the coast there are still groves of the native takamaka and badamier trees, and at the base of the hill there are swamps and drainage ditches where flying insects abound. Here the flycatchers are most abundant, the females feeding high up in the canopy, the males flitting darkly through the shady vegetation nearer the ground. The comings and goings of people living in the houses scattered among the trees do not deter the birds from nesting nearby; the tiny, cup-shaped nest is woven at the very tip of a down-hanging twig of a takamaka or badamier tree, often above a busy footpath. The base and cup are strengthed with spiders' webs, which bind the twigs and fibres of the nest together and secure them to the support. They lay one egg, which the female incubates alone, but raise the young together. Only one nest in six fledges a chick, but this may improve in a reserve that has now been created in their major stronghold. Their best defence must be the affection in which the 'Diguois' hold them – and their economic value as an attraction for visitors.

The lowland forests of La Digue are the last remaining breeding habitat of the Black Paradise Flycatcher.

The islands of Seychelles:
A paradise lost – a fragment regained

The Seychelles are like no other islands. They have not always been islands – 100 million years or so ago they were joined to India, Africa, Madagascar, Australia and Antarctica in the giant super-continent of Gondwanaland. As that southern landmass broke up, some continental fragments were left trailing between India and Madagascar; and there they remain, tiny, scattered specks in the western Indian Ocean, with only their granite rocks and their primitive palm trees, pitcher-plants and amphibians as reminders of their continental ancestry.

The Seychelles Grey White-eye (*Zosterops modesta*) was believed to be extinct until it was rediscovered in the 1960s in the highlands of Mahé Island.

Introduced plants can often invade native vegetation and pose a threat to endemic birds. The survival of the Seychelles Magpie Robin is largely due to its successful adaptation to the introduced flora of Fregate Island.

Their birds, however, have reached them over water; there are no descendants of the ancient stock of Gondwanaland. They are distinctive enough, with ten endemic species, but all have close relatives in modern Madagascar and Asia and must have colonized Seychelles relatively recently. But no less than 13 of Seychelles' endemic species and subspecies are endangered; more than in any other archipelago outside Hawaii.

One important reason for the parlous state of Seychelles birds is the small size of the islands. They are tiny: all 83 of them together cover an area of only 277km², which is substantially smaller than the smallest of the main Hawaiian islands and could be fitted 38 times into the area of the largest. A small island can support only small populations to start with, and offers no hiding place from alien predators and competitors once they are introduced. Its habitats can be quickly cleared and planted over. All these things have happened to Seychelles birds, and at least one-third of the island populations have become extinct.

One of the rarest Seychelles birds was once one of the commonest. The endemic Magpie Robin (*Copsychus sechellarum*) was found on almost all the larger islands, but was exceptionally tame; it was vulnerable to cats when feeding on the ground and to rats when nesting low down in trees. Now some 25 birds on Fregate Island are the sole survivors of their species. They are thrush-like birds, hopping long-legged and alert for prey among the leaf-litter below shady trees, and still coming into houses for scraps in the confiding manner of their ancestors.

Magpie Robins survive because they have adapted to a totally alien flora. Their native habitat of coastal woodland is gone from Fregate; indeed it is hard to find a single native plant there. The birds live now on flat land near the shore, where planted sang-dragon and breadfruit trees cast a deep shade and produce a leaf-litter rich in large insects, scorpions and lizards for the birds to eat. They nest in the crowns of coconut trees or, rarely, in holes in tree trunks, and raise a single chick once in every two or three attempts. They also feed on soil turned for planting vegetables, like robins in an English garden. The tangled vegetation of the hill that covers most of the island holds no attractions for them, and they live and breed in only 11 territories, on patches of flat ground near the coast. These lowlands are now filled with birds; they can expand no further, and to increase must be taken to other islands. And it is important that they should be translocated, for the single population on Fregate will always be vulnerable. This risk was emphasized in 1981 when only 24 birds remained from the 41 of three years before. Cats had spread throughout the island in that short time and had begun to prey on young robins. Only quick and expert action in eradicating the cats was able to halt the birds' decline. However, the population has so far failed to recover its former numbers – largely due to the lack of suitable feeding and breeding habitat but also perhaps because of competition from introduced Indian Mynahs.

The only known daylight photograph of the rare Bare-legged Scops Owl (*Otus insularis*) of Mahé Island in the Seychelles. The owl's decline is due in part to competition from introduced Barn Owls (*Tyto alba*).

The Magpie Robins share their island with another threatened bird, the Seychelles Fody (*Foudia sechellarum*). This small, sparrow-like bird survives also on two much smaller islands, Cousin and Cousine, but on Fregate it is rather scarce and seems overshadowed by the related Madagascar Fody, introduced by men who preferred its brighter scarlet plumage. On Cousin the native fody far outnumbers the alien, and feeds on insects in the bark of native trees, on the nectar that flows from flowers in the early morning, and on fruit and scraps around the houses. Those whose territory includes a house will bring their youngsters in for breakfast at the table, an even smarter tactic than it seems, for young fodies plague their parents for food for three months after fledging and this must slow the species' reproductive rate.

On Cousin, the fody thrives alongside a bird that is confined as strictly to that island as the Magpie Robin is to Fregate. The numbers of the Seychelles Brush Warbler (*Acrocephalus sechellensis*) had dropped to less than 30 before the island was bought by ICBP in 1968 to run as a reserve. The 'warblers' natural habitat of scrubby woodland had been shaded out by planted coconuts, and most of the warblers had taken refuge in the tiny patch of mangroves on the coast. To manage the reserve for native birds, ICBP allowed the native trees to grow among the coconuts, and in that warm, wet, tropical environment they responded at a gratifying rate. The warblers spread, and bred, quickly swelling their numbers to several hundred.

Cousin is separated by only two kilometres of sea from the much larger island of Praslin, which is famous for its palms and parrots. The palms are the legendary double coconuts, once worth a fortune and now carefully guarded in the Vallee de Mai reserve. The parrots are the Black Parrots (*Coracopsis nigra*), which feed on fruit of native and exotic trees alike, but concentrate on another endemic palm whose range has been severely depleted by cultivation. Populations of the parrot on other islands were destroyed by persecution, especially when the parrots raided crops. Their numbers now are limited probably by availability of nest sites, for which they need tall old trees which are in short supply, and there may well be fewer than 100 birds left.

The Seychelles Brush Warbler has made a spectacular recovery since ICBP took over Cousin Island to run as a bird reserve.

A Seychelles Fody feeding on the egg of a Fairy Tern (*Gygis alba*) laid, in characteristic fashion, in a slight depression on an exposed branch.

Mauritius Kestrel: Doomed to follow the Dodo?

The Dodo was not the only victim of mankind's aggression on Mauritius. Many less obviously bizarre and vulnerable species have become extinct since Europeans first settled on the island in the seventeenth century. The three Mascarene islands — Mauritius, Réunion and Rodrigues — in the western Indian Ocean east of Madagascar, shared an extraordinary avifauna, including many grotesque and flightless birds, all of which proved disastrously tame and confiding when man arrived on the scene.

The kestrels (*Falco punctatus*) of sixteenth-century Mauritius shared the dense subtropical forest of the lush volcanic island with at least one other raptor and two or three kinds of owl. Yet the pitiful remnants of the rich food chains that supported all those predators can now barely sustain the small number of surviving kestrels. The varied forests of ebony, olive and makaka that clothed the steep mountain gorges have been cut, burned, planted over, invaded by browsing deer and rooting pigs, and choked with invasive alien plants.

Mauritius was once completely covered in forest. Now the fertile low ground is intensively cultivated, mainly for sugar-cane production. Only on the steep volcanic slopes do a few scattered patches of virgin forest survive.

The kestrels are well adapted to the forests. Their short, rounded wings and long, mobile tails enable them to manoeuvre expertly below the canopy, twisting and turning between the branches to seize their prey. Sometimes they chase small birds like the Grey White-eye (*Zosterops borbonicus*), or grasshoppers, beetles and other flying insects; but mostly they stalk and snatch the bright green day-geckos which, like the kestrels, are endemic to the native forest. The kestrels take advantage of the lizards' trick of changing colour. In the heat of the day the geckos are a vivid green and forage in the canopy, where they are very hard to see. But in the early morning and in cloudy weather, when temperatures are low, the cold-blooded geckos crawl on to the bare branches of emergent trees and turn black in order to absorb the feeble heat of the sun. Then they are easy to see, and sometimes male and female kestrels will hunt together, one scaring a gecko to the far side of a branch, where the other snaps it up.

When the kestrels hunt below the forest canopy they are too elusive to count; but as the breeding season starts in September they take to soaring and swooping on the updrafts over cliffs and gorges, and then they can be counted. Several areas are known where kestrels will display like this, and in the past few years, diligent searching by biologists has located about 15 breeding pairs. The kestrels are confined to steep valleys providing native forests to feed in and cliffs to nest in. Their numbers have apparently increased over the past ten years or so, and in 1985 had reached about 50 birds, but until very recently they were producing very few young each year.

Fortunately this sad fact was recognized and preventive action taken. Falcons like the kestrel can be raised, and ultimately bred, in captivity. But the task is long and arduous, and demands the very special skills involved in raising young birds. First, the nest must be found; in a cliff cavity, safe from the cyclones which rip through the devastated forest with numbing frequency, but shared perhaps with roosting troops of alien monkeys which relish a meal of kestrel eggs or young. Then, if the nest has eggs, they must be carefully removed and carried to the ground, undamaged by the frantic attacks of the mother kestrel. The eggs must then be turned every few hours in their incubator, as their mother would turn them in the nest; and if the power supply should fail, as in such places it is bound to do, the eggs must be kept warm some other way. The eggs that hatch — and not all are fertile — release a precious but totally helpless chick that must be tended constantly, day and night.

Kestrel numbers have been low for many years; in 1974 only six were counted, and in 1985 there were still only 16 breeding pairs in the wild. Such a small breeding stock is vulnerable to the genetic problems of inbreeding, which may already have doomed the species. And the wild birds are part of a devastated and poisoned ecosystem from which no aviary can protect them. In 1978, several eggs were laid with thin, brittle shells, and failed to hatch: they carried levels of pesticide high enough to cause severe damage to the female and her eggs. Mauritius depends for its prosperity on productive agriculture, and relies on modern chemical pesticides to protect its cash crops and its food. These insidious poisons have penetrated not only the remotest forest ecosystem in the country but also the surrounding seas, which are now sufficiently polluted to put at risk the country's few remaining seabirds.

Even the kestrels' food supply is now threatened: introduced birds like Mynahs and Red-whiskered Bulbuls relish the same day-geckos that the kestrels feed on, and are far more widespread and successful breeders. Mynahs, and the White-tailed Tropicbirds that we have already met competing with Cahows on Bermuda, choose similar nest sites to the kestrels. Almost every part of their native niche has been invaded or depleted, and the remaining suitable habitat is probably already supporting as many wild kestrels as it can.

The small population of Mauritius Kestrels is doubly threatened by loss of its native forest habitat and by fierce competition from introduced birds.

Black River Gorge:
Vital refuge for parrots and pigeons

The forests of the Black River Gorge in Mauritius are the last stronghold of two more of the world's rarest and most threatened birds. Perhaps five to ten of the slim green, long-tailed Echo Parakeet (*Psittacula echo*) remain alive. They have not bred successfully since 1976, and have to fight for nest sites with the very similar introduced Ring-necked Parakeet (*P. krameri*). Like most parrots, they nest in tree-trunk holes, and these too are rare now in the managed forests that have replaced the island's native forests. A programme of captive breeding is thought to be the only remaining hope for the species, but to date the few remaining birds have evaded capture.

Unlike the parakeets whose habitat it shares, the Mauritius Pink Pigeon (*Nesoenas mayeri*) is threatened by predation rather than any shortage of nesting sites. Like others of its tribe, the Pink Pigeon builds a flimsy nest of twigs in the branches of a tree. Here, the two white eggs are desperately vulnerable to marauding monkeys, and the wild population of these handsome birds has dwindled to less than 20. They nest now in one grove of native trees, which is guarded in the breeding season, and feed on the flowers and fruits of the native trees. Consequently they are especially at risk when cyclones strip areas of forest bare of food. But unlike the kestrels and parakeets, Pink Pigeons breed well in aviaries, and the captive population in Mauritius and in Jersey is now large enough to provide birds for return to the wild. A programme of reintroductions is currently under way.

The Ring-necked Parakeet poses a serious threat to the handful of surviving Echo Parakeets on Mauritius. In the long term it may also become a pest on fruit and grain crops, as it has in Africa and India.

Successful breeding in captivity provides a lifeline to survival for the threatened wild population of Mauritius Pink Pigeons.

A rare photograph of one of the world's rarest birds: an Echo Parakeet — one of a known population of less than ten.

Black River Gorge — one of the few areas of relatively undamaged forest on Mauritius, and a vital refuge for several endangered species.

Puerto Rican Parrot: Rescued by conservationists

When Columbus first set eyes on Puerto Rico in 1493, the varied types of forest cover swarmed with parrots of two kinds. Not today. The smaller long-tailed green parakeets were extinct by 1900, and the large, short-tailed Puerto Rican Amazon (*Amazona vittata*) retains a precarious hold on life only through the dedication of conservation workers over the last two decades.

The aboriginal inhabitants of this large West Indian island kept parrots as pets, ate some, and used their feathers as adornments and to fletch their arrows. They cultivated pockets of land, but most of the forest remained a perfect habitat for parrots. But by 1750 European settlers had cleared one-third of the island, and by 1900 barely one per cent of the virgin forest still stood. The Amazons were still traded as pets and eaten, but they were also killed to keep them from raiding crops, and their habitat was destroyed on a vast scale. In the 1960s their decline suddenly became much steeper. Confined now to 1600ha of the Luquillo Forest in the eastern mountains, the population crashed from 200 in 1954 to 70 in 1966 and 13 in 1975. It has remained below 30 in the wild since then. This forest has been a reserve under United States law since 1918, but in the 1960s it was subject to shooting, road construction and extensive forestry activities. Experimental exposure to atomic radiation, then military training and testing of defoliants connected with the Vietnam war also took their toll.

Parrots nest in holes in trees and a big parrot like an Amazon requires a big hole and thus a big, old tree. But big, old trees are selectively felled by hurricanes, and two bad ones, in 1928 and 1931, not only killed many parrots and blew away their food of fruit and seeds, but blew down many of their nesting trees as well. Tall trees are also selectively felled by foresters; for timber if they yield good wood, for burning if they make good charcoal, as 'weeds' if they do neither. People hunting parrots as pets usually take chicks out of nests, and rather than risk life and limb by climbing tall, rotten trees they often cut the tree down. Many Puerto Ricans hunt for wild honey, and they, too, either cut the tree down or destroy the cavity while extracting the honey.

Somehow the parrots survive not only these setbacks, but also a variety of biological complications that were probably even more significant. Red-tailed Hawks prey on fledglings and probably even on adults. The large flocks in which the parrots used to move may well have deterred the hawks from attacking, but the small parties that are all the remaining parrots can muster are much easier prey. The nestlings are parasitized by bot-flies, bees may take over nest holes and force parrots into unsuitable sites, and Ship's Rats, introduced long ago, climb the nest-trees and eat the eggs or kill the young.

A new factor has entered the Amazons' struggle in the last 30 years, in the shape of another native West Indian bird, the Pearly-eyed Thrasher. This aggressive bird is a good deal smaller than the Amazon, but it eats parrots' eggs and young, likes the same nest sites, and is prepared to fight for them. Against the weight of the thrashers' much greater numbers, the Amazons have stood little chance of breeding in recent years.

Nest sites are now the key to the survival of the parrots. The Amazons confine their nesting activities to four areas covering a mere 27ha, where their favourite nesting trees – the Palo Colorado – are concentrated. These areas contain only seven good natural nest sites, which are contested so vigorously that many parrots are scarred with wounds that could lower their survival chance or at least their ability to breed. Artificial nest sites have been provided, and all the natural ones improved by making them deeper, darker and drier, and by modifying them to keep out rats and thrashers. Nest-boxes more suitable for thrashers have also been erected close to parrot sites – a cunning move that profits from the territorial behaviour of the thrashers. Once they have adopted the site provided, they keep all other thrashers away from the parrots' nests as well as their own.

The nesting success of wild parrots has been improved, and a captive breeding programme has also been started. Eggs are hatched and raised safely in captivity, often using hand-raised foster-parents of the closely related Hispaniola Amazon. The total population has slowly improved – to 46 in 1982 – but continued intensive management will be needed to restore the wild population to a viable condition.

Artificial nesting boxes carefully blended into the forest environment have been successful in easing the pressure on the dwindling number of natural nest sites.

Fierce competition from Pearly-eyed Thrashers (*Margarops fuscatus*) has been a major cause of breeding failures in Puerto Rican Parrots in the last 30 years.

The Caribbean Amazons: Under threat from the cage-bird trade

Amazona parrots live only in the American tropics, where their 27 living species range from Mexico to Argentina. Nine species are confined to Caribbean islands and five of these, including the Puerto Rican Parrot, are endangered, liable soon to join the 14 species of West Indian parrot that have already become extinct. St Vincent and St Lucia, tiny islands in the Lesser Antilles each less than one-twentieth the area of Puerto Rico, boast two of the most spectacular Amazons of all. The St Vincent Parrot is the island's national symbol – a magnificent and highly variable species, much prized by keepers of cage-birds and threatened most seriously by illegal traffic for the international avicultural trade. In a major volcanic eruption in 1979, a number of parrots were killed by gas and ash and some areas of prime forest were destroyed, but the birds still occur in several forested valleys along the mountainous spine of the island.

The St Lucia bird is equally prized by St Lucians, and an intensive conservation programme in the last few years has given it greater protection from hunters, and new, artificial nest sites. It has been declared the island's National Bird and has become the focus of rainforest nature tours which help to educate residents and visitors alike in the value of the forest and its birds. In the first year of operation, this programme earned the country the equivalent of US$200 for each parrot.

The island of Dominica has more rainforest than any other island in the Lesser Antilles, and hosts two species of Amazon. The Imperial Parrot is the largest of its genus, and one of the rarest. It occupies the more remote mountain forests, while the smaller and more common Red-necked Parrot lives lower down. Both species are hunted, and collected for the cage-bird trade, and both were badly hit by hurricane 'David', which devastated the island and its inhabitants in 1979.

These parrots live in small impoverished countries most of which are making commendable efforts – which they can ill afford – to conserve their birds. The parrots are an international heritage as well as national ones, and these islands need and deserve international help to conserve them.

Magnificent parrots of the West Indies
Distinctive species of the *Amazona* genus are endemic to many of the West Indian islands.

1. Cuban Parrot (*A. leucocephala*) Cuba, the Bahamas and Cayman Islands
2. St Lucia Parrot (*A. versicolor*) St Lucia
3. St Vincent Parrot (*A. guildingii*) St Vincent
4. Imperial Parrot (*A. imperialis*) Dominica
5. Red-necked Parrot (*A. arausiaca*) Dominica

Hillside forest on the island of Dominica begins the slow process of recovery after being stripped by hurricane 'David' in 1979.

Crested Honeycreeper: Survival against all odds

The Hawaiian islands form the most isolated landmass in the world, 4000km from the nearest continent. They also have by far the greatest concentration of endangered birds. No less than 15 threatened subspecies (of 10 species) belong to a single endemic family, the honeycreepers or Hawaiian finches.

The birds are called mainly by their Hawaiian names; that of the Crested Honeycreeper (*Palmeria dolei*) is '*Akohekohe*'. They are smallish songbirds, about 10 centimetres long, with a distinctive grey or white crest above the base of the bill and an equally characteristic orange-flecked black plumage and striking orange hindneck.

Honeycreepers have an extraordinary variety of bill shapes, ranging from deep and parrot-like to long and downcurved like a miniature curlew's. The '*Akohekohe's*' is an intermediate, conventional kind of insect-eater's beak, straight and pointed like that of a warbler. It uses it to feed on flower nectar, especially of the '*ohia* tree, and on insects among the foliage. Crested Honeycreepers once occurred on two islands, Molokai and Maui, but are now extinct on Molokai and confined to an extremely narrow belt of wet '*ohia* forest on the windward slopes above 1200m on the Haleakala volcano on Maui.

There are still substantial tracts of fine-looking rainforest, dominated by '*ohia* trees and apparently little disturbed. But no Hawaiian forest is as it was before man found the islands, 1500 years ago. Pacific Rats were brought by the first Polynesian settlers, and Ship's or Black Rats a thousand years later by Europeans. Pigs that escaped into the forests from their Polynesian masters were later ousted by pigs that escaped from European settlers. Cats were set to catch the rats, and so were mongooses. Cage-birds were brought in, and many escaped; some colonized the forest, and some brought with them avian malaria, and bird pox from domestic fowl. The mosquitoes that someone else imported carried these diseases from the blood of the immigrant to the blood of the native bird, which had no resistance and so died out. Pigs, rats, birds, mosquitoes and invasive alien plants infest almost all the Hawaiian forests, even those on the windswept, rain-sodden slopes of Maui's Haleakala volcano, where the Crested Honeycreeper fights for survival.

The permanently wet '*ohia* forests clothing the upper slopes of Hawaii's Haleakala volcano are the last refuge of the island's Crested Honeycreeper.

The Hawaiian Honeycreepers: Island specialists with an uncertain future

The Crested Honeycreeper is not alone in its plight. Haleakala's 'ohia forests are the last refuge of several other rare members of the same family.

Least distinctive of these is the 'Akepa, a small bird with a finch-like bill which feeds on insects in the higher branches of the trees. It is now so rare on Maui that a recent survey found only three birds in more than 200 kilometres of transect through the forest.

The Maui Parrotbill is another highly endangered species. It is characterized by a sharply downcurved upper bill, and like a parrot it uses both mandibles to chew its food. It is often seen in the company of the more abundant slender-billed Maui Creeper, one of five related forms formerly found on different islands. Of the five creepers, those of Oahu are extremely rare, those of Molokai probably extinct and those of Lanai certainly so.

As recently as 1973 a previously unknown species was discovered in the Haleakala forest. The Poo-uli is a secretive short-tailed, brown-backed little bird with a smart black face-mask and a short stubby bill. It is apparently confined to a small area of about 400ha in the least-altered band of 'ohia forest between 1450 and 1800m above sea level.

The Alaka'i Swamp on Kauai at the opposite end of the Hawaiian island chain is a truly extraordinary habitat – a mixture of wet bog and rich subtropical montane forest. Searches here for rare forest birds could hardly be more difficult: with more than 1100cm of rain every year, the island is among the wettest places on earth.

The swamp holds almost as many gravely threatened honeycreeper species as the Haleakala volcano on Maui. Perhaps the most bizarre is the 'Akialoa – a large green and yellow bird with a grotesquely long downcurved bill. Those inhabiting the forests of Kauai are the last remnants of a species that was formerly widely distributed throughout the islands. Sadly, the 'Akialoa has not been seen since 1973 and if the bird is not found again soon the entire species will have to be presumed extinct.

The Kauai race of the Hawaiian Creeper also has its last stronghold in this remarkable habitat, maintaining a precarious hold there along with the parrot-billed 'O'u, two endemic species of thrush and the islands' only member of the honey-eater family of Australasia and the western Pacific. The yellow-thighed Kauai 'O'o (or for those preferring its full Hawaiian name, the 'O'o 'A'a) was hunted by Polynesians for its plumes, and its more richly coloured relatives are all now extinct. It, too, was thought extinct until 1960, when it was rediscovered in these dense forests, but although several have been found nesting since then, there are fears that no more than two birds may now remain. In six man-months of searching the Kauai swamp in 1981, only one pair of birds was seen.

The Hawaiian avifauna is surely the most remarkable on earth. The evolutionary radiation of its honeycreepers outshines that of any other group of island birds, including the renowned but rather dull Darwin's Finches of the Galapagos. Some of the most beautiful are still quite common; the brilliant scarlet 'Apapane and 'I'iwe, for example, have survived generations of hunting by Polynesians yet are still locally abundant. But even more remarkable is the rate at which so many of these birds became extinct. More than half the bird species of Hawaii became extinct before European man ever set foot there. His introductions, especially of rats, exotic plants, mosquitoes and avian diseases, have wiped out a significant proportion of the remainder. As many birds are now in serious danger of extinction as have been lost in the course of the last 200 years.

As a microcosm of the planet earth the example of the Hawaiian islands does little credit to man and his ability to live in harmony with the natural world. Conservation programmes already established on the Hawaiian islands will require total commitment and dedication from our own and future generations if this exceptional laboratory of evolution is to be preserved.

Untouched virgin forest on the steep volcanic slopes of Molokai – an increasingly rare sight as most of Hawaii's native forests have long-since been destroyed.

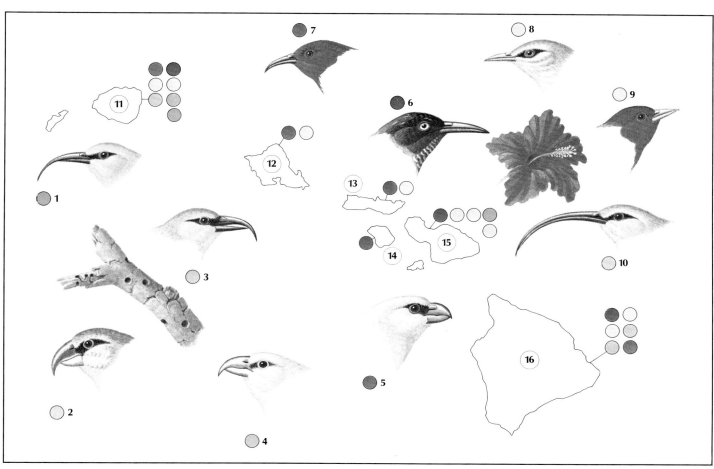

Hawaii's specialists
The honeycreepers of Hawaii are all descended from a common ancestral stock, but millions of years of adaptation to the islands' varied habitats have produced a remarkable degree of diversity and specialization – ranging from the slender curved bills of nectar-feeders to the massive finch-like bills of seed-eaters.

Undamaged forest-floor vegetation in the Olokui Forest of Molokai (*far left*) is rich and varied – a stark contrast with the devastation (*left*) caused to ground-level vegetation in areas inhabited by feral pigs.

1. Nkupu'U (*Hemignathus lucidus*)
2. Maui Parrotbill (*Pseudonestor xanthophrys*)
3. 'Akia Pola'au (*Hemignathus wilsoni*)
4. O'u (*Psittirostra psittacea*)
5. Palila (*Psittirostra bailleui*)
6. Kauai O'o (*Moho braccatus*)
7. 'Apapane (*Himatione sanguinea*)
8. Hawaiian Creeper (*Loxops maculata*)
9. 'Akepa (*Loxops coccinea*)
10. Kauai 'Akialoa (*Hemignathus procerus*)
11. Kauai
12. Oahu
13. Molokai
14. Lanai
15. Maui
16. Hawaii

Hawaii's avian extinctions:
A startling new perspective

Hawaii's remarkable bird fauna provides an insight into the manner and extent of the extinctions that island bird communities have suffered. Until recently the remaining species, together with historical records dating back to 1778, seemed to give a fair picture of Hawaii's original bird-life. This by itself was extraordinary enough. The 49 known species, of which 15 are now extinct, included a goose, a hawk, a flightless rail, a crow, 2 thrushes, 5 honeyeaters, a flycatcher and 27 of the uniquely Hawaiian honeycreepers, now known to be descended from finches. The extinction of so many of these remarkable birds after the islands were colonized by Europeans was widely deplored, and was often contrasted with the apparently harmonious relations which the Polynesian natives of the islands seemed to enjoy with the remaining species of indigenous birds.

A catalogue of disasters

Since 1970, newly discovered fossil remains have transformed our knowledge of the original Hawaiian avifauna. Deposits of bones in or near the kitchen middens of Polynesian settlers who arrived there about 1000 years ago contain the remains of nearly as many extinct species as the previous total of extinct and surviving species combined. The islands' earliest human colonists evidently exterminated at least 39 species before European man arrived. He, in his turn, wiped out 14 more. The bird-life that greeted the first Polynesians must have been truly magnificent. There were no fewer than seven species of geese — several of which were flightless — two flightless kinds of ibis, seven rails, a sea-eagle, a hawk, three species of owl, two large crows and at least 15 species of honeycreeper that did not survive into European times.

It is not surprising that so many flightless birds were exterminated. They would have made easy prey and were probably wiped out directly, by being killed for food. The only goose to survive into modern times, the

Nene, nests on the ground, where its eggs are vulnerable to feral pigs and other alien mammals, and was saved only at the eleventh hour by a captive-breeding programme. The mammals introduced by the Polynesians no doubt hastened the extinction of species not already wiped out by the Polynesians themselves. But the loss of so many species of small forest bird — the honeycreepers — is not likely to have been due directly to man and his camp followers, though rats may have accounted for some. Most of these small birds probably died out because their lowland forest habitat was destroyed.

A sad story repeated

It is clear now that the Polynesians also exterminated many of the indigenous birds of New Zealand, where they arrived about the same time that they colonized Hawaii. At least 30 species, including 13 large moas and 9 other flightless species, had disappeared by the time the Europeans arrived. The island continent of Madagascar suffered a similar fate at a similar time, losing up to 12 species of its giant elephant-birds (the 'Roc' of the legend of Sinbad the Sailor) as well as many giant ground-living lemurs and other members of the richest primate community on earth.

Hawaii, New Zealand and Madagascar are all too remote to have been colonized by large herbivorous mammals, and so birds evolved to take over the ecological roles of large grazing mammals, many of them becoming flightless in the process. The original avifauna of Hawaii, like that of New Zealand and Madagascar, was thus not only much richer than it is now but also much more varied, with birds filling many of the ecological niches that on continents are occupied by mammals. Hawaii shows us especially clearly just how much these island faunas have been devastated by mankind. European man no longer shoulders the sole responsibility for this carnage; it seems that whoever he is, and wherever he is, man is likely to have the same impact.

Waimea Canyon on Kauai Island, Hawaii, is one of the few remaining unaltered habitats for rare honeycreepers.

Hawaii over the past 200 years: a visual checklist
Waves of immigration by Polynesians and Europeans have at various times in the past caused the extinction of many of Hawaii's unique bird species.

 Native species not under immediate threat

1. Short-eared Owl (*Asio flammeus*)
2. 'I'iwi (*Vestiaria coccinea*)
3. 'Amakihi (*Loxops virens*)
4. 'Anianiau (*Loxops parva*)
5. 'Akepa (*Loxops coccinea*)
6. Hawaiian Creeper (*Loxops maculata*)
7. Apapane (*Himatione sanguinea*)
8. Hawaiian Thrush (*Phaeornis obscurus*)
9. Elepaio (*Chasiempis sandwichensis*)

 Native species threatened with extinction

1. 'Akiapola'au (*Hemignathus wilsoni*)
2. Hawaiian Hawk (*Buteo solitarius*)
3. Kauai 'Aikaloa (*Hemignathus procerus*)
4. Hawaiian Crow (*Corvus tropicus*)
5. Maui Parrotbill (*Pseudonestor xanthophrys*)
6. Small Kauai Thrush (*Phaeornis palmeri*)
7. Palila (*Psittirostra bailleui*)
8. Crested Honeycreeper (*Palmeria dolei*)
9. Laysan Finch (*Psittirostra cantans*)
10. Po'o Uli (*Melamprosops phaesoma*)
11. Nukupu'u (*Hemignathus lucidus*)
12. 'O'u (*Psittirostra psittacea*)
13. Kauai O'o (*Moho braccatus*)

 Native species extinct in the last 200 years

1. Akialoa (*Hemignathus obscurus*) No date
2. Koa Finch (*Psittirostra flaviceps*) 1891
3. Mamo (*Drepanis pacifica*) 1898
4. Hawaiian Brown Rail (*Pennula millsi*) 1864
5. Hawaii 'O'o (*Moho nobilis*) 1934
6. Ula-ai-Hawane (*Ciridops anna*) 1892
7. Hawaiian Spotted Rail (*Pennula sandwichensis*) 1893
8. Black Mamo (*Drepanis funerea*) 1907
9. Hopue (*Psittirostra palmeri*) 1896
10. Grosbeak (*Psittirostra kona*) 1894
11. Kicea (*Chaetoptila angustiplumaes*) 1859
12. Molokai 'O'o (*Moho bishopi*) 1915
13. Oahu 'O'o (*Moho apicalis*) 1837
14. Greater Amakihi (*Viridonia sagittirostris*) 1900

 Native species extinct before *c.*1780

Even before European man's impact was felt on the Hawaiian Islands, human persecution had already taken its grim toll. Gone forever were (at least); 1 sea eagle, 2 flightless ibises, 3 owls, 7 geese, 15 honeycreepers, 7 flightless rails, 2 crows, 1 honey-eater and 1 small hawk.

Lord Howe Island Woodhen: Survival by a lucky chance

The finches of the South Atlantic islands share their remote and inhospitable refuges with a very different kind of bird which also shows a remarkable propensity for speciation on islands. On Gough, and formerly on Tristan, the familiar Moorhen produced distinct endemic forms, both of which lost the power of flight. The Gough Island rail, and the tiny mouse-like *Atlantisia* rail of Inaccessible Island, are the remnants of a richer fauna of at least six Atlantic island rails on Gough, the Tristan group, St Helena and Ascension, of which four are now extinct.

The Woodhen (*Tricholimnas sylvestris*) of Lord Howe Island is a typical island rail, and one that long teetered on the brink of extinction. Lord Howe is a small island of about 13km² lying east of the northeast coast of Australia. It was discovered in 1788 and settled 46 years later, at which time it had 15 kinds of landbird of which 14 were found nowhere else. Fifteen kinds still breed there, but nine of these are newcomers and nine of the endemic ones, including four full species, are extinct. The Woodhen survived by an accident of landscape — a low, steep cliff that prevented pigs from reaching the remotest parts of the island, scattered patches of moss-forest lying at an altitude of over 860m on the summits of Mts Gower and Lidgbird. These areas could accommodate no more than a dozen pairs between them. Rats penetrated even there; pigs have altered the rails' former habitat; and men, cats and dogs have hunted them. The rails have adapted well to forest rather than the swamps that their ancestors presumably inhabited. It is remarkable that they have survived at all.

The history of the extinction of Lord Howe Island birds parallels that found on many islands. The first visitors to the island in 1788 found the birds abundant and suicidally tame. This was as true of the seabirds as of the landbirds. Like so many islands Lord Howe was as important as a breeding ground for seabirds as it was for landbirds. The island became a staging post where ships stopped for food and water, and at the very beginning the sea- and landbirds supplied much of that food. The local white gallinule, and the pigeon, were eaten out within 25 years of the first settlement, and mainland colonies of several seabirds were also wiped out. Farmers soon turned their attention to the parakeets that ate their crops, and had exterminated them by 1870. So there was a first wave of quick extinctions of landbirds and mainland colonies of seabirds. The birds died out quite simply because people killed them all.

The next wave of extinction was even quicker and more dramatic; but it was accidental. In 1918 the supply ship *Makambo* ran aground, and Ship's Rats ran ashore. Within five years these ubiquitous and nimble climbers had wiped out five more native birds. The rats accounted directly for these

five, and indirectly for another. To control the rats the settlers brought in owls, and one of these was so closely related to the endemic Lord Howe Boobook Owl that they interbred and both forms became extinct.

Lord Howe's introduced birds have replaced the extinct ones in numbers only, and not in any ecological sense, as they live in habitats disturbed or created by man. Much good forest remains on Lord Howe, and for that we can thank the rather small number of people who have settled it. But the forests have been infested with pigs, goats, cats and rats, and many native animals other than birds have been exterminated or depleted. Most of the pigs were eradicated during the 1970s, and other feral mammals are also now being controlled.

Those native birds that remain on Lord Howe generally nest out of reach of even the nimble Ship's Rats — the landbirds on twigs too thin to bear the weight of a rat, the seabirds on offshore stacks and islets, or on steep cliffs. The Woodhen nests in neither of these places. Its survival is an enigma. But in the last few years its future has been more firmly assured — largely through the most spectacularly successful captive breeding programme ever mounted for an endangered bird. In the two and a half years from May 1980 the population increased eightfold, from 15 to 120. In three breeding seasons, 66 Woodhen were raised in a specially constructed captive breeding centre on the island, and many of the 57 birds released into the wild have since bred successfully. The simultaneous control of feral pigs, goats and cats should, if maintained, ensure the survival of this resilient bird.

Other flightless rails maintain toe-holds on other islands. On Aldabra Atoll, north of Madagascar, the flightless White-throated Rail — the last of the legendary flightless birds of the Indian Ocean islands — maintains a population of several thousand in the face of large numbers of Ship's Rats. They live only on those parts of the atoll still free of feral cats, but may resist even feline predators in their inhospitable habitat of dense scrub and jagged limestone rock. The flightless rails of Aldabra, Lord Howe and a few other islands are the last survivors of a group of birds that are both especially good at reaching islands and adapting to them and especially vulnerable to invasion of their islands by mankind.

The White-throated Rail of Aldabra Island (*Dryolimnas cuvieri*) probably owes its survival to the inhospitality of its island habitat.

Although benefiting now from well-implemented and successful conservation policies, Lord Howe Island has, in the past, suffered almost every one of the major negative impacts — from hunting and habitat destruction to predation by feral rats and cats.

The Gough Island Rail (*Gallinula nesiotis*) pictured here, and the tiny Inaccessible Island Rail (*Atlantisia rogersi*) are the only survivors from the six species of flightless rail that formerly inhabited the South Atlantic islands.

Grosbeak Bunting:
Safe in an island fortress

The Tristan da Cunha islands in the South Atlantic are nearly as remote as Hawaii; 2800km from South Africa and 3200km from South America. They are classic examples of volcanic islands arising on a mid-ocean ridge. The three islands lie within 40km of each other and are small, wet and windswept, with scrubby vegetation. Few landbirds live there, but those that do make interesting comparisons with the more varied bird-life of the tropical Galapagos and subtropical Hawaii. All three groups have been colonized successfully by finch-like birds. In the Galapagos Islands these have radiated to produce 13 species, all but one clearly recognizable as a finch. On Hawaii, around 42 species evolved, many of them so unlike a finch that the true ancestry of the group was realized only very recently. The much smaller, cooler and ecologically impoverished Atlantic islands support three species of bunting, members of the finch family, in a total avifauna of only seven kinds of landbird.

On Tristan itself, the Tristan Bunting or Small-billed Bunting (*Nesospiza acunhae*) did not survive human settlement later than about 1870. But different races of the species are still abundant on the neighbouring uninhabited islands of Nightingale and Inaccessible, feeding mainly in the tussock grass that covers most of both islands. Its larger relative, the Grosbeak or Big-billed Bunting (*N. wilkinsi*), also still occurs on both islands, but it is very much rarer. On Nightingale there is room for only 30 or so pairs in the *Phylica arborea* woodland to which they are confined. On the aptly-named Inaccessible Island, ringed with sheer cliffs, the woods are more extensive and support an estimated 200 pairs. Though the area of woodland was reduced greatly by introduced livestock, it is enlarging again since the livestock have been removed. Ship's Rats, which have colonized Tristan itself, have not yet reached the outlying islands; if they do, not only the buntings but also the endemic flightless rail of Inaccessible will be seriously threatened.

Atlantic island finches
In the isolation of the South Atlantic islands, three bunting species (members of the finch family) have followed separate lines of evolutionary development.

1. Tristan Bunting (*Nesospiza acunhae*)
2. Gough Bunting (*Rowettia goughensis*)
3. Grosbeak Bunting (*Nesospiza wilkinsi*)
4. Nightingale Island
5. Inaccessible Island
6. Tristan da Cunha
7. Gough Island

Status report – Islands:
Threatened jewels of the natural world

Half the world's endangered birds are island species, and clearly they are particularly at risk. It is often suggested that island species are in some way degenerate, less fit to survive than mainland birds. But the normal processes of natural selection are not somehow suspended on islands, and island species are probably just as well suited to their own environments as mainland species are to theirs. The problems they face are attributable to the island ecosystem as a whole, rather than to any inherent deficiencies in the birds themselves.

The main problem with living on an island is that you cannot safely leave it. The sea is as much a barrier to the island species as it is to mainland ones. If a bird's habitat is destroyed or the bird is driven out by predators, it cannot simply move to the next patch of habitat as a continental species might. There is nowhere else to go. It is likely, too, to have a small population and so fewer individuals need to die to make the species extinct. Also, the extinction of an island population is much more likely to constitute the loss of a species than the loss of one population on a continent would be, because of the concentration of endemic species on islands. So not only are island populations more likely to go extinct because they are trapped on the island, and are small, but they are also more likely to be unique. These geographical and evolutionary factors contribute to the disproportionate vulnerability of island birds, quite apart from any biological deficiencies in their make-up.

Grim legacy of the island settlers
There was often a very long lapse, perhaps of several hundred years, between an island's first recorded discovery — commonly by Portuguese explorers in the sixteenth century — and its first settlement. Many islands at high latitudes had large breeding colonies of fur seals, or were close to whaling grounds, and so were first occupied by sealers or whalers who would stay often for weeks or months at a time but would not settle permanently. They took birds' eggs and killed adults for food, but rarely introduced alien plants or animals. Other islands, such as Lord Howe, Mauritius and the Falklands, were convenient staging posts on trading routes and were permanently settled soon after discovery.

The huge numbers of eggs to be found in Sooty Tern (*Sterna fuscata*) colonies provided a ready source of food for seafarers and settlers, and even today play an important part in the food economy of many islands, for example. the Seychelles.

At this stage, tropical islands in particular began to suffer severe damage. Their lush vegetation promised fertile agricultural land, and lowland forests could be cleared very quickly. Landbirds suffered as the forest was cleared, but so did seabirds. Some of these nest in forest too, but most breed on the ground and were easily wiped out. Seabirds increase the fertility of the island where they nest by leaving guano on it, so their loss would impoverish the island's nutrient cycles. Some islands were so thick in guano that it was mined commercially – usually with the loss of all native wildlife.

Ground-nesting birds, and flightless ones like the Dodo and Solitaire of the Mascarenes, Lord Howe's white gallinule, and rails everywhere, were wiped out in the next wave of extinction – caused by predatory mammals introduced by people. Rats and

cats were the worst of these, and Ship's Rats are the worst of the rats because they climb so well. They came ashore from the ships usually by accident, or following a wreck, but sometimes deliberately. James Cook built wooden walkways to encourage the rats aboard his ships to infest the land instead.

Rat plagues were no more welcome to the settlers than to the wildlife, and the invariable response was to introduce bigger predators – always cats, and often mongooses as well – to eat the rats. Between them they finished off whatever ground-nesting or ground-feeding birds were left. Often they in turn became a nuisance so the settlers brought in dogs to catch them. The usual result is a thriving population of rats, cats and mongooses (dogs fare less well when feral) – and few, if any, native birds.

Settled agriculture involved introducing alien plants, some of which invaded the native vegetation, and domestic animals like pigs, goats and cattle, which invariably did so. Goats were also put ashore from ships on any island they passed to ensure supplies of meat for future visits. Between them these herbivores have wrought as much damage to native vegetation, by accident, as people did deliberately by cutting it down or by burning it.

More subtle effects followed. Many settlers in strange and distant lands brought with them familiar cage-birds to make them feel at home. The scale of these introductions is astonishing; 160 species have been introduced to the Hawaiian islands alone. Some of these birds compete with native species, others may interbreed, and all may bring in diseases that can be devastating to the local birds.

It is hard to evaluate the relative importance of these different effects. It does not really matter which kills most native birds; all these processes have affected most islands, often simultaneously. Each is potentially disastrous, and their combined effects are guaranteed to be so.

Few island birds are as brilliantly coloured as the Aldabra Fody (*Foudia eminentissima*), a relatively recent arrival from Madagascar. Despite being a tree-nester, the Fody has been badly hit by predation by Black Rats.

Islands in the Pacific and Indian Oceans have inevitably come under enormous pressure from the growth of international tourism. Nowhere is this more obvious than along the magnificent Waikiki Beach in Hawaii.

Today, a new kind of colonization has become a threat to many islands. The threat is from tourism; from the millions of people from industrialized countries who seek sunshine and relaxation far from the stresses of their normal environments. In doing so they can all too easily contribute to the destruction of the very thing that attracted them – the exotic charms of an island paradise.

Few tropical and subtropical islands today are without their airport complexes, rows of beach-front hotels and sprawling leisure facilities; and without controls these developments will inevitably ruin a fragile island ecosystem. Yet it need not be so. With enlightened planning, tourism can make its much-needed contribution to an island's economy – and can also be made to pay for essential conservation programmes. In return, the conservation work will ensure the long-term health of the tourist trade, for without the beaches, palms, flowers and birds there will be no tourists. If moral arguments alone are not enough, sound business sense should prove the case for carefully planned island conservation.

Hope for the survivors

Many of the endemic islands birds that still exist do so in small populations on ravaged islands for which there are two main conservation strategies. One, which is rarely possible, is to make the whole island a reserve, and manage it solely for the native wildlife. Cousin Island in the Seychelles is a classic case, but a rare one. Another course of action is to move some of the threatened birds to islands better suited for them, and such translocations have proved spectacularly successful with Saddlebacks, Chatham Island Robins and a number of other birds on New Zealand islands.

The rarest birds in the world belong on islands. In relation to the insignificant area of land they occupy, these isolated refuges harbour an astonishing diversity of wildlife which represents a valuable genetic resource for mankind. Island ecosystems, so well endowed with unique species, are especially vulnerable because of their isolation, but that also makes them potentially easier to conserve. And conservation efforts on these small, self-sufficient areas yield rich returns for man and birds alike.

A daring and dramatic operation to save a species on the brink of extinction: translocation to a neighbouring island and clever manipulation of the breeding pairs have increased the population of Chatham Island Black Robins (*Petroica traversi*) from 5 individuals to 30.

Cousin, the ICBP-owned island in the Seychelles, provides a safe habitat for over 250,000 breeding seabirds of 7 species, one endemic landbird, and another found only on two other small islands.

Fed by nutrients swept in by the sea and washed off the land by rivers, the junctions of land and sea are as productive as any habitat on earth. Flat coastlines, alternately flooded and exposed by the ebb and flow of the tides, are very much the domain of birds, whose mastery of flight allows them to exploit dangerous tidal flats far beyond the reach of predatory mammals.

Each kind of coast has its own bird community, uniquely equipped for that particular environment. Steep, rocky cliffs provide huge colonies of seabirds with nest sites safe from ground predators, close to rich sources of food in the adjacent seas. Muddy estuaries provide equally rich feeding grounds, and roosting sites so frequently awash that few predators will venture there. They also provide safe staging grounds for millions of migratory shorebirds on their annual journeys.

Throughout the tropics, mangrove forests and coastal swamps, coral reefs and coldwater kelp beds act as nurseries for the vast stocks of fish that support the world's seabirds, in addition to major human fisheries.

Coasts and Estuaries

Cliff, shore and river-mouth

Estuaries and coastal habitats are among the most productive environments on earth. In relation to their area they produce about five times their expected share of the world's primary production. This luxuriant plant-life supports an equally impressive animal biomass; in fact only tropical forest can match the plant and animal production of the coastal and estuarine ecosystems.

The transition zone between the land and marine systems is particularly fruitful because it receives nutrients from both directions; washed off the land by rivers, and brought in from the sea by the tide. Here the sea is shallow enough to be lit and warmed by sunlight right to the sea bed, so plant production can make maximum use of the abundant nutrients.

Where coasts are washed by cool water and the sea bed is at no great depth, beds of giant seaweeds form enormous underwater forests in which individual plants can reach the size of terrestrial trees. These kelp beds contain great reserves of nutrients, and concentrate from the sea some elements, such as iodine, that are in short supply on land. They have traditionally been used as fertilizer — and, more rarely, as human food — in many parts of the world. In the warmer waters of the tropics, kelp beds give way to reefs of coral, constructed by tiny colonial animals whose skeletons of calcium carbonate form the massive barriers that protect the shoreline from erosion. Coral reefs play an important role in ocean chemistry by locking up vast quantities of calcium and carbon dioxide in their skeletons. Kelps and corals are among the most productive habitats known; though poor in bird-life they are vital to the food chains that support many birds. In tropical waters muddied by the discharge from rivers, corals give way to mangroves, and these quiet, shady forests, their tangled roots exposed at low tide, are a valuable resting place for many coastal birds, safe from land-living predators.

Coastal and estuarine waters are most important not directly for birds but as nurseries for fish. Many species which spend their adult lives at sea come inshore to spawn, and their young may stay in shallow water for some time. Nearly 85 per cent of the species that are fished commercially in the United States spawn or feed in estuaries or coastal waters, and two-thirds of the world's commercial fisheries are dependent on the fragile fertility of coastal waters.

Accommodation to suit all tastes

The land meets the sea in a variety of habitats, each offering a different environment for birds to live in and each supporting its own characteristic community of birds.

Many seabirds of the northern hemisphere crowd their nesting colonies on to coastal cliffs where they are safe from foxes, people and other ground-living predators. The highest cliffs fringe the northern continents, and here are found some of the world's most spectacular concentrations of seabirds. Nearer the equator, coastlines are gentler and rarely form steep cliffs. Low, rocky shorelines offer rich pickings for suitably specialized shorebirds — especially at low tide when crabs can be chivied from the seaweed and molluscs chiselled from the rocks.

Barriers of sand dunes, stabilized by thick vegetation and separated by zones of marshland fed by a small stream, provide a wealth of feeding opportunities for shorebirds.

Bizarre stilt-rooted plants of the mangrove family fringe the coast of Queensland, Australia — part of the Cape Hillsborough National Park.

Sandy beaches form where cliffs or offshore reefs shelter the coast from the full force of the sea. They form an unstable shifting environment where plants cannot root, and the worms and crabs and shrimps that live there depend for food on material washed in by the tide. The plovers and sandpipers that feed here are quick of eye and foot, dashing nimbly over the sand to pick their tiny prey from the surface.

In the most sheltered bays and estuaries the movement of the sea is stilled enough to allow the finest sediment to settle to the bottom and form mud-banks or, where land plants can take root, coastal marshes. Where fine mud can settle, so can the finest detritus, and the wealth of waste matter renewed twice daily by the tide is the basis for an enormously rich community. On the surface of the mud itself is a thin skin of microscopic algae, often underlain by a film of bacteria, whose production adds to that provided by incoming detritus to support a profusion of small invertebrates – worms, crabs, snails, clams and other molluscs.

Birds are particularly well suited to exploit this environment because of their ability to fly as well as walk. The mudflat is a constantly changing environment, alternately covered and exposed by the tide, and its soft slippery surface offers treacherous temptation to mammals that can move around only on foot.

Muddy shores are not only rich in food for birds, but their inaccessibility to mammals makes them doubly attractive. They offer better protection from predators than any other coastal habitat and are especially important to many small waders that are 'shorebirds' only outside the breeding season. These birds breed far inland, in upland or tundra habitats, but migrate to muddy coasts on passage, and often also in winter.

Huge breakers continually batter these sheer cliffs, but even such turbulent waters are rich fishing grounds for seabirds such as auks and sea-ducks.

Flat tropical coastlines are favoured wintering grounds for many northern waders. Here, Whimbrels (*Numenius phaeopus*) from the Eurasian tundra spend the winter on the Indian Ocean coast of northeast Africa.

Sea lavender in flower on the salt marshes of the River Deben estuary in Suffolk, England. Such highly specialized plant communities are common on coasts.

127

New Zealand Shore Plover: The reluctant colonist

Until European settlers brought cats and rats to New Zealand, Shore Plovers (*Thinornis novaeseelandiae*) nested around the mud-flats and rocky coasts of both the North and South Islands, as well as in the archipelago of the Chatham Islands. But these tame and confiding birds soon fell victim to the marauding aliens, and their range shrank so rapidly that as early as 1880, barely 40 years after settlement began on a large scale, the Shore Plover was already one of New Zealand's rarest birds. By 1900 it was extinct on the main islands, and on its last stronghold, the Chatham Islands, 800km east of the South Island, it was also wiped out rapidly on all the islands that rats and cats could reach. For over 70 years, Shore Plovers have been confined to the 220ha of South East Island in the Chathams, where rats and cats have so far been kept at bay. Yet even there the plovers have not been safe. Between 1890 and 1910, professional collectors of rare birds and their eggs inflicted serious damage.

Shore Plovers look strikingly like Turnstones, which frequent rocky shores throughout the world, but they are not closely related and Shore Plovers behave more like Oystercatchers than Turnstones. They feed mostly on rocky shores, especially where fresh water seeps across rock platforms, but they also use the salt-meadows farther inland, and a few live in the grassland on higher parts of the island. Like many coastal salt-meadows those of South East Island make rich grazing for sheep and cattle, and until the 1950s sheep kept the plover's favourite meadows cropped short. Sheep and cattle were then removed from the island and the grass regenerated so vigorously that much of it may now be too long for the plovers to feed in. The surviving Shore Plovers must represent one of the smallest shorebird populations in the world — a total of about 120 birds of which perhaps 80 breed annually.

Most species of plover lay their eggs in a scrape on bare ground, right out in the open. They rely for protection on the highly effective camouflage of their eggs and young, and on their own ability to see approaching predators a long way off. But New Zealand Shore Plovers evolved in an environment that was quite without ground predators and their nesting behaviour is correspondingly ill-adapted to them. The nest is much bulkier than other plovers', and is rarely open to the sky. It is usually under a tussock or a bracken frond, but it may be at the end of a horizontal tunnel of some kind — a crevice among boulders, the burrow of a Muttonbird, a hollow log, a tunnel in thick vegetation, or among the roots of a shrub. The incubating bird is therefore quite unable to see the approach of a predator. To make matters worse the birds' own confiding behaviour made them easy prey for the alien predators, human and four-footed alike, that swept through New Zealand with such devastating effect in the nineteenth century.

South East Island has been a reserve since 1959, and the plover is totally protected by law. But any population that is confined to a single island must be vulnerable, and one of the most important strategies for ensuring the plovers' survival, apart from protecting their existing habitat, must be to establish them on other suitable islands. Such translocation has been very successful in New Zealand with Saddlebacks (*Creadon carunculatus*) and, close by the plovers themselves, the Chatham Island Robin (*Petroica traversi*); but the plovers proved more difficult to move. Unlike the sedentary Saddlebacks and Black Robins that stay wherever they are put, the 15 Shore Plovers that were moved to Mangere, a rat-free island of the Chatham Group, simply flew right back to South East Island. Later attempts to move juveniles and wing-clipped adults were just as unsuccessful. Efforts are now being made to breed New Zealand Shore Plovers in captivity.

The Chatham Islands are the last refuge of two other endangered shorebirds. The Chatham Island Snipe (*Coenocorypha aucklandica*) also has its last refuge on South East Island, where it feeds in the damp leaf-litter on the forest floor and in long grass around the coast. It is closely related to the New Zealand Snipe, which has several races confined to different island groups around New Zealand. Like them, it is much smaller than other snipe and so distinctive that it is thought to be a remnant of an ancient stock that was overtaken elsewhere by present-day snipes and woodcock, and survived only on the remote refuges of southern and subantarctic islands. Some were transferred successfully to Mangere Island in the 1970s, and others have colonized Star Keys near South East Island without help.

The Chatham Island Oystercatcher (*Haematopus chathamensis*) is not confined to South East Island as the plover and snipe are, but more of its 50 or so remaining birds nest there than on any other of the Chatham Islands. Its general appearance is very similar to other oystercatchers; a large, strikingly black-and-white wader with long, stout pink legs and toes, and a straight, heavy bill ideally suited to chiselling mussels and limpets from rocks on the shore. Unlike most oystercatchers though, they are sedentary and do not form flocks. Their generally solitary behaviour limits their opportunities to indulge in the vociferous social 'piping' displays that are such a spectacular feature of rocky shores inhabited by other kinds of oystercatcher, but the birds do display when opportunity arises.

The Chatham Island Snipe occurs on five widely separated islands near New Zealand. Because of their long isolation, the birds have evolved into five distinct subspecies.

The feeding habitat of the New Zealand Shore Plover – flat, rocky platforms along the coast, almost at sea level and washed by each tide. The birds nest in the nearby coarse grassy cover.

129

White-tailed Sea Eagle:
Victim of Europe's changing land-use

The huge silhouette of the White-tailed Sea Eagle (*Haliaeetus albicilla*) was a common sight along the rocky coasts of northern Europe until about two hundred years ago. The birds' main stronghold was in steep coastal cliffs, but they also ranged widely, if more sparsely, over most of northern and central Eurasia, along river valleys and on inland lakes. Like many coastal birds they can make a living near fresh water inland as well as by the sea, though they reach their greatest densities along the coast.

The White-tailed is Europe's largest eagle, with a wingspan of over 2m. Its heavy build, long, broad wings and short, wedge-shaped white tail give it a distinctive silhouette, more ponderous and vulturine than the Golden Eagle (*Aquila chrysaetos*) whose range it overlaps. It is also more like a vulture in its behaviour. Many eagles will take carrion as well as meat they have killed themselves, but the Sea Eagle takes a higher proportion of dead meat than other European species. Its heavy, laboured flight is poorly suited to

the ferocious dashing attacks typical of Golden Eagles, and when it does hunt it relies more on surprise than speed to kill its prey. Sea Eagles spend much time sitting on an exposed perch, or soaring, looking for an unwary victim or a carcass on the ground and then approaching as stealthily as possible before striking at the last moment. One of their commonest foods in many areas is sea-duck, which sit in flocks on open water where they cannot be surprised, and these the eagles kill by repeated attacks that eventually exhaust the victim so that it can no longer dive or take flight and is finally plucked from the water like a fish.

The present stronghold of White-tailed Sea Eagles is the jagged coastline of Norway, where steep cliffs lining deeply indented fiords offer hundreds of kilometres of wild and unspoiled habitat. Here, a pair will patrol a territory of 600–800ha, which may contain several traditional nest sites. The nest itself is a huge pile of sticks and branches that is added to each year and may be over 3m deep and 2 across. They lay two large white eggs, and the female does most of the incubating while her mate gathers fresh green nest material and food for them both and, later, for the chicks. The nest site is often close to a colony of seabirds, or in inland territories of herons, so that a ready supply of food is on hand. Birds make up two-thirds of the eagles' food in Norway, and although they take fish and mammals too, birds are the most important food throughout the year.

The history of the White-tailed Eagle's decline in Europe reflects the changing land-use of the region. The birds are opportunist feeders and will exploit the carcass of a sheep as readily as that of a rabbit. Farmers finding eagles at the body of a lamb do not question whether the lamb was dead before the eagle started eating it: they kill the eagle.

The White-tailed Eagles of Scotland began to decline when the Highlands were stocked with sheep, from the late eighteenth century to halfway through the nineteenth. At a time when people were being cleared wholesale from the land to make way for sheep, it is hardly surprising that eagles were ruthlessly removed, by shooting and with poisoned bait. Their removal was not always deliberate; in Iceland, poisoned baits put out for Arctic Foxes and owls reduced the eagles from 150 pairs in 1880 to seven in 1921, when there were as many Arctic Foxes and owls as ever. By the early twentieth century White-tailed Eagles were extinct in Britain and had declined sharply across most of Europe.

Then began a second steep decline. Persistent insecticides and mercury compounds found their way into both the aquatic and terrestrial food chains of which the eagles were the final link. Some birds died; others failed to hatch their eggs because DDT had caused the shells to become so thin they could not bear the weight of the incubating birds. Most European countries now number their White-tailed Eagles in tens of pairs, except for Norway, where 45–60 per cent of the European population of 500–750 now breeds.

There has, however, been at least one recent success in the troubled history of the White-tailed Sea Eagle. In 1959 and 1968 attempts were made to reintroduce the birds to Scotland, in Argyll at first and later in Fair Isle. The attempts were unsuccessful, but paved the way for a much larger-scale reintroduction programme that began in 1976. Since that year, 82 young White-tails have been shipped from Norway and released on the rocky island of Rhum off the west coast of Scotland. The survival rate was encouraging – more than 50 per cent – and as the young birds approached sexual maturity there were strong hopes that they would breed. Unsuccessful nestings were recorded in 1983 and 1984, but in 1985 four pairs mated and produced eggs. Three failed, but one was successful, and in that year the first native-born White-tail for 70 years took to the skies over the Scottish Highlands.

Like its Eurasian relative the White-tailed Sea Eagle, the Southern Bald Eagle of America (*Haliaeetus leucocephalus*) is in grave danger. These magnificent birds have suffered from habitat destruction, interference with their nest-sites and from the effects of toxic chemicals in the bodies of their fish prey. Wide, straight wings and a short wedge-shaped tail identify the bird in flight.

Steep cliffs and quiet bays are typical of the wild and remote northern coasts that are the favoured habitat of White-tailed Sea Eagles.

The survival of the White-tailed Sea Eagle in Europe is dependent now on research and conservation efforts throughout its range. Ringing eagle chicks is an important method of gaining information about their movements in adult life.

Chinese Egret:
Slaughtered in the name of fashion

A strict Buddhist protects the birds that nest in his sacred trees, even if they do share the produce of his fish-pond. The last few pairs of Chinese Egrets (*Egretta eulophotes*) that nest in Hong Kong owe their survival to the 5000-year-old teachings of the Buddha, and to those who still observe his teachings.

Chinese Egrets once bred widely in the coastal provinces of China and in North Korea. After breeding they migrated to Japan, Malaysia and the Philippines. They nested in huge colonies, mixed in with other species of heron and egret in clumps of tall trees close to water. Many colonies probably enjoyed the protection of traditional religious beliefs, but there was plenty of unspoiled habitat to support not only the Chinese (or Swinhoe's) Egret, but also many other related species.

Two of these have played an important part in the recent history of the Chinese Egret; the Little Egret, which feeds in fresh water and by the sea, and the Eastern Reef Heron, which feeds among rock-pools and in muddy creeks of the sea coast. The Chinese Egret is squeezed, ecologically, between the two. It feeds in very shallow water on tidal mudflats, especially in estuaries, in a niche that the other two species can exploit almost as effectively. The Chinese Egret is much more narrowly specialized than its competitors, which can take advantage of a wider range of habitat if their favourite one is denied them.

All three are probably descended from ancestors that looked and lived like bitterns and pond herons still do — heavily camouflaged in brown and buff streaks and feeding and nesting solitarily in the dense cover of reed-beds. In the more open water where egrets feed, cryptic camouflage is ineffective and a pure white plumage evolved. The egrets also use different behavioural tricks to catch their food. Sometimes they wait patiently in the shallows for prey to approach or stalk it cautiously until they are close enough to strike. At other times they dash madly about, flapping and flicking their raised wings above their backs, frightening their prey from their hiding places under stones and seaweed.

The white plumage that suits the more open-water feeding habits of egrets also allows them to nest in colonies instead of singly; indeed it may force them to do so since they are too conspicuous to conceal their nests and so need the protection of greater numbers. In the colonies they are surrounded by others who will compete with them for mates, so an evolutionary pressure exists for each bird to be more beautiful than its neighbour. Egrets have developed the most elegant adornments for the courting season – delicate, long, white plumes on the back and neck, which are raised in display to create a graceful tracery of white against the dark green of the nesting-trees.

The beauty of the egrets' plumes has been their downfall. In the nineteenth century it became the fashion for women to adorn their hats and capes and evening dresses with the plumes of slaughtered birds. Throughout the world birds were killed indiscriminately, and the gentle Buddhist traditions crumbled before the commercial onslaught of the plume trade. Egrets were not the only victims, but they were among the most vulnerable because they nested openly and conspicuously in colonies, many of which were well known and could be approached easily. And because their plumes are grown only in the breeding season, so the birds had to be killed on the nest. Thus the toll was concentrated on the breeding stock at a time when they had eggs, or dependent young that were doomed to starve when their parents died.

Whole populations of herons and egrets were wiped out by the plume trade. Estimates of the numbers of birds killed each year range from five million to two hundred million. A furious campaign against the trade was waged from the 1860s until 1922, when ICBP itself was born in response, not least, to the clearly international dimensions of the plume trade. The sale of feathers was finally outlawed, and the carnage ceased.

In China, as elsewhere, some egrets began to recover from their losses. But the Chinese Egret has never recovered as fully as its relatives, which can use a greater variety of habitats as they expand their numbers. The Chinese Egrets' habitat itself is threatened by pollution from burgeoning townships nearby. One group of three pairs abandoned its nesting grounds in Hong Kong after smoke drifted through the colony from a growing township nearby. The enormous increase in rice-growers along the east coast of China has also squeezed out many egrets, but especially the Chinese. How many remain in mainland China is not known, but they are desperately scarce in their winter quarters and only one or two pairs are left in Hong Kong.

Delicate plumes like those of the Little Egret (*Egretta garzetta*) have long been highly prized fashion accessories – an attraction that brought disaster to many egret and heron colonies.

The Eastern Reef Heron (*E. sacra*) is usually seen alone when hunting along the shores of the Pacific, but like most herons the birds often gather at communal roosts at nightfall.

Damara Tern:
No hiding place from man

The Damara Tern (*Sterna balaenarum*) is closely related to the Little Tern (*S. albifrons*) which is widespread in the northern hemisphere and is also threatened in many parts of its range. But the Damara Tern's problems are more acute because the species is confined to a very small area where many different pressures are concentrated.

The cold waters of the Benguela current which sweep up the west coast of southern Africa support a breeding population of Damara Terns that probably numbers only one or two thousand pairs; certainly far fewer than the tens of thousands of Jackass Penguins that the same current sustains farther south. The terns range from the southern tip of Africa northwards to Cabinda in the breeding season, and as far as Nigeria

outside it. But they are known to breed only along the coast of Cape Province and, especially, Namibia. They nest in scattered groups among barren sand dunes and salt-flats, normally within a kilometre or so of the shore, and feed in shallow coastal waters immediately offshore.

Their favoured feeding grounds are in estuaries, bays and lagoons. These are popular with people too, as recreation areas, and to service the rising numbers of visitors to the coast there has been a rapid increase in industrial development and housing. In some places estuaries have been dredged, and large areas of coastal water have become polluted by industrial and domestic effluents.

Damara Terns do not nest in dense colonies like most terns do. Instead, they breed in loose colonies or in scattered pairs along hundreds of kilometres of coastline. Each nest is a small scrape, usually in a bare unvegetated slack between sand dunes, or on a salt-flat. In dunes the terns space themselves out so widely that even the closest nests may be hundreds of metres apart.

The steady winds typical of these coasts threaten to cover the nests with drifting sand, so most are placed in the lee of a dune. In the De Mond Reserve the winds also tend to blow the dune sand on to adjacent farmland, so much of the sand has been planted artificially to stabilize the dunes. Unfortunately, if this policy continues it will destroy the bare ground that the terns need to nest on.

Damara Terns lay only one egg. This is a most unusual habit for an inshore-feeding species (most of which lay two or three) and argues either that their food is scarce and unpredictable or that they are descended quite recently from a species that fed farther out at sea. After the chick fledges it depends on its parents for a further ten weeks while it learns to fend for itself. This prolongs the breeding period enough to make it impossible for the birds to lay a second clutch.

The coastal desert of Namibia is a vast expanse of rolling dunes, broken only by patches of scrub vegetation and here crossed by the Kuiseb River. This is the harsh habitat of the Damara Tern, which occurs only along the arid coast of Southwest Africa.

Sandy beaches close to townships in warm climates are vulnerable to disturbance by people coming there for recreation. People on foot frighten chicks off the nest, leaving them exposed to predators on the bare dunes or driving them into the territory of a neighbouring gull or tern, where they are viciously attacked and perhaps killed. Motor vehicles, especially those designed for use among the dunes, can also do serious damage to the dunes themselves and may eventually destroy the birds' nesting habitat.

A further conflict threatens some of the terns' nesting grounds near the estuary of the Orange River. Here, deposits of diamonds are found on the beaches and in shallow water, and these are exploited by beach mining — a crude operation that involves completely stripping the beach to a depth of as much as 20m. This not only destroys the birds' nesting habitat but also increases the amount of silt in the waters offshore and so threatens their feeding grounds as well. Diamond deposits have been found in other parts of the birds' range, and the Damara Tern may soon face as direct a conflict with the diamond-mining industry as Abbott's Booby does with the miners of phosphate on Christmas Island.

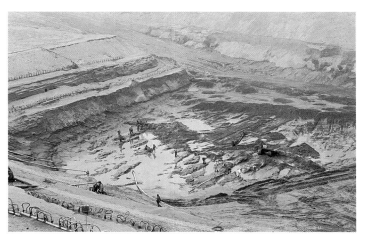

Behind the protective barrier of an artificial sea wall, workers at the Oranjemund diamond mine in Namibia strip the diamond-bearing sediments right down to bedrock.

Kleinschmidt's Falcon:
Mystery falcon at the world's end

Along the remote and windswept coastline of Tierra del Fuego, a few specimens have been collected of this mysterious falcon. It is evidently closely related to the Peregrine Falcon (*Falco peregrinus*), but at least until recently has been regarded as a distinct species. However, the Peregrine is very variable, with well-marked races in many parts of the world and a distribution that is practically worldwide. It is now suspected that Kleinschmidt's (*Falco kreyenborgi*) may be simply another race of the Peregrine, but if this is so it is certainly one of the most distinctive. Whatever its taxonomic status, Kleinschmidt's is probably the least known of all the world's falcons. Indeed, so little is known of it that it is impossible to say just how rare it really is; its remote and rocky refuge on the barren subantarctic coast at the very southern tip of the South American continent is perhaps as effective a protection against our acquiring further knowledge as it is against the threat of extinction at the hand of man.

About one-fifth of the birds thought to be endangered are in the international *Red Data Book* category 'Indeterminate', for which the most urgent conservation need is simply to find out more about them. Some are little known because they are extremely rare, while others, like Kleinschmidt's, owe their obscurity perhaps as much to the remoteness of their habitat as to their rarity.

The wild and rocky coastal terrain of Tierra del Fuego off the southernmost tip of South America; home of the elusive and little known Kleinschmidt's Falcon.

Status report – Coasts and estuaries: Collision zone for man and nature

Placed as they are at the junction of marine and terrestrial ecosystems, coastal and estuarine habitats suffer all the indignities borne by those systems as well as many peculiar to themselves. Their exceptional biological productivity and diversity multiplies the consequences of any harmful impact on them.

Coastal waters are the spawning grounds and nurseries for many fish, some of which contribute to commercial fisheries while others provide food for coastal birds like Damara Terns. The pollution of estuaries is very often due to misuse of the river farther upstream, but the impact is felt at the coast and even far out to sea. A classic case is the stifling of tropical coral reefs by silt that may originate hundreds or thousands of kilometres away in mountains that were once thickly forested. Clearing the forest on steep mountain slopes allows tropical rainstorms to sweep tonnes of topsoil into the rivers, which then carry the silt into the ocean where it settles offshore and chokes the reefs. The effects of this are not confined to the coral, for the reef makes a natural breakwater for the coast behind, and when it dies the erosion of the shoreline increases dramatically. People who live along the shore, making their living by fishing over the reef, find their livelihood buried under metres of clay. The entire biological system that depended on the living coral can thus be destroyed by acts committed hundreds of kilometres away.

The threat of human recreation

The most obvious damage to coastal habitats is very often inflicted at the site itself. People the world over experience a powerful pull to the seashore. Many primitive peoples have made a living by the sea for countless generations, and have survived by understanding its biology and obeying its natural laws. The damage is inflicted by those who go there not to live and work, but to relax. They have no need to adapt to the environment, and all too often simply extract as much as they can in the short time they are there.

The kinds of coasts most attractive for human recreation are sandy beaches. These are often rather sterile biologically but they make excellent nesting sites for a variety of ground-nesting birds because their bareness makes approaching predators clearly visible and they are often close to fertile feeding-grounds offshore. The mere presence of people can disturb the birds enough to cause them to leave their eggs and expose them to predators like crows and gulls. Later in the season, people can scare chicks away from the nest site and into the territories of neighbouring birds which may attack them. Disturbance by holidaymakers has been a major cause of the decline of many birds nesting on sandy coasts, notably the Little Terns of Europe and North America.

Undisturbed shores are indispensable resting areas for birds on migration from one part of the world to another.

Tourism and conservation clash in many parts of the world. Terns, perhaps more than any other bird group, have suffered from the pressures of holidaymakers on the sandy shores of Europe and America.

Pressures from industry and agriculture

The remote and desolate nature of much of the coast makes it an attractive site for certain kinds of building which people do not like to have close by their homes. Power stations — especially nuclear ones — are often built there, not only because they are remote from habitation but also because there is a plentiful supply of water close by that can be used for cooling. Damara Terns used to breed on a site near Cape Town that is now occupied by a power station, and there are many other places where less endangered birds have lost their breeding sites to power stations. The rise in water temperature caused by discharge of cooling water may favour a few aquatic creatures, but it also eliminates many more.

Estuarine mudflats are very important to far more birds than those that breed there. Millions of shorebirds use mudflats on migration, as wintering grounds or, in the case of such birds as European Shelduck, as specialized moulting grounds. Shelduck from many parts of western Europe migrate each summer to a strictly limited number of estuaries in northwest Europe — the Severn and the Wash in England, the Waddenzee in the Netherlands and the mouth of the River Elbe in northern Germany — solely to moult. No other places combine the necessary features of a rich and dependable food supply and a large enough area to give safety from predators. To millions of smaller shorebirds the mudflats where they spend winter, or where they refuel for the next stage of a twice-yearly migration that covers several thousand miles, are at least as important to them as their breeding grounds — and often under much greater threat.

Muddy estuaries contain two resources that are attractive to mankind. The estuaries of many large rivers cover enormous areas of land, submerged at high tide by only a metre or so of water. That land is potentially valuable for agriculture, especially in countries like Britain and the Netherlands that are densely populated and short of land. Reclamation of coastal mudflats has converted thousands of square kilometres of shorebird habitat to agricultural land in the past few hundred years, especially in Europe, and if it continues it will seriously threaten the survival of many species.

World-famous Copacabana Beach at Rio de Janiero is an extreme example of large-scale human impact on the coast.

Industrial developments often have a profound impact on the coastal environment. Their wastewater outflow pollutes areas that are vital to the reproductive cycles of many marine animals.

In many parts of the tropical world, logging of coastal mangrove forest is destroying the stability of this fragile and complex habitat.

The other resource that large estuaries offer is water, and especially its potential for producing electricity by the harnessing of its tidal power. Several ambitious schemes for impounding estuaries with barrages are under way in Europe. Between them they will change the estuaries so drastically that they too threaten the survival of many waders that migrate through western Europe or winter there. There is hardly an estuary used by shorebirds in western Europe whose future ability to support those birds is not threatened by one kind of development scheme or another.

A habitat too important to lose

Coastal birds therefore face a bewildering variety of threats to their survival, the most serious of which are human disturbance, exploitation of beaches for minerals, industrial development, land reclamation and impoundment by barrages. To these direct threats must be added the more insidious ones that originate elsewhere, either out at sea where ships discharge oil and other noxious chemicals that end up on the coast, or upstream in the catchment area of the rivers that feed the estuaries. In a world in which producing enough food is the major daily preoccupation of the majority of its people, we can ill afford to jeopardize the most productive habitats we have. We have much to learn from them about the natural laws of biological productivity.

The environments of the coast provide an object lesson in the mutual interdependence of different ecosystems. Population declines in coastal birds are indicators of environmental damage that might originate anywhere between a mountain watershed and an offshore fishery. However much we try to divide up the natural world into separate and self-contained systems — be they geographical, political or biological — nature contrives to demonstrate that she is not to be divided. At the coasts land meets sea, and terrestrial habitats, freshwater wetlands and marine ecosystems are linked by the physical, chemical and biological interchanges that take place between them.

Dykes like these in the bay of Nordstrand destroy the mud-flats of the European North Sea coast. The impact is severe, as these are important staging areas for migrants from a vast area stretching from northern Europe across to central Siberia.

Oil-slicks not only destroy shore-life but their effects often persist for years. The techniques available for combating such environmental disasters are always inadequate, and cannot prevent the deaths of great numbers of birds.

Flood control measures like the huge Thames barrier that now protects the low-lying parts of London require years of research to assess their likely environmental impact.

Linking one habitat to another like a silver thread, the waterways and wetlands of the world are, like the bloodstream of the body, vital and highly efficient distribution and cleansing systems.

Freshwater habitats can be as productive as any on earth, and support natural communities of great beauty and diversity. Many wetland birds are large and spectacular creatures, nesting in huge colonies. Many are also long-distance migrants, with long-established flyways linking one wetland habitat with another. Migrating birds carry the seeds of wetland plants with them on their journeys, and so aid the spread of entire living communities.

Thousands of years ago the vast and fertile wetlands of the Middle East provided the perfect setting for man's transition from nomad to settled farmer, and ultimately to the building of the first great civilizations of that region. Today we treat wetlands as wastelands – dumping our refuse in them or filling them in order to provide farmland or building land. Natural wetlands, their birds, and much of their potential value to mankind, are disappearing before our eyes.

Lakes, Rivers and Marshlands

The bloodstream of the biosphere

Water is essential to the survival of any plant or animal, and natural wetlands are vital cogs in the ecological machine. Most rain falls over the oceans and is evaporated back into the atmosphere; the small fraction that falls over land runs eventually into the sea, but on the way it is recycled again and again through many kinds of plant and animal, and several kinds of wetland. As it passes from one biome to another, water functions as a biological transport system, an ecological bloodstream carrying nutrients throughout the system and washing away waste products.

Rivers, lakes, marshes and swamps offer an enormous variety of habitats, and to call them all simply 'wetlands' reflects man's tendency to dismiss them all as wasteland, fit only for turning into something else, such as farmland, building land, recreation areas or dumping grounds for rubbish and toxic waste materials.

The life of the river

Most of the rain that falls on land descends on mountains, and the first stages of its journey to the sea are through fast-flowing mountain streams. The water is cold and clear, the bottom stony. The stream is usually too fast for plants to take root in its bed of shifting stones, but the turbulence makes it rich in oxygen and many insects and fish can make a living among the stones.

As a river reaches lower altitudes it flows more slowly and becomes clouded with an ever-increasing burden of silt. And so the life of the river changes; in its broader, warmer reaches, plant life flourishes and fish and frogs can build up populations big enough to support carnivorous birds. As the river matures, its biology becomes increasingly varied and complex until, eventually, it meets — and becomes one with — the sea.

Lake and marshland sanctuaries

Safety from predatory mammals is one of the great gifts that wetlands offer their inhabitants. Not many land mammals are in the habit of swimming, and most that are, such as otters and mink, commonly feed more on fish and other aquatic life than on birds. Freedom from predators is one of the reasons for the abundant bird-life of many wetlands, but high productivity is another.

The most productive wetlands are lakes and marshes. Lakes develop where a river flows into a basin or where its outflow is blocked, and marshes where the movement of water is slowed almost to a standstill by the flatness of the land. In both cases nutrients are concentrated in the lake or the swamp, where they accumulate by sinking into the mud and by being taken up by plants. The wetland literally drinks in nutrients from a vast area around it and so enhances its productivity.

Principal wetlands
1. Yukon Delta
2. James Bay
3. Salton Sea
4. Mississippi Delta
5. The Everglades
6. Chesapeake Bay
7. Venezuelan llanos
8. Amazon Delta
9. The Pantanal
10. Altiplano lakes
11. Wet chaco and Parana–Paraguay floodplains
12. Lake Myvatn
13. Waddenzee
14. Coto Doñana
15. Danube Delta
16. Volga Delta
17. Mesopotamian marshes
18. Ob and Irtish marshes
19. Lena River Delta
20. Lake Furen
21. Indus Delta
22. Bharatpur
23. Ganges Delta
24. Irrawaddy Delta
25. Banc d'Arguin
26. Niger River
27. Lake Chad
28. Nakuru and Naivasha
29. Okavango Swamp
30. Cobourg Peninsula

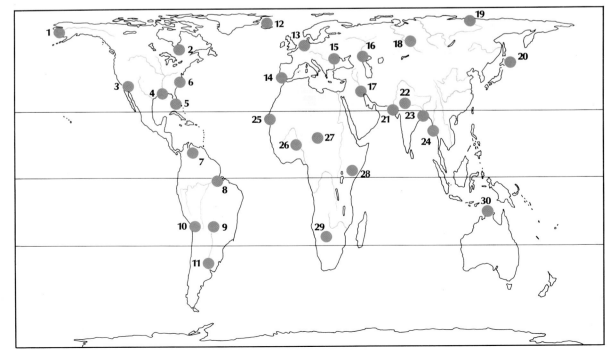

Lakes may be deep and steep-sided, or shallow with gently sloping banks. Life in deep lakes suffers many of the problems of life at sea. Plants can find a roothold only around the edge, and productivity in the deep water is limited. Deep, steep-sided freshwater lakes are often nearly as sterile as the open sea – and as poor in bird-life. But shallow lakes are among the richest and most productive habitats on earth because rooted plants can grow wherever the water is shallow enough, and plankton and floating plants can thrive in the water too. Light can penetrate to the bottom of the lake, and it is shallow enough to be constantly mixed by the wind so nutrients that sink to the bottom are rapidly recirculated. Shallow lakes and marshes are to deep lakes what upwellings are to the open ocean indeed they achieve similar levels of productivity, and are even richer in bird-life.

Habitats under siege

Wetlands are changeable habitats, dependent on fickle cycles of flood and drought. In many, the water level rises and falls in a continually changing pattern that alters the bird community from month to month. But these are natural rhythmic changes to which the birds have adapted over many generations. The changes faced by modern wetland birds are of a different order entirely: birds cannot simply 'adapt' to the wholesale destruction of their environment.

Clear mountain torrents feed the life-sustaining lowland rivers with fresh, oxygen-rich, unpolluted water.

Lake Ifni in the High Atlas mountains of Morocco is a classic oligotrophic lake, with virtually no organic production either in the water or on the banks. Such lakes are important natural reservoirs and their conservation becomes increasingly important.

Flocks of Sudan Crowned Cranes (*Balearica pavonina*) on the Sudd marshlands of the southern Sudan – one of the largest remaining natural wetlands in Africa.

The aftermath of a tropical storm: a brown and swollen river floods its banks, depositing fertile mud and silt over a wide area.

143

Birdlife of the world's wetlands

The great diversity of wetland habitats creates viable niches for many very different types of bird. A few are confined to fast-flowing streams and rivers. Wagtails feed on the insects that hatch from the water, and return there to lay their eggs. Dippers are wonderfully specialized for walking under water, using their wings to hold themselves down against their natural buoyancy while they forage for aquatic insects and fish eggs on the stream bed. In the forested mountain streams of South America, little Torrent Ducks pursue similar prey by quite different means, their powerful webbed feet holding their lithe streamlined bodies against the current while they dive or dabble for their prey. And on the far side of the world, Blue Ducks in New Zealand and Salvadori's Ducks in New Guinea lead strikingly parallel lives.

The river banks are patrolled by herons and egrets, their long legs allowing them to wade a few metres out from the bank, where they watch and wait for an unwary victim to approach close enough to strike at. A few cormorants fish the rivers here too, though they usually fish on lakes. In tropical rivers, darters swim submerged with only the snake-like head and neck above the surface. The highly specialized anatomy of the bird's neck turns its dagger-shaped bill into a spear that is stabbed forward to impale its prey. Other fish-eaters seize their prey between the tips of the mandibles, and then have to subdue it before it can be swallowed. Kingfishers perch on bare branches low over the water, diving down to chase their prey underwater then carrying it back to a tunnel hollowed out in the river bank. Pratincoles hawk for insects over the water, returning to the safety of a mid-river mud-bank to eat, and to roost.

The shallow lakes of East Africa are the habitat of the Lesser Flamingo (*Phoeniconaias minor*). The birds feed in dense flocks, filtering tiny organisms from the water with side-to-side sweeping movements of their bills.

Safety in numbers

The beds of tall aquatic plants that fringe the shores of shallow lakes and marshes are the most productive parts of the lake and also provide the best protection. The plants grow so close together that no predator of any size can force its way through without making its presence very obvious. A bird that stays still – especially if it is well camouflaged – can become invisible from only a few metres away. Reed-dwelling birds like bitterns are intricately patterned in reed-coloured stripes, and when alarmed will remain motionless with their necks stretched up so that they blend perfectly with the background. Other birds rely not on concealment, but on their numbers. Herons and egrets of many species, often gaudily plumed, crowd together in noisy colonies often several hundred strong, with open water or dense reed-beds as their only protection. Such behaviour works well against four-footed predators, but is desperately vulnerable to men in boats.

144

A world of specialists

The ways in which wetland birds make their living are as varied as the food they prey upon. Fish-eagles and ospreys plunge from the air to pluck large fish from the water — and often other waterbirds as well — while smaller fish are pursued by a variety of grebes, ducks, cormorants and pelicans that dive for them from the surface. Nearer the shore, where the shallow water teems with fish, frog and insect food, herons and egrets, storks and spoonbills, ibises, avocets and others exploit their own kinds of food in their own ways.

Wetlands support some of the most specialized feeders of the bird world: flamingos, sieving plankton from salt lakes with their grotesque bills held upside down; Shoebilled Storks of the East African papyrus swamps and the equally bizarre Boatbilled Storks of South America, wielding their enormous clumsy bills to prise frogs and lungfish from the mud; Open-billed Storks crushing African snails with their nutcracker bills, and Everglade Kites delicately prising American snails from their shells with their slender, curving mandibles.

Birds of the wetlands are often nomads, flying large distances in search of fresh water. Some, like the flamingos of East Africa, may patrol a string of lakes, hundreds of kilometres apart, for years before they find one at the right stage to breed in. For others, migration between nesting grounds and wintering areas takes on the predictable regularity of commuting. For residents and visitors alike, the wetlands are an essential part of life. A threat to one of their habitats translates immediately into a threat to many individual species.

Waterbirds show a wide range of specialization of both form and behaviour. This Great Blue Heron (*Ardea herodias*) stands motionless among mangrove roots in the Galapagos Islands, waiting to strike at a fish with its formidable bill.

The Mallard (*Anas platyrhynchos*) is perhaps the best known and most abundant waterfowl species in Europe and North America. It nests everywhere — even in city parks.

The strikingly coloured Purple Swamphen (*Porphyrio porphyrio*) inhabits reed-beds, swamps and riverside vegetation from south-west Europe, across southern Asia and south to Australasia.

Atitlan Grebe:
Final threat to an ancient community?

Lake Atitlan, in the mountains of Guatemala, is perhaps the most spectacular lake in the world. Steep volcanoes surround it, and until a few years ago dense forest descended the mountain slopes to the shoreline and hot sulphur springs bubbled to the surface in swirling clouds of steam. The open water is buffeted by storms sweeping across the mountain ridge as air-masses from the Pacific and Caribbean battle for supremacy. Atitlan is a big lake, with a shoreline of 125 kilometres and depths of over 340 metres. It has played its part in the history of mankind as well as in the evolution of birds: the people who live around it are descendants of the ancient civilization of the Mayas. Well over 50,000 of them live within the lake's catchment area and for generations they have depended on it for water, transportation, reeds, fish, crabs and waterfowl.

Until now. The destruction of the Mayas, started by the swords of Spanish invaders in the sixteenth century and left unfinished for four hundred years, is now being completed by cultural and biological changes. The lake ecosystem that supported the people for so long has been changed so drastically that it can no longer meet their protein needs. The mountain forest is separated from the shore by a rising tide of cultivation, and the lake level has fallen far enough to destroy the sulphur springs.

The fate of the Giant Grebe (*Podilymbus gigas*) of Lake Atitlan is bound up with that of the lake and its people. It is a distinctive bird, related to (and perhaps descended from) the Pied-billed Grebe (*P. podiceps*) that is widespread in the Americas; but it is bigger, with a more bulky head and bill, and is entirely flightless. The build of its head and neck, and its short, deep bill, suggest that it evolved to eat the crabs that were once abundant in the aquatic vegetation along the shallow margins of the lake.

But in 1958, and again in 1960 when there were over 200 grebes on the lake, alien fish were introduced to Lake Atitlan. One of these species, the aptly-named Large-mouthed bass, grew well, bred profusely, competed with the grebes and the people for small fish and crabs, and found young grebes a most acceptable item in its diet. Soon, the few remaining crabs had moved from the beds of pondweed in shallow water to the much deeper water farther out, where they could not be reached by Indians or grebes. The local fishery collapsed. The people could not catch the bass because they could not afford the expensive rods and lines of the sport-fisherman. The grebe population collapsed too – down to 80 in 1965, and apparently doomed. But the birds did survive, and now feed mostly on small fish, aquatic insects and the few crabs they can reach. Their numbers rose again to over 200, and for a time they apparently reached an equilibrium with their new neighbours, but their numbers have since fallen yet again.

The Mayas have always used the beds of reeds and cat-tails that used to line 25km of the sheltered southern shore. They have cut the stems and made them into sleeping-mats and chairs, which they use or sell for the pitifully few dollars that have been their only cash income. The reed harvest has sometimes clashed with the birds' breeding season, and the grebes' floating nests, built among the reeds and attached to reed-stems to stop them being blown away, have often been destroyed by the flashing knives of the reed-cutters. But enough reeds survived to maintain the habitat and meet the needs of both human and avian populations.

But now other people are taking an interest in the resources of the lake, and new threats loom for both Indians and grebes. City people have found the lake an ideal weekend and holiday retreat. They are buying land and building houses along the shore. To improve the view of the lake from their property, they cut the reeds and cat-tails along the frontage. They bring in powerful motorboats for water-skiing, scuba-diving and sport fishing; and sewage from their homes, hotels and shops threatens the health of the lake.

The lake has supplied all the washing, drinking and cooking water for generations of Mayas. Very few streams run into the lake, but none leave it. All the outflow is through underground fractures in the rock, renewed by frequent earth tremors. In 1969 a proposal was made to use Lake Atitlan's water to generate hydro-electric power — a scheme that would have lowered the surface of the lake by several metres. This would have been disastrous, for the birds, the fisheries and the Mayas all depend on the reed-beds, which would have been killed when the water retreated. Tragically, in 1976 a natural disaster — an earthquake — demonstrated just how harmful a lowered lake level could be. The earthquake opened up new outlets beneath the lake, whose level dropped by over four metres in five and a half years. By 1980, 60 per cent of the reeds and cat-tails were gone and the grebe population was down to 80: by May 1985 there were believed to be no more than 50–60 adults remaining.

To compound the grebes' problems, the guerilla warfare that has plagued Guatemala in recent years has curtailed wildlife patrols around the lake, and in May 1982 claimed the life of a warden dedicated to the protection of the grebes.

The incredibly beautiful ecosystem of Lake Atitlan has been important to a vanishing human culture as well as to a vanishing endemic bird. It has already been ravaged by the wholesale reconstruction of its food web by introduced fish; the destruction of nesting habitat by reed-cutting Indians and now, much more seriously, by property development. The recent drop in water level threatens to administer the *coup de grâce* to a magnificent ecosystem that has proved remarkably resistant to the outrages already perpetrated on it, while political unrest poses a further threat to the valiant efforts of local conservationists to protect the grebes.

Volcanic peaks provide a spectacular backdrop to Lake Atitlan in Guatemala, only known habitat of the Giant Grebe. But introduced fish, tourism and exploitation of the lake's reed-beds have placed the birds under great pressure. Now, following an earthquake, the lake level has dropped by several metres. Has all this altered the lake and its wildlife beyond recovery?

South America's Mountain Grebes: Survivors of the Andean lakes

The Atitlan Grebe is one of four waterbird species clinging to a precarious existence in the high lakes of the Andes mountains. Another flightless grebe lives an equally isolated life on Lake Junin in the highlands of Peru, thousands of kilometres to the south of Atitlan. Lake Junin covers a greater area than Atitlan but is extremely shallow, barely 12m deep at most. It lies above the tree-line, over 4000m above sea level in the bitter cold of the *puna* zone of the Peruvian Andes, and its vast fringing beds of reed and sedge shelter a large and varied waterbird population. The local people graze sheep, cattle and llamas on the floodplain, and on the lake itself hunt fish, birds and a giant edible frog. Wild guinea-pigs take refuge in the reed-beds; they are a popular local delicacy and large areas of reed-bed are regularly burnt to drive them out to be killed.

The people hunt from flat-bottomed boats with spears, not guns, and disdain the flightless grebe because its shrunken breast muscles offer little meat. Junin Grebes (*Podiceps taczanowskii*) were extremely common 50 years ago, and they were still abundant in 1961. But by 1969 they had declined drastically, and by 1979 there were 100 pairs at most. They feed mainly on small fish, supplemented with a variety of insects which they catch in open water; but in October they move into the reed-beds to breed, and they then compete with another species of grebe, the White-tufted, which is common on the lake.

Some of the threats faced by Junin Grebes are like those faced by their relatives on lake Atitlan. Introduced trout may have ousted native fish. The level of the water in the lake is now controlled by a hydro-electric plant on its outflow. But the gravest danger of all is from poisoning caused by nearby copper mines which wash deadly copper, lead, iron and zinc into the lake. By 1969 the lake was stained yellow by effluent from the mines, and by 1979 one-third of the lake-bed was dead — choked by toxic silt. Unless the outflow from the mines is properly treated, all animal life in the lake is likely to be extinct within a decade or two.

But paradoxically the best hope for the future is offered by yet another development scheme. There are plans to use the lake as a storage reservoir for domestic uses in the city of Lima; and if the water of Lake Junin is destined for Lima it will have to be properly purified first. Thus the best hope for the future of the grebes, and the whole ecosystem of the lake, may be just the sort of development that would have been fiercely opposed if the lake had not been so badly abused already.

The future of the Junin Grebe might, ironically, be secured by further exploitation of its habitat. If the lake is to be used as a reservoir for the city of Lima, its waters will have to be cleaned.

The flightless Junin Grebe breeds in the vast reed-beds of Lake Junin in Peru, at an altitude of 4000m. Fewer than 100 individuals survive, probably because the lake waters are polluted by nearby copper workings.

Grebes of the Andes
Four lakes in the High Andes support endemic species of grebe. All have only small populations, and all are threatened.

1. Atitlan Grebe
   (*Podilymbus gigas*)
2. Junin Grebe
   (*Podiceps tac-zanowskii*)
3. Colombian Grebe
   (*Podiceps andinus*)
4. Hooded Grebe
   (*Podiceps gallardoi*)

Two other species of South American grebe are also seriously threatened. The Hooded Grebe (*P. gallardoi*) — unique among grebes in that it nests colonially rather than in scattered pairs — made headline news when it was first described, as recently as 1974, from a remote district of southern Argentina. But the excitement of discovery soon gave way to concern when, by 1981, no more than 75 birds could be found. The original population was believed to breed only on one lake, whose level depended on the melt of snow in the nearby mountains, and it was thought that when the lake froze in winter the birds departed for some site yet to be discovered — probably somewhere on the coast of Chile or Argentina. But these remote mountains hold many surprises. Later in 1981 a second breeding population of over 250 birds was discovered on a plateau 120km north of the original colony, and in 1983/4 more headlines were made when new colonies were discovered on small volcanic lakes high on the plateau of Meseta de Strobel.

At the other end of the continent the least known of all the four species — the Colombian Grebe (*P. andinus*) — is known only from Lake Tota, over 3000m high in the Colombian Andes. The lake is surrounded by agriculture, and was stocked with trout in 1944. Colombian Grebes were abundant there until that date, but have since been seen only in ones and twos.

The Hooded Grebes of southern Argentina build floating nests of water weed. They are the only grebes that breed in colonies. An increase in predatory gulls may be the main reason for their decline.

150

Bachman's Warbler: Lost songbird of America's swamplands

In the closing decades of the nineteenth century, Bachman's Warblers (*Vermivora bachmanii*) were common enough to be collected in dozens. On their breeding grounds in the dense swamp forests of the southern United States, on migration through Florida, and in their winter quarters in the lowland swamp forests of Cuba, they were conspicuous members of the bird community. The handsome males sang with a passion and intensity that impressed itself on all who heard them, pouring out their rattling song for minutes on end with their heads raised to the forest canopy.

Their habitat attracted only the most assiduous of bird-watchers. The hot lowland swamp forests were a dense, sodden, tangle of gnarled trees – festooned with vines and alive with red bugs, ticks and venomous snakes. It was the sort of habitat that makes few friends, and around the turn of the century it came under concerted attack from lumber interests and drainage experts. It was felled, drained and turned over to agriculture, as much in the warbler's winter quarters in Cuba, where it gave way to sugar fields, as on the breeding grounds in the United States.

No nest of Bachman's Warbler has been seen since 1937; no Bachman's Warblers have been seen in Cuba since 1964; and only two have been seen in Florida since 1949. They are reported – anywhere – only extremely rarely; no more than six times in any year. But until the remaining breeding grounds are found, perhaps in the inaccessible I'On Swamp area of South Carolina, little can be done to save this elusive bird that so impressed all who saw it.

Bachman's is one of a small group of North American wood-warblers that share similar feeding habits. They all have a long, sharply pointed bill which they use to probe into tangles of dead leaves and vines, forcing them apart with a gaping action of the bill-tip like a starling probing soil. Sadly their feeding habits, and their habitat, are perhaps too highly specialized to survive in a world so changed by man that only the most adaptable of birds can survive.

No nest of Bachman's Warbler has been seen since 1937. The dense forests of tall Elliott Pines and dwarf Palmetto Pines that were its habitat have largely been felled to make way for agriculture.

Dalmatian Pelican: Persecuted for the fish it takes

'A wonderful bird is the pelican,
its beak can hold more than its belly can'
So runs the old children's rhyme, imprinting on countless childhood memories the image of the grotesque beak that makes pelicans so instantly recognizable. But the efficiency as a fish-catching mechanism of the long, flat bill and the huge pouch slung beneath it now threatens to be the bird's undoing. No fisherman seeing the huge mouthfuls that a pelican can take out of the water can believe that the bird does not threaten his livelihood, and fewer still can resist the inevitable temptation to remove the competition.

Dalmatian Pelicans (*Pelecanus crispus*) are the largest of the seven species in the pelican family, and probably the most seriously endangered. Their distribution is now centred on the Balkan region of south-eastern Europe, with scattered outliers in Russia, Iran and Turkey; but this is a paltry relic of their former distribution. Remains preserved in peat bogs show that Dalmatian Pelicans were widespread in western Europe in the Neolithic Period, 5000 to 3700 years ago, and we have the evidence of the Roman historian Pliny that Dalmatian Pelicans nested in the estuaries of the Scheldt, Rhine and Elbe nearly two thousand years ago. They were common in eastern Europe until the nineteenth century, numbering 'millions' in Romania as late as 1873 but declining to 'thousands' within 20 years, and their numbers and distribution shrank equally rapidly throughout their range around that time. As human populations increased, so did disturbance of the pelicans' nesting colonies, and much of their habitat was destroyed by drainage in the course of agricultural improvement.

No more than 1300 pairs of Dalmatian Pelicans remain in the world, and these are scattered among about 20 nesting sites. Half breed in Russia, the rest in Bulgaria, Greece, Iran, Romania, Turkey and Yugoslavia. In some countries their numbers are holding their own, but one of the biggest concentrations, on the Danube delta in Romania, decreased from 1300 pairs in 1939 to only 100 in 1975, and another large concentration in the Volga delta halved in size between 1949 and 1974.

Dalmatian Pelicans breed in rivers, lakes, deltas and estuaries, as far as they can from human disturbance and from ground predators. They nest normally in scattered groups, on islands or in thick aquatic vegetation. Reed-beds are favourite sites, and nesting islands in them are commonly made of floating debris from trees and reeds. The nest is a pile of vegetation up to 1.5m across and 1.5m above the water, though as the season progresses it becomes sealed with droppings and often settles lower in the water. The nests may be as little as 30cm apart and take three or four days to complete; days in which the female guards and builds while the male goes to and fro, carrying up to 40 pouchloads of twigs and reed stems. The birds lay one to six eggs (normally two) and share the month-long task of incubation. In many colonies eggs are often lost when the adults are disturbed and leave the nest unguarded. Then, waiting predators — especially Hooded Crows, Magpies and gulls — swoop in to break and eat the eggs, which weigh up to 195g and so make a very worthwhile meal. Disturbance of the colony by people accounts in this way for many of the nesting losses, but natural causes — especially floods — also take their toll.

The young are naked when they hatch, but soon grow a coat of white down. They hatch several days apart, and the eldest often kills its nest-mate or causes it to starve by taking more than its share of food. The parents swallow the food before feeding it to their young, so the chicks must reach right into the adult's gullet rather than into its pouch. When they are six or seven weeks old the young pelicans leave their nests and spend much of the day in the water, gathered together in 'creches'. They become independent at about 15 weeks old and leave the breeding grounds between the end of August and October. They and their parents disperse for the winter, mainly to coasts and estuaries. The most notable wintering grounds now are probably those in Iran, Iraq, Greece and Italy, though the Nile delta was once important too. Throughout the winter they divide their time between wandering, roosting (often on the water) and fishing, before returning to the breeding grounds between the middle of February and early April.

One of the many branches of the Danube which together form the river's vast delta on the Black Sea coast of Romania. Yet even this quiet river bears the marks of extensive human interference.

A group of Dalmatian Pelicans incubating their eggs in the shelter of a dense reed-bed in Greece. The huge nest-mounds are so close together that they merge into a communal 'island' of sodden reeds and other vegetation. Intensive exploitation of these reed-beds threatens the birds' nesting grounds.

Pelicans incur the wrath of fishermen all over the world. A broad black edge to the underside of the wing distinguishes the White Pelican from the Dalmatian Pelican.

A small price – for survival

Pelicans are ungainly creatures on land, but afloat and in flight they have a powerful grace that transforms them into things of beauty. They take off clumsily, with much thrashing of wings, but once aloft they fly strongly with the head retracted on the breast, and can soar for hours on end in rising air currents. They swim strongly too, powered by strong legs and large feet webbed between all four toes, like those of a cormorant. On the water they float buoyantly, dipping the head and bill beneath the water to fish. Commonly they fish alone or in small groups of two to five birds, usually in water less than eight metres deep. When fishing in groups they often dip their heads in unison, striking at a shoal of fish from several directions at once and so confusing the fish.

On the deep lakes of Prespa in Greece, Dalmatian Pelicans and cormorants fish together in a partnership that combines two quite different fishing techniques to the apparent advantage of both birds. The cormorant seeks out a pelican, and dives beneath the water; the pelican follows above it, flying very slowly, low over the water. After following the cormorant for ten or twenty metres, the pelican suddenly drops to the surface and plunges its head underwater to catch a fish. A few moments later the cormorant surfaces, also triumphantly swallowing a fish. The water in these lakes is deep, without the shallows that pelicans usually prefer, and this behaviour has been seen nowhere else. A curious feature is that the pelican seems to benefit most by following the cormorant, but the cormorant always seeks out the pelican and never the reverse; perhaps the pelican can see fish from the air better than the cormorant can underwater.

The Danube delta in Romania is one of the three most important wetlands in Europe, and supports the largest Dalmatian Pelican population outside the USSR. The birds, however, are under threat from loss of their nesting habitat and through conflict with the traditional local fisheries.

A colony of cormorants in the swamps of the Danube delta. These vast tracts of riverside wilderness are almost unique in Europe.

Pelicans and cormorants fish the same waters not only in harmony but apparently to their mutual advantage. The same cannot be said for pelicans and people. Fishermen and birds alike have suffered a drastic reduction in their inland habitats in the last few hundred years, and now must make their living in a handful of places in Europe. Only the most productive and extensive wetlands can support colonies of large fish-eating animals, be they birds or people, and such places have been drained over most of the western world in the last few hundred years of burgeoning populations and industrialization. Many of the remaining wetlands are so polluted that they support fewer fish than they used to. Seeing his food supply declining, and huge pelicans gulping in enormous mouthfuls of his precious livelihood, a fisherman is quick to reach the obvious conclusion and take appropriate action. Pelicans are shot throughout their range simply to stop them fishing, but their meat also makes good eating and they have long been killed for food as well. The skin of the pouch is soft and supple, and has been used for centuries to make tobacco pouches and sheaths for hunting knives. Young pelicans are also relished in some areas, especially for their fat. These traditional uses of the birds by men were legitimate in the days when the birds were plentiful and their habitats extensive, but the pelicans' numbers have now reached the point where any mortality added to the deaths that are inevitable in the natural world could tip the balance and plunge the species into extinction.

The Danube delta now holds probably the largest colonies of Dalmatian Pelicans outside Russia. The reed-beds where they nest are harvested by the local people, and pelican nests are still sometimes burnt or their sheltering reeds cut down in the course of the harvest. The pelicans are protected by Romanian law, but nestlings are still killed and adults shot by fishermen who fear competition from the birds. Fishing quotas are in force, but they are set too high for the present fish stocks, which have been depleted by over-fishing, and the fishermen can no longer reach their quotas. Naturally they blame the birds for this, rather than unrealistic quotas or their own mismanagement, and so they kill more pelicans.

Fishing techniques are now changing from simple hunting to organized 'farming', and the fish-ponds that are springing up throughout the Danube delta are attracting increasing numbers of pelicans. The birds are easy to shoot there, and there is no doubt that they do take fish from the ponds; but whether they really affect the yield, and if so by how much, has not been studied, and effective methods of scaring the birds away have not yet been developed. Yet surely these must be tried. No-one would deny that the livelihood of the fishermen and fish-farmers must be protected, but the Dalmatian Pelican is an endangered species that is surely worth the few tonnes of fish that are needed to ensure its survival.

Dalmatian Pelicans have readily accepted the man-made nesting platforms built on the shores of Lake Manyas by Turkish conservation authorities.

New Zealand Black Stilt: The hidden threat of interbreeding

These elegant and graceful birds survive in only one area, and then only by intensive management to protect them from the battery of hazards ranged against them. They were never very common, but did breed throughout both the North and South Islands of New Zealand in the nineteenth century. Now they maintain a scattered population in the upper valley of the Waitaki River in the South Island, especially around Lake Tekapo. The total population is down to an estimated 50 birds, of which no more than a dozen are likely to be active breeders. The most successful breeding now takes place in two small enclosures of four to five hectares each, fenced off with electrified wire to keep out predators.

The New Zealand Black Stilt (*Himantopus novaezelandiae*) has been brought to this parlous state by a succession of different factors. The first, and perhaps still the most important, was the predatory mammals — especially ferrets — introduced by European settlers and kept at an artificially high population density by the abundance of their main prey, the European Rabbit. The stilts nest in swamps and on beds of shingle and gravel on the banks of rivers high up in the mountains, where the water runs fast and clear over stony beds. They lay four beautifully marked eggs on the open ground, where they are vulnerable to the natural hazards of floods and the alien danger of predators. An extra threat accompanied the spread of European agriculture from the coastal lowlands into the mountains, in the innocuous guise of the Pied Stilt, a bird so closely related to the Black that many ornithologists regard them as varieties of one species. Beside a Pied Stilt, the Black appears short-legged, longer-billed and more robust; the Pied is white beneath and on the head, on the front of the neck, and in a band across the shoulders. It nests in a much greater variety of habitats than the Black, from the seashore to salt lagoons, lakesides, swamps and river beds, from sea level to 800m altitude. Its broad tolerance of nest sites has helped it to spread throughout the South Island and into the North. Pied and Black Stilts frequently interbreed where they meet, and this interbreeding is now one of the main threats to the survival of the Black Stilt. Pied Stilts colonize their territories, and the Blacks are finding it increasingly difficult to find mates of their own kind.

Black Stilts survive today because every stage of their nesting cycle is now closely managed in a concerted effort to boost their chances of success. The two electrified enclosures (actually exclosures, designed to keep predators out rather than birds in) contain three of the ten remaining breeding pairs. The first clutches, even those in the enclosures, are usually lost to bad weather, so now wildlife biologists take these clutches and incubate them artificially. Just before they hatch they are exchanged for eggs laid by Pied Stilts, which then raise the young as foster-parents. Pairs of Black Stilts that lose their eggs before they can be switched are often given dummy eggs to incubate. These can then be replaced later by the second clutches of pairs whose first clutch was taken to be incubated artificially. Taking the second clutch from these birds stimulates them to produce a third, which they are then allowed to raise by themselves. The second clutch is also incubated artificially, and exchanged for the dummy eggs of the 'foster' pair just before they hatch. Most predation on stilts occurs at the egg stage, so it is crucial to protect this most vulnerable part of the life-cycle as rigorously as possible.

Only intensive management now stands between the Black Stilt and extinction. Having narrowly survived the threat of introduced predators, this elegant bird (*below left*) is now threatened by interbreeding with the much more adaptable Pied Stilt (*below right*). The result of such mixing is a marked increase in the number of hybrids (*bottom*) and little prospect of recovery for wild Black Stilts.

The danger with allowing Pied Stilts to raise young Black Stilts is that the youngsters may grow up thinking they are Pied Stilts, an illusion that may last for the two years that it takes a Black Stilt to become sexually mature. Chicks of most birds acquire their sense of identity from the birds that raise them. In a world without mirrors, it makes good sense to assume that the kind of bird that raised you is the kind of bird you are, and when the time comes to look for a mate you naturally choose one that looks like your parents. Often this 'self-image' is engraved on the bird's mind within a few days of birth, and remains with it for life. This process of 'imprinting' can be irreversible, and if it is misdirected can make it impossible for a bird to mate with a partner of the right species. Fortunately, Black Stilts raised by Pied Stilts seem not to have had their behaviour distorted in this way, and have later bred with mates of their own species.

Hybrid stilts have occurred naturally as the Pied Stilts have invaded Black Stilt country. Some of these hybrids have also been used to foster Black Stilt chicks, with as much success as Pied Stilt foster-parents. Other Black Stilts have been raised in captivity. These combined techniques of increasing the breeding output of Black Stilts — by protecting some nests from predators, and removing vulnerable eggs from others and raising them in captivity or under foster-parents — have been very successful and have certainly raised the breeding success of the Stilts. But the crucial stage is the entry of those young into the breeding population two years later, and it is this 'recruitment' that has so far proved elusive. The extra young produced have not survived long enough in the wild to add significantly to the wild breeding population, so captive-raised birds that now breed in captivity are being used as a source of eggs for the cross-fostering programme in the wild. Clearly, Black Stilts are going to need continued intensive management if they are to survive.

Wooden dummy eggs are used to replace Black Stilt eggs taken into 'protective custody', and to keep birds that have lost their eggs on the nest until they can be used as foster parents.

The last refuge of the New Zealand Black Stilt is among the marshes, coarse grasses and gravel banks of the South Island's upper Waitaki valley.

Crested Ibis:
Protective custody – the last resort

The several species of white ibis are among the most beautiful of all birds, but the Crested Ibis (*Nipponia nippon*) is also one of the rarest and most gravely endangered. It is a species that refuses to fit into a neat habitat category since it nests in deciduous trees and feeds in farmland as well as in swamps and marshes. This curious combination of requirements has made the species doubly vulnerable since it suffers from the decline of both wetland and woodland habitats.

But the natural requirements of the Crested Ibis are now a matter of history. Only 21 birds are known to remain; 17 in the wild in China, one in captivity in China, and three in captivity in Japan. In the early nineteenth century these elegant birds graced the marshy woods of northeastern Eurasia, breeding from the far southeast of Siberia and the neighbouring Chinese province of Manchuria, south and west through China to Chekiang Province and west to Shensi Province. They were also found in the Korean Peninsula and bred widely in Japan. Mainland birds migrated as far as Hainan, Taiwan (Formosa) and the Ryukyu Islands between Taiwan and Japan.

Like the Chinese Egret and others unfortunate enough to be adorned with beautiful nuptial plumes, Crested Ibises were hunted almost to extinction in the nineteenth and early twentieth centuries to satisfy the demands of the fashion trade. At the same time, their woodland nesting habitats were cut down for fuel and timber and their marshes were drained and converted to agriculture.

The birds' range coincides with one of the most densely populated regions of the world. Land is at a premium, and every available hectare is now used to help feed the burgeoning human population. Nothing is left for the graceful birds that inspired Chinese watercolour painters for thousands of years.

Crested Ibises have not been known to nest in the USSR since 1917, and the last colony in China was thought to have disappeared in 1958; but persistent searches by Chinese ornithologists in recent years were rewarded in 1981 when two pairs were found nesting in the Qinling Range in Shansi Province. In 1983 three pairs tried to nest in China: one pair laid two clutches, each of two eggs, but lost them all to crows; another pair raised three young; but the third did not lay, and were probably young birds. The known population of wild ibises in China has increased from four in 1981 to 17 in 1985, so despite the setbacks there is a glimmer of hope that Crested Ibises may yet survive in the wild.

The Ibises maintained known breeding sites in Japan for so much longer than in China or the USSR that the species even came to be known as the 'Japanese' Crested Ibis. By the 1930s their former wide range along the entire archipelago had contracted to the Noto Peninsula of Honshu Island, and little Sado Island just offshore. Since 1969 it has shrunk even further – to Sado Island alone. The Sado Island birds have not bred since 1973, so the situation there has become as desperate as that of the Mauritius Parakeets and Kestrels.

Forlorn reminder of a spectacular bird: the deciduous forests of Sado Island, Japan, are the nesting habitat of the formerly widespread Crested Ibis, now reduced to just three birds in Japan and less than twenty in mainland China.

Yet the Japanese have long recognized the rarity of their ibises, and have done much to help them. They were declared a 'Natural Monument' in 1934, and have not only been fully protected but have lived for many years in a large reserve set up specifically for them. There they have been given supplementary food in the winter months when supplies of their natural food have run short. Even the occasional birds sighted in Korea (possibly part of the known Chinese population) have enjoyed the status of 'National Treasure No. 198' since 1968, and the species is also fully protected in the USSR. Why, then, have these birds continued to perform so feebly in spite of decades of protection over most of their range?

In the 1950s and 1960s, many Crested Ibises in Japan were poisoned by mercury, BHC and other pesticides applied to paddy fields to protect the rice from pests and diseases. Many died, and many others were sterilized. Only those that lived in the highlands of Sado Island escaped, and even those were desperately few because in autumn young birds would descend from the hills and feed in the contaminated lowland areas.

The survivors in Japan tried to nest each spring, but their eggs were invariably eaten by crows or jays. Because they were in a nature reserve these predators were not controlled – even though the reserve was there to protect the ibises and the birds were eating ibis eggs. Such misguided reluctance to undertake distasteful but essential management on nature reserves is all too common throughout the world. The three surviving Crested Ibises in Japan have now all been taken into captivity in an attempt to improve their chances of breeding.

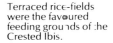

Terraced rice-fields were the favoured feeding grounds of the Crested Ibis.

Not much is known about the way of life of Crested Ibises before the wholesale slaughter of the nineteenth century. The wild pairs in China are widely separated from each other and defend breeding territories, but other populations in the past are known to have nested in large colonies, as most of their relatives do. In those halcyon days before guns and feathered hats and agricultural drainage schemes, a large mixed 'heronry' would commonly contain tens of thousands of nests of many species of herons and egrets, as well as ibises and perhaps storks and spoonbills too. They must have filled the swamps with a deafening clamour, a pungent soup of smells and a dazzling spectacle of waving wings, clattering beaks and frenetic displays. It is hard to visualize now because these kaleidoscopic exhibitions no longer exist, but the few large water-bird colonies that can still be seen give some impression of the way they must once have been.

These huge associations of birds were not just impressive natural spectacles; they were part of the birds' essential biology. Over thousands of generations of growing up in groups of thousands, and of finding a mate and raising young year after year only pecking distance from a dozen other birds, the patterns of behaviour of the birds became adjusted to the wild infectious excitement of life in a crowded colony. It is possible that Crested Ibises not only adapted to those conditions but may even have become dependent on them, and that this may go some way to explaining the difficulties they have in breeding now that they have declined to just a few isolated pairs.

Biologists believe that for birds that nest in dense colonies, there may be a threshold of colony size below which the birds cannot breed successfully. We know that the sight of other birds displaying or carrying nest material can stimulate the most prosaic laboratory pigeon to produce the hormones and behaviour appropriate for breeding. Could the same be true of the Crested Ibis? The last resort of the would-be saviours of the Crested Ibis is to keep the captives next to an aviary containing a large colony of the closely related Oriental Ibis (*Threskiornis melanocephalus*) and hope that this will trigger them at last into successful breeding.

In Japan, the immediate future for the Crested Ibis lies within the confines of a cage. In China the species' survival in the wild will depend on vigilant protection not just of the birds but of an environment under ever-increasing pressure from that country's vast rural population.

Several rare species of ibis are currently being bred in captivity at the Tama Zoological Gardens in Tokyo. Young from these two broods of Oriental Ibis (*Threskiornis melanocephalus*) were later reintroduced into the wild.

Mr Takaji Takano of the Sado Crested Ibis Centre with 'Kin' – an adult female Crested Ibis he raised from a chick. When this photograph was taken in 1981, 'Kin' was thirteen years old.

Slaty Egret:
A recent addition to the list

The Slaty Egret (*Egretta vinaceigula*) is one of ornithology's most recent and curious discoveries. Until 1971 it was thought that one species of blackish-coloured egret was widespread throughout Africa south of the Sahara. Known, unimaginatively enough, as the Black Egret (*E. ardesiaca*), this species has the curious habit of holding its wings over its head while it is feeding. Its bashful appearance is deceptive. The trick of 'umbrella-feeding' shades the surface of the water from the glare of the tropical sun and so improves visibility underwater. But a few specimens of 'Black Egret' were rather different. They had narrower wing-tips, a reddish throat, a pale base to the lower part of the bill, white bases to the primary wing-feathers, and shorter toes and bill. These birds were thought to be merely colour variants of the Black Egret — until it was noticed that the 'variant' birds were not umbrella-feeders. Once the specimens were linked with their respective behaviour patterns it was clear that the smaller reddish-throated birds were a quite separate species.

The seasonal rains that flood vast areas of the Kafue Flats and Okavango Swamp provide food-rich habitats for thousands of wetland birds.

162

Slaty Egrets live mainly in northern Botswana and southern Zambia, though the first specimens came from northern South Africa and they may also occur in Angola. Since they are so similar to Black Egrets, which are much more widespread, and since there are very few bird-watchers in south-central Africa — and even fewer who can tell the two species apart — they may yet prove to range more widely. They are most regularly seen in two of the most spectacular wetlands in Africa, both of which are extremely important to wildlife in general and to waterbirds in particular. The Okavango Swamp of Botswana is a vast basin into which the Okavango River drains after a 1000km descent from the highlands of Angola. The Kafue Flats of Zambia form the flood-plain of the Kafue River, which passes through them on its way to the great Zambezi, 100km downstream.

The Slaty Egret and its close relative the Black Egret were separated partly on the grounds of the Black Egret's characteristic umbrella feeding. This series of photographs shows how the bird stalks through the shallows, then raises its wings over its head to cast a shadow on the water before striking at its chosen target.

Both wetlands experience great changes with the seasons. Rainfall in this part of Africa is highly seasonal, and water level in the rivers and swamps rises and falls in time with the rains in the distant mountains, where the rivers arise. Both these great wetlands are characterized by a distinctive landscape of grassland pockmarked with curious circular thickets: each clump of bushes is centred on a giant termite mound after which this habitat, the 'termitaria zone', is named. This zone is bordered on one side by a mosaic of channels and lagoons which hold water through the dry season, and on the other by open grassland with scattered trees and bushes. The termitaria zone is flooded during the rains by the rising river, which reaches the fringing grassland much later and retreats from it sooner. Water level changes month by month, giving a fluctuating succession of habitats that supports, at times, hundreds of thousands of birds of dozens of species, and vast numbers of game animals.

Slaty Egrets stalk their prey quietly, searching keenly and then stabbing at a fish that ventures too close. Sometimes they stir up the water with their feet to flush out fish as many other egrets do. They feed in extremely shallow water, normally less than five centimetres deep, or even on land that is merely wet rather than submerged. These shallow-water inundation zones are temporary features of both the Okavango and Kafue wetlands, and the egrets may well have to

wander in search of suitable habitats at times of year when these wetlands are either too dry or too deeply inundated. Their nesting habits are not known, but may contain clues to their low numbers and limited distribution. Like the Chinese Egret of coastal Southeast Asia, they may perhaps be victims of too narrow a specialization.

Status report – Wetlands:
Ecological threads at breaking point

Freshwater wetlands occupy less than three per cent of the land area of the earth, but they support vast populations of birds quite out of proportion to the extent of the habitat. It is difficult to say just how many species of bird depend on wetlands. Several orders of birds contain several hundred species that depend chiefly or entirely on freshwater wetlands – the swans, geese and ducks; herons, egrets and storks; cranes and rails; gulls, terns and waders. But there are hundreds more, much less obviously wetland birds, that are linked so closely with the wetland habitat that its loss would spell extinction for them. Weaverbirds building their colonies of globular grassy nests in the papyrus swamps of Africa; warblers and wrens, tits and blackbirds, making their solitary nests in beds of reed and sedge all around the world; swallows and martins roosting in reed-beds by the hundred thousand on migration and in their winter quarters; all these depend on wetlands for their survival just as much as pelicans and herons do.

The wetlands chemical factories

Birds play an important role in the nutrient cycles of most wetlands. The enormous flocks of ducks and geese that pass through on migration or spend the winter there contribute vast quantities of droppings, and are a vital link in the cycling of nitrogen and phosphate. In this way they help to maintain the spectacular productivity of the system.

But many wetlands play a more subtle role in the chemistry of the biosphere. In the sediments of many swamps and marshes the oxygen concentration becomes very low at some times of year because of the enormous concentrations of bacterial decomposers, sustained in their turn by the masses of organic matter produced by higher plants. In these 'anaerobic' conditions, specialized bacteria can flourish which break down the nitrates and nitrites that are the waste products of protein metabolism, and return free nitrogen to the air. These 'denitrifying' bacteria are the final link in the nitrogen cycle; without them, the free gaseous nitrogen of the atmosphere would gradually be depleted, and nitrates and nitrites would build up in the soil and water to toxic levels.

Life itself would be endangered not only by this new and unfavourable chemistry, but by an even more devastating hazard.

Nitrogen is an extremely inert element and it makes up four-fifths of the earth's atmosphere; most of the rest, of course, is oxygen. Now oxygen is anything but inert; it is a very lively element, and in its pure state is extremely flammable. The oxygen in the atmosphere would ignite instantly and burn the entire planet to a crisp were it not for the fire-blanket of nitrogen that keeps it diluted to a safe concentration. Of course only a minute fraction of the nitrogen in the atmosphere at any one time is produced by bacteria in wetlands, and if wetlands were to disappear entirely it would take a very long time for the atmosphere to become explosive; but the link between wetlands and the composition of the atmosphere is a real and important one.

Florida's Everglades are classic eutrophic wetlands – rich in nutrients and able to support high levels of productivity. Unfortunately, misguided management and drainage schemes have damaged much of America's only semi-tropical wetland habitat and imperilled much of its unique plant and animal life.

The Scarlet Ibis (*Eudocimus ruber*) inhabits the coastal mangrove swamps, estuaries and shores of tropical Central and South America, often breeding in large, spectacular colonies.

A source of livelihood – and leisure

Wetlands are of direct and immediate importance to millions of people, who put them to uses almost as varied as the wildlife. Water itself, of course, is as vital a mainstay of life for people as it is for any living creature, and there is hardly a river in the world that does not contribute to the local economy by supplying water for drinking, cooking and washing.

But we use wetlands for much more than their water. Those who live close to the land recognize the productive value of wetlands, and in different parts of the world make use of the various resources they offer. Wild rice is harvested throughout the tropical and subtropical regions of the world, and indeed supports millions of migrating waterbirds as well, while cultivated rice supports millions of people, often in wetlands maintained artificially for raising fish as well as rice. Inland freshwater fisheries support countless millions of people and in many cases the productivity of the fisheries is undoubtedly enhanced by the presence of birds, which help to fertilize the waters and distribute the aquatic plants.

From Neolithic Europe to modern-day Central America, men have utilized the dense beds of reeds that line the shallow-water shores of lakes and marshes. Reed boats, indeed, even took ancient peoples across the oceans from one continent to another. Reeds have been harvested for thatching houses and making sleeping-mats, screens, walls and even chairs, ever since mankind first lived by water. The distinctive trees of swamp-forests, too, have yielded valuable harvests of timber for generations. But trees have more varied uses than reeds, and grow much more slowly. All too often they have been over-exploited and the swamp-forests have been destroyed.

The estuary of the River Dart in Devon, England, illustrates the age-long attraction of coasts and estuaries as places for sport and relaxation. Space at the water's edge is running short, and in many places plants and animals have fallen victim to the demands of our leisure-oriented society.

The conversion of land to rice paddies creates no problems for the adaptable Indian Pond Heron (*Ardeola grayii*), but for many other birds, such as the Chinese Little Bittern (see page 59), the loss of natural reed-bed cover can be disastrous.

The modern uses of wetlands in the developed world are related more to leisure and recreation than to survival. In North America, Europe, Australia and New Zealand, people visit lakes and rivers in enormous numbers at weekends and on holiday. They use them for sailing, water-skiing, swimming, fishing, watching birds and other wildlife, and for taking photographs, painting pictures, and generally relaxing. Often these uses conflict; there may be so many water-skiers and power boats and sailing dinghies on a lake that there is barely room for any birds. The development of lakes for recreation is one of the greatest threats faced by wetlands in the industrialized world, where people so value the beauty and spiritual refreshment provided by a natural wetland that they will pay a great deal of money to enjoy it, even though the enjoyment can last only until the number of people trying to share it actually destroys it.

Many people in the industrialized world satisfy their ancestral hunting instincts by shooting waterbirds. The duck-shooting industry is big business in North America, where hundreds of millions of dollars are spent every year in raising ducks and geese, shooting them, manufacturing the guns and ammunition to do it with, and in licensing the sport and administering it. Shooting satisfies a behavioural need rather than a

nutritional one on the part of the hunters, but that need is powerful enough to sustain a major industry and a significant political lobby. The hunting industry is bad news for individual ducks, but in the long term probably maintains higher populations of waterbirds than could otherwise be supported if their habitats were not preserved – and often managed very intensively – specifically to sustain the sport.

Habitats altered beyond recovery
The extraordinary fertility of wetlands proved their undoing as soon as man learned how to drain them. From grazing his cattle on the floodplains of lakes and rivers, following the advance and retreat of the waters in a nomadic existence not very different from that of desert people, he was able to settle down and grow crops on the fertile alluvial soil that the wetland had created. It is no accident that human civilization began in the 'fertile crescent' of Asia Minor, on the floodplains of two great rivers. Ecologically this was the obvious habitat in which to settle down. Reclaiming wetlands has now become such an ingrained human habit that it is often done without assessing the long-term costs and benefits. Mankind has come to regard drainage as the only

European agriculture regularly produces large surpluses, stored for years at great cost. Yet ever more wetlands are being drained for agriculture – a trend that endangers not only the local birdlife but also the water-balance of the surrounding area.

sensible thing to do with a wetland. In the industrialized world at least, the wetlands that were easy to drain, and yielded the best agricultural land, have long since been put to the plough.

The great rivers of the world are also coming under increasing pressure as sources of hydro-electric power. Where the river already has a constant steady flow this can often be done with very little damage to the environment. But in those parts of the world where power is needed most urgently — chiefly in the tropics — the flow is often seasonal and unreliable. To increase the head of water and ensure its supply throughout the year, a dam must then be built upstream, and this inevitably changes the pattern of the rise and fall of water on the floodplain, usually to the detriment of the wildlife and often also of the people who fish the river and graze their cattle on its banks.

Upsetting the chemical balance

Wetlands are fertile because they concentrate nutrients from the whole of their catchment area. Unfortunately they do the same with any chemical, whether a nutrient or a pollutant; and some nutrients can become pollutants if they are too concentrated. Some of the pollution suffered by wetlands is put directly and deliberately into the water: 'throw it in the river' is the oldest and still the commonest method of disposing of garbage and human waste alike. But much pollution originates not in the water itself but on the land, in the catchment area. Toxic chemicals applied as pesticides on agricultural land, and artificial fertilizers applied to the same fields, end up eventually in the streams that drain the land. The chemistry of the fresh waters of agricultural land has become extraordinarily complicated by this noxious soup whose effects extend throughout the waterways and out into the open ocean.

Wetlands link the atmosphere with all the ecosystems of the land, and those systems in turn with the sea. They transport nutrients around the biosphere just as our bloodstream carries nutrients around our bodies. Modern wetlands are being drained and poisoned at accelerating rates, and can be purified and protected only by more sensitive treatment of the planet as a whole. There is no ecological equivalent of a blood transfusion. Wetland birds are declining at alarming rates, and their fate signals grave dangers to the health of the planet.

A flight of Spur-winged Geese (*Plectropterus gambensis*) crossing Lake Nyabor in the Sudd marshlands of southern Sudan. These are among the world's largest wetlands; they are fed by the Nile and form an essential reservoir for lowland Egypt.

From India eastward to Indo-China the Painted Stork (*Mycteria leucocephala*) is held in much the same esteem and affection as the White Stork in Europe. Yet like its European relative this handsome bird is suffering from widespread loss of its habitat.

The construction of a large dam, although often an important part of a nation's economic development has long-term effects on the ecology of the entire catchment area.

167

Climbing a mountain is very like travelling from the equator to the pole: increasing altitude and increasing latitude are accompanied by almost identical zones of vegetation. Rich and varied lowland forest is followed by dark stands of coniferous forest, then by windswept grasslands and moors beyond the tree-line and finally the ultimate extreme of barren rock and ice.

Mountain ranges shape the climate over very large areas. Rising steeply in the path of the wind, they deflect the flow of moisture-laden air, forcing rain to fall on the windward slopes and leaving a barren rain-shadow to leeward.

Carrying their own special assortment of habitats, mountains are separated from each other by their surrounding lowlands just as effectively as islands are separated by the sea. And like islands, mountains make stern demands on their resident birds. Many mountains are populated by species that live nowhere else, or whose nearest relatives are marooned on other distant peaks. And some montane species have become so highly adapted to their high-altitude life-style that they can live nowhere else.

Mountains

Islands in the sky

Mountain-tops are specialized regions, so strictly fashioned by their physical conditions that they are as different from the surrounding lowlands as islands are from oceans. Like islands they are not, strictly speaking, habitats in themselves, in the way that wetlands or forests are, but environments that exert a strong unifying influence on all the habitats upon them. Mountain-tops from the Arctic to the equator have more in common with each other than with the lowlands that surround them.

Mountains have an enormous influence on climate, and so on the distribution of habitats. They are the source of most of the world's major rivers, and they create some of the most arid deserts. A moving air-mass that meets a mountain is deflected upwards. As it rises it is inevitably cooled and, since cold air can hold less water vapour than warm air, much of the moisture condenses and falls as rain. Thus the windward side of a mountain is often very wet, clothed in luxuriant forest and a source of mountain streams that water the drier lowlands below. By the time the rising air currents reach the summit they have often lost all their moisture and so the leeward side of the mountain is much more arid: the driest and most barren deserts in the world lie in the lee of the Andes and the Himalayas.

Volcanic mountains also play a major role in nutrient cycles. Eruptions of hot gases are an important source of atmospheric nitrogen and sulphur, while the dust, ashes and lava spewed out by volcanic eruptions bring fresh supplies of minerals into the biosphere. By their effects on climate and the composition of the atmosphere, and of soils over areas vastly exceeding their own, mountains exert an influence on the biosphere that is quite out of proportion to their modest distribution on the face of the globe.

Life-zones of the mountains

The changing temperature and rainfall at increasing altitudes on a mountain result in bands of different vegetation types. The ascent of a tropical mountain, in particular, is a dramatic reminder of the influence of climate on vegetation. Seasonal woodland at the foot of the mountain gives way to luxuriant evergreen forest, bearded with mosses and adorned with air-plants. Higher up, sheer cold defies all attempts of trees to grow and they in turn give way to montane grassland, studded with the weird and fantastic shapes of giant woody heath plants and higher still of giant groundsels, lobelias and other plants of families more familiar as lowly lowland herbs. In many ways the zones of vegetation that ascend a mountain are like the vegetation bands that ring the earth itself from the equator to the poles. At the summit there is nothing but the ice, snow and barren rock that typifies the polar regions themselves.

Each zone on the ascent of a mountain is more rigorous than the one below and supports fewer forms of life. Many plants and mammals are highly specialized for the upper zones of mountains, and share many adaptations with species of polar regions; in fact the Arctic and alpine zones require such similar adaptations that they are often treated as a single 'arctic-alpine' biome. Their birds and other wildlife are so highly specialized for that habitat that they are ill-equipped to live in any other — or to withstand much alteration of their ecosystem.

Perpetual snows cover the awesome peaks of the Himalayas, yet these mountains harbour a rich avifauna, with many species unique to the region. Even at altitudes of 5000m there are many birds to be seen.

Knife-edge ridges and valleys worn wide and deep by the glaciers of the Ice Ages dominate the relief of the Alps. Climatic conditions vary greatly from one locality to another, creating specialized plant and animal communities.

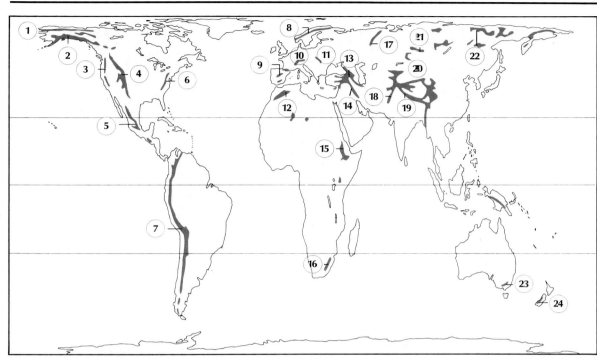

Major mountain ranges
1. Brooks Range
2. Alaska Range
3. Coast Range
4. Rocky Mountains
5. Sierra Madre
6. Appalachians
7. Andes
8. Scandinavian Range
9. Pyrenees
10. Alps
11. Carpathians
12. Atlas Mountains
13. Caucasus
14. Zagros Mountains
15. Ethiopian Highlands
16. Drakensberg Mountains
17. Ural Mountains
18. Pamir Range
19. Himalayas
20. Tien Shan Range
21. Altai Range
22. Verkhoyansk Range
23. Great Dividing Range
24. Southern Alps

Above 3000m on Mount Kenya the bamboo forest belt gives way to a mist-shrouded high moorland clothed in sedges and coarse tussock grass and dotted with giant tree heaths (*Erica* spp.) whose branches are festooned with mosses and lichens.

The Scarlet-tufted Malachite Sunbird (*Nectarinia johnstoni*) is one of the many bird species adapted to life in the high moor zone of the East African mountains.

171

California Condor:
The million dollar gamble

No bird symbolizes the wildness of the mountains more perfectly than the condor. These magnificent vultures ride the mountain winds on broad, splay-tipped wings three metres across, sailing effortlessly over enormous areas in search of food. The California Condor (*Gymnogyps californianus*) has patrolled the mountains of western North America since the Pleistocene Ice Ages. Formerly extending east to Florida and north to British Columbia, it is now confined to two small areas on the coast and in the Sierra Nevada range of southern California.

The condor population has declined steadily since the 1940s, when there were between 60 and 100 in the wild. In 1983 there were perhaps 20 wild condors left, but during the winter of 1984/5 the birds suffered a disastrous decline. By early 1986 the known population was down to three in the wild and 24 in two zoos in California.

The wild birds formerly ranged over an area of 130,000km², nesting at between 450m and 1400m in a breeding area of some 8000km². They nested in holes in steep cliffs, and roosted on exposed trees and rock outcrops. The raising of a single chick was so protracted that a breeding pair could never produce more than one young every two years. And even then they needed a good nest site within easy reach of water and food — the carcasses of dead mountain animals.

The main causes of the recent decline are thought to be lead poisoning caused by hunters' shot in the carcasses on which the birds feed, and accumulation of toxins through consumption of poisoned bait left out by farmers for the coyotes that prey on their livestock. The bait carcasses are readily taken by condors, and levels of pesticide residues found in the tissues of some dead condors have been as high as any ever found in landbirds. Eggshells, too, have exhibited up to 50 per cent thinning compared with eggs laid before organochlorines came into widespread use.

Uncertainty over the causes of the condor's plight contributed to a controversy over the best course of action to be taken. One school of thought believed that the remaining wild birds should be taken into custody and that their genes should be used to enhance existing captive breeding programmes. Others were violently opposed and felt that provision of a large uncontaminated feeding range for the remaining wild birds should be the main priority. A third group believed that marker tags and radio-tracking should be used in an intensive study of the habits and breeding behaviour of the wild birds, while others condemned this as too drastic an intrusion of technology into the world of nature.

This nest site — one of the last known occupied sites in the Sierra Nevada — was abandoned while this book was being written.

Condors are carrion-feeders and require very large territories over which to search for their food. This photograph shows part of the range of the last remaining wild California Condors.

Fortunately the gravity of the condor's situation has united many of these opposing views. More knowledge about the birds' biology and habits will undoubtedly be needed and will form a vital part of long-term conservation plans. But in the immediate future, hopes for the survival of this magnificent species must lie in captive breeding, which has already proved successful, and in order to utilize the largest possible gene pool it seems likely that eventually the three remaining wild birds — all males — will be taken into custody. In the longer term, and before anything can be gained from releasing captive-bred birds into the wild, large areas of unpopulated, uncontaminated land must be purchased, despite the high cost, and be set aside and managed solely for the benefit of the condor.

There are many who believe that in this way up to 100 condors could be re-established in the wild by the end of the century. Without an effort on this scale, the California Condor has little future beyond the confines of a zoo enclosure.

Three California Condors wait impatiently for a Golden eagle (*Aquila chrysaetos*) to finish feeding on the carcass of a mountain deer.

For years, teams of scientists have been trying to save the California Condor. Yet despite all efforts the species' only chance of survival now appears to lie in a programme of captive breeding.

Western Tragopan:
A common future for man and bird

Tragopans belong to the pheasant family, many members of which are noted for the astonishing beauty and complexity of their plumage and display. Typical pheasants have long and elaborate tails, but the tragopans have short, stumpy tails and at first sight are no match for the splendour of the true pheasants. But what the male tragopan lacks in beauty at the rear, he makes up for in front, though he saves his striking ornaments until he needs them most — in courtship display.

Even when he is not displaying, the male Western Tragopan (*Tragopan melanocephalus*) is a strikingly beautiful bird whose richly mottled back and wings brighten the shady undergrowth of the Himalayan montane forest. When he courts his mate in the spring, he circles around her with his back and upper wings angled towards her to achieve the maximum effect. But the dazzling effect of his intricately mottled plumage is eclipsed when he suddenly stops and turns towards her, freezing for a moment as two huge blue, fleshy horns, five to seven centimetres long, spring up from the silky feathers of his crown while a brilliantly patterned bib of purple, pink and pale blue appears out of the feathers of his chest, like a gorgeous silk scarf. Both the horns and the bib — known as a lappet and up to 15cm long and 8cm across — are of bare skin that can be erected in a few seconds, and deflated just as quickly. Normally they are hidden beneath the feathers, and their effect when produced in display must be quite stunning for a susceptible female tragopan.

Certainly the tragopans will need all the reproductive success that they can muster if they are to produce enough young to compensate for the losses that the species has suffered over the past hundred years. Their natural range extends across the northwestern Himalayas from northern Pakistan through Kashmir to Himachal Pradesh in northern India. They are still found throughout this range, but their distribution is now broken up into small isolated fragments, few numbering more than a hundred birds and with a total world population of probably less than 5000.

Western Tragopans inhabit the dense undergrowth of wild rhododendron and bamboo in temperate and subalpine forests on the slopes of the world's highest mountain range. They range in summer from altitudes of 2400m to as high as 3600m, but in winter they may descend as low as 1350m. They feed mainly on leaves and buds, with some insects, seeds and berries.

Many pheasants will fly up into trees to roost, even though they feed and nest or the ground, but the tragopans nest in trees, often in an old nest of another bird such as a crow. They are solitary, shy and wary birds, revealing their presence more by their raucous calls than by offering any sight of themselves.

The people of the Himalayas are a hardy race, and eating birds is a part of their survival strategy that the more prosperous people of the world have little right to decry. They do eat tragopans, and other kinds of pheasant too, probably in sufficient numbers to lower the birds' populations, especially near villages. But the greatest cause of the tragopans' decline lies in the loss of their habitat, which has been felled wholesale over huge areas. Even where some forest remains it is heavily browsed by goats, and is cut and pruned for firewood by mountain people desperate for fuelwood and animal fodder. The combined effects of hunting, felling, grazing and collecting firewood have fragmented the Western Tragopan's habitat and depressed its numbers to a level where its survival is now in doubt, even though vigorous captive breeding programmes are under way in Pakistan, and the densest population in Himachal Pradesh is included in a proposed National Park.

Three other species of tragopan are also at risk from hunting and the loss of their mountain habitats. Blyth's Tragopan (*T. blythii*) lives in dense damp montane forests in Tibet, Bhutan, Assam and northern Burma, and little is known of its numbers. Cabot's Tragopan (*T. caboti*) is confined to the mountains of southeastern China, where its forests have been razed in an effort to satisfy the land hunger of an inexorably increasing human population. In the Himalayas, the Satyr Tragopan (*T. satyra*) still maintains a wide range and reasonably high numbers, but is likely to suffer a decline and increasing fragmentation of its range as its habitat, too, is destroyed.

Like other montane forests, those of the Himalayas protect vital catchment areas that are the sole source of water for millions of people living in the distant plains. The future of the mountain tragopans will be ensured by exactly the same measures that will assure the survival of millions of lowlands people — the conservation of the mountain habitats that protect and sustain the life-giving rivers.

Temminck's Tragopan (*Tragopan temminckii*) in full courtship dress. This species inhabits the forests of southeastern Tibet, western China and North Vietnam.

The Western Tragopan's foraging habitat is the deep shade provided by stands of chestnut, hazel and walnut trees growing along the banks of mountain streams in the Himalayan forests.

Puna Rhea:
Hunted to the verge of extinction

The *puna* is a habitat unique to the mountains of the Andes; a bleak, windswept moorland that extends from the tree-line, 3500m to 4000m above sea level, to the ice and snow of the jagged rocky peaks. The *puna* is often warmed by bright sunshine but is frequently shrouded in cloud and swirling mists. The winds are bitter and persistent, too cold for trees to grow in, and the bleak rolling uplands are dominated by bunch-grass and sedges. The high, cold plateau seems almost as inimical to wildlife as to people.

Yet the *puna* not only supports a unique and diverse variety of plants and wildlife but is also home to several million people. It is naturally a habitat for grazers; not the wild sheep or goats of North America or Eurasia but specialized descendants of the camel tribe, the llama, alpaca, guanaco and vic-uña. The last two have suffered from hunting by man, who not only grazes much more stock than the environment can support but also tries to till the hostile ground to raise potatoes and other crops.

The rhea (*Pterocnemia pennata tara-pacensis*) of the *puna* zone is a huge flight-less bird, over 1.5m tall; slightly smaller than the more familiar Ostrich of Africa but similar in its habitat and behaviour. The Puna Rhea is one of two varieties of Darwin's Rhea, named after its illustrious describer. The southern race, 'Darwin's Rhea' itself, is still abundant in parts of Chile and Argentina, but in the northern parts of those countries, and in Peru and Bolivia, the northern race – the 'Puna Rhea' – has been hunted and persecuted to the brink of extinction.

Darwin's Rhea (*P. p. pennata*) has been studied more than the *puna* race, but the two are probably very similar in their biology. Female rheas are among the most sexually liberated of all birds. They group together to watch a lone male's display, and line up to lay in the nest he scrapes in the bare ground; then they leave him to incubate the eggs and raise the young alone. There may be up to 50 eggs to a nest, and once the male has begun to sit tight on the eggs, he defends them vigorously by hissing and snapping. Visiting females have to lay their eggs either when he is away, taking a drink or feeding, or else sufficiently close by for him to roll them into the nest with his bill.

Darwin's Rhea is smaller than the African Ostrich, which it closely resembles. The rhea occurs in Argentina and in parts of southern Peru and northern Chile.

The *puna* is the high grassland zone of the Andes range. It extends from the tree-line at 3500–4000m right up to the perpetual snow-fields of the high peaks. The short, dense grasses are grazed by herds of alpacas and llamas.

The newly hatched young soon stagger to their feet and walk around in search of their own food of insects, seeds, leaves and roots. When all have hatched they herd together and leave the nest, guarded by the male, and very often the broods of several different males combine into large groups of young of very different ages.

Like Ostriches, rheas make up in running speed for their inability to fly. Their long, muscular legs propel them in a swift swerving run, faster than a galloping horse. At full tilt the body is held horizontally with the neck stretched out in front, one wing flung out to the side as the bird dodges and weaves. A running rhea could outstrip its fastest pursuer were it not for its fatal habit of dropping down into long grass and trying to double back. Hunters long ago perfected the technique of chasing rheas on horseback and bringing them down with the *bolas*, a three-thonged sling weighted with stones, which entangles the rhea's legs. The birds are hunted for sport, for their meat and skin, and for their feathers, which are used not for ornament, as Ostrich feathers are, but as feather dusters. Their habitat, too, has been shrinking rapidly in the face of over-grazing and inappropriate agriculture.

Puna Rheas are legally protected over much of their range, but the legislation is largely ineffective. Dusters of rhea feathers are still sold openly in Bolivian shops; their skins are still sold; in Chile their fat is used as a medicinal remedy; and hunters chase them in dune-buggies around mining settlements in the Peruvian Andes. The rheas' decline is a sad testimony to the misuse of their bleak but magnificent environment, and to mankind's insensitive exploitation of one of the most ancient forms of bird-life.

After courting and mating with a large group of females, the male Darwin's Rhea collects all their eggs together – sometimes as many as 50 – and incubates them all by himself in a large hollow scraped in the earth.

Takahe: Third time lucky?

A remote mountain range can sometimes act as a refuge in which a species can survive pressures that would wipe it out elsewhere. The Fiordland region of New Zealand's South Island has performed just such a function for the Takahe (*Notornis mantelli*), a large flightless gallinule that maintains a precarious existence deep in the inaccessible Lake District of the South Island.

Takahes have twice before been resurrected from the dead. The early European settlers in New Zealand found the bones of a large flightless rail among those of the huge Ostrich-like Moas that dominated the deposits of fossils in both the North and the South Islands of the new colony. Not surprisingly they added the species to the list of those that had become extinct before the arrival of the settlers. But in 1849 one bird was run down and killed by seal hunters on the South Island coast, and the description of the species could be filled out to include the brilliant glossy indigo, blue, green and white of the plumage, and the red of the massive bill and strong thick legs. Other birds were captured on three more occasions in the nineteenth century, the last in 1898, but for the next 50 years there were only occasional unconfirmed rumours of live birds, and the species was again assumed to be extinct.

In 1948 a determined expedition to the Fiordland region created an ornithological sensation by capturing and filming living Takahes. The part of the Murchison and Kepler Mountains in which they lived was declared a reserve and began to be managed solely for the preservation of the birds. Further exploration revealed that the population of several hundred birds is spread over about 650km² west of Lake Te Anau, and a small area to the north. Studies of the biology of the birds, and their interactions with their habitat and the other wildlife of the region, revealed a worrying picture of continuing and varied threats to the survival of the species.

These ponderous but splendid birds — over 60cm tall — use several different montane habitats in the course of a year. In the summer they breed in wet alpine grasslands between 1200m and 1800m above sea level. They build a bower-like nest under tussocks of grass, and there they lay two eggs. The male and female pair for life, and together defend a territory of between 10 and 350 hectares. They eat the leaf-bases and roots and seeds of the alpine grasses, and seem to be sensitive to the condition of

the grasses. Young growing leaves are rich in protein and other nutrients, but on poor soil they may not supply enough of the birds' needs, and both the reproduction and survival of the birds may be affected. This seems to be the explanation of a steady decline in numbers in one of the areas, Takahe Valley, where the birds have been studied. When winter storms bury their food under several centimetres of snow, the Takahes move along the valleys into the forests of Southern Beech to feed on ferns, grasses and herbs.

Before Europeans came to New Zealand there were no large mammals feeding on the alpine grasslands or in the beech forests, and no predatory mammals either. Despite New Zealand's enormous size, its animals have evolved without large mammals to eat them or their food supply. And New Zealand has been isolated for so long that large mammals have not reached it from other continents. The shock to the New Zealand ecosystem when Europeans settled there was profound, for they brought with them as many as they could of the animals that were familiar to them at home and released them into the unsuspecting and defenceless island environments. The aliens that most affect the Takahes are Stoats, which have penetrated even the remote mountain grasslands and are voracious predators, and surprisingly, perhaps, Red Deer. The deer were brought in for sport, and found the landscape of New Zealand's mountains greatly to their liking. They graze the grasses that the Takahes graze, and in the forests – where they too shelter from the winter snowstorms – they browse so intensively that they leave little food for the birds.

Between the poor quality of much of their grazing, extensive losses of their eggs and young, and competition for food from deer, the unfortunate Takahes are struggling to hold their own. All three problems are being tackled by the assiduous Wildlife Service and associated agencies in New Zealand. They are attempting to improve the grasslands, to control the numbers of deer and keep them from the forests, and to eliminate the Stoats from the area. The Takahes

number only 120 or so birds, and seem to be few enough to be suffering from the genetic problems that threaten small inbreeding populations. A pilot programme to breed Takahes in captivity – partly as insurance and partly to learn more about them – has successfully hatched young from eggs taken from the wild. In due course these will be returned to the wild. All the resources of a major conservation programme will be needed to keep Takahes from a third and final descent into the oblivion of extinction.

Stoats were introduced into New Zealand in an attempt to control the escalating numbers of introduced small mammals. Unfortunately the eggs and chicks of the Takahe proved just as palatable – and vulnerable – to this voracious little predator.

In this valley the Takahe was rediscovered just 40 years ago. The valley is very remote and is accessible only on foot.

The Takahe: twice believed to be extinct, and now totally dependent on the careful management of its remote upland habitat.

Algerian Nuthatch: Discovered just in time

In 1975 the remarkable discovery of a new species of bird was made in a most unlikely place. Algeria has an image of remote and barren deserts, but it also has a fine range of mountains barely 20km from the Mediterranean shore. The summits of the Kabylie Range, over 2000m high, are in striking contrast with the hot, dry deserts inland. In winter they are deep in snow and bitterly cold; in summer a cool, damp refuge which attracts herdsmen with their goats and cattle from the burning plains below.

The ridge of Djebel Babor holds the remnants of a unique forest which shelters the tiny population of Algerian Nuthatches (*Sitta ledanti*). The dominant trees are Mirbeck's Oaks, Atlas Cedars and the endemic Algerian Fir, which cover about 1200ha of the shaded slopes and four-kilometre ridge. The area has been a National Park since 1934, but excessive grazing and browsing were not allowing the trees to replace themselves, and were causing the forest to shrink year by year. The nuthatch was the 'flagship' of a successful campaign to preserve this very special habitat. In 1982 the population was estimated at about 80 pairs, each occupying a territory of about four hectares in the oaks and firs of the ridge-crest and ten hectares in the oak-cedar forest in the valleys lower down.

The nuthatch is a typical member of its family, named after its habit of jamming a nut into a crevice in the bark of a tree while chiselling it open with its strong, tapered beak. The birds forage up and down the trunks of trees for insects and fruit as well as nuts, moving quite differently from woodpeckers and tree-creepers, which brace their bodies against the trunk with their specially stiffened tail feathers and so can climb only upwards. Nuthatches move obliquely, hanging from one foot and pushing down on the other, and so can climb down as easily as up.

The Kabylian Nuthatch was discovered only shortly before it might have become extinct, and will survive only if its habitat is helped to regenerate and cover a large enough area to support a viable population.

Until April each year, deep winter snows cover the montane forests of Djebel Babor in Algeria – home of the Algerian or Kabylian Nuthatch. The species was named after J. P. Ledant, the scientist who discovered the species in 1975.

Status report — Mountains: The fragile giants

The varied habitats found in mountain regions suffer all the problems that beset them individually elsewhere — and a number of additional risks incurred by being on a mountain. These extra threats are often rooted in the isolation of the mountain, and especially in its role in generating the rain that washes nutrients out of the barren rocks and down into the plains. Land at high altitude is usually wetter and potentially more fertile than the lowlands around, and if those lands are dry, or too densely populated, then the mountain habitats often come under intense pressure as people climb ever higher in search of water and productive land.

People use mountains most often for grazing their stock, and the pattern of use is usually seasonal. In cold climates the mountains are abandoned in winter and the animals moved lower down, to be brought up again to the high mountain pastures when spring thaws the snow and warms the grass and flowers into life. In hotter climates the animals are moved in response to rainfall rather than to cold and heat. In the wet season the stock can find fresh grazing in the lowlands, but as those pastures dry out the cattle are moved higher up to the permanent streams and springs of the mountains.

In many arid countries an isolated mountain may provide the water catchment for a very much larger area of surrounding land. In such places a rapid increase in the population of people and their grazing animals can spell disaster for the fragile habitats of the mountain and so, in due course, for the people and their animals. Habitats tend to be more fragile on mountains because the soil on the steeply sloping ground is more easily blown or washed away than it is on flat land. It is held in place very largely by the roots of plants, and if these are cut down for fuelwood, grazed too close, or trampled by too many hooves, the soil is washed away by the next rainstorm and the habitat is very quickly degraded.

The mountains in richer countries have different problems. They are often the sole remaining source of wilderness in a sea of regimented agriculture and urban ugliness. The amount of trouble and expense that millions of people will go to, simply to escape into a mountain wilderness, is a measure of the special place that mountains hold in the human spirit. But that very power to draw people holds the seeds of the mountain's own destruction, for its habitats are as vulnerable to trampling and disturbance as those of any other mountain. Far too many highland parks in the western world are suffering serious erosion, degradation and habitat alteration simply because they are too popular with people.

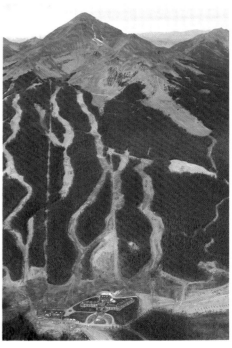

Human impact on the montane ecosystem is nowhere more dramatic than in the European Alps, where valleys and high passes are now dominated by highways built to carry huge volumes of commercial and tourist traffic.

Despite the knowledge that trees are a hillside's only protection against avalanches and soil erosion, developers do not hesitate to cut clearways on even the steepest slopes to provide thrilling runs for visiting skiers.

Cold winters or long, dry summers dominate many of the world's climatic regions, and these conditions favour forests that can withstand an annual period in which growth is slowed or even brought to a standstill. Often immensely rich in their plant and animal life, these forests and woodlands have provided man with shelter, timber, game, fuel and medicines throughout his long history. Their soils have been cleared to provide fertile farmland, and as the forests have dwindled, so too has their associated wildlife.

A few forest species can eke out a living in even the coldest winter or the longest dry season, but many of the resident birds are migrants – responding to the annual onset of lean times by moving *en masse* to more favourable climes. These annual migrations have excited the wonder of mankind for generations, and continue to enchant and mystify us to this day.

Seasonal Woods and Forests

The changing face of the seasonal forest

The zones of vegetation that pattern a mountain-side are a microcosm of the zones that circle the globe from the equator to the poles. One of the most obvious divisions is between the various kinds of forest, from the lush rainforest of the tropics, through mixed woodlands and bush, to the stunted conifers at the very limit of tree-growth fringing the alpine zone of mountains and the tundra of the polar regions. Seasonal woods and forests are an enormously varied group of habitats that share a need to adjust their life-cycles to a strongly seasonal environment. This includes at least one time of year when conditions for tree-growth are so rigorous that the trees must shut down their metabolism in the arboreal equivalent of a mammal's hibernation. Broad-leaved trees do this by shedding their leaves altogether; conifers, on the other hand, grow needle-shaped leaves that do not lose too much heat and moisture in the bitter cold of winter and so can remain on the tree, ready to take advantage of brief periods of wintry sunshine or the first full sun of springtime.

Silent pines and teeming woodlands

The lean season that all these forest types have in common may be either very cold or very dry. Passing southwards from the arctic tundra of northern Eurasia and North America – or down from the sub-alpine zone of almost any mountain outside the tropics – the first kind of trees to appear are evergreen conifers. Right at the limit of growth they are low, gnarled and twisted forms, scattered through the barren landscape, but soon they form dense stands of dark and gloomy trees with a thick soft carpet of fallen needles underfoot. The dense shade and the acid soil produced by the needles inhibit the growth of any but the hardiest ground plants. The forests are dark and largely silent, characterized by the uniformity of their tree-growth and paucity of wildlife.

Where summer temperatures are higher, and the winter winds less chilling, the growing season is kinder and much longer. Here, conifers are largely replaced by broadleaved trees that shed their foliage in winter. The long, mild summers, with their abundant rain, enable the trees to build up a store of food in their trunks and branches, and this is sufficient to carry them through the winter months when they are unable to photosynthesize. Though varying through the seasons, both plant-life and wildlife is much richer here than in the coniferous forests.

The changing seasons of spring, summer, autumn and winter in the mixed deciduous woodlands of Europe. For thousands of years these forests gave food, fuel and shelter to a growing human population. Today, greatly reduced in area, they provide an important leisure resource and a vital refuge for Europe's native wildlife.

Too useful to be left in peace

Seasonal forests once covered enormous areas of the earth but they have suffered greater destruction than any other habitat because they have supplied so many of mankind's basic needs. Broadleaved woodlands make deep, rich, brown soils that are easy to till and cultivate. The trees make fine fuel, and their wood can be used to make almost anything from houses and furniture to spears, ships and telegraph poles. The forests shelter game animals that can be hunted for food, and for their hides and horns and sinews. They also shelter bees, whose honey was the commonest source of sugar until cane and beet were cultivated. The herbs and grasses and shrubs that thrive in the benevolent shelter of a woodland not only delight the senses but have always provided a rich source of medicines and potions for those who know their secrets.

But as human populations spread, their need for land to cultivate was more pressing than their need for any other resources of the forest. The woods were felled and converted to fields, and the forests were plundered for timber and for fuel. In Europe the destruction of deciduous hardwoods has reflected human history, accelerating in periods of great naval warfare when large trees were used to build the ships, and in the industrial revolution when any size of tree was fit to fuel the greedy furnaces. Many birds of northern seasonal forests have had to adapt to the scattered woodlots and the long lines of hedges that are all that remains of the primeval forests.

Miombo woodland is a dry seasonal deciduous type of woodland found over large areas of tropical South America, Africa and India. It contains a rich and varied avifauna, but during the dry season (illustrated) many species migrate to areas offering more plentiful food supplies.

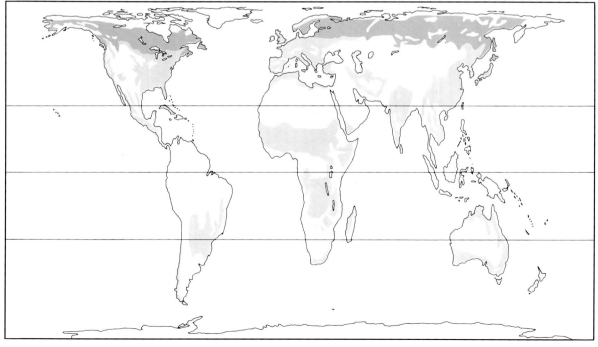

Seasonal woodlands
Cold winters or long drought periods prevent continuous growth in many parts of the world. The result is a series of woodland zones with markedly seasonal cycles of growth.

Temperate forest

Seasonal woodland

Birdlife of the forests

The montane and boreal pine forests offer a striking contrast to the mild deciduous forests and woodlands of the temperate regions in both the numbers and variety of their wildlife residents.

The coniferous forests are sombre and austere, dominated by their pines and firs and with few wild flowers to relieve their monotony. They are silent too, for few birds can survive on the limited food resources available. The lack of flowers means a similar paucity of insect life, so birds must make what use they can of the brief growing season and then depart for more favourable climes for the winter months. The only birds that can withstand the rigours of winter are those that specialize in eating the seeds of the conifers.

Crossbills in the northern forests and parrots in the highland pine forests of the tropics can extract the seeds from cones with their curved and pointed bill-tips. Large-billed finches such as grosbeaks, and the nutcrackers of the crow family, are the other birds characteristic of the conifers, but even they, like crossbills, must sometimes abandon the evergreen forest when the seed-crop fails every few years. At these times they wander far afield in vast 'irruptions', searching the unfamiliar deciduous woodlands for seeds and fruit. Birds are important dispersers of seeds in these forests, and in the summer insectivorous warblers, chickadees and titmice may also affect the numbers of caterpillars that can sometimes reach plague proportions and strip the needles off all the trees over enormous areas.

By contrast, the deciduous forests and woodlands are constantly changing, from the bare-branched austerity of winter through the fresh bright green of spring leaf-buds, and then through the darker hues of midsummer maturity to the kaleidoscopic yellows, browns and reds of autumn. The longer and more benign growing season produces a profusion of plant growth — climbers, shrubs, herbs, mosses and fungi of every kind — and on these live countless flying, crawling and burrowing insects. Consequently the woodlands can cater for a wide variety of avian lifestyles — woodcocks feeding in the leaf-litter; woodpeckers taking

The cone-feeders
Similar feeding habits have produced almost exactly the same kind of bill-shape in these two very different and widely separated bird families.

1. White-winged, or Two-barred, Crossbill (*Loxia leucoptera*)
2. Red-spectacled Amazon (*Amazona pretrei*)
3. Thick-billed Parrot (*Rhynchopsitta pachyrhyncha*)
4. Common, or Red Crossbill (*Loxia curvirostra*)
5. Parrot Crossbill (*Loxia pytyopsittacus*)

their insect food from trunks and branches; chaffinches, hawfinches, siskins and flycatchers dividing up the food resource of a tree between them by feeding at different levels; and jays — ever the opportunists — taking a variety of seeds and fruits in addition to preying on insects and the eggs and young of other birds.

Yet even in this rich habitat resources fluctuate with the seasons, and when times are hard the birds of the forest must either be prepared to change their feeding habits in tune with the varying abundance of their plant and animal foods, or migrate to other areas where supplies are more plentiful.

The Woodcock (*Scolopax rusticola*) is still hunted in many European countries and its steady decline calls for urgent legal measures to protect it.

The Greater Spotted Woodpecker (*Dendrocopos major*) is the best-known member of a group of very similar species with strikingly patterned wing-feathers. The birds' drumming sounds, made as they excavate beetle larvae from decaying wood, can be heard in most northern hemisphere forests.

A cock Capercaillie (*Tetrao urogallus*) in full display. These magnificent forest birds are very sensitive to disturbance of any kind, and the increased use of forests for leisure activities has led to a sharp decline in their numbers.

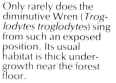

Only rarely does the diminutive Wren (*Troglodytes troglodytes*) sing from such an exposed position. Its usual habitat is thick undergrowth near the forest floor.

São Miguel Bullfinch:
A fatal attempt to adapt?

The remote Atlantic islands of the Azores, 1800km west of Portugal, were once forested with a dense cover of an evergreen laurel forest unique to the subtropical islands of the North Atlantic. These forests have enjoyed 20 million years of isolation, and in that time have developed their own endemic floras and faunas. The endemic bullfinch (*Pyrrhula murina*) of São Miguel island in the southeast of the archipelago is a distinctive descendant of the European Bullfinch, and for a long time it was treated as a race of that species; but its long confinement to the native laurel forests has induced such clear differences in its appearance and behaviour that it is now regarded as a full species.

The bullfinches live in the native laurel forests in the Pico da Vara area of eastern São Miguel. The forests clothe the flanks of two mountains, Pico da Vara and Pico Verde, and the great valley of Ribeira do Guilherme. The region is a jumble of jagged crests and steep ravines whose rich variety of habitats has encouraged the evolution of a profusion of endemic plants and insects. For the 500 years since human settlement began, the forests of Pico da Vara have been used intensively for grazing sheep and goats and, more recently, cattle and pigs. The timber has been cut for fuel and for building, and so the quality of the forest has been eroded and its area greatly reduced. Yet of all the remnants of native laurel forest in the Azores, those of the Pico da Vara are the richest and best preserved. The steep terrain has no doubt helped to keep them more

intact than other forests on flatter ground, and has made the area so difficult to explore that the relict population of bullfinches there, though reported by local people from time to time, evaded searching scientists for over 40 years.

Steep slopes and a lack of access roads have helped to preserve the unique mountain forests of the Pico da Vara area and provide a sanctuary for the endemic Bullfinch of the Azores.

Until 1968 there had been no reliable reports of bullfinches on the island for 40 years; yet in the mid-nineteenth century they had been so abundant that a bounty was put on their heads because they had become a pest on fruit crops. European Bullfinches, too, can do great damage to orchards because of their fondness for the buds of fruit trees, and the Azorean species has retained this distressing propensity of its ancestors. But whereas the European bird is unlikely to be seriously affected by measures taken against it, the island birds have nowhere to go to escape their human predators: their natural habitat declined drastically just at the time the birds themselves came under attack from the farmers.

It is too late now to know for certain what caused the bullfinches to decline from pest status to near-extinction in only 40 years. The people who urged the government to protect the birds as long ago as 1920 certainly thought that hunting was responsible, and no doubt it played a major part; but the overgrazing and felling of the forest must surely have played their part as well.

The bullfinch's massive bill looks well suited to cracking open large seeds and nuts, and indeed European Bullfinches do feed chiefly on seeds, but they are clearly fitted too for opening the tight-wrapped juicy leaves of young fruit-tree buds. The European birds turn to these buds when their natural food of wild seeds and buds is scarce. If the same is true of their descendants on São Miguel, it may well be the damage to their natural habitat that led them to turn to orchards in the first place. Their fate at the guns of the farmers may itself have been a result of the changes inflicted on their habitat, and the birds' attempts to adapt to those changes.

Whatever the causes of their decline, the unique and gravely threatened bullfinches of the Pico da Vara will survive only if they and their habitat are rigorously defended and preserved. Forestry plantations, mainly of species foreign to the islands, continue to encroach on the native habitat; useful timber trees are still extracted from the forests without control; pastures within them are still heavily grazed, and road-building and water projects threaten the fragile integrity of much of the remaining forest. There may now be as few as ten bullfinches left, and their fate is inextricably linked with that of a rich and varied habitat that has no counterpart anywhere else on earth.

Human impact has taken a heavy toll of the ancient forests of the Azores – mainly through large-scale timber felling and replacement of the natural forests with huge plantations of introduced Japanese Cedar (*Cryptomeria japonica*).

Buds and berries are the favourite food of the European Bullfinch (*Pyrrhula pyrrhula*). When food becomes scarce in winter, the birds often congregate in city parks and gardens.

Kirtland's Warbler:
A drastic but vital intervention

Few birds can be as fussy about where they will live as these small songbirds. They breed only in a small area where the southern edge of the great Jack Pine forests of North America overlap a particular soil – the Grayling Sands – and 90 per cent breed in the drainage area of a single stream. They nest only among pines between eight and 22 years old – the youngest about the size of a domestic Christmas tree. The sandy soil is important because the warblers embed their nests in the ground, among long grasses, and the heavy summer rainstorms would flood them if the water did not drain away quickly. Such a preference for a particular stage in a habitat succession – especially one so short-lived – is probably unique in birds, and must have played a large part in their decline and slowness to recover. Another aspect of their life history that has made them vulnerable is their migration, which takes them every winter to the scattered islands of the Bahamas.

The first Kirtland's Warbler (*Dendroica kirtlandii*) known to science was on its way to the Bahamas in 1841 when it was collected on a boat. It was over 60 years before a nest was found, and in that time the wholesale cutting and burning of the Jack Pine forests of northern Michigan State had probably created more suitable habitat than the bird had ever known before. It must surely be the only bird now endangered whose numbers in the wild actually increased as the tide of human immigrants swept inexorably westward through America. But the drastic changes to its habitat favoured not only the Kirtland's Warbler but also another bird whose arrival in their breeding range very nearly wiped out the warblers.

Brown Cowbirds (*Molothrus ater*) like open grassy country scattered with young pine trees as much as Kirtland's Warblers do, and are a great deal less particular about the type of soil that they will tolerate. They lay their eggs in other birds' nests, and their young are reared either at the expense of their hosts' offspring or side-by-side with them. They are very successful parasites, not least because they do not specialize in one kind of host. If one species of victim becomes extinct, the cowbirds can always find another.

Brown Cowbirds swept north into Michigan as the settlers opened up the pine forests by lumbering and burning, turning much into grassland and increasing the area of growing young Jack Pines. When the warblers were first counted in 1951, 500 pairs were found; at that time, about 55 per cent of their nests were parasitized by cowbirds and the production of young warblers was reduced by more than one-third. By 1971 the warblers had declined to around 200 pairs, and the cowbirds were parasitizing as many as four nests in five. So few young warblers were being produced that the population could not persist unless the cowbirds were removed.

So began a programme that nobody can have enjoyed; killing cowbirds to save Kirtland's Warblers. The cowbirds proved easy to catch in baited traps placed throughout the warblers' nesting area, and several thousand have been caught each year since 1972. Before this programme began, each pair of warblers was producing on average less than one young per year; now they raise over four, more than any other species of American warbler.

Yet curiously, the number of breeding pairs has hardly changed; there were 200 pairs when the programme began in 1972, and 200 pairs six years later. More recent years have, however, witnessed a slight improvement. In 1985 there were estimated to be about 440 adult breeding birds. Between leaving their nests and returning to breed, something has been happening to young Kirtland's Warblers; something that was not suspected when so few were being produced, and so was not looked for, but which still remains a mystery.

A male Kirtland's Warbler in full song. This is one of the world's rarest migratory birds, having a known breeding population of only 200 to 220 pairs.

Most of the warblers' breeding grounds are now in public hands, and the amount of suitable habitat for them is being increased by management to arrest the natural succession from grassland to dense mature pinewoods. Perhaps this will be enough; but the mysterious loss of so many young birds, somewhere on their long migration to the Bahamas, reminds us that a migrant bird needs more than safe nesting grounds if it is to survive.

The Brown Cowbird lays its eggs in the nests of other birds, including those of Kirtland's Warblers. This poses a serious threat to the small population of warblers, whose breeding success has declined dramatically.

Many of the problems facing Kirtland's Warbler arise from its very specific habitat requirements. The birds will breed only in ten- to twenty-year-old stands of Jack Pine (*Pinus banksiana*).

Cheer Pheasant:
Warning sign in the Asian hill-forest

The pheasant family is predominantly Asian; the familiar species that is now so widespread in the western world as a game bird was introduced for sport from several different stocks in various parts of Asia and eastern Europe. The family contains some of the most spectacularly beautiful and elaborately plumaged of all birds, and their splendour has undoubtedly contributed to the parlous state of many pheasant populations.

The Cheer Pheasant (*Catreus wallichii*) is a dull-looking bird by pheasant standards, intricately patterned in muted browns and greys rather than the dazzling colours of so many of its relatives. It is related to the 'eared' pheasants of China, which are unusual in the family as a whole in that the male and female are very similar, differing chiefly in the presence of a spur on the leg of the male but not of the female. The Cheer cannot blame its decline on its beauty, but rather on its preference for a habitat that is under great pressure from increasing human populations, and on the succulent and tasty flesh that is characteristic of even the plainest of the pheasant family.

The range of the Cheer Pheasant overlaps that of the Western Tragopan and several other endangered Asian pheasants; from eastern Pakistan through Kashmir to central Nepal. Although their total range has probably not contracted, their distribution within it has become increasingly patchy as one small population after another has disappeared. They occupy forests at a lower altitude than many other species of pheasant, and so are the first to be inundated by the rising tide of human pressure.

Cheers eat a wide variety of shoots, roots, fruits, leaves, berries, grubs and other insects, scratching their food from the ground with their strong bills. They breed in dry oak forests on steep, rocky hillsides between about 1200m and 4000m altitude, but often move to lower levels in winter.

A Cheer Pheasant bred in captivity is released into thick undergrowth in the Margalla Hills of Pakistan. Where the natural cover has been lost through cultivation or grazing, the pheasants are vulnerable to hunters and predators.

The Margalla Hills in Pakistan, where captive-bred Cheer Pheasants are being released in a programme designed to boost the small wild population. Such methods can, however, be successful only where the habitat can also be protected.

In Nepal they show some preference for open scrubby forest dotted with grassy cliffs, and throughout their range they survive best in the steepest and craggiest parts of the oak-forest zone. But much of that zone is no longer forest; it is fast being converted into grassland, with scattered scrub left only in patches on slopes too steep for woodcutters or grazing animals to reach. In west Nepal, forest as high as 2300m is cleared for cultivating crops, and most of it is cut for fuel, grazed by livestock, and burnt each year to improve the grazing. Cheers like the thick cover that long grass afforcs, but when it is burnt and closely cropped by sheep and goats it gives them little shelter and they fall easy prey to hunters.

In spite of being so clearly affected by the things that people do, Cheers are unaccountably often found close to villages. They seem able to adjust successfully to the simple presence of people, at least until the people destroy their habitat. As the steep slopes are increasingly stripped of vegetation they will of course become less suitable for people too, since soil erosion, lack of forage, and drought are bound to follow. The disappearance of the pheasants is a harbinger of disaster for the mountain people.

The species itself can be maintained by captive breeding. The birds are not beautiful enough to attract many zoos or aviculturists, but those that do care to breed endangered species can breed Cheers quite successfully, and birds raised in England have been released into the Margalla Hills in Pakistan and Himachal Pradesh in India. But the ultimate success of these projects lies in the conservation of the mountain forests and the control of hunting, and in the first of these, at least, lies also the key to continued human life in the habitat.

Imperial Woodpecker: Last seen in 1958

The world's largest woodpecker is well named. It is as regal and magnificent as its name implies, and as close to extinction as the historic title of 'Emperor'.

This huge and splendid species – reaching over 57cm in length – is so closely related to the Ivory-billed Woodpecker of America and Cuba that the two may be races of a single species. For such a rare bird the Ivory-billed Woodpecker (*Campephilus principalis*) is quite well known because its decline has been closely recorded by the ornithologists of the United States, a country almost as rich in bird-watchers as in birds; but the Imperial Woodpecker (*C. imperialis*) is confined to Mexico, where ornithologists are almost as scarce as Imperial Woodpeckers, and too little is known of it even to be sure whether or not it is a separate species.

Imperial Woodpeckers seem always to have been confined to virgin forests of tall pines and oaks in the highlands of northwest Mexico, above an altitude of about 2000m in the north of their range and 2500m in the south. They can never have been very common because each pair occupies an area of about 25km², a vast home range for any forest bird. None have been seen for certain since 1958, though unconfirmed reports persist and enough suitable country remains for a few to have survived.

The male is a magnificent bird with a brilliant red crest; the female lacks the red but has an equally splendid black crest that curls up and forward. In the breeding season they advertise themselves – and no doubt their territory and their readiness to mate – by drumming loudly with the bill on wood, and giving out an incongruous nasal call like the sound of a tin trumpet. Both sexes have a bright yellow eye, and a heavy bill that they use for excavating nest-cavities and for feeding, very probably using techniques similar to those of Ivory-billed Woodpeckers. These strip bark from the trunks of dead and dying trees to expose the beetle grubs underneath, and also dig deep pits in the wood, as deep as 12cm, to extract the deeper-boring insects. On larger side-branches they exploit the underside as well

as the top, shuffling upside-down apparently oblivious to the pull of gravity on their huge bulk. They nest in stumps high up in pine trees, in an unlined cavity in which they lay the white eggs characteristic of woodpeckers, and share the duties of incubating the eggs and raising the young. We can surmise that the Imperial has similar habits, but the details of their private lives are secrets they may yet take with them into extinction.

Although the Imperial Woodpecker's natural history remains unstudied, its anatomy is sufficiently well known to show that they share the extraordinary adaptation of all woodpeckers to their highly specialized way of life. The tongue, like that of any other bird, is divided at the back into two horns; but in woodpeckers these are enormously elongated and pass right around the back of the skull, over the top and down again to be rooted either above the base of the bill, inside a nostril, or around the eye-socket. This elongated root enables the tongue to be protruded well beyond the end of the bill. When it is sticky with saliva it can be used to pick up ants, and the tip is often fringed with brush-like bristles that can trap a juicy grub many centimetres beyond the tip of the long bill.

A woodpecker's tail-feathers have specially strengthened shafts that the bird uses to brace itself against the tree-trunk, and its feet have very mobile toes that can be spread wide to improve its grip on the bark. The bill is like a heavy chisel, driven by highly developed neck muscles and mounted on a greatly strengthened skull to perfect a weapon that is the natural prototype of a motor-driven hammer. As the largest of its kind, the Imperial Woodpecker represents a peak of woodpecker evolution in which all these specialized characteristics reach their greatest development. The loss of this magnificent species would diminish the whole family of woodpeckers as well as the environment of the species.

The pine-oak forests of northern Mexico are under enormous pressure from selective felling of the most valuable trees. Although this method of exploiting the forest is less damaging than wholesale clear-felling, it requires that roads be constructed into the forest just as clear-felling does, and these logging roads bring people into areas that used to be remote from human impact. The people bring guns with them and shoot wildlife, especially the larger kinds, with no control; and the slow-flying, conspicuous Imperial Woodpecker, flying lazily across the road in its undulating flight, is an easy target. Like other large birds occupying the top levels of their food chains, Imperial Woodpeckers are naturally rare and sparsely distributed. If both birds of a breeding pair are shot, that represents the total loss of the species from 25km^2 of forest. At such low densities, the vacant territory will probably never be reoccupied.

Hunting is probably the most important cause of the species' decline, though the hunters could not have reached the birds without the logging roads, so the exploitation of their habitat has played a major part in the birds' demise.

Despite widespread and accelerating logging activities, the hinterland of northern and central Mexico retains large areas of wild and remote mountain forest in which the elusive Imperial Woodpecker may yet survive.

Red Siskin:
The 'bird lovers' who turn a blind eye

This strikingly colourful little finch has become so rare so suddenly that in spite of its great beauty, and the numbers that have been taken into captivity, so little is known of it in the wild that it is difficult even to be sure of its typical habitat. Much of its range is now occupied by scrubby grassland, but much of that was probably originally an open seasonal woodland. The birds' diet of seeds and their habit of feeding at the forest edge suggest that deciduous forest may have been their favoured habitat. Such forests are often much grassier than evergreen ones because enough light reaches the ground, when the trees are bare of leaves, for grasses to grow, whereas the dense shade that persists all year round in an evergreen forest inhibits the growth of grasses.

The range of the Red Siskin (*Spinus cucullatus*) originally extended from northeastern Colombia (where none have been recorded since 1947) through northern Venezuela to Trinidad, though so few have been seen in Trinidad that it is not quite clear whether they were wanderers from the mainland of Venezuela — barely 15km away — or truly part of the Trinidadian fauna. They feed on the seeds of a variety of wild herbs and grasses and on small insects, often at the edge of forest.

Red Siskins are closely related to the canaries that are so popular with the cage-bird trade, though their song is weaker. However, their brilliant colours more than outweigh their feeble song, and around 1900 they began to be imported into Europe and North America in large numbers because it was soon found that they could be crossed with cage-bred canaries to introduce the genes for red plumage colour into the canary stock. A wild male Red Siskin crossed with a female canary could produce male hybrids that were fertile, and so could be re-crossed with canaries to give a new variety of red or bronze-coloured canaries.

The Siskin proved so popular for this purpose, and was apparently so easy to catch, that very soon the supply of wild-caught birds began to dry up. The Government of Venezuela responded by banning their capture, and the few that still find their way to Europe and North America are almost certainly caught illegally. Unfortunately they are still in such great demand for this esoteric purpose that unscrupulous collectors of cage-birds will still pay hundreds of dollars for a wild-caught male, without troubling too much about the legality of the transaction or its effects on the wild population.

A modern textbook of aviculture bemoans the dismal prospect that, '. . . in the more or less immediate future, European collectors will have to be satisfied with species bred in their aviaries'. Another puts the blame for the birds' scarcity in collections squarely on the shoulders of the Government of Venezuela for banning their capture. Such attitudes are unfortunately not rare in the cage-bird trade, which continues to pay huge prices for endangered birds while stubbornly refusing to acknowledge its own part in the decline of many colourful species of tropical bird.

The forests of Venezuela are probably the original habitat of the threatened Red Siskin.

A captive-bred canary showing the intense red-orange factor derived from cross-breeding with the brilliant red male Siskin.

The little that we know of the Red Siskin's life comes from those few that have survived to breed in the aviaries of collectors sufficiently interested in the birds to record some of their habits. The female siskin is much less brilliant than her mate, reddish-brown on the back and wings and white beneath, without the black hood of the male. She lays four bluish-white eggs, spotted with red, and incubates them for 12 days while her mate feeds her on the nest. They feed the young together, not only for the two weeks they remain in the nest but also for the further month or so that it takes the young to become independent. The siskins' tropical origins are betrayed by their need for temperatures of at least 23°C; at lower temperatures they are inactive and will not breed, and many of the aviaries in which they were first kept in Europe and America were simply too cool for them.

It seems quite clear that Red Siskins will become extinct primarily because too many have been caught to put in cages. Other factors may have operated too, but the importance of collecting in bringing about their decline is not seriously questioned. The loss of this exceptionally beautiful little bird will be an indictment of the selfish exploitation of foreign faunas by nations that have failed to practise abroad the conservation morality that they preach at home.

So-called 'red' canaries like this one for sale in a small Spanish village form a significant part of the cage-bird trade.

Kakapo:
Dramatic return of the booming parrot

The extraordinary Kakapo is one of the most endangered birds on New Zealand's sadly swollen list of critically threatened birds. It is also, by any standard, among the most bizarre that has ever lived.

This giant nocturnal parrot (*Strigops habroptilus*) was once widespread throughout the podocarp and beech forests of the North, South and Stewart Islands of New Zealand. Their decline may have begun before the Maori people colonized New Zealand from Polynesia around A.D.950, but it was certainly well advanced when Europeans began to settle the islands nine hundred years later. Maoris and Europeans have cleared over three-quarters of the vast forests that once covered most of New Zealand, and have infiltrated the rest with introduced predators such as cats, stoats and dogs, and alien herbivores like deer, chamois and opossums, which drastically affect the forests' structure. Kakapos are flightless herbivores and so are affected by almost everything that mankind has done to their habitat. Even in their best-known stronghold, in the mountainous Fiordland region of the South Island, the tiny population dwindled rapidly throughout the 1960s. As recently as the early 1970s they were pronounced effectively extinct because all the birds known to be alive were males.

In 1976 the tide of Kakapo history was turned when a small population was found in a remote area of about 550km² on Stewart Island. This population included some females, so hope for the continued survival of the species was dramatically rekindled. Intensive research on these birds, and a programme of translocation to safer sites, have been in operation ever since. By 1985 the population was thought to be about 50, of which 12 were known to be females. However, in that year no chicks were believed to have survived beyond the end of the breeding season.

Kakapos are unlike almost any other parrot; only the Night Parrot (*Geopsittacus occidentalis*) and the Ground Parrot (*Pezoporus wallicus*) of Australia look at all like them. Kakapos are huge: males weigh up to 3.5kg when they are breeding, and are up to 66cm long; females are much lighter, rarely over 1.5kg. Their breast-muscles are very much reduced and they cannot fly, though they can leap or drop with wings outstretched for four or five metres. However, they run with surprising speed and agility and live in such dense undergrowth that they can easily evade capture.

The present range of the Kakapo has contracted to small areas of temperate forest just below the tree-line on Stewart Island and in Fiordland, where the birds have access to both the low, dense scrub-forest and the sub-alpine grasslands. It may be important to them to be able to reach both habitats, for they feed extensively in the grassland zone but need the forest for shelter and for nesting as well as feeding. They seem to make considerable movements up and down the mountain slopes in relation to food supply and also — especially in the males — to breeding, for the display grounds of the male are located on the crests of ridges.

The Kakapo's breeding behaviour is perhaps the most intriguing and mysterious of all its eccentric habits. The Maoris and early European explorers knew of a complex system of well-defined paths running through the forest of the mountain ridges where Kakapos lived. Europeans thought they were the tracks of Maori hunters, and were puzzled to find them still fresh and clear many years after the Maoris had left. The tracks led between curious bowl-shaped depressions in the ground, and the plants that lined the paths were often chewed in a very distinctive fashion, with tiny balls of chewed leaf or stem left hanging from the plant. The Maoris knew that the tracks were made by Kakapos and thought they used them for commuting through the forest. They also knew that the extraordinary booming sounds that shattered the summer nights were made by Kakapos and said they boomed only one year in five, when the fruits of the *kiekie* vine were ripe. The bowls along the paths were thought to be dusting-bowls, used by many birds to keep their feathers in good condition.

The Kakapo is one of the world's rarest and strangest parrots. Small numbers survive in the remote mountain areas of southern New Zealand. The males build complex courtship arenas, with winding tracks and 'booming bowls'. Only very recently have the bizarre habits of these secretive birds come to light after years of patient observation from hides like these in the Fiordland hills of the South Island.

For many years the Kakapo was feared to be extinct. Then a few males were discovered in Fiordland. Ten years later another small group, including some females, was found on Stewart Island.

This well-trodden Kakapo track is part of a courtship arena made and shared by a group of breeding males.

The focal point of the male Kakapo's display is the 'booming bowl' (above), hollowed out beneath tree roots to create an echo-chamber for the mating calls.

To produce its deep, booming call the bird inflates its body with air (right) until it is distended like a balloon. Enhanced by the effect of the bowl, the bird's calls carry far and wide through the hills.

Recent studies of the few surviving Kakapos have found that the paths are indeed made by Kakapos, and so are the bowls, but neither is used for quite the purpose that people had once thought. Only the males make the paths, and several of them share a system of tracks and bows which together make a courtship 'arena'. Each male uses a different bowl, which he uses like a megaphone to amplify the strength of the bittern-like booming call which he makes to attract a female. No other bird is known to build its own megaphone in this way. The Kakapos' breeding system is in fact a 'lek' like that used by a number of birds in the northern hemisphere – such as Black Grouse and Ruff, for example, in Europe, and some tropical forest species like birds of paradise and manakins. Males of lek species advertise their breeding wares on shared courting grounds, the 'arenas', where females come to make their choice. Once mated, the females go off to nest by themselves some distance from the arena. In typical lek species the males are a good deal bigger than the females – as they are in Kakapos – partly because they have to compete with each other for the females and this may involve fighting with other males. Nineteenth-century accounts of Kakapos suggested that they were fierce fighters, even going so far as killing each other, but there are no recent eye-witness accounts to confirm this.

Kakapos probably do not 'boom' and breed as regularly as every five years as Maori tradition maintained; but certainly the males do not boom every year, and there seems to be no breeding without booming, so their breeding interval is certainly irregular. It is very probably related to the availability of food, which must be abundant close by. A male must spend many nights booming to ensure a mate for himself. He may boom a thousand times an hour and this activity, together with assiduously cleaning the tracks connecting the bowls of his arena and defending them from rival males, must make the breeding period an extremely demanding time. Females too must incubate and raise the young alone, so for both sexes breeding can be attempted only when they can be sure of abundant food supplies nearby.

The curious balls of chewed leaf and stem that festoon the plants lining Kakapo trails are produced by the birds' unique habit of chewing the plant without detaching it, sucking out the nutrients and leaving the fibrous tissues attached. When feeding on some kinds of plant, their secateur-like bills leave a crisp cut edge that is equally characteristic. They feed on a wide variety of plants and on many different parts, from leaves, flowers, fruits and seed-heads, to roots, which they grub up from the ground. The most extraordinary aspect of their feeding is that they do all their chewing with the bill. Other birds use a muscular part of the gut — the gizzard — to grind their food, often with the aid of small fragments of grit swallowed for the purpose, but the Kakapo's gizzard is rudimentary and its function has been taken over by the bill.

One of the hardest aspects of studying Kakapos is simply finding them. Their dense habitat and nocturnal habits make this especially difficult, but a combination of old and modern techniques promises to overcome the problem. Dogs, suitably muzzled but specially trained to find Kakapos, have been used with great success; and some birds have then been fitted with small radio transmitters whose signals enable researchers to find them again at any time.

Kakapos nest on the ground under vegetation, rock piles and in holes under tree roots, and lay two to four white eggs. They roost in holes, under overhangs, or low down in trees or bushes. Consequently they are desperately vulnerable to stoats, cats and rats: no fewer than one-quarter of all the known Kakapos in one area were killed by cats in a single year. The control of cats is a major part of the Kakapo recovery programme, but the best hope is perhaps to transfer the birds to islands that have suitable habitats but no predators or competitors. The first attempts to do this seem successful, and there is every hope now that these amazing birds can be helped to survive to delight future generations.

Scientists have spent many months in the remote mountain areas of New Zealand, looking for new Kakapo colonies and studying the habits of these rare and elusive birds.

'Sinbad' — one of several Kakapos being kept under observation by conservation scientists. Small radio transmitters have proved an invaluable aid in following the movements and activities of these secretive nocturnal birds.

Status report – Seasonal forests:
Scattered remnants of a once-great biome

The varied kinds of seasonal woods and temperate forests of the world account for a very high proportion of its biomass and production. They cover perhaps one-fifth of the surface of the land, but produce more than two-fifths of its plant biomass and nearly one-third of its biomass of animals. Their disproportionately large contribution to the production of the biosphere is accounted for chiefly by the huge numbers of trees they contain: they are so much bigger than other plants that they carry a huge weight of leaves with which to do the work of production and a great volume of wood in which to store their products.

These forests hold a large proportion of the biosphere's reserves of carbon, and as they are burnt as fuel they add to the amount of carbon dioxide in the atmosphere, inexorably changing its composition. The burning of wood is now known to add as much carbon dioxide to the atmosphere as burning oil and gas has long been known to do. The possible consequence of this we will discuss again in relation to tropical rain-forests, for the two kinds of forest between them have more influence on the balance of chemicals in the various parts of the biosphere than all the other land habitats combined.

As an environment for birds the forests are extremely attractive for most of the year because except at the limits of tree growth in the coniferous boreal and upper montane forests they are rich in a great range of food resources and nesting sites. Yet the seasonal check on production, in the form of cold winters or hot, dry seasons, imposes a ceiling on the number of birds that can live there, and demands an adjustment – in numbers, in feeding behaviour, or by migration – on the part of its resident birds.

A hillside forest in New Zealand, destroyed by sheep-grazing – a common example of the increasing conflict between man and nature.

In many parts of the world the ecological diversity of natural vegetation and mixed farming has been replaced by large-scale monoculture more suited to mechanization.

The impact of man

Outside the flood-plains where civilization began, the woods and forests of the northern hemisphere were the first habitats to experience the terrible force of man's ingenuity and ruthlessness in exploiting his environment. They offered abundant food, fuel, shelter and building material, and their deep, brown soils grew crops prolifically after the trees were felled. As they swept through the Old World, people felled the forests and turned them into the patchwork of fields and hedges and woodlots and settlements that have been shaped to serve the needs of the northern hemisphere peoples over the past few thousand years. In the New World, European immigrants took just a few hundred years to do to the woods and forests of the western hemisphere what had taken them thousands of years in the Old World. We are still seeing rapid changes in the life-styles of many birds as they try to adjust to the changes mankind has wrought on their habitats. The clash between Brown Cowbirds and Kirtland's Warblers is only one of many recent changes in the distribution and abundance of birds in response to the dizzying speed of environmental change in North America.

Heavy rains falling on land parched for many months can have a highly damaging effect. Here, near Lake Shala in Ethiopia, flash floods have caused severe gully erosion in light woodland.

Fire is a natural part of the forest and grassland ecological cycle, but its excessive use by man to clear ground for agriculture can quickly lead to erosion.

An all too familiar sight in the forests of southern Germany: mature forest being cut to make way for new motorway developments.

The seasonal forests of the tropics are now coming under similar pressures to those suffered by forests of the northern hemisphere, but at a much faster rate because more people are now being added to the human population each year than at any time in history. It is easy for those who live in industrialized countries to forget that more than half the people in the world depend for fuel not on the oil or gas or electricity that are wrested from the earth at such great expense, but on wood; and mostly on wood that is gathered by the families themselves.

The dry wood that litters the floor of deciduous tropical forests and scrublands makes good fuel; and when that has gone, the dead trees are felled; and when they are gone, the living trees soon follow.

The logs that littered the ground were infested with ants and termites and beetles, all food for a variety of birds. Dead trees were similarly infested, and the living ones offered yet another range of resources to feed yet more kinds of bird. At each stage of human exploitation of the forest, plants, birds and other wild creatures are affected. And ultimately, when the entire forest is destroyed, that whole community of plants and birds and other animals goes with it.

And what of the people? The resources of the forest, on which they depended, are gone as much for them as for the birds of the forest, and the death of the forest carries grim forebodings for those who killed it. In those parts of the tropics where people are most desperate for fuel and land, they have no choice but to cut down the trees if they are to survive the next few weeks or months. To argue that by doing so they leave no reserve for the future carries no weight because they have no choice. Where the pressure is rather less, and comes from logging companies, the local people may co-operate to defend their forests against destruction, as is happening in parts of India. But there can be no doubt that for as long as people are desperate for fuelwood, animal fodder and land, the outlook for such forests and their wildlife is a dismal one indeed.

Nearly half the world's population, some 2000 million people, depend on wood for domestic heating and for cooking their food. Already, nearly 96 million are unable to find enough wood for even their basic needs, while 1000 million more can satisfy their needs only by depleting the dwindling wood reserve. By the year 2000, it is estimated that 2400 million people will be forced into consuming wood faster than it can be grown.

Six goats hungrily feeding in a single tree graphically illustrate the impact of livestock in semi-arid areas like the hills of Morocco.

Adaptability: the key to the future?

Though the forests still cover large areas of land their original extent must have been truly enormous. Most of the agricultural areas of China, for example, where every scrap of land that can grow food now does so, were once wooded. How many species of bird have vanished into extinction there as the forests were felled we shall never know. The few birds still to be seen in parts of China and other densely settled northern countries are the hardy remnants of an avifauna of largely unknown size and variety. Yet the ability to adapt to change is a fundamental part of any bird's adaptation to life in seasonal woods and forests, because the passing seasons themselves impose constantly changing demands. Perhaps these forests more than any others are by the very nature of their seasonal environment better fitted to adapt to the changes forced upon them by

mankind. Their birds are used to a diet that changes from month to month, and some of them are even used to leaving the forests altogether to avoid the leanest times of year. In Europe and North America, many woodland birds maintain thriving populations in the tiny scraps of woodland that are left, and some do even better in the artificial 'woodland' habitats of hedgerows, farms and gardens, and urban parks.

Seasonal woods and forests sheltered and fed mankind as he spread across the northern hemisphere. They occupy a special place in the folk memory of our species and still exert a powerful attraction. Their loss, to people no less than to the birds that live there, would not be measured only in terms of global chemistry.

Throughout large areas of western Europe, Scandinavia and North America, forests are being damaged by acid rain. The effects may be felt close to the source of pollution or hundreds of kilometres away: the effluent gases of industry have joined oil, DDT and other pesticides on the growing list of global pollutants.

Although protected by law, the Spanish Imperial Eagle (*Aquila heliaca adalberti*) (*above*) is still persecuted in many areas by farmers. Its main stronghold is now in the Coto Doñana (*left*), where third and fourth chicks – which normally never survive – have been successfully transferred to the nests of breeding birds whose eggs have failed to hatch.

The richness and diversity of life in tropical forests, especially rainforests, far exceeds that in any other habitat on earth. Within just a few hectares of rainforest, hundreds of plant species crowd together, rising up, layer upon layer, from the dark, almost bare, forest floor to the unbroken canopy far above. The trees are festooned with climbers, stranglers and epiphytes; fruit, nuts, berries and nectar-rich flowers are available in abundance throughout the year, and the dense vegetation is alive with burrowing, wood-boring, flying and crawling insects.

Not surprisingly, the bird-life of the forest is equally rich. In just one small area of Central American forest, scientists recorded 15 species of ground-dwelling bird, 75 different species living in the understorey, and more than 130 inhabiting the main forest canopy layer. In all, more than 2500 bird species live in the tropical rainforests, almost one-third of all known birds.

Tropical Forests

The biological power-house

The hot and humid conditions of the equatorial lowlands create a natural hothouse where life can flourish free from frosts and droughts. Elsewhere, most plants and animals are checked at some time in their lives by low temperatures or a lack of water, but in lowland tropical forests water is always abundant and temperatures close to the optimum for growth. Where temperatures rarely fall below 20°C and there is at least 10cm of rain in every month, tropical rainforest dominates the natural landscape.

Since they grow in the most favourable climate on earth it is not surprising that tropical forests are the richest and most productive habitats on the planet. They cover no more than six per cent of the land area yet contain probably half of all the living species of plant and animal, and about 30 per cent of all known species of bird. As a store of species and genetic resources, as a source of organic production, and as producers of the oxygen that sustains all animal life, tropical forests are by far the most important ecosystem on earth.

Worlds within worlds

One secret of the forests' richness lies simply in the size of the trees. A mature specimen can be well over 50 metres tall, so light can be harnessed into energy to a height of 50 metres above the ground. In a virgin forest, trees of this or even greater size stand proudly isolated above a continuous canopy of lesser trees whose crowns intermingle so closely that they cast a dense shade on the forest floor. No more than one per cent of the light that floods the canopy reaches the ground. There, the shade is so deep that very few plants can grow.

The huge forest trees create a climate of their own. As much water is 'breathed' into the atmosphere from the enormous biomass of plants as evaporates from the surface of a lake. As it rises into the air the moisture condenses into clouds to fall again as rain. Within the forest, falling rain is intercepted by the leaves and funnelled down branches and trunks to the spongy soil, where it is sucked up at once by thirsty roots to be recycled again and again.

The forest is a green city containing a wealth of different micro-habitats. The walls and roof of the forest are exposed to the full force of wind, rain and sun, but inside the air is still, dark and cool, and the atmosphere is saturated with moisture. From the base of the canopy to the ground 30m or more below is a still, shady world as different from the sunlit crowns and forest edge as a cave is different from a field.

With no autumn o winter to check their growth, tropical forest trees can flower at any time of the year – brightening the forest canopy with great splashes of colour and providing a year-round food resource for fruit, leaf and nectar feeders.

The tropical forests
Tropical rainforests and monsoon forests cover about 11 million square kilometres of the earth's surface and account for half the world's forested area. Of this total, about 40% is true rainforest, and this occurs in three main blocks. Central and South America hold the largest, with 56%; Southeast Asia and the Malay Archipelago account for about 26%; and the forests of West and Central Africa have the remaining 18%.

A system easily unbalanced

The warmth and moisture of the forest fuel the chemical reactions of life to run faster than in other habitats, and the process of decomposition is no exception. Every fragment of debris that falls to the ground is devoured by a host of decomposers, from ants and termites to microscopic bacteria, which rapidly break it down into its essential elements. If a plant is to tap these nutrients its roots must be as near the surface as possible or else some other shallow-rooted plant will get them first. In order to compete, trees of the tropical forest spread their roots in a dense mat just below the surface.

Between 75 and 90 per cent of the nutrients of a tropical forest are stored not in the soil but in the living plants, and this is why, when farmers clear the forest to grow crops, they can cultivate the land for only a season or two before the soil is exhausted. The soils of a tropical forest are not themselves productive; without the living forest they are among the most sterile on earth.

The shallow-rooted trees are supported partly by the trees around them, and are sheltered by them from the full force of the wind. At the edge of the forest, trees are deeper-rooted and act as a windbreak. When the forest edge is destroyed, the whole interior becomes vulnerable to storm damage.

The web of interdependence

Many of the animals and plants of tropical forests are linked together in complex inter-relationships. Many flowers are pollinated by particular kinds of bird, and may have fruits that are dispersed by other species. Some even have seeds that will not germinate until they have passed through a bird's intestine.

Many forest birds feed only on fruits, which supply them with all the food they need and are available all year round; some can obtain their entire day's food supply in a few minutes' foraging. Such birds, like the birds of paradise and bowerbirds of New Guinea and Australia, and the manakins and cotingas of the American tropics, can therefore devote most of their time to elaborate mating and territorial displays of astonishing complexity and beauty. Many South American species need a certain kind of fungus for the foundation of their nest, and line the nest with a grass for which they are probably the main agent of dispersal. Others use spiders' webs as a foundation and support.

The loss of one species from the forest can send shock-waves far and wide; for example, the loss of a spider might cause the disappearance of a bird that needed its web for its nest, and in turn cause the loss of the plants that the bird pollinated, or whose seeds it dispersed. Biologists used to think that the complexity of the tropical forest lent it great stability and resistance to change, but now they see how far-reaching the effects of interdependent relationships can be. The tropical forest as a whole is much more than the sum of its parts; the parts depend upon and influence each other to a degree unknown in other habitats, giving this complex but delicate ecosystem the fragility of a house of cards.

Food chains in tropical forests are more complex than those of any other habitat. Most of the larger mammals, reptiles and birds are known, but scientists have barely begun to catalogue the staggering variety of insect and plant life.

Almost synonymous with tropical forest – a tiny Violet-eared Hummingbird (*Colibri thalassinus*) pauses to feed at a large *Passiflora* flower in the forest of Guatemala.

A world of plenty

The larger trees of the tropical rainforest provide a lavish variety of niches that are exploited by many other plants and animals. The branches support whole communities of plants that live only there, never making contact with the ground. Bromeliads cluster on the larger trees like fantastic pineapple plants, supporting miniature communities of insects and frogs in the water trapped between their leaves. Hummingbirds feed on the nectar of their flowers, and other birds, like the Wild Pine Sergeant of Jamaica, on their microscopic pond-life. Lianes hang down from the branches, and mosses festoon the trees, creating a micro-habitat for specialized invertebrates that in turn attract insect-eating birds. Even the hollow cores of older, dead or dying trees are roosting and nesting sites for birds and bats.

A world upside down

Leaves are food for the herbivores of the forest, where primary production takes place high above the ground. The plant-eaters here are not ground-dwelling deer and antelopes but the insects, monkeys, apes and squirrels that live high in the maze of slender, swaying branches. Fruits provide food for squirrels, monkeys and bats and a wealth of brilliant birds, including pigeons, parrots, macaws, toucans, hornbills, tanagers, barbets and cotingas. Flowers attract nectar-sipping butterflies, moths and beetles, and brilliantly plumaged sunbirds, hummingbirds and honeycreepers.

Most of the forests' herbivores are insects that feed on leaves or on the stems or under the bark of trees. They in turn support insect-eating birds, each patrolling its own particular 'beat' within the forest. Warblers and vireos glean busily from the surfaces of leaves and twigs; woodcreepers and wood-hoopoes probe the nooks and crannies of the bark for hidden beetles, grubs and spiders; and woodpeckers dig into the wood itself in search of grubs.

A young Three-toed Sloth (*Bradypus tridactylus*) of the Brazilian Amazon, its thick coat characteristically stained green by the algae growing in it.

Sharp-eyed and alert, the Spot-backed Antbird (*Hylophylax naevia*) of South America specializes in hunting the large invertebrates flushed out of the forest floor leaf-litter by marching columns of army ants.

The tiny arrow-poison frog *Dendrobates auratus* of Panama is one of the many small creatures that live in the pools of water held by leaves.

A formidable array of hunters

Among the smaller predators, flycatchers sally forth from perches above, below and within the canopy, constantly darting after flying insects, while down on the forest floor, antbirds and ant-thrushes follow the battalions of army ants to pounce on the insects and small animals that scuttle in panic from the path of the all-devouring hordes.

At the higher levels of the forest food-web, hawks patrol by day and owls by night, feeding on frogs, lizards, snakes, birds and mammals. The ecological pyramid is crowned by the huge forest eagles – the Crowned Eagle of Africa, the Harpy of the tropical Americas and the Monkey-eating Eagle of Asia, each capable of carrying off a full-grown monkey and each requiring a vast territory over which to hunt.

Food for all seasons

Each kind of bird follows its own way of life secure in the predictability of an environment fashioned by aeons of evolution in the most benign conditions in the biosphere. For though the tropical forest does have its seasons they involve no drastic changes. They are enough to impose some seasonality on the annual cycles of birds so that they have seasons for breeding and moulting just as other birds do, but they are not enough to force birds to change their diet from one month to the next. Whereas a thrush in a temperate woodland has to forage at one time of year for caterpillars, at another for worms, another for berries and another for snails, in a tropical forest a different kind of thrush can specialize on each different diet because each is available all year round.

The rich diversity of life in a tropical forest is a reflection of the almost seasonless environment in which the forests grow, and which they themselves help to create and perpetuate.

The male Blue-crowned Manakin (*Pipra coronata*) performs his courtship display along with other males in a shared arena on the forest floor. Such complex behaviour is possible only in habitats so rich in food that a few moments' foraging can satisfy a bird's needs.

The Banded or Blue-tailed Pitta (*Pitta guajana*) inhabits the dark forest floor of Thailand, West Malaysia and the Greater Sunda Islands. The bird feeds on leaf-litter insects and despite its bright colouring is very hard to find.

Butterflies often cluster together on tracks and in dry stream beds. The adults need extra nitrogen for egg-formation, and this they get from the damp ground, where a passing animal has urinated.

Blue Bird of Paradise: Virtuoso performer of the forest

Fruit-eating forest birds have such a dependable supply of food that they can devote much of their time to patrolling their home ranges and attracting mates. Over countless generations, competition between males to attract females has led to the evolution of increasingly bizarre and beautiful adornments and spectacular displays, which reach their most extreme development in the birds of paradise of New Guinea and Australia.

In most species the males are brilliantly coloured and have some groups of feathers elongated or otherwise specialized as adornments which are shown off in display. The males pose and strut on high branches and perform elaborate ritual dances, either silently or accompanied by a few harsh calls. But the male Blue Bird of Paradise (*Paradisaea rudolphi*) takes his display to spectacular extremes. He displays *upside down,* hanging from a branch and swaying very gently back and forth, accompanying himself with an extraordinary penetrating mechanical whirring like the engine of some extraterrestrial machine. His main adornments are plumes of brilliant blue sprouting from tufts of reddish-brown feathers on each side of the breast, and two slender tail feathers like long black ribbons, tipped bright blue. Like most of his kind, his plumage is generally blackish, so he is hard to see in the

Early morning mist fills a deep valley in the central highlands of New Guinea, habitat of many of the most spectacular birds of paradise.

forest until he reveals his rich colours in display. Much of the colour of his feathers is iridescent, caused by the physical structure of the feathers rather than by their pigments, and is most strikingly shown off by the rhythmic swaying movements that the male makes in display. As the light catches the feathers at subtly changing angles, they shimmer and flash with an exotic metallic brilliance that no mere pigments could match. Even two small but striking patches of white above and below the eye are expanded, leaving the bird only a narrow slit to peer through.

Remarkably little is known about this superb bird; even its extraordinary display has rarely been seen. The female is duller-coloured than the male and does not share his ornate plumes and tail-feathers. She displays by bobbing rapidly up and down. The Blue is almost certainly polygamous, as are most birds of paradise, and each female lays one egg, coloured cream with brown and grey streaks, in an unlined basin-shaped nest of screwpine leaves and palm-leaf fibres in a low tree. The Blue is confined to the mid-level tropical forests of eastern New Guinea, between about 1100 and 2000 metres above sea level. At lower altitudes it is replaced by the Raggiana Bird of Paradise (*P. raggiana*), a close relative with a yellow head, rich maroon back and tail, and an enormous train of orange flank-feathers. The Raggiana is better equipped than the Blue to exist in forest country that has been settled and cultivated. The latter is confined to intact forest, and is becoming increasingly rare.

The exceptional beauty of the Blue Bird of Paradise is one of several good reasons for regretting its increasing scarcity, and is also one of several causes of its decline. All the richly ornamented species of the family suffered in the nineteenth and early twentieth century at the hands of the same bird-plume trade that dealt savage blows to populations of egrets and other birds burdened with natural beauty. That trade, originating from the wealthy western world, added an extra toll to the steady attrition of birds of paradise at the hands of the indigenous people of New Guinea, who hunted them with bows and arrows, primarily for plumes with which to decorate their elaborate head-dresses. This traditional hunting has been going on for centuries, but now it is often carried out with modern firearms, and birds are being taken from a population already greatly reduced by the loss of habitat to agriculture.

Feathers taken from birds of paradise and many other brightly coloured forest species are used in the ornate head-dresses worn by the tribesmen of Papua New Guinea.

A fledgling Blue Bird of Paradise, brought to a scientific research base in the highlands of Papua New Guinea. The parents had either deserted the young bird or been taken by feather hunters.

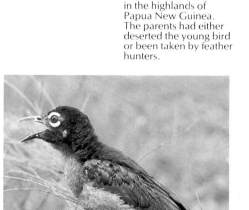

Birds of Paradise:
Legendary sun-birds of New Guinea

Until European travellers set foot on New Guinea, birds of paradise were known only from feathers of incredible beauty that came from the East. Their mysterious appearance, and the fact that specimen skins usually had their legs removed, encouraged fanciful ideas that the birds came from the sun, or from Paradise.

The fate of these legendary birds has been closely linked with mankind, certainly for hundreds of years and probably for the tens of thousands since their forests were first colonized by people. Almost all the 43 species have at least a patch of brilliant colour, a vivid wattle or an unusually shaped adornment, and more than 25 have ornamentation so bizarre that they are exceptional among birds.

Such a concentration of spectacular beauty in one family of birds, in one of the remotest parts of the inhabited earth, has fascinated men for centuries. For a time the plumes were more valuable than gold, and from the time of European settlement in New Guinea in the sixteenth century until the worldwide trade in bird plumes was stopped in the 1920s, a vigorous trade flourished throughout the Papuan region. At its height at least 80,000 skins left New Guinea each year. For many years these skins were the only source of cash income for European settlers struggling to establish plantations in a largely hostile environment.

Yet it would be wrong to think of the European influence as the birds' main link with mankind. The indigenous people of New Guinea had prized the birds' plumes for generations as the most spectacular components of huge and elaborate head-dresses worn by the men on ceremonial occasions.

New Guinea islanders – or Papuans – were among the most warlike tribes in existence; in some clans a boy could not achieve the social status of manhood until he had killed a man. Yet their appreciation of the beauty of birds of paradise, and their skill in weaving the plumes into artefacts of breathtaking beauty, shows a highly developed aesthetic sense. They show a complete knowledge of the birds' habits in tracking down the display sites of the males and approaching close enough to shoot them with three- or four-pronged arrows. In some cases, ownership of a traditional display site is considered to belong to the man who owns the tree itself; in the Wahgi valley, for example, the brilliant red-plumed male Raggiana Birds of Paradise display on trees whose owners are as much the 'owners' of the birds as they are of the trees on which they display.

Birds of Paradise
There are 43 species of Bird of Paradise in Papua New Guinea. The four illustrated here can only hint at their spectacular variety of form and colour.

1. White-billed Sicklebill (*Drepanornis bruijnii*)
2. Ribbon-tailed Astrapia (*Astrapia mayeri*)
3. Long-tailed Paradigalla (*Paradigalla carunculata*)
4. Macgregor's Bird of Paradise (*Macgregoria pulchra*)

How is it that there are any birds of paradise left at all, if they have been hunted for thousands of years by Papuans and slaughtered on an even greater scale by Europeans for several hundred years? For although the Blue Bird of Paradise is, as we have seen, in real danger of extinction, most species are not; and the Blue seems to be threatened more by the loss of its habitat than by hunting alone. Some of the species whose plumes are most popular with Papuans are still among the most common. Probably only the Blue, Macgregor's and Black Sickle-billed Birds of Paradise are threatened by hunting at present, though more may become so as Papuans turn from their traditional bows and arrows to modern firearms.

The birds' resilience lies in their social structure. In the most gorgeously plumaged species males take five to ten years to reach sexual maturity, and for that time they are dull-coloured like the females. Before they can breed they must obtain a display site, and this may entail contests with rival males. At any one time, relatively few adult males hold display sites; the rest of the population waits on the sidelines, the females assessing the relative splendour of the displaying males while the young males wait their turn to mature. It seems that they cannot attain their full finery until they can occupy a display site so, when a fully-plumaged male is killed by a hunter there is always a young or surplus male ready to moult into full plumage and take his place.

Not all species have a reserve of males. In Macgregor's Bird of Paradise (*Macgregoria pulchra*) the sexes are alike and lack plumes, and they share in raising the young – unlike the plumed species which are polygamous and in which the female raises the young alone. Such monogamous species are very vulnerable to a selective cull of the males, and the population of Macgregor's Bird of Paradise has been seriously depleted through being hunted for food.

A male Emperor Bird of Paradise (*P. guilielmi*) in his initial display – bobbing up and down and flicking his wings before swinging round underneath the perch with his magnificent tail plumes fanned open.

A native hunter with a 'bag' of four Raggiana Birds of Paradise (*P. raggiana*) taken in the forests of the Aru Islands, Indonesia.

Bowerbirds:
Avian artists and architects

Side by side with the birds of paradise lives another exotic family of birds whose response to the same environmental conditions is without parallel in any other group of animals. The bowerbirds of New Guinea and Australia build dance halls, decorate them with ornaments, paint them with brushes loaded with pigment, and create gardens around them.

The bowers of the Vogelkop Gardener Bowerbird (*Amblyornis inornatus*) can be as large as 2.5m long, 2m deep and 1.4m high; large enough to be mistaken for man-made structures. They are called bowers because they are used solely as display grounds by the males: the actual nest is built in a tree some distance away by the female, who rears the young alone. A female looking for a mate visits the bower, and is courted there by the male with a vigour and variety of behaviour that few other birds can match. In some species the visual effects of the bower are supplemented by a versatile exhibition of vocal mimicry, the male imitating bird calls and other sounds of the forest with extraordinary accuracy.

The ornaments which decorate the bowers vary from species to species and from place to place. In remote forests they are natural objects – snail-shells, flowers, moss, insect fragments and brightly coloured fruits; closer to villages they include shotgun cartridges, film cartons, buttons and plastic bottle tops. Within each group of species building a particular type of bower there is some tendency for the species with the most brightly endowed males to build simple bowers with little decoration, and for those with less spectacular adornments to build more elaborate and richly decorated bowers. This tendency, and the males' habit of offering a decoration (often an edible fruit) to a female during his display, suggests how these extraordinary mating habits might

have evolved. In many birds the male feeds the female during courtship, and this 'courtship feeding' is important in cementing the relationship between the birds, in overcoming the female's fear of the aggressive male, and often in helping the female obtain the extra food she needs to lay her eggs. Brightly coloured birds displaying on the ground – as bowerbirds and some birds of paradise do – are very vulnerable to predators. Perhaps transferring the bright colours to other objects enables a male to be less conspicuous.

Two species of this remarkable family have small isolated populations that are vulnerable. Archbold's Bowerbird (*Archboldia papuensis papuensis*) and Sanford's Bowerbird (*A. p. sanfordi*) are each confined to a few localities in the highland forests of New Guinea, where Sanford's is particularly threatened by timber operations. This extraordinary family of avian architects and artists can surely tell us something of the origin of aesthetics; that any of them should become extinct through human neglect is surely unthinkable.

Artists of the forest floor
Of the 18 species in this family, 14 are bower-builders, and the structures they build are of three kinds. Archbold's Bowerbird builds a simple flat platform on which to display. Five species build a 'maypole' with a central pillar and surrounding moat or cleared display area. The eight species remaining construct avenues of varying complexity, with decorated pathways enclosed between high 'fences' of interwoven sticks and grasses.

1. Macgregor's Bowerbird (*Amblyornis macgregoriae*)
2. Yellow-fronted Bowerbird (*Amblyornis flavifrons*)
3. Golden Bowerbird (*Prionodura newtoniana*)
4. Vogelkop Gardener Bowerbird (*Amblyornis inornatus*)

Maleo:
Easy prey for the nest robbers

Most birds incubate their eggs with the heat of their own bodies or, like cuckoos, that of other birds they have deceived into fostering their eggs. But the Megapodes — the mound-builders or 'incubator birds' of Southeast Asia and Australia — use the inanimate heat of their environment. Some species build a compost-heap of rotting vegetation in which the female lays her eggs, and whose temperature the male controls by adjusting the amount of overlying vegetation. Others, like the Maleo (*Macrocephalon maleo*) of the island of Sulawesi (formerly Celebes) in Indonesia, lay their eggs in sand heated by hot springs, volcanic gases, or by the sun.

Maleos are birds of the lowland rainforest, where they live on invertebrates and fallen fruit. In the breeding season they move to the few areas of hot sand between 32° and 38°C, mostly on sea beaches, where they dig as deep as one metre to lay their eggs. These hatch about 78 days later and the chicks struggle unaided to the surface. There, the secret of their long incubation period is revealed; the young are so advanced that they can immediately take flight into the comparative safety of the forest.

But Maleo eggs are large and tasty, and a high proportion are dug up and eaten by monitor lizards, Sulawesi pigs and macaque monkeys. Local people have also traditionally harvested the eggs, adding human predation to an already substantial loss to wild animals. Over the past 40 years some populations have become extinct and others have been reduced by 90 per cent or more. The species is protected by law, but not very effectively, though it would be perfectly feasible, with good management, to harvest a proportion of the eggs and still maintain the population. The birds' feeding grounds in lowland forest need proper conservation and strict protection from over-cropping, and artificial incubation of eggs and management of the nesting habitat are also essential if these extraordinary birds are to survive.

An adult Maleo on one of the few remaining breeding beaches on the island of Sulawesi.

Maleos lay their eggs up to 1m deep in the hot sand, which acts as a natural incubator. After 78 days the chicks emerge, fully developed and ready to fly to the safety of the forest.

Natives mark the Maleo nests with sticks, and harvest the eggs as soon as the adult birds return to the forest. If these rare birds are to survive, the laws that theoretically protect them must be strictly enforced.

Kagu:
Pushed back by the colonists

The black tropical nights of New Caledonia once resounded to a shrill yelping bird call that carried up to two kilometres through the forest. The bird that made it was a fitting resident of these unique and ancient forests, a relict of the fauna of ten million years ago. New Caledonia is a fragment of the Australasian continent that became detached long ago, drifting out into the western Pacific Ocean with a captive 'cargo' of plants and animals. While those on the mainland either succumbed or adapted to the challenges of immigrant species, the inhabitants of the New Caledonian forests were isolated and protected in their floating time-capsule. The forests retain a high proportion of species of plants and animals that are found nowhere else, and give us a glimpse of the tropical forests of ten million years ago.

The Kagu (*Rhynochetos jubatus*) is so special, so different from any other bird, that it is hard to recognize its closest relatives among other living birds and it is usually classified in a family of its own, related to the rails and the Sun Bittern. It is a little larger and more long-legged than a domestic chicken,

rather like a squat heron in appearance, and lives now in the remote dense forest of the mountains of New Caledonia, about 1000km east of northern Australia. Kagus were once much more common and more widely distributed there, but human colonists — Melanesians first, followed in the mid-nineteenth century by European settlers — brought rats, pigs, cats and dogs into the forest and drove the Kagu before them.

Kagus nest on the ground and are flightless. They are hunted with dogs, which also kill them when they are supposed to be hunting deer; and during their wartime occupation of New Caledonia, Japanese soldiers snared and trapped considerable numbers of the birds. Their forest habitat — every bit as unique as the Kagus themselves — is diminishing in the face of felling for timber and agriculture, and nickel mining, which is of course a valuable source of revenue but also extremely destructive of the forest.

The relict forests of New Caledonia provide a living record of the forests of ten million years ago. They are as unique, as important and as threatened as the Kagus they shelter.

The plight of the Kagu highlights the problems of endemic island birds facing habitat destruction and predation by aliens. Without urgent conservation measures, captive specimens could soon be the sole survivors of their kind.

The Sun Bittern (*Eurypyga helias*), pictured here in its spectacular display, is probably one of the few close relatives of the Kagu. It is a resident of the dense tropical riverine forests of South America.

Kagus are attractive birds and in addition to their distinctive calls have a spectacular display in which the wings are spread and fanned. The displaying bird then looks very like a Sun Bittern, whose wing-fanning display also shows off a similar barred wing-pattern. They have long been in demand by bird-keepers; they can live 20 to 30 years in captivity, and there is a steady demand for them by zoos and aviculturalists and by local people wanting to keep them at home.

Their main food consists of snails, earthworms and other invertebrates found in the leaf-litter and soil of the forest floor. They have a special way of dealing with snails; they crack the shell around the middle with a blow of the heavy bill, then pick up the snail by the body and shake the shell loose. Earthworms, sometimes as much as 40cm long, are pulled gently from the soft soil and usually emerge intact. The pigs that run loose in the forest root up the soil and litter, destroying the habitat for the Kagu's food. Cover for the birds is damaged by the browsing of introduced Sambar Deer, and the forest itself is being steadily reduced by frequent and widespread burning, and by wholesale clearance by mining companies.

Although hunting for Kagu is now forbidden by law, enforcement is weak, and protection of the habitat and eradication of alien predators and browsers may well be more important in their conservation.

Kagus do breed in captivity, so some will probably survive the extinction of the wild population. They can still be found in the remoter forests of New Caledonia, but they will probably continue to decline there unless a vigorous programme is enforced very soon, aimed at conserving the habitat as well as the birds. As a flightless relict in a remote island forest, the Kagu is as nearly equivalent to a Dodo as anything in the modern world. Have we learned enough, in the 400 years since the last Dodo died, not to repeat that mindless crime?

Helmeted Hornbill: Threatened by loss of its habitat

The Helmeted Hornbill's scientific name, *Rhinoplax vigil,* embodies two of the bird's most distinctive characteristics; the huge casque on the bill, like a horizontal rhinoceros' horn, and the great vigilance with which the birds keep out of harm's way in the dense canopy of the forest. A less wary bird could not long survive with such an adornment, for the casque is made of ivory, as valuable as elephant tusk or rhinoceros horn.

Hornbill ivory was known as 'Ho-ting' by the ancient Chinese, who valued it more highly than elephant's ivory, jade, and even gold. They imported it from the forest people of Borneo and Sumatra, who had long worked it into beautiful and delicate ornaments of a beautiful golden colour. In life both the casque and the bill are coloured a deep red. The pigment is the avian equivalent of make-up, an oily secretion from the preen gland at the base of the tail, which the bird wipes directly on to its bill and casque. The Helmeted Hornbill shares the lowland forests of Indonesia and Malaysia with the Rhinoceros Hornbill, and both species are important in the mythology and traditions of the forest people, especially in Borneo.

The heavily ridged bill of Blythe's Hornbill (*Aceros plicatus*) used an an adornment, along with the tusks of a wild pig, by a tribesman of the Hali tribe of Papua New Guinea. In China, the bills of these birds were once more highly treasured than gold.

Hornbills are the Old World equivalent of the toucans of the New World, but in addition to their grotesquely long, deep, curved bill many hornbills have a large casque on top of the bill — outwardly like that of the Helmeted Hornbill but filled with light 'honeycomb' material rather than being of solid ivory. The Helmeted Hornbill is the only bird that produces ivory, so the species is of special interest to scientists as well as to the forest people in whose culture it has figured so prominently for thousands of years. In spite of its cumbersome appearance, the heavily weighted bill is clearly a very useful tool. It enables the bird to reach out to fruits that would otherwise be hanging out of reach, and to catch and quickly subdue more lively prey such as squirrels and small birds. It also makes an effective pick-axe for digging into wood to reach insects, and for excavating nest holes.

The Helmeted Hornbill shares the bizarre nesting habits of most hornbills. The female lays her egg in a cavity in a tree and then walls up the entrance hole with a mixture of mud and saliva which sets rock-hard when it dries. She leaves a narrow slit, just wide enough for the male to pass food through to her in the tip of his bill. And there she sits — for up to three and a half months — while her egg develops and hatches and her chick grows big enough to leave the nest. She moults all her feathers while incarcerated, and overcomes the obvious sanitary problems partly by casting pellets, partly by defaecating through the narrow entrance slit, with astonishing accuracy, and partly with the aid of a specialized community of scavenging insects. Each pair raises only one young, which stays with its parents for two or three years. They do not breed again until their offspring leaves to join a roaming group of other juveniles.

Helmeted Hornbills prefer primary forest and eat many small animals as well as wild figs, which ripen sporadically and often at widely scattered places. Like most really large animals (they are over 1.2m long and weigh over 3kg) they need a very large area to live in. Pairs defend a territory of 300-500ha, declaring their ownership with a bizarre hooting call that gets faster and faster until it ends in peals of cackling 'laughter' from both birds.

Some species of hornbill can be found in forest that has been logged, and give the impression that they can survive there as easily as in primary forest. Often, however, they have simply flown in to a fruiting tree, and may not be able to live there permanently — especially as suitable large nesting trees are unlikely to have been left standing. Loss of habitat is now an acute threat to the Helmeted Hornbill. Most primary forest in Sumatra and Borneo has already been allotted to lumber contractors, and lowland forest is disappearing faster in this bird's range than anywhere else in the world.

The beak of the Rhinoceros Hornbill (*Buceros rhinoceros*) is made of ivory like the tusk of an elephant. In this immature bird the characteristic casque is already beginning to develop along the top of the massive bill.

Grey-necked Rockfowl: Safe — but for how long?

Tropical forests are so rich and complex that they can contain within them other habitats so distinctive and self-contained that they appear to function independently of the forest that surrounds them. Caves in the forests of West Africa support rich communities of insects, snakes and bats, and a rare bird which lives most of its life inside the caves.

These caves too are rare. They are found only in rocks rich in iron ore, in hilly country covered in primary forest. They are surrounded by dense thickets within the forest, and all have a stream flowing through them, which raises the humidity to near 100 per cent and helps to maintain a characteristically moist environment. Perhaps the most important members of the cave community are the bats, usually of four species and present in such vast numbers that in the largest colony of rockfowl, in Gabon, it takes three and a half hours for the cave to empty of bats every evening. The bats are prey to Bat Hawks, which patrol the cave entrance during the short period of dusk when there are bats to catch and still light to see them by. The hordes of bats produce a steady rain of detritus on to the floor of the cave, and this supports vast numbers of insects — including a giant species of cockroach found nowhere else.

The exquisitely delicate colours of the Grey-necked Rockfowl (*Picathartes oreas*) disappear as the bird steps gracefully out of the sunlight into the darkness of the cave. Each pair returns to the cave to spend the middle of the day roosting, often on an old nest under an overhang in the interior of the cave. The birds move mostly in pairs, taking little notice of any other inhabitants of the cave except for the insects, on which they feed and which, in their turn, feed on the accumulated bat guano.

Each morning and afternoon the birds leave the cave to feed in the forest nearby, bounding restlessly after their prey of small invertebrates and constantly jumping or flying up on to roots and fallen tree-trunks. Outside the cave they are usually silent and appear harassed and furtive, but when alarmed, the whole neck swells up as they give a deep, unbirdlike, growl. They return frequently to the cave, and in the breeding season spend very little time outside it.

In March or April they lay two speckled eggs, much more brightly coloured than those of other cave-dwelling birds. The nests, built under an overhang, are made of red mud and are reinforced with grass in the same way that local tribespeople build the walls of their huts. They may last for several years, relined and repaired as necessary. Little more is known of the rockfowls' breeding habits; the sites of breeding colonies are often very remote and hard to reach, and have not encouraged detailed research.

Unfortunately the breeding colonies are not sufficiently remote to deter collectors for zoos and private bird collections. The rockfowl population is so small that collectors catering even to this relatively small and exclusive market can exert a harmful effect. The largest known colony holds only 10 birds, and the breeding sites are so distinctive that most are well known to the local people. The species occurs mainly in Cameroon, with a few sites in Gabon.

About 1100km to the west a sister species, the White-necked Rockfowl, lives a similarly sheltered life in caves and along rocky cliffs from Guinea in the west, through Sierra Leone, Liberia, Ivory Coast and Ghana to Togo in the east. Both species of rockfowl have bare heads with brightly coloured skin that seems oddly out of place in the darkness of a cave. The function of these colours remains as mysterious as the relationships of the birds themselves. Few other small birds have bare heads, or the peculiarly loose plumage that rockfowl share with a few species of forest babblers. Rockfowl have been classified variously as crows, starlings or babblers, birds so different from each other that attempts to link the rockfowl with them show just how special the rockfowl is.

Both species may be able to withstand a limited amount of collecting for zoos and aviaries, but this remains to be proved. Their extremely specialized habitat may also protect them to some extent from the destruction of the forest that proceeds apace through almost all of West Africa except Gabon. Yet even this protection, if real, could be only temporary; for the water that flows through their caves, and the dense thickets that shade the surroundings, are ultimately dependent on the survival of the forest itself.

Like its relative in Cameroon and Gabon, the White-necked Rockfowl (*P. gymnocephalus*) of West Africa is represented in several major zoos. But the captive breeding record is poor: only determined conservation efforts will ensure the species' survival.

A Grey-necked Rockfowl on its nest of mud and grass, plastered onto the dripping rock wall of a cave in the tropical hill forest of Gabon.

Kupe and Uluguru Bush-shrikes: Africa's elusive mountain shrikes

On opposite sides of Africa, shrinking forests shelter remnant populations of two species of bush-shrike that have evaded searching ornithologists for decades. Both species are handsome birds, medium sized but chunky, with the large head and heavy hook-tipped bill typical of shrikes. Both are greenish above: the western species on Kupe Mountain (*Malaconotus kupeensis*) is grey below with a striking white throat, black stripe through the eye, and grey crown; its counterpart in the Uluguru Mountains of East Africa (*M. alius*) is yellow on the breast and throat with a greenish belly and a glossy black crown that accounts for its alternative name of Black-cap Bush-shrike.

Mount Kupe is an isolated peak in Cameroon. That part of Africa holds one of the richest bird faunas in the continent, but also one of the most immediately threatened. Forest is being cleared so fast that many mountain tops formerly rich in forest are now degraded bush and grassland, and the remaining patches of forest on isolated mountains like Kupe are islands in a sea of cultivation. Kupe Mountain's endemic bush-shrike was first found there in 1949 and has only once been seen since – in 1951 when scientists reported seeing a group of three. Its nest, food and habits are unknown, and unless the forest on Kupe is conserved there can be little hope that the species will ever be rediscovered.

There is more hope for the Uluguru species. A few Black-cap Bush-shrikes were collected at one site on the eastern side of the mountains between 1947 and 1962, but for the next 19 years successive expeditions failed to find any. The Uluguru Mountains are in eastern Tanzania, where population pressures are rather less intense than in West Africa, but the forest is under considerable threat nonetheless. However, in 1981 two birds were seen and their very distinctive call was positively identified. The call was later heard in several other parts of the forest, suggesting that the birds may still be quite widespread though they are very hard to see in the topmost layers of the canopy.

The Mount Kupe Bush Shrike was discovered in 1949, but since then has been seen only once – in 1951. This painting by Norman Arlott is one of the very few illustrations ever made of this bird.

Part of the summit area of the Uluguru Mountains falls within a forest reserve, so providing at least some protection to the locally endemic bush-shrike, whose habitat has been greatly reduced by felling.

224

Madagascar Ground-rollers: Migrants to an unknown destination

The forests of the island continent of Madagascar harbour a unique bird fauna that has evolved in isolation since Madagascar separated from India and Africa about 70 million years ago. Much of that avifauna is now extinct, and the rest is gravely threatened by the destruction of its ancient rainforest habitat.

Some of the least known and most specialized of Madagascar's endemic forest birds are the ground-rollers, a small subfamily of five species closely related to the true rollers of Africa and Asia. True rollers are named after the acrobatic somersaults they perform in their aerial courtship display; the ground-rollers, in contrast, are largely terrestrial and though their displays have not been described they must be quite unlike those of true rollers. Four members of the ground-roller family are confined to Madagascar's rainforests, and one to its arid semi-desert.

The forest species are all beautifully patterned in blue, green, buff and chestnut. They run and stand much like thrushes, and take flight on their whirring stubby wings only when disturbed. They feed on insects, spiders, small reptiles and amphibians on the bare ground beneath the very densest shade of the forest.

Ground-rollers apparently lay their eggs in a tunnel dug in the soil of a bank, or in a tree-hole. Malgache natives maintain that ground-rollers hibernate, but this story — reminiscent of the belief in eighteenth-century Europe that swallows hibernated in mud — probably springs, like that myth, from an ignorance of the phenomenon of migration. But where the birds go, and why, is as much a mystery to us now as swallow migration was two hundred years ago.

Madagascar's ground-rollers are just one example of the many threatened forest birds of that magical and mysterious island continent. The once rich and exotic forests, whose flora and fauna have a higher proportion of endemics than any other continent, have been devastated since mankind colonized the continent only 1400 to 1600 years ago.

The Long-tailed Ground Roller (*Uratelornis chimaera*) is restricted to small areas of dry deciduous woodland and semi-desert scrub in the southwest of Madagascar.

Huge erosion scars and a mud-laden river show the extent of soil loss following forestry operations in Madagascar. The light green trees dotting the hilltop landscape are Travellers' Palms (*Ravenalia* sp.) — a clear indication of secondary forest, the new growth that is replacing the felled primary forest.

Resplendent Quetzal:
Living echoes of a lost civilization

The clouds that shroud tropical forests at higher altitudes create a distinctive habitat known simply as cloud-forest, which is recognizable throughout the tropics and has its own distinct communities of plants and birds. The cool climate, abundant water, and soils that are generally more fertile than those found at lower altitudes, have encouraged human settlement and agriculture. The pre-Columbian peoples of Central America populated their cloud-forests quite densely, and venerated one of its birds with such religious passion that the bird was valued more highly than gold.

The Resplendent Quetzal (*Pharomachrus mocinno*) is surely one of the worlds's most beautiful birds, and the metre-long train of brilliant green feathers that the male trails behind him was long ago incorporated in the plumed serpent Quetzalcoatl, a deity worshipped by the Aztec and Maya Indians. Such a gorgeous bird might seem very vulnerable to predators, but though the colours glow brilliantly in full sunlight, Quetzals live in cloud-forest which is normally overcast. Their leaf-green upper-parts are perfect camouflage and they take care to keep them facing intruders. They sit very still and upright on a high branch, normally 23m or more above the ground, occasionally turning the head from side to side. They feed by darting out to pluck a fruit or an insect or occasionally a lizard or frog from the canopy, or to take flying insects in mid-air.

Males patrol their home range of six to ten hectares at dawn and dusk, calling repeatedly from favourite tree-top perches. They keep to the upper one-third of the canopy, but in the breeding season they often have to descend lower as the nest is built in a rotten tree-stump 4 to 24m high, in which the birds dig out a nest cavity. Wood soft enough to excavate a nest in is rare, and suitable trees are vulnerable to earthquakes, lightning, wind storms, wood-cutters and honey-hunters. The female lays two plain blue eggs, normally between March and June in highland Guatemala, and both birds share the task of incubating.

Quetzals occur throughout the cloud-forests of Central America at altitudes above about 1500m. But within this extensive range they are now rarely found in forests that are used and visited by people. The cultural and religious values placed on them by the pre-Columbian Indians have survived sufficiently strongly for the birds still to be hunted locally for feathers, which are used in religious ceremonies. In addition, the sheer beauty of the bird makes it very attractive to bird-fanciers throughout the world, who keep up a steady demand for the export of live birds.

The Quetzal has become the national symbol of Guatemala. It is commemorated in the name of the unit of currency, whose coins bear its image, and the highest civic honour is the Order of the Quetzal. However, the state's recognition of the part the birds have played in the nation's heritage has backfired as a conservation measure by encouraging people to keep captive Quetzals as a patriotic gesture.

The shimmering metre-long tail plumes of the breeding male Resplendent Quetzal were used in the religious ceremonies of both Aztec and Maya civilizations. The bird was worshipped as the god of the air, and was closely associated with the god Quetzalcoatl.

Quetzals are by no means the rarest species in tropical cloud-forests. Many other birds are threatened at least as seriously, and some considerably more so. But the Quetzal serves well as a symbol of the problems afflicting the whole community of cloud-forest birds. Most of the traditions and beliefs of the Aztecs and Mayas died with their civilization under the swords of the *conquistadores* 400 years ago; but the Quetzal, both as a cultural symbol and as a living thing of extraordinary beauty, lives on in its remote forest fortress. The Quetzal and the remnants of the human culture with which it has been so intimately involved are now threatened by the destruction of the habitat they have shared for centuries.

Quetzalcoatl – the Plumed Serpent – represented in stone on the walls of the Temple of Quetzalcoatl at Teotihuacan in Mexico.

Guayaquil Great Green Macaw: Endangered by its own popularity

The lowland forests of tropical South and Central America owe much of their place in the popular imagination as the tropical forests *par excellence* to the spectacular flights of brilliantly coloured macaws. Their raucous calls and distinctive flight pattern are evocative of the forest itself.

Macaws are large, long-tailed members of the parrot family, confined to South and Central America. They are the largest members of the family, and the Great Green (or Buffon's) Macaw (*Ara ambigua guayaquilensis*), at 85cm, is one of the largest. The birds live in the lowland tropical forests of southern Central and northwestern South America, and are divided into two quite separate populations. The southern race, the Guayaquil Great Green Macaw of western Ecuador, is now very scarce and may even be restricted to the Chongon Hills near Guayaquil. The northern race, for many years believed to be reasonably common in parts of Central America, is now also thought to be threatened.

Parrots are among the most distinctive of all birds. The deep, short, hooked bill, the thick tongue, and the strong rough-scaled grasping feet with two toes pointing forward and two back, are used to break into the toughest nuts and to climb about the birds' feeding and nesting trees. They are well known, too, for their apparent intelligence, legendary longevity, and the ability of many species to imitate a remarkable range of sounds – including human speech.

In spite of the fact that very few of us ever see one of this tropical family in the wild, parrots are familiar to all of us because we are used to seeing them in captivity. Their intelligence, long life, vegetarian diet, bright colours, large size, and amusing 'conversation' have made them the world's most popular cage-birds. But this very popularity now constitutes one of the biggest threats they have ever faced. Combined with the accelerating loss of habitat in the wild, the cage-bird trade threatens many macaws with extinction.

Parrots, whether the small budgerigars of Australia or the large macaws of South America, are favourite cage-birds all over the world. Unfortunately, many rare species are now threatened by the thriving and often illegal international trade in wild birds.

One serious problem with controlling the cage-bird trade is that a number of endangered species are very similar to others that are still quite abundant, and are easily mistaken for them by enforcement officers, and indeed by dealers. Many specialists could not tell a caged Guayaquil Great Green from a Great Green, and both races are very similar to the Military Macaw (*A. militaris*), which is much more widespread and abundant. Similarly, the Scarlet Macaw (*A. macao*) – perhaps the most familiar of all its kind – has declined alarmingly and commands huge prices, but some still slip through the legislative net as Green-winged Macaws (*A. chloroptera*), which are almost identical to the untutored eye.

Macaws are large and tasty as well as beautiful, and are still shot for food. Amid such a barrage of potential threats it is hard to pick out one as the most important, but in the long term the loss of its forest habitat is probably the greatest danger on the Green Macaw's horizon. A thriving population in a healthy habitat could probably withstand a reasonable harvest for food, and even for the cage-bird trade; but when those pressures are inflicted on a population already declining through loss of habitat there is little chance that the race can survive. A further problem is that the birds live for so long. Although this is in one way an advantage, in that it gives adults many years in which to recover from losses, it can also be a drawback because it can disguise low breeding output for many years. For as long as plenty of birds are seen flying around, people believe the species is in good shape, even though the birds are not breeding. By the time the decline of adults is evident it may be too late to reverse the trend. The gloomy prospect that is faced now by the Guayaquil race of the Green Macaw is one that will soon be faced by its sister race – and eventually by most other species of these most spectacular and widely loved birds.

Dense luxuriant rainforest on the slopes of the Andes in western Ecuador is the original habitat of the Guayaquil Great Green Macaw.

The pheasants of Asia:
Safe in captivity — threatened in the wild

The domestic fowl is one of mankind's most important sources of food. It is descended from the Red Jungle Fowl (*Gallus gallus*), a native of tropical Asian forests which shares parts of its range with several other species of the pheasant family. Some of these are among the most beautiful, least known, and perhaps most endangered of all forest birds.

Pheasants are terrestrial birds; they feed and nest on the ground, flying up into trees only to roost or to escape sudden disturbance. They are strong-legged birds with long toes and claws, which they use for scratching their food out of the soil. Many species also have sharp spurs on the legs, especially in the males. In most species the males are much more beautiful than the females and, like birds of paradise, spend much time in display and mate polygamously. In these species the females are camouflaged in obscure browns and greys to protect them while they incubate and raise the young alone. The chicks are well advanced when they hatch, and can soon run after the female and even fly up into trees to roost within a few days of hatching.

Several closely related species of the tropical Asian forests are seriously endangered. All belong to the genus *Lophura*, the so-called 'gallopheasants'. The Imperial Pheasant (*L. imperialis*) was discovered as recently as 1923, in the rugged interior hills of Vietnam. A single pair was brought into captivity in Europe and bred for several years. However, their descendants were crossed with other species, and much of the remaining stock is therefore of hybrid origin. The bird is hardly known at all in the wild; its range coincides most unfortunately with the former border between North and South Vietnam, which was heavily sprayed with defoliating chemicals during the Vietnam war. The pheasants are likely to have suffered both directly through poisoning and indirectly through loss of their habitat, but their present status is unknown.

The same inhospitable region is shared by a very similar species, Edwards's Pheasant (*L. edwardsi*), which has been known longer than the Imperial but was always shy and hard to see in the wild. None were seen between 1895, when the first skins were collected, and 1925, when live birds were first imported into Europe. There have been several reports of their fate during the war, one reporting them commoner in the secondary forest that sprang up after the primary forest was killed, another that some

The handsome Red Jungle Fowl (*Gallus gallus*) is the ancestor of all the world's domestic fowl. It lives in the dense sal and teak forests of the Himalayan foothills and also in dense stands of bamboo, but often moves out into scrubland, rice paddies and other cultivated areas to feed on grain, bamboo shoots, fruit and insects.

The devastating effect of 'Agent Orange' — one of the defoliating chemicals widely used to destroy the forest cover during the war in Vietnam.

were shot for food by American troops. Their true status in the wild remains unknown, but they are well established in captivity. The male's display is characteristic of this group of pheasants, though it is one of the simplest. The white crest is raised, the back feathers fluffed out and the wings whirred rapidly while the male parades around the female.

Swinhoe's Pheasant (*L. swinhoii*), which is confined to the island of Taiwan (Formosa), is an altogether more dramatic bird with a more spectacular display. The white feathers of the back and tail are raised, and the red face-wattles erected while the male bobs his head up and down, jumps erratically around and whirs his wings. It has been bred in captivity since 1866, but in the wild is threatened by a multitude of pressures on its natural habitat of primary hardwood forest. The forests are being cleared for agriculture, mining, hydro-electric power, tourism, road-building and all the associated developments. Reserves have been created for Swinhoe's and the long-tailed Mikado Pheasant (*Syrmaticus mikado*), but their effectiveness remains to be seen. Both species are still subject to live-trapping for the aviary trade, in spite of legal protection. A number of captive-bred Swinhoe's Pheasants have been released back into the wild in Taiwan, but the success of these reintroductions depends on the effectiveness of the protection enjoyed by wild birds and their habitat.

The most extravagantly adorned of the *Lophura* pheasants is Bulwer's Pheasant (*L. bulweri*) of Borneo. The male's face wattles are enormously elongated, and are dramatically engorged during display when the combined length of each upper and lower pair can reach over 18cm. These wattles are a bright sky-blue, tipped with black, in striking contrast with the red eye and facial skin. The contrast is increased further by the white tail, which has more feathers than the tail of any other bird, and is first flattened from side to side then fanned fore-and-aft so that it looks like a flat, white disc reaching above the back as far forward as the head. The outermost tail-feathers are spikes which drag along the ground and make a loud rustling sound among the leaves.

Bulwer's Pheasants occur in deep gullies in the forested interior of Borneo, up to 670m above sea level. Like other forest birds of Borneo their main threat is the loss of their habitat; almost all the primary forest on that huge island has already been contracted to logging companies, including forest in some of the National Parks. Bulwer's Pheasants have recently been bred in captivity, so there is some hope of saving the species. That hope does not exist for the other birds of the Borneo forest. Pheasants are fortunate to have captivated enough dedicated people willing to devote their lives to raising them in aviaries. Less spectacular and less tractable species do not have that option.

Threatened pheasants of Asia's forests
Many factors contribute to the plight of Asia's pheasants, but for all of them survival rests entirely on whether or not man will preserve at least some portion of their virgin forest habitat.

1. Swinhoe's Pheasant (*Lophura swinhoii*)
2. Edwards's Pheasant (*Lophura edwardsi*)
3. Bulwer's Wattled Pheasant (*Lophura bulweri*)

Status report – Tropical forests:
Local destruction with global consequences

Well over 2500 different species of bird inhabit the world's tropical rainforests – an environment so different from any other that most of those species could live nowhere else. The loss of large areas of this habitat would therefore cause the extinction of a correspondingly large proportion of the world's avifauna. The same conclusion is true for almost all other kinds of living thing; more species live in this habitat than in any other. The fact that tropical forests are being cut down very rapidly therefore has grave consequences not only for birds but for all kinds of life. We are facing the prospect of extinction of species on a scale rivalling the extinction of the dinosaurs, but in a very much shorter time.

Man himself is also being affected by the loss of tropical forests, though he is not specialized for life there. A very small proportion of the human race lives in tropical forest, and although the loss of those relatively few people is a valid humanitarian concern it does not constitute the extinction of a species. So could we not, perhaps, simply accept the loss of the forest, albeit sadly, in the knowledge that most of us will not be directly affected?

A look at the consequences

To answer that question we need to remind ourselves of the roles that tropical forests play in the global ecosystem – the biosphere. We need to remember that plants produce the oxygen we breathe and turn the energy of the sun, and the carbon dioxide that we exhale, into our food. We must also remember that one-quarter of the carbon fixation that takes place on land is carried out by tropical forests. They are still extensive enough to play a significant part in the regulation of the atmosphere. If they are lost, the chemical balance of the entire biosphere must be upset.

The loss of the forests will affect the global carbon budget not just by the loss of the biomass of the forest, but also by the *way* in which it is lost. Most forest clearance involves burning at some stage, and clearance is now proceeding at such a pace that burning tropical forests are adding significantly to the amount of carbon dioxide in the atmosphere. Not all of the additional CO_2 will remain there; some will be absorbed by the oceans and some will be taken up again by whatever plants grow on the land cleared of forest, but enough is likely to remain in the atmosphere to double its concentration. This has truly been called the greatest ecological experiment of all times. It is also a potentially very dangerous gamble to take with such a precious resource as the air we breathe.

The likely consequences are controversial. Carbon dioxide absorbs the infra-red radiation given out by the earth, thereby increasing the temperature of the atmosphere. The net result is likely to be that the average temperature of the world will rise due to the so-called 'greenhouse effect'.

The Monkey-eating Eagle (*Pithecophaga jefferyi*) is the top avian predator of the Asian tropical forests. As such it was never an abundant species, but its rapid decline to an estimated population of only 500 individuals is a clear warning of the disastrous impact of rainforest destruction.

Burning forests add not only carbon dioxide to the atmosphere but also minute particles of dust from the burning vegetation itself and later from the bare soil that is left behind. The concentration of dust in the lower atmosphere has trebled in the last 60 years, and most of that is due not to the smoke and other pollution that we produce in the western world, but to the loss of forest cover, especially in the tropics. Atmospheric dust adds to the insulating effect of the carbon dioxide in the atmosphere and so contributes to the rise in world temperature.

The consequences of that warming are by no means certain, but they could include a rise in sea level due to the release of meltwater from the polar ice-caps, which would affect millions of people living very close to sea level. They could also include widespread crop failures since modern crops are sensitive to quite small changes in average temperature.

The possible climatic effects of global warming would also be increased by the effects of local changes in temperature in the deforested areas themselves. Forests are dark, and reflect little heat; the crops or bare soil that replace them reflect more heat, raising the temperature of the atmosphere in the tropics. The tropics play an important role in determining the patterns of world climate. Some of these effects are well known and spectacular; the ferocity of tropical hurricanes and cyclones needs no emphasis, and extends well outside the tropical zones in which they originate. But apart from their obvious role in spawning hurricanes, tropical zones initiate other climatic processes that are global in their effects.

Thousands of hectares of virgin tropical forest have been burnt during the construction of the Trans-Amazonica Highway. Little, if any, will be replaced.

The effect on the water cycle

The effects of tropical forests on the global water cycle are small compared with those of the oceans, but they can be very important regionally. In an extensive forest area such as Amazonia, for example, less than half the rainfall reaches the rivers; the rest is returned to the air by the trees. This internal cycle means that the region generates much of its own rainfall. When the forest that drives that cycle goes, so will the rainfall. One consequence is that even if some areas of forest are set aside as reserves, they are unlikely to survive much beyond the lifetime of the trees themselves because the rainfall of the entire region will become inadequate to support the remaining forest. The 'domino effect', beloved of politicians, has its awesome counterpart in the ecology of tropical forests.

In addition to generating and recycling their own water supplies the forests also regulate the flow of water to other areas, often hundreds of kilometres downstream. Rainfall in the tropics is often extremely heavy, and a half-hour thunderstorm can dump forty times as much water on the land as falls in a half-hour shower outside the tropics. A forest will intercept one-third to one-half of this rain, reduce the violence of its impact on the soil, and release it slowly and steadily into the soil and eventually the rivers. When the forest is removed, the steady flow of water changes to a devastating succession of floods and droughts.

In large areas of the tropics, most of the population lives at or near the water's edge. The people depend directly on the quality of the water as well as on its quantity and the pattern of its flood cycles. In India, for example, the catchment area of the River Ganges, which accounts for over 70 per cent of the subcontinent's flood-prone land, has been deforested by over 40 per cent in the last 30 years, increasing the severity of floods and the associated losses to human and animal life and to crops and property. In much of Southeast Asia, the 'miracle' strains of rice that brought about the Green Revolution will not tolerate the raised flood levels that have occurred as a result of deforestation. Most human settlements in Amazonia are along rivers, on which the people depend for their agriculture and their animal protein. And most of these rivers rise in the Andes, where forested land is being cleared to provide subsistence agriculture. The people who invade the forested eastern slopes of the Andes are therefore seriously affecting the livelihood of people 2000km away by changing the flood cycles and the silt loads of the rivers that support them.

Stripping the land bare

Heavy rain falling on unprotected soil washes huge quantities of silt into the watercourses and eventually deposits it downstream or even out at sea. In Indonesia, a country once covered almost entirely by tropical forest, one-fifth of the land is now seriously eroded. On the island of Java alone, the soil that is washed into the sea from former forest land each year could grow sufficient crops to feed 15 million people.

On its way to the sea, silt can raise the level of a river bed and so further increase the severity of floods. It also changes the turbidity of the water so that the aquatic life is changed. People in Southeast Asia, like those in Amazonia, depend on freshwater fish for most of their animal protein and are finding fish supplies dwindling as the rivers become choked with silt.

Even in normal conditions, tropical rivers like the Sepik in New Guinea carry huge volumes of mud and silt into the sea. When inland forests are cut down the flow becomes a flood as millions of tonnes of soil are stripped from the land and lost forever.

About 85 per cent of the world's energy needs are still met by burning wood, and this use of wood alone accounts for a large proportion of the clearance of tropical and other forests. To meet their energy needs, many tropical countries try to harness their abundant rainfall into hydro-electric power. Huge dams are built with the intention not only of generating electricity but also of controlling floods. But all too often the catchment area is deforested at the same time: the dammed reservoirs silt up so fast that they can generate only a fraction of the power for which they were designed, and many soon become unusable.

The forests' commercial potential

The loss of the tropical forests will also diminish the quality of our own daily lives much more than we may realize. We use many raw materials from tropical forests, quite apart from the timbers with which we are familiar. Essential oils, gums and latexes, resins, volatile oils, tannins, waxes, edible oils, flavourings, sweeteners, spices, balsams, pesticides, dyes and many others, are ingredients of cosmetics, food, polishes, insecticides and countless more everyday items. So far, very few of the 100,000 or so tropical forest plant species have been tested, much less exploited, and many useful plants are bound to become extinct before their value is realized. Even with a low level of exploitation, the world trade in the essential oils camphor, cassia, cinnamon, clove, nutmeg, cardamom and ginger is worth more than US$1000 million each year. Oils from the oil palms of tropical

forests are widely used in margarine, cooking oil, ice-cream, mayonnaise and other foods, as well as for making lubricants for engines. Many synthetic products now made from petroleum oil can be made more cheaply from the oils of tropical forest plants – plastics, man-made fibres, adhesives and formaldehyde among them. It will also cost us much more to construct buildings when supplies of cheap imported timber dry up, because alternative materials cost much more in energy to produce. Cement, for example, takes 4–5 times as much energy to produce as sawn timber; the equivalent factor for steel is 23, and for aluminium no less than 126.

Some authorities estimate that tropical forests are being cleared at an average rate of 30 hectares a minute.

More than 2000 million people depend on wood for their domestic energy needs and throughout the Third World much of that wood is used in the form of charcoal. Here, charcoal production forms the basis of a thriving village economy on the island of Madagascar.

A vital resource under threat

Tropical forests are often cut down to grow food, but in the long run this will reduce our food supply, not increase it. Many of the world's staple crops are descended from tropical plants, many of which lived in rainforest, and very few of the species which might be used or cultivated have yet been investigated. In Papua New Guinea, for example, there are over 250 species of tree with edible fruits, but fewer than 50 of these have been cultivated. Forest tribes eat over 4000 species of plant in Indonesia, but fewer than 10 per cent of these have been cultivated widely. There is clearly an enormous reserve of potential foods waiting in the forest to be tapped, if the forest can survive long enough for them to be discovered.

Modern food crops are the result of intense selective breeding and this genetic manipulation requires a constant supply of genetic material from the same or closely related species. A perennial variety of maize was discovered recently in a Mexican forest. If the part of its genetic code that makes it perennial can be 'spliced' into cultivated maize, farmers will no longer have to plant anew each year. Sugarcane, coffee, cocoa and banana are all valuable crops that have been saved in recent years by infusions of genetic material from tropical forest stock.

The forests hold a vital reservoir of potential new crops, and the genetic resources that will be necessary to keep cultivating the ones we already use. Tragically, scientists are now finding that the genetic resources they need are becoming scarce as the wild ancestors of many food crops approach extinction.

About one-quarter of the medicines we buy in the developed world have their origins in tropical forest plants. Many such medicines are still produced much more cheaply by isolation from the plant than by synthetic processes, and many cannot be synthesized at all. Morphine, quinine, ipecac, atropine, caffeine and nicotine are all well-known derivatives of tropical forest plants. Over a thousand species of tropical forest plants are believed to be potentially effective against cancer. One such plant, the Rosy Periwinkle, a herb of the tropical forest edge, has already provided two drugs that have quadrupled the chances of remission for children with leukaemia.

Worldwide pressure on the forest lands

The rate at which tropical forest is being cleared is the subject of hot debate, but satellite photography is providing increasingly accurate measures of the scale of the problem. Worldwide, the area of tropical forest cut down each year is at least the size of England, and some estimates would double that. Why is the forest being cleared so fast that in many parts of the tropics there will be very little, if any, left by the end of the century?

By far the greatest cause of tropical forest destruction is the small-scale forest farmer. Throughout the tropics people have traditionally farmed by cutting down a small patch of forest (about one hectare per family per year), burning or selling the timber, and planting crops for two or three years until the soil is exhausted or the patch becomes overgrown. Then they move on to a new patch,

Small circular clearings like these in the rainforest of Venezuela are the work of shifting cultivators

The Rosy Periwinkle (*Catharanthus roseus*) is just one of the many tropical forest plants known to have valuable medicinal properties. Used wisely, the forest resource will yield many more benefits to mankind.

allowing the former one to regenerate. Such shifting agriculture has persisted in some regions for thousands of years as a successful system of sustainable harvesting. It could persist without damaging the environment so long as population density was low. But population densities have risen to at least three times the level at which shifting agriculture can be sustained. Consequently the land is now used again before it has recovered; it produces less food, and the farmer must cut more forest to feed his family. Human population growth rates are higher in the tropical forest countries than anywhere else in the world, often over three per cent a year; and this combination of soaring population, poor farming methods and a rapidly diminishing supply of suitable land, threatens to wipe out the forest in many countries.

The patterns and causes of forest clearance vary greatly from region to region. In Amazonia and Central America most forest is cleared for cattle ranching and the beef is exported, chiefly to North America, where it is made into hamburgers. North America (and Europe) could easily grow their own beef, but it is cheaper, on paper, to buy Brazilian. The real cost – of the forest destroyed – does not appear in the accounts. In Indonesia and Borneo most of the lowland forest has already been allocated to logging companies. Here, the timber trade is very important and, added to the accelerating inroads made into the forests by the burgeoning human population, contributes to one of the fastest rates of forest clearance in the tropics.

So the extinction of hundreds – possibly thousands – of bird species will be but one of many tragic consequences of the loss of a large proportion of the world's tropical forest. It will undoubtedly be matched by an increase in human suffering on a scale which even mankind has not previously inflicted on the world.

Cattle fattened on dry pastures formerly covered in rainforest are the first link in an economic chain that ends with the frozen beefburgers on sale in a European or North American supermarket.

Grasslands dominate the heartlands of the continents. Originally they supported vast herds of grazing animals, including many huge flightless birds; today they supply us with most of our food — either through the animals we graze on them or through the cereals we grow where wild grasses once flourished.

Grassland often grades into forest, through various types of scrub, and some climates support permanent kinds of woody scrubland. Heathlands are special kinds of scrub, and each type has its own special wildlife community. In all these habitats trees are scarce and birds must exploit the opportunities available at, or just above, ground level. Many grassland and scrub habitats are now intensively managed by man, and few natural examples remain of the kinds of habitat in which mankind evolved and whose plants and animals he domesticated in his transition from hunter-gatherer to farmer and city-dweller.

Grassland, Heath and Scrub

The grassland habitat

Man is basically a grassland animal. We evolved on the grassy plains of Africa, and grassy habitats still provide most of our food. The cereal crops that provide the bulk of our staple diet are simply domesticated grasses. Since man first learned to exploit them, grasslands have borne the brunt of his efforts to carve out a niche for himself.

Grasslands and forests exist in an uneasy equilibrium, and men and other animals can easily tip the balance from one to the other. Grasslands grow naturally where there is too little rain or soil for trees to grow. But they are also often found where forest could grow, their dominance maintained either by grazing cattle, which eat the tree seedlings and encourage the growth of grasses, or by burning. Fire is widely used to burn off dead grass and woody growth and encourage the sprouting of fresh young grass for cattle to eat. Many of the world's great grasslands are maintained by a combination of fire and grazing.

Left alone, many grasslands would revert to forest, passing through a stage with many low bushes scattered among long grass. Scrubland is often such a succession which has been arrested by fire, grazing or cutting to prevent it turning into forest. But some scrublands are permanent, notably the *chapparal* of western America and the Mediterranean *maquis,* though even these are often swept by natural fires. Heaths are a special kind of scrub, herbaceous rather than woody, some of which, notably in western Europe, also owe their continued existence to human management. We treat grassland, scrub and heaths together because they frequently grade into each other, their bird-life has much in common, and they share similar problems.

The birds of these predominantly grassy habitats have many fewer niches to exploit than forest birds. In pure grasslands there are no trees to nest in, and birds must conceal their nests on the ground. There are few perches to sing and display from, so aerial songs and displays are conspicuous; the European Skylark, the Singing Bushlark of Australia and the longspurs of the North American prairies are well-known examples. The wide open plains also supported many large flightless grazing birds such as ostriches, emus, rheas, bustards and cassowaries.

Red-billed Queleas (*Quelea quelea*) nest and roost in huge colonies in Africa's savanna grasslands. The birds are a major pest, especially on rice crops, but are difficult to control because of their frequent and erratic migrations to follow the rains.

The world's grasslands
Broad zones of grassland form the main intermediate type of vegetation between forest at one extreme and desert at the other. The grasslands fall into two principal subdivisions; those of tropical regions are called savanna, while temperate zone grasslands are variously called steppe, prairie or pampas.

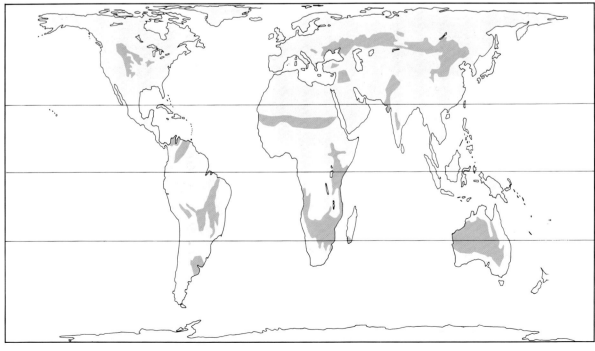

Wind Cave National Park in South Dakota, USA, is typical of the prairie habitat once roamed by millions of buffalo. Within a bare half-century, the vast herds were gone; the buffalo hunted to the brink of extinction. Fortunately, conservation measures were taken in time, and small but stable herds now live in several protected grassland areas.

Many grasslands had associated faunas of large grazing mammals that dominated the habitats until they were wiped out or domesticated by man. Birds soon learned to exploit these herds, and on the African plains such partnerships can still be seen. Vultures soar overhead, waiting for the inevitable carcasses; Cattle Egrets sit on the backs of buffalo or stalk through the grass picking up insects disturbed by the animals' hooves, and oxpeckers bustle busily from one animal to another, picking ticks from wrinkles in their hides. Most of the great herds of grazers are gone now, and the birds have had to adapt to a habitat with fewer opportunities and more people.

The incubator mound of Australia's Mallee Fowl (*Leipoa ocellata*) is up to 5m in diameter and nearly 1m high. It consists of a metre-deep hole, filled with dry leaves then thickly covered with sand and leaves. The clutch of between 5 and 35 eggs is maintained at a constant 33°C by the male, who regulates the temperature by adding or removing overburden.

The savanna grasslands of Africa support huge numbers of grazing and browsing mammals which in turn form the food resource of predators such as lions, cheetahs and hyenas, and the vultures and other carrion feeders that ensure that nothing is left to waste.

Bengal Florican:
Cash crops versus conservation

For many years ornithologists in India were preoccupied with the fate of the huge and magnificent Great Indian Bustard (*Choriotis nigriceps*), a spectacular denizen of the grasslands, whose numbers were declining seriously. Only very recently did they realize that the smaller and less prominent Bengal Florican (*Houbaropsis bengalensis*) had declined to a point where nobody could name a single Indian breeding site.

The birds breed in areas that contain at least two types of grassland. For his main feeding and display area the male needs short grass where his spectacular display can be seen to its best effect. This takes place in the early morning and evening, and consists of an athletic leap four metres into the air with the glossy black feathers of the head, neck and body fluffed out, and the snow-white wings arched downwards and clapping together loudly enough to be heard a kilometre away. From the top of his leap, the male flutters down like an animated black-and-white beach-ball. He and his performance are very conspicuous, and attract females who mate with him at his display ground before going off to nest by themselves. In the heat of the day, the gaudy males retire prudently to the shelter of long grass, which may be as tall as ten metres, and makes them very difficult to find. The females are well camouflaged and always much harder to see, even though they nest in short grass which provides very little cover against predators.

This lovely, graceful bird has been found in only four countries — India, Bangladesh, Kampuchea and Nepal — but its present breeding distribution has contracted to scattered pockets of grassland, mainly in Nepal, and in Assam in India. Most of the floricans remaining in Nepal are in National Parks or other kinds of reserve. Outside the reserves, the grasslands are all subject either to intensive agricultural use or to human disturbance at a level the birds cannot tolerate. No more than 75 floricans could be found in a survey of the country in 1982.

A similar fate has overtaken the closely related Lesser Florican (*Sypheotides indica*). Unlike the Bengal Florican, Lessers are migrants, wintering in central India and following the monsoon to the northwest of the country for the breeding season. The return of the floricans to their breeding grounds once involved flocks of hundreds, and they were shot in considerable numbers. Now they are almost gone. In Jamnagar District in the State of Gujarat, once a major stronghold of the Lesser Florican, an intensive search in 1982 revealed only 77 birds.

Only 30 years ago undulating grassy plains abounded throughout Jamnagar District. Now, there are only 60km² of native grassland, all confined to 'vidis' — state-controlled grasslands reserved for producing hay to support the villagers' cattle through the winter. During this century, the area of land devoted to cultivation has risen from 42 per cent to 75 per cent, mostly at the expense of the grassland beloved of floricans. This extra land is devoted not to feeding people but to growing cash crops such as peanuts, sugar and cotton. The land producing food has actually declined to little more than half the area it occupied in 1909.

Bengal and Lesser Floricans clearly depend on particular kinds of grassland for their survival. Their habitats were once very extensive in the Indian subcontinent, but this region experiences some of the severest food shortages in the world and it is hard to argue that land that could grow food should be set aside for floricans. Yet this is not really the issue; less land now grows food for the local people than was the case when floricans abounded. If land can be taken out of food production to grow cash crops, can some not be spared to preserve two kinds of bird that are part of the nations' heritage?

The original grasslands of the Jamnagar District in India are rapidly disappearing as land is converted to sugarcane, peanut and cotton production. Another major threat to the habitat comes from the grazing of large cattle herds. The animals remove the long grass cover that is essential for ground-living birds like the Florican and the Great Indian Bustard (*Choriotis nigriceps*).

The Lesser Florican: one of the small populations remaining in the Jamnagar area, where the species was once common.

Waldrapp:
Last of the line of Abu Mengel

The Waldrapp's historical record goes back over 5000 years to the hieroglyphs of Ancient Egypt, but the bird made its historical debut in European records in 1555 when a Swiss physician described it and recommended its flavour. The young were protected by law for the next 200 years in parts of Europe, but were widely eaten none the less, and this persecution, combined with increased cultivation of their habitats, perhaps hastened by climatic changes, led to their extinction in Europe by the middle of the seventeenth century.

It was more than 200 years before a species of ibis from North Africa and Asia was recognized as belonging to the same species as the Waldrapp or Hermit Ibis (*Geronticus eremitus*). Once this was known, collectors throughout Europe wanted specimens, and the ibises were rapidly exterminated in Syria and throughout most of Algeria. Today they breed in 12 scattered colonies in Morocco (total population about 320 birds), one small colony in Algeria, and a small, declining colony in Turkey.

The Turkish colony has survived so long because the birds are associated with a religious belief and so have been protected by the local people. They believe that Noah released from his ark not just the dove, as a symbol of peace, but also a swallow, to represent a new era, and Abu Mengel, a black sickle-billed ibis, as a symbol of fertility. Abu Mengel was the Waldrapp, and was believed to have led Noah and his sons from Mount Ararat to a small house in a valley. The only place where the Waldrapp has managed to retain a toehold on the Eurasian continent is the village of Birecik, whose name is Turkish for 'little house'. From June to February, when the Waldrapps winter in eastern North Africa and southern Arabia, they were believed to be leading pilgrims on their 3500km round trip to Mecca.

Birecik is on the River Euphrates, and in 1911 several hundred pairs of Waldrapp nested on the rocks bordering the river as well as on cliffs above the village itself. Fifty years later none nested along the river and only 120 pairs above the town. The catastrophic decline has continued in Turkey, and also in the scattered colonies of Morocco and Algeria.

A Waldrapp on its nest in a small protected colony on the outskirts of Birecik. The colony is guarded by Turkish conservationists.

The town of Birecik completely surrounds Turkey's main colony of Waldrapps. New nesting ledges were cut into the cliffs in an attempt to improve the birds' breeding rate, but so far without success.

One of the small breeding colonies of Waldrapps in southern Morocco, where hunting pressures are adding to the problems already created by habitat disturbance.

The ibises nest on rock ledges and feed in grassland. In their former distribution these grasslands were either mountain meadows or the lush grasslands of riverine floodplains. Cultivation of alpine meadows for crops and cattle grazing squeezed them out of the montane part of their range in Europe, and the same process, repeated in Asia and combined more recently with the extensive use of toxic pesticides, has led them to their present dire position in Turkey. An added pressure has been the growth of the human population of Birecik, and the influx of immigrants from farther east who did not share the local veneration of the Waldrapp.

The Birecik colony, situated above the village 70 years ago, is now within what has become a town. Houses have encroached on the nesting ledges so much that there are roofs on a level with the ledges, and houses above them. A major cause of nesting failure has been the disturbance caused by this human encroachment.

The ledges have been protected to some extent by walls built above them, and artificial wooden ledges have also been built for them. In 1976, 85 per cent of the population used the man-made sites. But the battle to preserve the Turkish Waldrapps will be lost unless the people revive their former concern for the birds. A project to dam the Euphrates at Keban may be the final blow if it is implemented, for it will bring into cultivation the last of their feeding grounds. The population – down to only 13 birds in 1984 – consists mostly of birds over 20 years old, reflecting the lack of recruitment of young birds in the past two decades.

In Morocco, the birds have declined almost as fast, and only about 400 remain. Threats there include hunting, disturbance and changes to their feeding habitat as in Turkey, and seem poised to exterminate Noah's messenger before the century is out.

Noisy Scrub-bird:
The bird that moved a town

Occasionally the ornithological world is set alight by the rediscovery of a species long thought to be extinct. The Noisy Scrub-bird (*Atrichornis clamosus*) is perhaps the most famous case of such a resurrection in recent times. Not one bird was seen between 1889 and 1961, surely long enough to pronounce it well and truly extinct; indeed, a monument to the bird and its discoverer was erected in 1949. Yet 12 years later a lone male was found, and two years after that a nest. The number of males rose from 45 in 1970 to 74 in 1976, but no further sites have come to light since then.

The Noisy Scrub-bird has short rounded wings, a long graduated tail, and long, strong legs. It is a ground-living bird, preferring to scramble mouse-like through the tangled vegetation of its environment rather than fly. It eats insects, frogs and lizards, and builds a round nest of rushes which it lines with a papier mâché-like layer of decayed wood and rushes. The female alone incubates the two eggs. The male lives up to its name by being extremely vocal, and has an impressive repertoire of piercing, if unmusical, calls and occasional imitations of other birds. Its loud voice, and frequent use of it, seems well suited to the density of its habitat, in which it would be very difficult to communicate by displays and other visual signals. The males' territorial songs are also very useful in revealing their presence to investigating scientists: an accurate idea of their numbers can only be obtained by mapping and counting the singing males. The birds' numbers have increased — to an estimated 80 pairs in 1983 — but are probably still well below the carrying capacity of their habitat.

The species was first discovered in 1842 in the Darling Range south of Perth in Western Australia. Over the next 50 years it was found in five other places in the southwest of the continent, most commonly in the Albany area, where it was later rediscovered. But over that period it was declining rapidly as its range was settled by colonists who cleared and burnt the bush to provide land for agriculture.

On the other side of the continent a similar species, which came to be called the Rufous Scrub-bird (*A. rufescens*), was found in several widely scattered localities from just south of Brisbane south to Mount Barrington in New South Wales. The Rufous Scrub-bird is more widely distributed than the Noisy,

nown localities are fortunately in Parks. It lives in several different kinds of forest but still requires a dense layer of scrubby undergrowth. The Noisy Scrubbird now lives in dense undergrowth of shrubs and rushes beneath eucalyptus forest in steep gullies, and under stunted gum trees on the flat heathland between the gullies. Its name aptly reflects its present habitat, but originally it may have occupied the marginal habitat lying between forest and swamp.

These two species belong to one of Australia's oldest families of birds, and are the only living members of it. They represent a case only slightly less dire than that of the Kagu – the prospect of an entire family being at risk. Like a number of other pairs of species in Australia, with close relatives now found only at opposite sides of the continent, they are relicts of a group that was probably much more widely distributed until it became separated into eastern and western populations when the centre of the continent became a desert. The amount of suitable habitat available to them was then further reduced by man, who destroyed large areas of forest and scrub and turned it into agricultural land. Much of the land was cleared by burning, which destroyed their scrub habitat and fragmented it into widely separated patches to which such weak fliers were unable to disperse.

When the Noisy Scrub-birds' continued existence was first revealed, part of the area in which they had been found was scheduled to be developed into a town. To the lasting credit of the authorities involved this was relocated to allow a 4640ha reserve to be established. The bird was given the fullest protection of the law, and a ranger is stationed permanently on the reserve. There was at first some controversy over the question of access; many people wanted to see this famous bird, so dramatically brought back from the dead, but others wanted the reserve to be strictly out of bounds to the public. Eventually a compromise was reached whereby visitors are allowed to visit half the reserve, under strict control, while the rest of the area remains strictly out of bounds to the public.

Scrub-birds, not unreasonably, require scrub; but as we have seen, scrub is very often not a stable habitat but a stage in a habitat succession that culminates in forest. The great fear when a few birds are confined to a single locality is that some catastrophe, such as a fire, will overtake them all at once; yet, paradoxically, it may be necessary to burn at least part of the habitat to ensure that it does not naturally cease to be scrub. A similar problem has overtaken the Seychelles Brush Warbler on Cousin Island, an ICBP reserve in the Seychelles. Like the Noisy Scrub-bird this warbler seems to need a more scrubby habitat than that provided by the forest to which the island's vegetation is returning. The unpleasant ecological reality for conserving birds of scrubland is that very often they cannot be left to their own devices, but must have their habitat managed for them.

The mixed habitat of wooded gullies and open heathland with dense ground vegetation where the Noisy Scrub-bird was rediscovered in 1961.

An Australian ornithologist with one of the special boxes developed for use in transporting endangered birds to new, and safer, localities. The technique has been used successfully with Scrub-birds, Black Robins and several other species.

Status report – Grasslands:
Exploited to the limit – and beyond

Permanent grasslands – including pastures – represent the world's largest land-use category, covering some 20 per cent of the land. Together with scrublands and heaths they probably account for a quarter of the world's utilized land area. Grasslands alone support over 3000 million head of domestic stock and thus produce most of our meat and milk, while scrublands are a very important source of fuelwood.

These habitats are generally unproductive and need careful management if they are to realize their full potential. Unfortunately, overstocking is now universal and is one of the main causes of environmental damage. Swelling populations crowd farmers off good agricultural land on to land that is marginal for farming, and as they encroach, they in turn push the pastoralists and their stock into scrub and grassland that is marginal for grazing. It is soon turned into desert. Here, more clearly perhaps than with any of the other ecosystems we have looked at, different environments and their bird-life clearly grade into and affect each other.

Maintaining an uneasy balance

Most of the world's wetter grasslands are now under crops, and some of their birds have adapted to the new environment, in a few cases even to the extent of becoming pests. But in the past 40 years a new dimension has been added to their habitat – the intensive use of persistent toxic chemicals to control pests. Chemical poisoning may well have been an important factor in lowering the breeding success of the Turkish Waldrapps, for example, and probably killed many of the 600 birds found lying dead around Birecik in 1959.

Outbreaks of bush fire are a natural part of the grassland ecological cycle; so much so that some plant seeds will not germinate until they have been scorched.

However, excessive use of fire as a management tool tends to promote growth of fire-resistant scrub at the expense of regenerating grass and woodland.

Cattle grazing on heavily degraded acacia scrub in the Awash valley of Ethiopia. In many parts of Africa the problem of overgrazing is difficult to tackle because of the great importance of cattle ownership in the social and economic traditions of the people.

The drier grasslands are usually invaded by cattle grazers. In many parts of the world the stock are not solely an economic resource but are also a badge of prestige, the major source of wealth and the unit of currency. A herdsman's flock is his bank account as well as his larder. As modern medicine has become accessible to both the people and their animals, human and livestock populations have swelled, exerting pressure that has converted many areas of scrub and grassland into desert.

On the other hand, new grasslands are also being created as farmers push their stock into forests and woodland. In the world as a whole, grasslands and scrub are perhaps being created as fast as they are being destroyed. If so, this is at the cost of other habitats which are potentially more productive. For these predominantly grassy environments are, biologically, among the least productive habitats on land; they must be treated with care to produce even one-fifth to one-half as much as a forest in the same climate. And even if pastoralists in the Himalayan mountains can survive by turning forest into grassland, that option is not open to the people of the Sahel, whose cattle and children are the ultimate victims of an attempt to wrest more from the land than it has to give.

Birds without a future?

Few species of bird in these habitats are critically endangered, but those that are indicate the dangers of misusing their environments. The floricans and bustards of the plains of Europe and Asia are on the same path to extinction that has already been followed by the Heath Hen (and of course the Bison) of the North American prairie grasslands, hunted for their succulent flesh while their habitat has been turned into cropland or pasture. The Waldrapp's grassland feeding grounds are now under pasture or crops, its few remaining fields poisoned with chemicals, its nesting ledges deep in human litter. The Noisy Scrub-bird is a relict, driven by destruction of its habitat into a remote corner of an almost empty continent, and dependent even there on the constant vigilance of conservationists for its survival. Sadly these most fragile environments support too many people for most of their native birds to survive much longer.

The natural cover of scrub heathland and wooded valleys in Malta has been almost entirely replaced by open fields offering virtually no protective cover or food to birds migrating between Europe and Africa.

The original habitat of the North American Prairie Chicken (*Tympanuchus cupido*) was tall grass prairie. Some birds have now adapted to open scrubland and farmland, but one race, on the east coast, has already become extinct while another, in the south, is small and currently declining in numbers.

True deserts are in no danger of disappearing. Quite the opposite: enough new desert is created each year to cover an area the size of Belgium. But these new deserts are formed at the expense of other, wetter, habitats that can support many more birds, many more cattle, and many more people. The transformation of semi-arid habitats into true desert is all too often accompanied by starvation and misery on a tragic scale.

The birds of arid lands show many adaptations of structure and behaviour designed to equip them for their harsh environment. Many birds, moving from waterhole to waterhole, or dropping down to oases on long-distance migrations, play a vital role in dispersing the few precious plants capable of colonizing desert regions. As lusher habitats degenerate into desert through prolonged drought or human mismanagement, the ability to survive in arid lands will become more and more vital to men and birds alike.

Arid Lands

Life in the deserts and semi-deserts

More than a quarter of the earth's land surface receives less than 50cm of rain a year and is thus classified as arid. And of this total, nearly half is desert. Yet some of these environments are surprisingly rich in birds, whose efficient insulation and great mobility enable them to survive where many other animals cannot.

True deserts have no life, but only the deep interiors of the frozen polar regions meet this strict criterion; the environments we normally think of as deserts have up to 20cm of rain a year, and are often vast areas of rock, sand and gravel where life is hard, but possible. Deserts are not simply very hot, they are also often extremely windy, so any surface moisture evaporates instantaneously. At night they can be bitterly cold, and some, such as the Gobi of Asia, are permanently frigid. Yet they are not truly barren. Scrubby bushes and tufts of grass are scattered here and there, and a rich variety of invertebrates lurks beneath the stones and the sand. The plants seem withered or even dead, but below ground their roots may extend for many metres and there are innumerable seeds among the sand grains. When rain does fall, the desert blooms as bushes turn green and seeds germinate.

Living with the desert

The many small mammals that inhabit these arid lands generally survive by burrowing underground to escape the heat. They obtain all their water from the food they eat, and conserve it by excreting a highly concentrated urine. Desert birds seem even less affected by these rigorous conditions. They do not burrow underground, and need not go without water; they can simply fly to the nearest waterhole. Some conserve water by excreting much of the salt they take in through special glands very like those of seabirds, but in general the basic structure of a bird needs little modification for desert life.

It may be many years before a sudden downpour fills this dry North African river bed with water – and even then the spectacular surge of a flash flood may last for only 15 minutes.

The arid lands
Deserts and semi-desert regions are the only natural habitats whose areas are increasing. Some are entirely natural; others have been created by misuse.

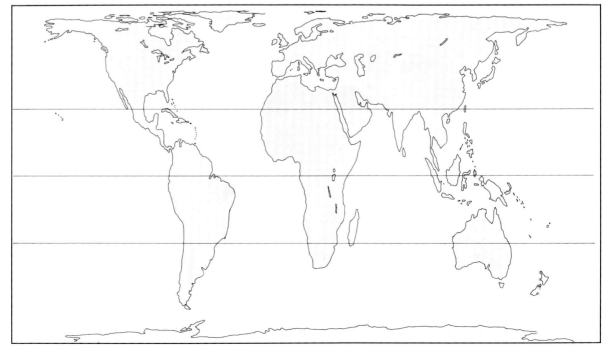

The mysteries of migration

Several major bird migration routes lie over deserts, and the twice-yearly crossings represent the greatest hazards in the lives of the birds that make them. The Sahara is crossed each year by many millions of small birds on their way from breeding grounds in Europe and Asia to winter quarters in tropical and subtropical Africa. They make these journeys with surprising frequency and success, but occasionally disastrous sandstorms can wipe out huge numbers in a few hours. The rare oases of permanent water and vegetation are as important to migrant birds as they are to the nomadic people of the desert.

Many other species move in and out of arid habitats in response to rain. These local migrations, together with long-range migrations and regular trips between waterholes, enable birds to perform an extremely useful function in the ecosystem by dispersing plant seeds.

The semi-arid regions are richer in bird-life but are still rigorous environments. Although rain is more plentiful it is still exceedingly unreliable; 50cm may fall in an average year, 150cm in a good one, but there are many years of below-average rainfall when the habitat fares no better than a desert. Many arid-land birds are nomadic opportunists, moving great distances to areas where rain has fallen and conditions are suitable for breeding. How they detect where rain has fallen, perhaps from hundreds of kilometres away, is one of many mysteries of the lives of desert birds.

Arid habitats are vulnerable because the life they support is already close to the limits at which life can exist at all. We shall have to learn how to exploit these environments ourselves if we are to support our own growing population, but we may never learn in time if we destroy the species that have already learned what the deserts have to teach.

Even the most arid desert is not devoid of life, but a high degree of specialization is required for any plant or animal to survive in such extreme conditions. This desert region in northeastern Brazil is, like many others, rapidly extending at the expense of marginal scrub- and woodlands.

At dawn or dusk, the male Namaqua Sandgrouse (*Pterocles namaqua*) leaves its nest in the desert of Namibia or South Africa and flies up to 80km to drink at a waterhole. In a unique desert adaptation the bird soaks the soft downy plumage of its belly, absorbing as much as 40g of water which it carries back to its nest scrape. The chicks drink by nibbling and 'stripping' the saturated feathers.

Houbara Bustard: Quarry of kings and princes

Bustards are large ground-living birds found in the grasslands and semi-arid plains of Africa, Eurasia and Australia. The Houbara (*Chlamydotis undulata*) is the species best adapted to truly arid lands, and has for centuries been the favourite prey of the sporting hunters and falconers of Arabia and the Far East.

Houbaras fly well and fast, but much prefer to walk or run. Their plumage is beautifully camouflaged, and their behaviour makes maximum use of its concealing effect. When alarmed they crouch and move stealthily, often crouching flat on the ground with the neck outstretched so that they are as inconspicuous as possible. When driven to run, they do so with great skill, reaching speeds of 40km/h. They defend themselves vigorously with bill and wings, and with a peculiarly effective trick of turning the back towards the attacker, fanning and raising the tail like a shield, and squirting sticky faeces that clogs the fur or feathers of the aggressor.

Houbara bustards are shot for food throughout their range across North Africa, the Middle East and the Russian steppes. But for the Russian population the greatest danger comes when they migrate to winter in Arabia, Pakistan and India, where they have long been the chief victims of falconry – the sport of princes. In the traditional version of the sport, Arab dignitaries would ride into the desert with their entourage to fly highly trained falcons at a variety of prey, on which the party would later feast. The quarry species included hares and Stone Curlews (*Burhinus oedicnemus*), but the great prize was the Houbara.

Some of the Houbaras that died in this way bred in the Arabian desert, but very few breed there now: nearly all the birds hunted today are wintering after breeding in the steppes and semi-deserts of the USSR. But now even the most remote breeding populations are declining because of the losses inflicted on the wintering birds. Houbaras have now become so scarce in Arabia that the falconers have moved to North Africa and Pakistan to pursue their sport – often as guests of the government.

The winter habitat of the Houbara Bustard of northern Asia: the arid semi-desert plains of the Sind region of southeastern Pakistan.

The traditional falconer was mounted on a horse or camel, flew only a few falcons, and normally killed only enough to feed his party for the day. The modern falconer uses cross-country motor vehicles loaded with supplies, and so can go farther into the desert, for longer periods. He also carries up to 90 falcons, and often uses firearms to supplement the kills of his birds. This modernization of a sport once in harmony with its environment has led to the extermination of many desert animals: now it threatens to send the Houbara into extinction too.

Houbaras are also declining throughout the rest of their range, from the Canary Islands in the west, through North Africa as far east as Egypt. Here they are victims not of falconry but of shooting for food, conversion of their habitat to agriculture, industrial development, and poisoning and disturbance during locust-control programmes. Even this most remote and arduous of earth's terrestrial habitats has not protected these spectacular birds from mankind's insatiable demands on its resources.

Status, wealth and power are represented by these Sakar Falcons (*Falco cherrug*) proudly displayed outside the palace of their owner in northeastern Africa. In addition to the pressure this style of hunting places on many endangered North African birds, the falcons themselves are now seriously threatened. The demand for falcons is so great that it supports a flourishing illegal trade in these rare and endangered birds of prey.

Small-scale traditional falconry, still widely practised in Pakistan (*right*), has a less dramatic impact on native wildlife, but in this country too, highly organized commercialized hunting is now taking a severe toll of the native bird and mammal fauna.

Splendid Parakeet:
Followers of the desert rains

This gaudy little bird (*Neophema splendida*) – also known as the Scarlet-chested Parrot – seems to have packed the brightest possible colours into the smallest possible space. It occupies the arid saltbush and spinifex plains of southern Australia, where it is rarely seen – partly because it seems to be extremely nomadic in its habits and never stays long in one place. It is hard to believe that such a brilliantly coloured bird could be so easily overlooked, but so long as they are feeding calmly and quietly they can be extremely difficult to see. They feed mainly on seeds, and so spend most of their time in low bushes or on the ground, where they display the characteristic parrot habit of using the foot to hold down food – in their case bending a grass stem to bring the seed-head within reach of the bill. Like the other 'grass-parrots' of Australia they fly swiftly and erratically, zigzagging from side to side in the manner of sandpipers.

Parrots have adapted as successfully to desert life in Australia as they have to tropical rainforest in South America. Many species live in the vast arid interior of the continent and share with Splendid Parakeets a number of features that are characteristic of desert birds in general. They may not be seen at all for many years, but then appear in a sudden irruption to breed in any area where rain has fallen. After breeding they disappear as suddenly as they came, and may not be seen again for many years. Normally Splendid Parakeets are seen in pairs, sometimes in small groups of up to 10; but in an irruption they may form flocks of 100 or more. Their ability to move long distances between places where food is sufficiently abundant to allow them to breed is vital in an environment where they can breed only after rain, and where rainfall is a very erratic and unpredictable event.

Like other parrots they nest in holes, usually in trees but sometimes in a log on the ground, or even in a fence post. The nesting season is variable, depending on the rains, but is usually between August and January. They lay the rounded white eggs characteristic of all parrots, from three to six in a clutch, and the female incubates alone for nearly three weeks. She lays the eggs on a soft bed of wood-chips, but also brings back to the nest the green leaves of aromatic plants. She carries these not in her beak, or with her feet, but tucked among the feathers of her rump. Some other parrots carry nest material in this way but no other birds are known to use this convenient method. Since she carries too few leaves to contribute to the structure of the nest, it is tempting to suggest that she uses them to scent the cramped quarters to which she will be confined for the next three weeks.

Splendid Parakeets seem to be naturally rare. Nomadic species with apparently small populations in remote areas are extremely difficult to study, and are vulnerable because they could die out without anyone noticing for many years. If 10 or more years can go by without their being seen in any numbers, how would we ever know that they were declining? The Splendid Parakeet is vulnerable for other reasons. It is, not surprisingly, popular with the cage-bird trade. It is sufficiently highly prized that in spite of the difficulty which biologists and naturalists experience in seeing it, it turns up regularly in aviaries and is now well established in captivity, both in Australia and elsewhere. These captive stocks are self-sustaining because the birds are relatively easy to breed in captivity. There is no longer any valid excuse for catching birds in the wild because the cage-bird trade could easily be supplied from birds already in captivity.

The semi-arid habitats of central Australia support huge numbers of brilliantly coloured parrots, parakeets and budgerigars, whose erratic movements take them wherever rains have recently fallen.

Two other species of parrot in the arid lands of Australia are also rare enough to be considered endangered. Naretha Bluebonnets (*Psephotus haematogaster*) are not as brilliantly coloured as Splendid Parakeets, but are eagerly sought as cage-birds. Trapping of adults, and especially the destruction of nest sites to extract the chicks, pose local threats to their survival. Princess Parrots (*Polytelis alexandrae*) are the most erratic of the three species, probably timing their movements in response to the appearance of temporary surface water and the flowering of *Acacia* trees.

A pair of Golden-winged Parrots (*Psephotus chrysopterygius*) at their nest burrow in a large termite mound (*above right*). The termites seal off the inside surface of the burrow and so protect the nest from other potential predators within the mound. Unfortunately the termite mounds are conspicuous in the flat, lightly wooded landscape and are easily found by hunters who dig out the burrows (*right*) and trap the birds for illegal trade.

257

Lear's Macaw:
Prime target for illegal hunters

The largest of all the parrots is the rich blue metre-long Hyacinth Macaw (*Anodorhynchus hyacinthinus*) of South America. This majestic parrot is regularly imported into North America by the aviculture trade, and over the years shipments have occasionally included specimens of a different species — only three-quarters the size of the Hyacinth but the same deep indigo colour and with a large bare yellow patch at the base of the bill. For a hundred years the smaller species was known only from these few captive specimens. It was not known for certain which country they came from, nor even the type of habitat they lived in. So little was known about them that it was even suggested they might be hybrids between Hyacinth Macaws and the smaller, greyer Glaucous Macaw (*Ara glaucus*).

After many years of diligent but fruitless searching by Brazilian ornithologists only one part of the country remained unexplored, and that was the remote and inhospitable Rasa da Catarina in Bahia State in northeastern Brazil — a hot, dry limestone plateau, dissected by deep canyons and dried-up river beds and covered with dense, low, thorny vegetation.

In December 1978 the intrepid biologists finally penetrated the Rasa da Catarina and found, at last, a wild population of Lear's Macaw (*Anodorhynchus leari*), also called the Indigo Macaw. It was the first time the bird had ever been seen in the wild, and the scientists were able to observe the colony for nearly a month. Up to 21 birds were seen at a time, flying in flocks to search for their favourite food — the small nuts of the *licuri* palm. The macaws would take these either perched in the trees or by walking along the ground below in search of fallen nuts.

Just before dusk the macaws would return to roost in hollows in the deeply eroded walls of a canyon. Here they scrambled about, climbing with their bills as well as their feet as many parrots do, and snapping at the dense swarms of flies that inhabit the canyons. Later in the year those same rough crevices and hollows would serve the birds as nesting sites.

The real threat to Lear's Macaw is that once the locality becomes known this last remote refuge will be invaded by hunters eager to trap the birds for the aviary trade – well aware that such a rare species will command a price of up to US$20,000 a head. By chance the area in which they were found lies inside a government Ecological Reserve, and so has some degree of protection; but to be properly safeguarded the reserve will need to be extended, and the birds and their habitat properly guarded.

The two species with which Lear's Macaw's history has been so long associated – the Hyacinth and Glaucous Macaws – are birds of forest rather than of arid lands, but their fates have some relevance to the conservation of Lear's Macaw. There are no recent records at all of wild Glaucous Macaws, and the last bird seen alive was a captive exhibited in 1936. The species is almost certainly extinct, and if so, it may be the first South American bird to become extinct since European colonization. Why it died out we shall probably never know. Its decline does not coincide with any major changes to its habitat, and although it was hunted and trapped, so were other species that are still quite common in the areas it formerly occupied. Hyacinth Macaws are also becoming more scarce year by year due to hunting for food and trapping for the cage-bird trade. The species' range coincides with that part of Brazil being colonized most rapidly, so its future status must also give rise to grave concern.

More relevant to the case of Lear's Macaw is the status of another arid-country species, the Red-fronted or Red-cheeked Macaw (*Ara rubrogenys*) of east-central Bolivia. This species has the smallest range of any macaw, extending over about 5000km^2 within which there are probably no more than 3000 birds. Until recently they seemed safe in their remote and unsettled refuge, but in the 1970s bird-trappers moved in and began to catch large numbers for export. More than 100 are now being exported each year – almost certainly more than the population can withstand.

The arid-land macaws are threatened much less by loss of habitat than by hunting and capture for the bird trade. Hunting for food, by people so poor they have no choice, cannot fairly be condemned: on its own this is unlikely to cause extinction. But the trapping of live birds for sale to people rich enough to pay tens of thousands of dollars for a single bird cannot be justified – least of all when such actions endanger the very existence of a species.

Scarlet Macaws (*Ara macao*) and Green-winged Macaws (*A. chloroptera*) flock to a salt-lick in the forests of Peru. Although still abundant, both species are trapped in large numbers for the cage-bird trade, and fetch high prices in North America. Their habit of congregating at natural salt-licks simply increases their vulnerability to the hunters: without controls, they too may soon join the catalogue of threatened forest species.

Jerdon's Courser: Risen from the dead

One of the most remarkable of recent re-discoveries occurred in January 1986 in the scrub jungle of Andhra Pradesh in eastern India. The bird in question was Jerdon's Courser (*Rhinoptilus bitorquatus*) – last seen in 1900 and believed by many to be extinct. Fortunately for science there were those who believed the bird might still be alive, and notable among these were Dr Salim Ali, India's foremost ornithologist, and other members of the Bombay Natural History Society who have searched repeatedly for this elusive little bird.

Even before 1900, so few people had seen Jerdon's Courser that little was known about it beyond the fact that it was a strikingly marked ground-dwelling bird, roughly the size and shape of a European Lapwing and a resident of thinly forested hill country.

Coursers are plover-like waders that have forsaken the wetlands frequented by their relatives and colonized instead the arid lands of Africa, Asia and Australia. They feed and nest exclusively on the ground, and are generally rather sedentary. Their eggs and young are beautifully camouflaged, and the chicks are able to follow their parents around within a few hours of hatching. All the other species live in arid country – some in full desert – but Jerdon's Courser seems to have adopted more thickly wooded habitats than any of its relatives. The few recorded sightings of the bird came from scattered parts of two river valleys – the Godvari and the Penner – in southeastern India, in hill country with thin scrub forest on rocky soils. One nineteenth-century observer remarked that the birds avoided open ground, always keeping to dense cover, but this may have been at least in part a response to the trigger-happy tendencies of many of the Europeans living in Imperial India in those days.

The lone specimen of Jerdon's Courser spotted at night in the headlight beam of a searching scientist was the ornithological high-spot of 1986. It was also just reward for many years of painstaking effort. In the most recent investigation, drawings of the bird had been shown to thousands of villagers until eventually contact was made with some who claimed to have seen it. How many of these elusive birds have survived we do not know. We can only hope that careful research and habitat protection will ensure their continued survival – and perhaps provide some insight into how they came so perilously close to extinction.

Puerto Rican Whip-poor-Will: Besieged by men and mongooses

Until January 1986, a great many experts were sure that Jerdon's Courser was extinct. In 1961 they were equally sure that the Whip-poor-will (*Caprimulgus noctitherus*) of Puerto Rico was extinct; sure, that is, until one of them found the birds again, in the parched scrub-forest that grows on the coastal limestone in the driest parts of this and other Caribbean Islands.

There are two other species in the Americas, and all are closely related to the nightjars, or goatsuckers, found in the Old World. Beautifully camouflaged in subtle and intricate patterns of brown, buff, grey and black they spend the day among leaf-litter on the ground, their great eyes firmly closed to avoid giving away their presence. By night they are transformed into agile, graceful hunters of moths and flying beetles, for which the broad mouth, fringed with long stiff bristles like that of a swift, seems perfectly adapted.

The Puerto Rican species is now confined to the driest parts of the island, where fewer than 500 pairs breed in three sites in the Guanica and Susua forests. They may well have been more widespread in the past, but like many other ground-living island birds were easy prey for the mongooses introduced to control rats infesting the lucrative sugarcane plantations. The wettest parts of the island support too few night-flying insects for whip-poor-wills, but there are large areas of apparently suitable habitat — drier than the mountain forests but lusher than the extremely arid coastal scrub where they now live — which they could probably populate if those forests were not also infested with mongooses. The birds' present habitat is so dry and inhospitable that it is unattractive to people as well as mongooses,

and the combination of human disturbance and mongoose predation probably confines the whip-poor-wills unnaturally to their present arid refuges.

One close relative of the Whip-poor-will, however, has achieved a degree of adaptation to its desert environment that no other bird can match. In the desert mountains of the central and western United States, the Poor-will (*Phalaenoptilus nuttalli*) overcomes the disappearance of its insect food in the bitter cold of winter by hibernating. Like a squirrel or a bear, it drops its body temperature and metabolic rate to levels so low that it appears to be dead. Poor-wills choose a narrow cleft in a south-facing rock, or a protected site under a desert shrub, and settle down to a winter of quiet content, their body processes so slowed that the few grammes of fat with which they start the winter can last them for 150 days. They can lower their body temperature to within five degrees Celsius of freezing without apparent harm, and if the days turn warm, as they often do in the Arizona winter, they can return to normal activity in a few hours. The Poor-wills' hibernation has been known to science for less than 40 years, but the Hopi Indians of Arizona knew their habits well and called them Holchko — the Sleeping Ones.

The Poor-will is clearly a species with a long evolutionary history of desert living; so long that it has achieved a degree of physiological adaptation unique among birds. Its relative in Puerto Rico owes its precarious status in part, perhaps, to being less rigidly adapted to the habitat into which it has been forced by man and his camp-followers.

Like most nightjars, the ground-nesting Puerto Rican Whip-poor-Will is perfectly camouflaged when at rest in the leaf-litter of the scrub-forest floor.

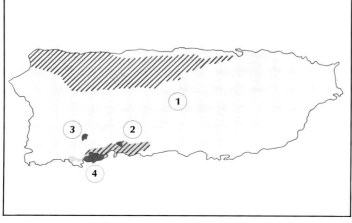

Puerto Rican Whip-poor-Will
The distribution of the Whip-poor-Will has shrunk to three tiny and widely separated areas.

Known locations
1. Central cordillera
2. Guayanilla Hills
3. Susua Forest
4. Guanica Forest

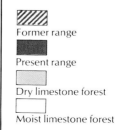

Former range

Present range

Dry limestone forest

Moist limestone forest

Status report – Deserts:
The worldwide advance of the arid lands

Arid lands are the only habitats that are actually increasing in area. Deserts can look after themselves, and are surely the last environments on land that man will destroy, but semi-deserts are under enormous threat. An average annual rainfall of between 20cm and 50cm can support low densities of stock in average or above-average years. But there are below-average years too, and these often arrive one after another in devastating succession. The prolonged droughts that ravaged sub-Saharan and northeastern Africa in the 1960s, 1970s and 1980s killed millions of cattle and tens of thousands of people. Many had come into the region attracted by a few years of good rainfall and a network of waterholes installed by well-meaning development agencies.

Deserts are expanding at an astonishing rate. Every year an area of nearly 60,000 square kilometres – the size of Belgium – turns into desert. Of even greater concern is the land that at present is merely arid, but is poised to become desert if its present treatment continues. This potential desert occupies an area equal to that of Canada.

About 80 million people are immediately threatened with loss of the land on which they depend, due to this process of 'desertification'. An area twice the size of Canada is already afflicted, and the total area of land already desert, plus the land at risk of becoming desert, covers 30 per cent of the land surface of the earth. The increase in this habitat is thus one of the greatest threats facing mankind. And it is caused entirely by the misuse, by man, of vulnerable land: climate may provide the opportunity, but it is man who now creates the desert.

This aerial view over northern Kenya, taken in 1979, shows the dramatic impact on the land of overgrazing. The land has been stripped almost bare of vegetation for dozens of kilometres around a remote waterhole.

The bones of dead stock litter the parched landscape of southeastern Niger, one of the worst-hit drought areas of the Sahel region.

The losing battle

We create it by moving too many people, cattle and goats into arid areas. To enable crops to be grown on land too dry for agriculture, the land is irrigated; but proper irrigation is enormously expensive in materials and human skills, and if it is not properly done the soil becomes clogged with salt or alkali and then will not grow anything. Irrigation now causes as much productive land to be lost each year as is gained. Boreholes are sunk to provide people and cattle with permanent water. The result is that the soil is stripped bare and compacted by hooves for large areas around each hole, vegetation is browsed to the ground or cut as fuel for the herdsmen's families, and the water table drops so far that the few remaining plants wither and die.

The desert so created is usually more sterile than a natural desert. Perhaps a few highly specialized birds of the extreme desert will be able to increase their range, but all arid-country birds need some vegetation, and man-made deserts usually have none. The many species that are exploiting those arid lands that are not now true desert, but are poised to become so, are doomed to disappear; just as the invaders who will turn that land into desert are doomed to starve.

The arid lands fringing deserts are often important habitats not only for the birds that breed there (many of which migrate to permanently wetter habitats outside their breeding season) but also for long-distance migrants that use them as staging posts, or even spend the whole non-breeding season there. The West African Sahel, for example, is flooded with small migrant songbirds from Europe each autumn and spring and some, like the European Whitethroat, may spend all winter there. Countless Whitethroats perished during the droughts of the late sixties and seventies, and the numbers breeding in Britain are still only one-quarter of their pre-drought levels. So it is that the degradation of arid lands in the tropics affects the bird-life of northern countries, just as it will ultimately affect the lives of their human populations.

As more and more lowland pasture is converted to arable use, or simply overgrazed, the pastoralist and his livestock are forced higher and higher into the hills. Here, at Shadi in India, barely a blade of grass remains.

Oases are refuges in the desert landscape. For many birds migrating between Europe and Africa they are vital resting-places.

These man-made habitats occupy less than one-tenth of the land area of the earth, yet on that small area is grown most of the food we eat. On average, agricultural habitats are less productive then many natural eco-systems, but at their best they outstrip most natural habitats. However, the more efficient they are the less attractive they are to most birds, because the most efficient agricultural production, in economic terms, is obtained by monoculture — huge areas devoted to the production of a single crop. The result is a uniform and monotonous habitat to which few wild species are adapted or attracted.

Birds and farmers are constantly at war. Monocultures attract few species, but those that are attracted often very soon become pests and the focus of intensive eradication campaigns. In countries favoured by good agricultural land — notably Europe and North America — so much land is devoted to agriculture that changes in land-use and farming practices may have far-reaching effects on bird-life and may even threaten the existence of some species.

Agricultural Land

Habitats under the plough

Agricultural land is the most important of all habitats for mankind. But it is not a natural habitat; it is man-made, and every one of the 14 million square kilometres of cultivated land exists at the expense of some natural habitat. As our populations and expectations rise, our need for food is growing so fast that the fate of many other habitats will be determined very largely by the future of farmland.

As the need for food increases, so more natural habitat is turned into cultivated land. At least attempts are made to do so; attempts which usually destroy the integrity of the original habitat but often do not produce much food. For the truth is that most of the land that can be cultivated has already been put to the plough: the rest is too wet, too dry, too poor in nutrients, too deficient in soil, or permanently frozen. The good land is not distributed evenly: those with least (and many Asian countries have 10 per cent or less of their land suitable for agriculture) are chiefly in the tropics; those with most – such as Europe (36 per cent) and North America (22 per cent) – are in the northern hemisphere. Countries with the densest human populations often have the least good farming land, making them vulnerable to famine and largely dependent on surplus food grown in the less populous countries.

A second-class habitat for birds

Although it occupies over nine per cent of the land area of the earth, farmland contributes less than eight per cent of world primary production and well under one per cent of plant biomass. In spite of the enormous investment of time, money, machinery and chemicals that go into growing food, agricultural land compares poorly with many natural ecosystems. The most productive agricultural land is as productive as any ecosystem, but most farmland produces well below its maximum potential, and the average performance is poor.

Agricultural ecosystems differ from natural ones in several respects that are important to birds and other wildlife. In most cases the biggest yields are obtained by growing a single crop in large fields, dressed abundantly with chemical fertilizers and pesticides. Intensive agriculture typically depends on such monocultures, but relatively few kinds of bird can thrive in these

Monoculture in North America: huge fields of ripening barley stretch as far as the eye can see across converted prairie-land in Alberta.

Kikuyu 'shambas' near Nairobi. When a Kenyan farmer dies, the shamba is divided between his children; but in a country with a high population growth the result is that the individual portions soon become too small to support a family. Nearly 30% of Kenyan farmers are now essentially landless.

conditions; tree-nesting species have nowhere to nest, and ground-feeding and ground-nesting birds are vulnerable to the heavy machinery used to plant, manage and harvest the crop. Those that do adapt often become pests – simply because of the huge quantities of food available; fields of peas naturally attract flocks of pigeons.

Which birds suffer most from conversion of land to monoculture depends on the type of habitat being replaced. The great wheat-fields of central North America, for example, were formerly prairie grassland, and ground-living grassland birds such as Prairie Chickens were the chief victims. In Europe, farmland generally replaced woodland, and until recently many woodland species were able to survive quite well because there were enough nesting and roosting sites for them in the hedgerows that bordered the fields. But in the last 30 years most of those hedges have been destroyed to increase the size of fields, and the consequent losses of birds and other wildlife have been matched only by the loss of topsoil from erosion.

Birds and farmers have probably warred since mankind first began to farm. When fields were small and surrounded by forest, many forest birds must have invaded the fields for easy pickings – retiring to the safety of the forest when disturbed, as they still do in areas of shifting agriculture in the tropics. Chickens allowed to wander by day were often picked off by birds of prey, and country people throughout the world still refer to the boldest local raptor as the 'chicken hawk'.

Yet many birds perform useful functions too, especially those insectivorous species that prey on insects which, if uncontrolled, would soon become pests.

As more and more land is brought into cultivation of some sort, birds that can adapt to agricultural land must increase at the expense of those that cannot, but in the long term the greatest effect of agricultural land on bird-life will be through the loss of the habitats that are destroyed.

Mixed agriculture in Western Europe. This type of farming, with its diversity of land use, its hedgerows and patches of old woodland, is fast disappearing today. Modern farming methods demand bigger fields in which large agricultural machines can be used efficiently.

Entire hillsides near Warang in Nepal are terraced in an attempt to produce sufficient food and fodder for the local people and their livestock. International agencies are now encouraging the planting of fast-growing fuelwood and fodder trees to increase productivity and, more important in the long term, to protect the steep hill slopes from erosion.

A small mixed farming community working the productive soils at 4000 metres in the mountains of Ecuador.

Chilean Woodstar: Confined to a man-made habitat

Hummingbirds epitomize the frailty and paradoxical resilience of birds. They are the smallest of all vertebrates — the smallest weighing less than two grammes — and are so specialized for flight that their feet are so vestigial they cannot walk. And yet they are one of the largest of all bird families, the 315 species occupying all habitats in the tropical Americas from desert to mountain-top.

The Chilean Woodstar (*Eulidia yarrellii*) is the only endangered bird that seems to be confined to a man-made habitat. This may simply reflect the replacement of its natural habitat by an artificial one rather than its adaptation and transfer to a new habitat: we do not know which because the bird has been very little studied, but the apparent pace of its decline suggests the worst.

This species seems always to have had a very restricted distribution in the northern part of Chile, where it is now found only in the cultivated valleys of the Azapa and Lluta rivers and in the gardens of the city of Arica and its suburbs. There are occasional records of the bird from as far away as 130km, but they have been seen regularly — and therefore presumably breed — only in the vicinity of Arica. The city and its two valleys are surrounded by desert; indeed the coastal plains of Chile hold some of the most arid deserts in the world. The Woodstar probably once lived in several of the narrow fertile valleys that thread their way through the desert, and were wiped out as the valleys were settled and cultivated. Until about 1948 they were common within their very limited range, but by 1971 they had become much scarcer. They used to be seen occasionally in substantial numbers at flowering trees in Arica city itself, but in recent years it has become very difficult to find more than one or two at a time. The aptly named Oasis Hummingbird (*Rhodopis vesper*), which is half as large again as the Woodstar, was scarcer in Arica in 1943 but is now much more common, and seems to have adapted much more successfully to the man-made landscape.

Just what it is about the conversion of its natural valleys into agricultural land that has led the Chilean Woodstar into its precipitous decline is not known, though several factors can be suggested. Hummingbirds depend on ample supplies of small insects and flower nectar, and it is likely that the cultivation of the valleys – carried out with extensive use of toxic chemicals – would have greatly altered the balance of the Woodstar's insect prey at the same time as the flowers it was used to feeding on were being replaced by crop plants much less rich in nectar. We can only speculate on its decline, because in that remote and inhospitable part of the world there is little chance that the Woodstar's plight will ever be properly researched.

A bird like the Woodstar, whose habitat is lost entirely to cultivation, cannot survive unless it adapts very quickly to life in agricultural land. But adaptation is possible. Some species, which had larger original ranges and so were less likely to lose all their native habitat in a short time, have made the transition so successfully that they are now more characteristic of agricultural habitats than of natural ones.

The Chilean Woodstar is the last of the species we shall discuss that is 'endangered' in the classic sense. The birds to be described in the rest of this section, and the next, are clearly in no immediate danger of extinction. On the contrary, they are extremely successful. Many of them have increased enormously in the recent past, and some continue to do so. These birds have successfully transferred from natural habitats to those completely dominated, or even created, by man. They illustrate the kinds of changes that wild birds can make in order to co-exist with people; the kinds of changes other species may have to make if they are to survive. Some of them also suggest that in making these changes they may cut themselves off so completely from their natural roots that they, too, may be threatened if people should ever cease to provide them with the resources on which they have now come to depend.

The Chilean Woodstar is perhaps the only bird that owes its survival to the creation of agricultural land. Near the Chilean town of Arica, in one of the world's harshest deserts, two fertile valleys have been cultivated. This is the only known habitat of this rare hummingbird.

A Chilean Woodstar nest with two nearly fledged young. Recently the population of this rare bird has declined sharply – a response, experts believe, to the increased use of pesticides which has reduced its food supply.

Cattle Egret:
New partners in an ancient lifestyle

One of the earliest forms of farming practised by man was the keeping of domesticated grazing animals for their milk, meat, blood and hides. Today, pastoral agriculture is still one of the most widespread kinds of farming in the world, and it affects a wider range of habitats than arable farming because cattle can be grazed in environments too extreme for the raising of crops.

Cattle Egrets (*Bubulcus ibis*) are exceptionally successful fellow-travellers of pastoral man. Until recently they were confined to the tropical and subtropical Old World, from Africa and southwestern Europe east through Asia as far as Japan. Throughout their range they are associated with cattle, feeding on large insects and small vertebrates which the cattle disturb as they move through the grass. The egrets walk slowly, with a rather clumsy goose-like gait, and when trying to catch up with a fast-walking cow or a particularly lively locust they hurry forward with a comical urgency quite unlike the graceful dignity of most egrets. The birds

divide their time between sitting on the backs of the cattle and foraging around their feet, and it has been proved that they benefit from the activity of the cattle by obtaining considerably more food than they do when they have to forage alone.

Until about 1930 Cattle Egrets were confined to the Old World, but then they became established in South America after crossing the Atlantic apparently unaided. They spread through the Caribbean islands and into North America, where they first bred in 1953. Half a world away, at the opposite end of their range, they colonized northern Australia unaided by 1948 — though their subsequent spread through Australia, into New Zealand, and through the Pacific islands as far as Hawaii, has been helped by deliberate introductions.

They had been recorded in South America in the nineteenth century, but did not begin to breed there for over 50 years. Probably they were not able to establish themselves successfully, either there or in the other areas they have colonized recently, until European and Asian man had introduced cattle. In the birds' original range, people and their cattle had been gradually replacing herds of wild herbivores for several thousand years, so the egrets were able to switch gradually from the wild species to the domesticated ones. In Africa they can still be seen accompanying herds of wild game as they must have done before people began to replace the game with cattle. The African Cattle Egret is just as much at home with the cattle of Maasai and other pastoral tribes as with the migratory herds of wildebeest, eland and other animals which are gradually being squeezed out of grasslands and bush as pastoralists and their cattle, or arable farmers, take over the land. Indeed, the egrets are probably better off with cattle than with antelopes, for cattle do not migrate the huge distances that wild game do, and never stray far from water.

Cattle Egrets with chicks in an Australian breeding colony. Formerly found only in Africa and Asia, the species has now spread to Australia and the Americas.

The Cattle Egret's success lies in its great adaptability. Where the birds used to follow the herds of grazing herbivores across the African savanna, they now adopt the same close relationship with man's domestic cattle.

Although Cattle Egrets are much less tied to the vicinity of water than most species of the heron and egret family are, they usually assemble near water before going to roost, and most roosting and nesting sites are in trees or bushes surrounded by water. This gives a measure of safety to the colony, at least from terrestrial predators. Often, the water surrounding the roost or colony is a temporary pool that dries out after the rains and so does not have a resident population of aquatic predators either.

As people and their cattle invade more and more of the world's forests and arid lands, Cattle Egrets will be able to increase their range still further. The limits to their numbers and distribution will probably be set by the availability of nest sites, since although they do wander considerable distances they do not usually migrate far to breed. They are useful rather than a hindrance to herdsmen and so have little to fear from man. They take insects that graze the same grass his cattle eat, fertilize the ground with their droppings, and even give warning of approaching predators. Cattle Egrets have occupied a new niche, created by man, and have even colonized regions where their natural niche does not exist. One of the major influences on their spread in recent years has been the widespread development of irrigation farming. Most of the world's Cattle Egrets are now probably dependent on man for their survival. They have thrown in their lot with the pastoralist, and their future will reflect the success or failure of that way of life.

Mammal and bird share the benefits of partnership. The egret feeds on the insects attracted to the wildebeest and flushed from the grass by its movements. In return it provides the animal with an early-warning service by flapping noisily into the air at any sign of danger.

The Rosellas:
Australia's farm-loving parrots

The eight species of rosella are all brilliantly coloured, long-tailed Australian parrots, 28–36cm long. Several of them have adapted so well to agricultural land that they are sometimes treated as pests, at least in parts of their range. They all have characteristically mottled backs, which make them remarkably difficult to see in spite of their bright colours, and a striking cheek-patch of a different colour from the rest of the surrounding plumage.

Eastern Rosellas (*Platycercus eximius*) rival the Splendid Parakeets in gaudy brilliance, but are nearly twice their size. They also spend much of their time on the ground eating grass-seed, and even when approached they often do not take flight until the last moment; sometimes even later, as frequent road-deaths testify. They chatter companionably while feeding, and their flight is swift and undulating unless they are travelling long distances over open ground, when they fly straight and high.

Their natural habitat is open woodland or lightly wooded grassland in southeastern Australia. Such country has been settled and farmed over much of their range, and they have adapted well to the mix of farmland and gardens that has replaced much of their native habitat. In the more thickly forested parts of their range, the closely related Crimson Rosella (*P. elegans*) was better adapted to the native habitat, but as the forests were cleared, farmed and settled, Crimson Rosellas were less able to adapt and have been replaced by the Eastern.

Eastern Rosellas are versatile feeders and have no difficulty in adding a wide range of agricultural produce to an already varied diet. They feed not only on fallen grass-seed, a habit predisposing them to take spilled grain in farmyards and fields, and seeding grasses in pastures, but also on seeds and blossoms in the tops of trees. They find the blossoms of fruit-trees at least as attractive as those of native species, and can do considerable damage in orchards. They were introduced to New Zealand around 1910 and within 20 years had already become a pest in that country's orchards.

Crimson Rosellas provide a dazzling splash of colour as they swoop in from nearby woodland to feed boldly in a city garden.

In the southwestern corner of the continent the Western Rosella (*P. icterotis*) occupies a similar niche to the Eastern, and has likewise taken enthusiastically to agricultural land. The Westerns are more unobtrusive birds than their eastern counterparts, except when they congregate on stubble after harvesting, or in farmyards, to feed on spilled grain.

In the northeast of Australia the Pale-headed Rosella (*P. adscitus*) is common in woodland and even in forest if it is close to grassland. It too can be a pest of orchards and of maize fields. In southern South Australia, two separate populations of the Adelaide Rosella (*P. adelaidae*) — intermediate between the Crimson Rosella and the Yellow Rosella (*P. flaveolus*) — are abundant in wooded country, often penetrating into the gardens of the city of Adelaide. They are common around farms, where they too collect spilled grain from farmyards, haystacks and stubble fields.

Each of these closely related species of parrot, in their widely separated ranges, has taken to agricultural land in a very short time. They seem generally to take grain that has already been spilled, and thus lost to the farmer, and probably do little actual damage except on the occasions when they take orchard blossom. Even then the numbers of flowers they take may very well not be reflected in a loss of fruit on the same scale. They certainly do some good too, since they take the seeds and berries of weeds as well as crops.

It is not clear to what extent any of these delightful species has become dependent on agriculture. Probably they make use of it without being totally dependent, but in time there is a danger that they will come to rely too much on a land-use that may not last forever. All these parrots are common, and give no cause for concern; but the same could have been said a hundred years ago of the Passenger Pigeon in America, and of many other species that have since died out. Human agricultural practices can change too fast for birds to keep pace with, as many European birds have found to their cost.

The natural habitat of the brilliantly coloured Eastern Rosella is open woodland and grassland, and this has enabled the bird to adapt readily to the farmland and gardens of human settlement.

The Pale-headed Rosella of northeastern Australia is one of several rosella species that have become pests in orchards and also on some grain crops.

Collared Dove:
The peaceful invader

Until the end of the last century, Collared Doves (*Streptopelia decaocto*) were found in southern and central Asia, east to Japan (where they had been introduced from China) and west as far as Turkey. They were found mostly in dry or lightly wooded country, usually close to human settlement and cultivation. Then they began to spread northwest through Europe, reaching Britain in 1952. They first bred there three years later and by 1969 had swept through the country to become common birds of garden and farmland from the Scilly Isles in the south to the Shetlands in the north. In the following decade their British population increased fourfold.

This astonishing expansion has few parallels. Only the Cattle Egret and the Fulmar have spread so far so fast. All these expanding populations have benefited from food provided by man, though its role in bringing about the range expansion is not certain.

Today the Collared Dove is a common resident of fields and gardens across much of northwestern Europe. What triggered its remarkable expansion is not definitely known, but genetic modification or climatic change could have been contributing factors.

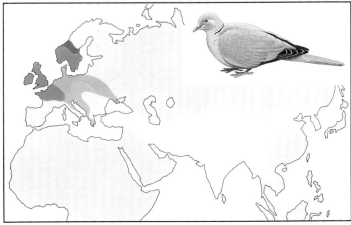

The peaceful invasion
In the last 50 years the Collared Dove has spread across Europe from its homeland in south-central Asia in one of the most dramatically successful colonizations of modern times.

Distribution

	1930
	1938
	1945
	1955
	1965
	1975

Collared Doves feed mainly on small seeds on the ground, and in Europe today they are virtually parasitic on man, taking grain spilled in farmyards or put out for poultry. They also compete with House Sparrows, Starlings and Domestic Pigeons for breadcrumbs at garden bird-tables and in city parks. In winter there is often no other food for them, and in most of Europe, and even in parts of their original range, Collared Doves probably survive through the winter only by eating food provided by man.

Although all three species whose ranges have expanded so rapidly this century could do so only because of food made available by man, the original cause of the expansion must have been different. Human cultivation, after all, preceded the arrival of Collared Doves in Europe by several thousand years. Possibly some genetic change in the Turkish population may have caused them to move so suddenly into cultivated Europe.

Yet Europe is not short of birds that eat grain in farmyards and chicken runs. House Sparrows thrive on small seeds in farmyards. Wood Pigeons often feed in the same rural gardens as Collared Doves; and Domestic Pigeons, House Sparrows and Starlings are well-established plunderers of breadcrumbs in city and suburban parks. How did Collared Doves manage not only to find enough ecological space to establish themselves, but enough surplus resources to increase at such an astonishing speed; and all, apparently, without causing any other species to decline? It is an ecological axiom that no two species can occupy precisely the same niche, yet the Collared Dove appears to make its living in ways already being followed by other species.

Probably the Collared Dove's secret lies in its versatility, and the fact that although its requirements overlap those of several other species, it does not overlap completely with any of them. It is smaller than the Wood Pigeon, and much less afraid of man, so it takes generally smaller items of food and forages where Wood Pigeons do not dare. Domestic Pigeons are more or less confined to cities, and frequent cultivated land much less commonly than Collared Doves. House Sparrows have very different nesting requirements and do not forage as far from houses as Collared Doves are prepared to do.

Within a few years of being first recorded in an area, Collared Doves have often become abundant enough to be declared pests. Certainly they eat a lot of food put out for chickens, but since most commercial chicken production in Europe now takes place under cover, their economic impact is not great. The noise of their penetrating courting call is probably their most annoying characteristic, at least to town-dwellers.

Like Cattle Egrets, Collared Doves have probably now become so dependent on man for their survival that they could not survive a major change in agricultural practice. They show that cultivated land offers opportunities for birds which may go unexploited for a very long time before a species becomes adapted to them.

Collared Doves are great opportunists and readily join other common woodland and urban birds in exploiting food resources provided by man's activities.

Status report – Farmland: The industrialization of nature

Mankind is abusing his most precious habitat at such a rate that one-third of it is likely to be severely damaged or even destroyed in the next 15 years. Good agricultural land, which is already inadequate for our needs, is being built over and degraded at such a pace that substantial increases in world famine, and in food prices, are inevitable.

Poor land-use is something we think of as a characteristic of developing countries, especially in the tropics, and there is no doubt that much of the low food production and loss of topsoil that occur in the tropics are the result of bad agricultural practices. But the scale of the problem is awesome. In India alone, over 40 per cent of the country's 3.3 million square kilometres suffers soil erosion, and large areas are degraded by floods and the accumulation of salt and alkalis. The loss of nutrients in the topsoil eroded from Indian farmland each year is greater than the volume of nutrients added to the land in the form of fertilizers. In many parts of the tropics, peasant farmers achieve only a fraction of the potential productivity of their land, often due to ignorance of appropriate techniques or to their inability to pay for the necessary equipment.

The spreading tide of concrete

Yet the developing countries account for a relatively small proportion of the world's agricultural production. Most of the world's grain is grown in the prairies of North America, and it is there that lost food production really counts. The USA has the largest and most highly developed soil conservation service in the world, yet 12,000 square kilometres of American farmland are degraded by soil erosion every year. But the most irreversible and scandalous abuse of farmland is through covering it with asphalt and concrete. In the USA alone, as much cropland is permanently destroyed in this way as is degraded by erosion; and in Canada more than 8000 square kilometres of farmland were submerged under roads and buildings between 1961 and 1971.

The consequences of this rampant destruction of good farmland are felt all round the world. The USA alone supports over 300 million people on the food it grows on about 1.6 million square kilometres. The area of farmland obliterated *each year* in that country would feed another two and a quarter million people, roughly the number of people added to the world population every 12 days.

Where traditional farming is practised, the White Stork (*Ciconia ciconia*) can coexist with man, but in areas of large-scale monoculture the available food supply is usually insufficient for successful breeding.

The gains of highly mechanized agriculture must be weighed against both economic and ecological consequences. Crops grown under such systems are often susceptible to pests and diseases. More and more agrochemicals are then applied – with serious repercussions on both production costs and the environment.

Other developed countries bury their farmland under roads and cities in equally profligate fashion. Japan – a country already poorly endowed with farmland – destroyed seven per cent of its agricultural land between 1960 and 1971, and European countries lost between 1.5 and 4.5 per cent. Many developing countries misuse their agricultural land, but until recently few actually buried it out of reach; unfortunately the habit is spreading as people throughout the world desert the land for the cities and can be housed only by enlarging urban areas.

No habitat is spared

We have already seen how the need to grow more food puts pressure on natural habitats as people try to turn them into agricultural land. In the Netherlands, the most densely populated country in Europe, farming land is so scarce that the Dutch have had to create land from the sea, distorting coastal and marine ecosystems in the process. Wetlands are being drained in many parts of the world to harness their prodigious natural productivity to grow food. Forests of all kinds are felled and replaced by crops regardless of their soil's ability to sustain agriculture, or are invaded by cattle who browse regenerating tree seedlings and trigger an inexorable regression towards grassland. Grasslands and drylands are overstocked with domestic grazing animals and turned into unvegetated arid wastelands.

Settlements move higher and higher up mountains, and ever-steeper slopes are cultivated as the valleys and plateaux are turned into farmland. The bare soil that is inevitable at some stage of cultivation is washed downstream, flooding rivers, silting up estuaries and coral reefs and choking the coastal spawning grounds of marine fish and shellfish. Even the polar regions and the oceans are now under increasing pressure to be exploited for their potential food resources.

To a considerable extent the fate of birds of all habitats will depend, directly or indirectly, on the efficiency with which agricultural land produces food. The lower that efficiency, the more natural habitat has to be put to pasture or the plough to make up the difference. Our fates, too, are in the same hands, for the accelerating rape of all natural habitats is a symptom of the widening gap between the amount of food we need and the amount we produce.

Urban man is often extravagant in his use of land, covering huge areas of viable habitat with sprawling housing developments and high-volume motorways. More modest developments would preserve habitats for the benefit of man and wildlife alike, and also conserve potentially productive land for future agricultural use.

Corn is a popular crop but also a damaging one. It leaves the soil totally exhausted, and so requires intensive use of fertilizers. After the harvest, the fields are often left bare, and vulnerable to wind and rain erosion.

The city is a habitat in which at first sight ecological principles seem not to apply. They are designed by man, for man, offering him security, a home and a place in which to make his living. But modern cities are dominated by concrete pavements, canyon-like streets between bleak walls, traffic noise, exhaust fumes, dust and smog. They are habitats far removed from any found in nature.

But the city-dweller's links with the countryside are stronger than many may think. His food comes from the surrounding land, and from lands far away, and he needs the fresh air, peace and spiritual renewal provided by mountains and lake-shores, forests and river valleys.

For most birds the centre of a large city is an inhospitable place: but not for all. Parks and gardens, canals and buildings can create many different habitats, some of which support an astonishingly varied avifauna. Such habitats may even be safer than natural ones: there are fewer predators, and far fewer lethal chemicals around. The result is that several species have adapted so successfully to city life that they are now seldom found in the wild.

Towns and Cities

The urban habitat

The price of our much-valued personal mobility is high. Vehicle exhaust gases pose a significant health risk in many crowded cities, as well as being a major factor in the corrosion of the stonework of historic buildings and ancient monuments.

The urban life-style which most people in the developed world pursue – and to which most of the rest of the world aspires – can be supported only by an efficient agricultural system. In a very real sense city-dwellers are symbiotic with farmers, and the future of this most man-made of all habitats depends as much on the future of agricultural land as does the future of any natural habitat.

The continuing burial of good farmland under concrete and asphalt is of course a reflection of the steady stream of people leaving the land for the city. This is the great human migration of modern times. It affects almost every country in the world, and is both cause and consequence of changes in agricultural practices. As it becomes harder to make a living, so more people abandon the laborious and uncertain life of a peasant for the apparent glamour of city life. Paradoxically, as agriculture becomes more efficient it also encourages people to leave the land because fewer are needed to grow the same amount of food.

A large city creates its own climate raising the air temperature by a degree or two and probably changing the pattern of rainfall by filling the air with acid fumes and with particles of dust and smoke. A city centre is an inhospitable habitat for most birds, though a few species have colonized it with great success. The tall stone buildings of older city centres are good nesting and roosting sites for the Domestic Pigeons, House Sparrows and Starlings that forage for food scattered accidentally, or put out deliberately, by people.

Residential areas and suburbs provide food and cover for a wider variety of birds. Suburban gardens often have denser bird populations than the woodlands that are the original habitat of many of the birds, but though a few species thrive in cities, urban bird-life is usually much less prolific and diverse than that of the natural habitats the cities have replaced.

Parks and ornamental gardens are peaceful oases for people and wildlife alike amid the noise and bustle of towns and cities.

For many city-dwellers the native and exotic waterfowl that crowd the ponds and lakes of public places in winter provide an important link with nature.

Feral Pigeon:
From cliff-ledge to window-ledge

The bird-life of a big city centre is remarkably uniform around the world. Domestic Pigeons, House Sparrows and European Starlings are the three most common species in city centres from Canada to Australia. These birds have been widely introduced, but have also spread from city to city of their own accord.

Feral Pigeons (*Columba livia*) are the free-living descendants of Domestic Pigeons, which in turn are descended from Rock Doves. They are now much more common and more widely distributed than their ancestors, which occur in Europe, North Africa and central and southern Asia, nesting and roosting in cliffs or caves. Feral Pigeons have spread out from the remote cliff ledges of their ancestors and adopted the cliff-like window ledges of stone buildings in most major cities of the world. They are probably the most successful of all urban birds, and the most tied to cities. Some populations do roost and nest among buildings and then fly out to feed in the surrounding countryside, but the largest populations feed, roost and nest within the city limits. They are primarily seed-eaters, and in former days the grain spilled from horses' feed-bags was a major source of food for them. Now, many subsist largely on bread, though it is a much less suitable food and the birds usually prefer some kind of seed if any is available.

Much of the food they eat is actually given to them by people. For city-dwellers, Feral Pigeons are a precious link with the natural world of living things, and the birds' huge success in colonizing such an artificial environment is eloquent testimony to the love that mankind has for birds. These personal feelings easily outweigh the advice of civic authorities, who point to the pigeons' negative contributions to city life: the droppings that foul pavements and sidewalks, and stain and rot the stonework of buildings; the nests that 'foul' fire-escapes and window-ledges; and the birds' possible role in transmitting some virus diseases. Pigeons even eat buildings. At egg-laying time, when the female needs extra lime to build her egg-shells, she may peck at crumbling mortar for the calcium it contains. It matters not. The Feral Pigeon has made the city its home, and there it is likely to stay, despite the disapproval of city officials.

Pigeons crowd the skies and open spaces, monuments and buildings of nearly every major city in the world; as popular with tourists everywhere as they are unpopular with the civic authorities whose buildings they all too frequently deface.

Feral pigeons have adapted all too well to the urban environment. The ledges and niches of the city skyline make ideal nesting and roosting sites, well out of reach of most predators.

European Starling:
Noisy, dirty — and very successful

No birds can drown the din of city traffic as effectively as a massed roost of European Starlings (*Sturnus vulgaris*). Black clouds of tens or hundreds of thousands, wheeling in complex aerial manoeuvres in the darkening sky before sweeping down to roost with a deafening rush of wings, are as familiar a feature of life in many cities as the traffic and the lights. For hours after dark the birds keep up a shrill cacophony of squawks and whistles, no doubt prolonged by the late-night bustle and lights of the city. The song of the Starling is not a pretty sound, and is not improved when offered thousands at a time. The birds are probably even more unpopular for their discordant evening chorus than for the inevitable deposits that accumulate beneath their roosts.

The natural range of European Starlings extends through Europe east into central Asia, and in the 1940s they colonized Iceland of their own accord. But their actual range is vastly greater than this. With a lot of help from people they have spread throughout populated North America, through southeastern Australia and New Zealand, and even across the southern tip of Africa, where Cecil Rhodes liberated 18 birds in 1899. In the USA the first successful introduction was in 1890 in Central Park, New York. It took only 50 years for them to cover the 4000km to the west coast, and they now range from Alaska to southern Mexico.

Starlings are as much birds of agricultural land as of towns, and their phenomenal spread across the American continent has been due largely to their ability to exploit farmland, rather than cities. But in many cities they have become as much an urban bird as they are in London or in New York, where many Starlings roost, feed, and breed entirely within the city. They feed among the pigeons and sparrows in parks and at garden bird-tables, swaggering confidently with a characteristic jerky gait. They are sociable birds and often dominate a feeding area by sheer numbers, although individually they are not especially aggressive, defending only the scrap of food on which they are intent at the time and not trying to claim an entire bird-table as a Blackbird or a Robin would. On lawns they have a distinctive way of probing for soil invertebrates, opening the two halves of the bill to part the grass and expose their invertebrate prey.

The large winter flocks break up in spring as pairs take up their nesting territories. For such very gregarious birds they show remarkably little tendency to nest in colonies. They nest in holes, in trees in rural areas but in cities commonly under house eaves, in drainpipes and chimneys, and in other convenient cavities in buildings. Chimney-pots, roof-ridges and television aerials are favourite song-posts for the male, who delivers a weird variety of croaks, chuckles, wheezes and whistles, often incorporating imitations of other birds, or city sounds like telephone bells and the chimes of ice-cream vans. They often continue to feed socially even while they are breeding, and birds that are not breeding, or have tried and failed, will often roost communally through the nesting period, just as they do in winter. These summer roosts are often overlooked in northern cities because dusk falls so late that the Starlings assemble long after city workers have left the city for their own 'roosts' in the suburbs.

Only in close-up is it possible to appreciate the colour and patterning of the Starling's plumage: from a distance the birds often look dark and drab. Although more often seen probing the lawn for earthworms, Starlings are opportunists like most city birds and a fallen over-ripe pear makes a welcome change of fare.

Thousands of European Starlings wheel high in the evening sky before swooping down to roost on the roof-tops and ledges of buildings.

It is difficult to see why Starlings have been so widely introduced. Almost all their interactions with mankind are negative; they foul buildings and ground alike with their droppings, block chimneys with their nests, wake us up too early on summer mornings by screeching on the roof, and in their roosts create a deafening din that can dominate a city's night-life. They may be implicated in transmitting diseases (though this is very far from being proved) and are frequently pests on farmland. Yet so familiar a part of urban life were they to Europeans that they went to great pains to introduce them to cities in the new continents. Starlings are now at least as successful on agricultural land as they are in cities and could probably survive almost any change in human life-style.

Power lines are a favourite resting and roosting place for flocks of Starlings. Here they may look very crowded, but each individual is careful to maintain a distance of about two bill-lengths from its neighbours to reduce the chances of unnecessary conflict.

European Swift: High flier of the city

Swifts (*Apus apus*) are the most aerial of all birds. They come to rest only to enter or leave a nest- or roost-hole, and they feed, collect nest material, drink, sleep and mate, all in flight. They are the closest living relatives of hummingbirds, which they resemble in their narrow, pointed wings and extremely short legs. But where hummingbirds are specialized for hovering, swifts are built for speed and are the fastest fliers of all birds, capable of speeds of more than 240km/h.

In many European cities, spring is truly ushered in by the sudden arrival of parties of swifts hurtling among the rooftops at breakneck speed with a shrill screaming that is one of the most characteristic sounds of summer. In ages past, the sudden appearance of their black scythe-like shapes, and their habit of circling, screaming, around church towers, was sufficiently ominous for the swifts to be called 'Devilbirds' in many parts of the English countryside.

European Swifts used to nest in caves and on sea-cliffs, and perhaps occasionally in holes in forest trees, but for many generations they have nested in buildings. A hundred years ago in Britain their favourite sites were holes under the eaves of thatched cottages, or in country church towers: today they nest in equivalent sites in our towns and cities. The construction of the swift's nest is presumably based on materials the birds have always used, and these consist of whatever lightweight debris can be found floating high in the early summer air. The main constituents are feathers and small plant fragments, firmly cemented together with the bird's own saliva.

Clinging to a house wall the European Swift demonstrates many of the physical characteristics of the aerial specialist. Four tiny claws, all pointing forward, help the bird to hang on to vertical surfaces. To launch into flight, the bird simply twists and drops clear of its perch. The enormous gape is opened wide to scoop insects from the air, and the deep-set eyes are protected from impact damage by jutting 'eyebrows' of short stiff feathers.

Their stiff, scythe-shaped wings take swifts higher and farther than swallows and martins, the other birds that feed on airborne insects. They regularly feed at heights of over 300m, and may travel 800–1300km in a day when foraging for food for their nestlings. Their greater flying range gives them an advantage over swallows and martins for city life because it allows them to feed beyond the polluted air of the inner cities, where insect life can be too sparse for a bird to raise its brood. A swift gathering food for its young may feed for several hours at a time, and store several thousand insects in a ball in its elastic-sided mouth. Provided the weather is dry and reasonably warm (10°C or over) the swifts can be sure of enough to eat, but cold, wet or windy weather reduces the supply of flying insects and then the birds have problems. When they are incubating their two white eggs, food may be so scarce that both adults have to leave the nest at the same time in order to feed, but swift eggs are unusually resistant to chilling and losses are minimal. If bad weather strikes when young are in the nest, the adults may not be able to brood them; but both young and adult birds are able to withstand low body temperatures by becoming torpid in the equivalent of a brief period of hibernation.

Cities in many countries have their urban swifts. In North America the city species is the Chimney Swift (*Chaetura pelagica*), which, in the few hundred years since Europeans settled the continent, has switched from its natural nesting and roosting sites of huge, hollow forest tree-trunks — which were felled very quickly by the colonists — to the chimneys of factories and other large buildings. The birds roost in these chimneys too, in large flocks, especially on migration, when as many as 12,000 may circle tightly packed above the opening of a chimney before dropping down in a funnel-shaped cloud to spend the night clinging to the vertical walls inside. In Africa, where cities with tall buildings are a phenomenon of the last few decades, they have none the less already been colonized by Little Swifts (*Apus affinis*). In Asia the same species is known as the House Swift and has long nested in temples and other tall buildings.

Swifts are vulnerable to the atmospheric pollution that haunts many of our cities, but they are such magnificent fliers that the city too big for them to nest in, and still find food elsewhere, has probably not yet been built. Let us hope it never will be.

A familiar sight during the nesting season; hundreds of Swifts join in 'screaming parties' over the city before climbing high into the sky to roost on the wing throughout the night.

Mud and straw are the principal materials used by Swallows (*Hirundo rustica*) in building their cup-shaped nests beneath eaves and in open barns and similar structures. These nestlings, eagerly awaiting their next meal, are almost fully fledged.

House Sparrow:
Cosmopolitan without a passport

The House Sparrow (*Passer domesticus*) is the most citified of all birds. It has colonized the cities of Europe and Asia on its own, and with man's help has spread throughout North America and much of Australasia.

The Sparrow is a born opportunist, quickly discovering and exploiting any available source of food. But despite their long association with man, Sparrows are exceptionally alert and always ready to dart away to safety at the slightest hint of danger.

House Sparrows probably evolved in the arid scrublands of the Mediterranean basin, where, like other species of sparrow, they would have fed mainly on grass seeds. It is intriguing to speculate that they may have included the wild ancestors of cultivated cereals in their diet. Over many generations they would have grown accustomed to the proximity of mankind as people learnt to cultivate those wild grasses and so become farmers. As the practice of agriculture led inevitably to permanent human settlements and the growth of cities, so the House Sparrow would have moved from the fields into the villages, feeding originally on spilled and scattered grain but gradually learning to scavenge other edible human refuse. As villages grew into towns, and towns into cities, so House Sparrows too became more urban. Yet they remain ubiquitous in farmland, though they rarely venture very far from buildings.

Sparrows have retained a wary mistrust of man in spite of their long and close association with him. They rarely become hand-tame, and even in cities they approach people closely only when shortage of food demands that they compete with Feral Pigeons and gulls for hand-outs. When efforts are made to control or exterminate them they learn faster than other urban birds to take appropriate evasive action. Their vigilance has surely contributed to their success from the earliest times, when they must have been regarded chiefly as grain thieves.

Other species of sparrow can also colonize towns and cities, provided they do not have to compete with House Sparrows. In eastern Asia, where there are no House Sparrows, the Tree Sparrow (*P. montanus*) is a city bird, though where its distribution overlaps with House Sparrows it is confined to the countryside. In the Canary Islands Spanish Sparrows (*P. hispaniolensis*) occupy the towns, but in the Mediterranean basin, where both species occur, House Sparrows firmly occupy the towns and Spanish Sparrows the surrounding countryside. In parts of North Africa, Desert Sparrows (*P. simplex*) take over the urban role of the absent House Sparrow.

House Sparrows were first introduced to North America in 1850, in Brooklyn, and later to 100 other cities in the USA and Canada. With this help they had conquered the whole country by 1905. They were brought in not just as familiar reminders of home but to help control insect pests, especially the dropworm. The birds do feed their young on insects, but most of the year they eat grain, and within 20 years of being introduced to eat insects these familiar little urban birds had been declared a pest in many areas.

The House Sparrow — the most familiar and successful of man's avian 'fellow travellers', here with feathers fluffed out for maximum warmth in the cold of a European winter.

Status report – Towns and cities:
A home for the bold and resourceful

The world's towns and cities are growing even faster than the human population, for they are swollen by immigration of people from the land as well as by their own off-spring. Since cities grew up where people settled to grow food, urban expansion is inevitably at the expense of agricultural land. And as the best land is swallowed up, so natural habitats are transformed into pro-gressively more marginal farmland. The fate of all birds' natural habitats is thus affected by the growth of cities.

Some birds will benefit by this. Feral Pigeons, Starlings and House Sparrows will continue to spread to new cities and multiply in those they already occupy. The House Crows of India, which now live only in association with mankind, will doubtless flourish as the citizens of India continue to swell their already desperately crowded cities. House Sparrows will continue to sup-port thriving populations of Kestrels in inner London, Tawny Owls in European suburbs and Screech Owls in suburban North America. Swifts, too, will benefit so long as cities do not become too polluted, or so large that the birds cannot reach clean feed-ing areas in a day's flight.

But these few species prosper at the expense of those of the natural habitats that have been destroyed. Cities and their at-tendant industry and road systems also affect existing habitats directly through their pol-lution of the atmosphere and waterways. Large cities consume vast quantities of water and demand that distant valleys be dammed and lakes and rivers harnessed to satisfy their thirst. Few birds live so far from cities that they are unaffected by them. From Junin Grebes on their chilly upland lake in the Peruvian Andes, whose waters are already earmarked for the city of Lima 160km away, to Chinese Egrets ousted from the outskirts of Hong Kong by clouds of smoke drifting over their nests, and from Waldrapps prevented from breeding in Turkey by piles of human garbage littering their nesting ledges, to Chilean Woodstars slipping into oblivion as their remote valleys are farmed and settled, few corners of the world are free from the pressures of man's growing cities.

We have discussed some of the endangered birds in the major natural environments of the world, and some species that have become characteristic of the two most arti-ficial habitats, agricultural land and human settlements. Although it is useful to treat these environments as quite separate, clearly they are all connected. None is self-con-tained; the whole planet is an ecological unit. All habitats share the resources of the biosphere, all affect each other directly or indirectly, and all are subject to the eco-logical laws of nature. Even urban man shares those habitats; they are our life-support systems too.

Most birds live in a specific habitat, and if that is lost they have nowhere else to go. Mankind has expanded his ecological niche to include all the earth's habitats. We use them all; we need them all too, and the fate of a habitat and its birds is a pointer to the fate of all mankind.

An image that reflects one of the underlying themes of this book: a Little Owl (*Athene noctua*) lies at the side of a busy motorway – not killed by any delib-erate act, but simply an innocent victim of the thoughtless haste of the modern world.

For birds in the city, adaptability is the key to survival. Birds that have become familiar with man often choose the most unlikely places to build their nests.

To say that mankind needs birds is no emotional flight of fancy. We may not need them directly, in the sense of being dependent on them for food, but our need for a healthy, thriving bird-life is synonymous with our need for a healthy, thriving planet. The two can not be separated.

Birds have been with us since the dawn of mankind. We breathe the same air, drink the same water and play our respective roles in the countless food chains and food webs that make up the living world. Like all other creatures, birds are an integral part of an infinitely complex and delicately balanced biosphere to which we all contribute and on which we all depend.

The more we study the natural world, the more we learn about the processes that support, drive and maintain earth's ecosystems. Many of these processes are still a mystery to us, yet we must learn to understand them – and we must do that before they become damaged beyond repair. Our future may depend as much on our better understanding of biology as it will on our knowledge of medicine, science and technology.

A world without birds is almost unthinkable. It would also, almost certainly, be uninhabitable. Saving the world's birds is an act of enlightened self-interest. By conserving birdlife we take the first important steps towards conserving all life on earth.

Save the Birds — We Need Them

ANTHONY W. DIAMOND

Why we need birds

To many people, particularly those swept up in the busy, consumer-orientated life of towns and cities, the very idea of mankind needing birds is a puzzling and even rather irrelevant concept. We might *like* birds, but do we really *need* them? Yet even to ask the question, 'Why do we need them?' betrays an attitude towards other living creatures that views their presence on earth almost entirely in terms of man's own needs and convenience. It is a viewpoint based largely on economic values, and on an assumption of mankind's inherent superiority. Morality hardly enters into the equation, yet do we really have any right to question other creatures' rights to exist?

In the following pages we shall try to show that birds are just as important today as they have been in ages past, not only for their economic value but also for the significant role they play in our cultures and religions, and in the well-being of our environment.

Mankind has been fascinated by birds throughout history. We have observed them, painted them, written and sung about them, and have kept them, protected them and revered them since time immemorial. Our concern for birds is an unbroken link with our earliest ancestors; it is a principal theme in our cultural and spiritual development as well as a source of insight into our contemporary world.

Primitive peoples today, and our own forebears, lived so close to the wildlife around them that they invested birds and many other animals with religious significance. The major Eastern religions, notably Buddhism and Hinduism, retain a profound respect for the separate identities and rights to life of other species, but the later Western religions swept aside such animist beliefs and came to regard species other than our own as being on this earth solely for man's use. Curiously, though they may take for granted their God's forbearance in not using the power they believe he has to destroy our own species, followers of these religions often do not hesitate to 'play God' with respect to the survival or extinction of other species.

Throughout history, and in some parts of the world even today, some people have adopted the same attitude towards others of their own kind. We suggest in this book that the attitude that prompts the question, 'What use are birds?' is, from an ethical point of view, fundamentally the same as the one that permits some people to hold over others the power of life or death. 'Racism' can easily translate into 'species-ism'. Both are ugly words, and both are extremely ugly phenomena: they have no place in a world that claims to be civilized.

The moral case for conservation

The ecological view put forward in this book is that mankind is inextricably a part of the ecological framework that sustains all life on this planet. Our close and continuing cultural relationships with birds can be seen as a recognition of our kinship with other species that rely on, and indeed make up, the life-support systems on which we, too, depend. This approach is partly one of self-interest, but not entirely so. We would not accept that if a species could be shown to be of no practical importance whatever it should be made, or be allowed to become, extinct. Such a course of action would be no more justifiable than to accept that a person or group of people that were of no direct 'use' to others should be put to death.

Our ecological viewpoint, based on fundamental scientific principles, thus leads us to an approach that is essentially a religious or philosophical one. Science cannot prove that other creatures have a right to exist, any more than it can prove that people have such a right. Fortunately, people do not act solely according to the dictates of scientific proof any more than they act purely for their own economic benefit. Morality has a crucial role to play in the formulation of our actions and judgements.

We will now consider some of the economic and practical benefits which birds have brought us, but we offer these examples only as one small part of the total case for saving species. The ethical case alone is overwhelming.

From time immemorial birds have been man's companions on earth. Their forms and colours fascinate us; their songs enchant us; their soaring freedom inspires us in countless ways. They are symbols of peace and harmony, the very spirit of life, and as such have found a special place in the cultures, religions and traditions of people throughout the world.

Top: Whooper Swans (*Cygnus cygnus*), Mute Swans (*C. olor*) and Common Coots (*Fulica atra*) share the peace and tranquillity of a Danish lake in winter. *Above*: Lesser Flamingos (*Phoeniconaias minor*) fly across the setting sun in East Africa.

Birds as a food resource:
Meat, eggs — and swiftlets' nests

The meat and eggs of birds provide around 15 per cent of the total animal protein consumed by mankind. Domestic poultry account for most of this, but significant amounts of meat and eggs of many other species also serve as human food. Chickens have been domesticated for at least 4500 years, and are more widely distributed throughout the world than any other domestic animal except the dog. They are small, easy to keep, will eat almost anything and are very hardy, so they can be kept by the poorest of people on very little land. In terms of their availability to the least privileged members of human society they are probably mankind's most important source of animal protein.

Other birds have been domesticated too. Turkeys were kept as domestic animals in North America long before Columbus set foot there, and are widely farmed now to supply the centrepiece of traditional festivals such as Christmas and Thanksgiving. Ducks and geese are also common as domestic stock, and ostrich farms produce not only feathers and leather but also eggs, which begin as the world's largest single cell and end as its biggest breakfast.

Wild birds provide substantial quantities of food for people all over the world. Rook and pigeon pies are traditional favourites of country people in Europe. Small songbirds on migration are widely trapped for food even now in southern Europe. The eggs of quail, guineafowl and plovers support specialized markets in richer countries, while there and in many poorer lands the eggs of gulls and terns often make important contributions to human diets. In the Seychelle Islands of the Indian Ocean, Sooty

Tern eggs have traditionally been harvested from the outlying islands. They provided such a welcome change from fish (often eaten salted or dried) that people would fight for a place at the dockside when the egg-boats came in. Sooty Terns are probably the commonest and most widely distributed of all tropical seabirds, and nest in such huge colonies that even though each pair lays only one egg, hundreds of thousands or even millions can be cropped in a season without reducing the tern population. This species probably contributes to the protein diet of more people in the world than any other wild bird.

Free-range chickens are an important source of animal protein in all parts of the world, but in many densely populated industrial countries this traditional method has been largely replaced by the controversial battery farming technique – now one of the world's most widely used high-intensity food production processes.

Breeding colonies of Puffins (*Fratercula arctica*) provide a traditional source of food in the Faeroe Islands. The birds are still caught with long-handled pole-nets – a technique that has been used for many centuries.

Living larders of the cliffs

Seabirds are harvested for their meat as well as for their eggs. Islanders on both sides of the North Atlantic have caught fulmars, puffins, murres and guillemots for centuries, and young gannets are still cropped each summer on Sule Skerry off northern Scotland. The economy of the islanders of St Kilda depended very largely on their being able to salt or dry enough fulmar bodies in the summer to last them through the winter. In Iceland, the Faeroes and St Kilda, the rights to take seabirds on particular cliffs or islands were jealously guarded, and the fowlers respected the bird-cliffs and protected them for the food they provided. Sadly, that respect and protection did not survive the end of fowling as a way of life earlier this century.

The Inuit (Eskimos) of Canada regularly crop the huge Arctic colonies of fulmars and murres. In Newfoundland, the Gulf of St Lawrence and western Greenland, the killing of guillemots, puffins and murres for food has seriously reduced these populations. Yet in Australia and New Zealand people have harvested young Sooty and Short-tailed Shearwaters – which they call Muttonbirds – in tens of thousands for many decades with no noticeable effect on the overall population.

The 'Caviar of the East' is bird saliva, used by several species of swiftlet to cement their nests to the walls and roofs of sea-caves in Southeast Asia. Some species make their nests entirely of their own saliva, which is prized, especially by the Chinese, as an ingredient of soup and sweets. The substance has supposedly beneficial properties, though hardly any nutritional value.

Eggs and young birds can provide important quantities of animal protein, especially for people who cannot afford to buy meat. Properly regulated, such cropping can continue indefinitely so long as people take fewer eggs or young than would have died anyway from natural causes. Killing adults for food is harder to sustain without causing population declines.

Glaucous Gulls (*Larus hyperboreus*) are an important winter food resource for Greenland Eskimos. The continued health of the bird population is crucial to the Eskimos' welfare and over-exploitation is carefully avoided.

Thousands of Short-tailed Shearwaters or Muttonbirds (*Puffinus tenuirostris*) are harvested each year from their nest burrows on Tasmania and the islands of Bass Strait.

Fulmar eggs are collected in their thousands from breeding colonies on the Vestmannaeyjar Islands off the south coast of Iceland.

Birds in culture and commerce:
Fish, feathers and fertilizer

Flying trained falcons at tasty quarry originated as a way of hunting for food and was then also developed as a sport. A more strictly utilitarian use of trained birds has long been practised in parts of China and Japan, where cormorants are used in a traditional night-fishery on lakes and rivers. The birds are fitted with collars to prevent them swallowing their prey, and are trained to catch fish and bring them back to the waiting fishermen. Birds have also been widely used as couriers. South Pacific islanders traditionally used Lesser Frigatebirds to carry messages from one island to another, while in Europe and many other parts of the world the Carrier Pigeon served the same purpose in peacetime and in war. Such is the fascination of the birds' swift homing flight that the breeding and racing of pigeons soon developed into a popular sport.

In Europe, falconry has been largely replaced by shooting for sport – an activity whose economic value to the landowners, travel operators and hoteliers greatly exceeds the value of the food obtained. In Europe and North America, bird-shooting and other forms of hunting are now major forms of land-use which can dominate the landscape, as they do, for example, in the grouse moors and deer forests of Scotland.

The incomparable insulating properties of feathers have been recognized and exploited for many centuries. The soft down which many waterfowl pluck from their own breasts to line their nests is by far the most efficient material known for filling sleeping quilts and cold-climate clothing, and in Iceland, Eider Ducks have long been farmed commercially for their down feathers. Another modern commercial use of feathers is in the manufacture of artificial flies for sport-fishermen, for which the colourful outer feathers are used.

Feathers, fashion and finery

The decorative properties of feathers have attracted people for millennia; indeed, very few of the world's peoples are without some tradition of decorating themselves with feathers. In Europe and North America the bright feathers of a Jay or a Mallard still adorn men's hatbands, though the worldwide onslaught of the millinery trade is thankfully a thing of the past. Most of the feathers used by today's milliners come from Ostrich farms. In times past, the long flowing head-dresses worn by the chiefs of some North American Indian peoples were made up of eagle and hawk feathers, and even today in South and Central America the brilliant feathers of macaws and parrots are still used in the head-dresses of many tribes. The ancient Chinese art of feather jewellery still uses the brilliant blue feathers of White-collared Kingfishers, while in Kenya, pink flamingo feathers are made into imitation flowers to sell to tourists. Ostrich plumes crowned the headgear of Maasai and Zulu warriors, and head-dresses of small birds' feathers still figure prominently in the initiation ceremonies of male Maasai. In the Indonesian islands, the black-and-white feathers of hornbills are used to decorate dancing cloaks and head-dresses, and the 'ivory' from hornbills was also formerly important in trade and ritual. The forest people of New Guinea make elaborate and spectacular headgear from the feathers of birds of paradise and cockatoos, and a widespread trade in feathers was big business in that region long before New Guinea was 'discovered' by Europeans.

Night fishing with captive cormorants is still widely practised in Japan. Attracted to the boat by the light of a blazing fire-basket, the fish fall easy prey to the diving birds.

The start of a race. In many countries, and particularly in the industrialized regions of Britain and Europe, the breeding and racing of domestic pigeons are traditional pursuits.

One of the most familiar of feather head-dresses – the Ostrich plumes of the Maasai warrior class.

The feather cloaks once worn by Hawaiian chieftains are among the most spectacular forms of feather adornment, but the price paid by the islands' avifauna is staggering. For each cloak, tens of thousands of birds were killed.

But perhaps the most elaborate and spectacular examples of feather ornamentation were made in Hawaii. Huge feather cloaks, four metres across the base, were made for royal chiefs from the feathers of native honey-creepers. The cloak of King Kamehameha I took at least 100 years to make and used about 450,000 feathers, mainly of the yellow *mamo* but with some red *'i'iwi* feathers around the neck. About 80,000 *mamo* must have contributed to it. Some birds were released after the few chosen feathers were removed, but often they were killed and eaten. Feathers were used as taxes as well as ornaments in Hawaii, which accounts partly for the strong association that birds came to have with royalty.

An overworked resource

The droppings of fish-eating birds have been recognized as the best organic fertilizers at least since the highly organized industry of the Incas of Peru was discovered by the Spanish in the sixteenth century. When seabirds nest on very dry islands in rich fishing grounds their guano can accumulate to prodigious depths. Sadly, it has been treated like coal and oil – as a mineral to be mined rather than as a renewable natural resource, and in most parts of the world the birds that produce it have been severely depleted or even destroyed.

Guano mining on one of the many small islands off the Peruvian coast. The accumulated bird droppings are loaded into sacks for transportation to fertilizer factories on the mainland.

In their natural habitat young Ostriches spend much of their time in tightly bunched groups – a behavioural trait that proves very useful to South African farmers rearing these huge birds for their feathers, eggs and skins.

Birds as symbols:
From storm gods to doves of peace

Birds have been particularly important to the cultural, religious and aesthetic aspects of human life from the earliest times of which we have any record. Their importance stems from the same attribute that makes them so useful in the modern world as indicators of the health of our natural environments: they can fly, and the freedom with which they can pass between earth and the heavens has given them a special place in human folklore, tradition and religion.

The image of the Thunderbird commonly surmounts the intricately carved totem poles that figure prominently in the Indian cultures of the American Northwest and western Canada.

Thunderers and sun-gods

Birds — especially birds of prey — played a significant part in our early spiritual strivings. The legend of a huge raptor with flashing eyes and rushing wings, bringing storms and welcome rain, recurs as the Thunderbird of the American Indians and as the Voc of Central America — messenger to the tempest god Hurakan, who gave us the word *hurricane*. The same awesome figure appears in the lore of the Caribs of Brazil, the Basuto of Africa, the Karen of Burma and the Cook Islanders of Australia. Such a Thunderer seems to have been ancestral to the God of Hosts, who was revealed to Hebrew prophets 2700 years ago and is now worshipped by more peoples than any other deity.

Birds of prey are often referred to in Old Testament accounts of the trials of the Israelites, who must have witnessed the spectacular migrations of raptors from Europe across the Sinai Peninsula and the Red Sea to North Africa. These movements can still be seen, though they must be a poor shadow of those watched by the ancient Israelites.

One of the first birds to appear in religious fables was Garuda, the great Asiatic god of the sky who bore the sun on his wings. In thirteenth-century Buddhist temple decorations he acquired a human body, and Hindu migrations took his worship east as far as Japan. He is now the national symbol of the Moslem state of Indonesia. His statue still stands in the ruined temples of Angkor Wat, and his worship survives among Brahmans, for whom he has the red wings and white face of the Brahminy Kite, a real and common raptor of modern India.

Emblems of might and empire

It is easy to see why birds of prey impressed our forebears, for they were predators too and must have envied the birds' speed and power. Wooden masks and totems of birds, and especially birds of prey, were important religious symbols in many cultures. The removal of the bird-mask during a dance often symbolized mankind's transition from a lowly animal state.

Remnants of totemism survive in almost every inhabited continent. Raptors soon acquired martial connotations, and representations of eagles, or their feathers, were used as military banners and imperial symbols by peoples as diverse as Babylonians of the sixth century BC, the Plains Indians of North America, the Aztecs of Montezuma's court, Roman legions, the armies of Charlemagne and the Holy Roman Empire, and the citizens of present-day America. Roman soldiers marched to war bearing standards of bronze or golden eagles, but their commanders often decided whether or not to give battle on the basis of auguries from domestic chickens, which they carried with them for the purpose. The Aztec emperors of Mexico were protected by a bird of prey — probably a hawk — caged in the temple, and the eagle and the jaguar were the totems of their two élite soldier societies.

Birds of prey were so prominent — and often so large — in early cultures that it is tempting to speculate that they were once both more common and larger than they are now. Huge condors, with wingspans reaching 5.2m in the aptly-named *Teratornis incredibilis*, became extinct in North America in the Pleistocene along with other raptors much larger than any found today. Before mankind and climatic change combined to wipe out the astonishing large-mammal faunas of the Pleistocene, there would have been plenty of food to support a population of predatory birds much larger in size, and much more abundant, than anything seen in modern times.

Omens and auguries

Vultures, too, would have thrived more widely in ages past. They are still venerated by the Parsees of India, descendants of the Zoroastrians who fled Iran when it was overrun by Islam in the seventh century. Parsees still do not bury or burn their dead, but expose them on a tower for vultures to consume. Vulture feathers were used as propitious charms by midwives in ancient Greece and Rome, and vultures were symbols of childbirth to the Mayas of Yucatan, and to ancient Egyptians, whose goddess Nekhebt was represented as a vulture. The Egyptians deified many birds, especially the ibis, still known as the Sacred Ibis, and the falcon-god Horus, chief god of the sun-cult of Heliopolis.

Owls have a chequered reputation in human folklore, and are feared as ill-omens as often as they are respected for their fabled wisdom. The Greek goddess Athene (Minerva to the Romans) was a goddess of wisdom, and was represented by an owl. She gave her name both to the city of Athens and to the Little Owl, *Athene noctua*.

Bird symbolism in art

It is evident from the earliest art that the veneration of animals is the oldest form of human worship. Cave paintings made by Stone Age people in Europe and Africa are concerned largely with animals, which assume a mystical significance far beyond their practical importance as a source of food.

In historic times European art was controlled by the Church, and reflected religious belief so closely that the two were inseparable — until the Renaissance, when artists began to interpret the world around them in a much more free and creative way. Until then, birds appeared in art solely as religious symbols. The migrant swallow represented resurrection; the goldfinch, with its red crown and predilection for thorns and thistles, symbolized Christ's Passion; the peacock, whose flesh was reputed not to decay, appears in paintings of the Nativity and the Annunciation (notably in Botticelli's *Adoration of the Magi*) and also as a symbol of vanity and pride, as in Rubens' *Judgement of Paris,* while the dove appears repeatedly as a symbol of purity and peace, often associated with the Holy Virgin.

Birds also figured prominently in Chinese art, though here they were not necessarily symbolic or connected with the religious or secular affairs of men, but were painted purely on their own merit — the subjects of portrait studies of astonishing beauty. Raptors were also popular subjects and it seems clear that falconry was one human activity that did have a direct influence on Chinese art. The practice probably began in China and later spread, along with certain Chinese painting techniques, to Japan. Throughout the range that falconry occupied before the spread of firearms, its practice was highly ritualized and stratified in relation to social class and status. It was also represented abundantly in all forms of contemporary art.

Among the giants of literature, Shakespeare — the Swan of Avon — was clearly an ardent bird-lover. Birds figure in all his major works, and more than 60 different species have been identified. Poets, however, more commonly used birds as symbols of the emotions, seldom observing or interpreting the birds themselves. Composers, too, have been inspired by the songs of birds, though the direct use of recognizable birdsong is limited to the calls of cuckoos, blackbirds and nightingales. Most composers have preferred not even to try to compete with the beauty and complexity of the songs of birds which, like the beauty of their plumage and the mystery of their migrations, enrich the world for all mankind.

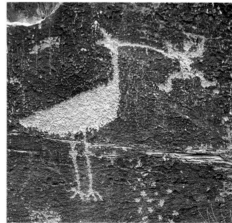

The Little Owl (*Athene noctua*) is found in many habitats, from the woods and grasslands of Europe and Asia to the semi-deserts of North Africa. In ancient Greece the bird was a symbol of wisdom.

An early Indian pictograph on a rock outcrop in the Mesa Verde of New Mexico has much in common with European illustrations of the Stork in its folklore role as the bringer of new-born infants.

Birds as warning lights:
Monitors of the environment

Pesticides are toxic chemicals applied to the land with the deliberate intention of killing. But many other chemicals also enter the natural environment quite accidentally. There is no intention to cause death or injury, but these chemicals can be just as lethal in their effects. The ancient Greeks used the entrails of birds as a means of foretelling the future. Three thousand years later we are still doing it: our scientists now analyse bird tissues in order to measure just how polluted our environment has become.

The invisible enemy

For centuries Britain's waterways were graced by Mute Swans, whose haughty elegance became a familiar part of the landscape. But in the past 10 years or so their numbers have declined drastically throughout most of southern England. Many have died from lead poisoning, drawing attention to the widespread pollution caused by the lead shot which anglers use to weight their lines—and which they often lose or discard.

Many of the countless paints and plastics that have been manufactured and widely used for 50 years or so in Europe and America contain chemicals known as polychlorinated biphenyls (PCBs). They are also important constituents of electrical transformers and insulators, whose use has increased to keep pace with our rising demands for electrical energy. These chemicals had been infiltrating the environment without any apparent ill effect until residues in the bodies of birds and other animals alerted people to their possible dangers. PCBs were found to be among the most abundant contaminants in the bodies of over 17,000 seabirds that died mysteriously in the Irish Sea in 1969, and are now so strongly suspected as a health hazard to people as well as birds that their use is now greatly restricted.

Mercury is one of a group of chemical elements known as heavy metals, which occur naturally but are known to be poisonous in some forms. Mercury was the cause of the infamous 'Minamata disease' which killed over 40 people in Japan in 1953.

Polluted waters do not always look or smell foul. Many dangerous colourless and odourless poisons now find their way into our waterways undetected: undetected, that is, until dying fish and birds draw our attention to the contamination.

Modern herbicides are devastatingly effective in removing unwanted plants. A few become inactive on contact with the soil, but many are extremely persistent and these pose the most serious long-term threat. Instead of breaking down they accumulate in the food chain, poisoning animal life and upsetting the balance of soil organisms.

Copper deposits stain and poison the Rio Tinto downstream of the mine-workings at Huelva in Spain.

Natural sources of mercury, harmless by themselves, are augmented to potentially dangerous levels by the chemical's use in seed-dressings and as a fungicide in paper-making. The deaths of White-tailed Sea Eagles and other birds warned of the increasingly dangerous concentrations of mercury in Sweden, where paper-making is a major industry, and led to the imposition of tight controls on its use and disposal.

A worldwide problem

The pollution of lakes, rivers and marshlands by chemicals has now reached almost every corner of the world. Some of its most serious consequences have been felt in the highly industrialized regions of Europe and North America, where awareness of the problem was slow to dawn and where appropriate legislation and control of effluent emission often lagged even further behind. Yet despite the appalling state of many waterways, major 'clean-up' campaigns have brought about dramatic rehabilitation of others. If the political will is there, and industry is required by law to face its environmental responsi-bilities, it is possible for industry and nature to co-exist. There is a price to pay — but many would argue that it is a price we cannot afford not to pay.

The situation in many developing countries is less optimistic. International and domestic pressures have convinced many that progress is synonymous with a head-long drive towards industrialization, often at devastating cost to the environment. It will take a major effort on the part of the developed nations and the international agencies to prevent the mistakes of the older industrial nations being repeated throughout the developing world.

In central Europe every year, tens of thousands of ducks, gulls and waders fall victim to botulism – a disease caused by bacteria that flourish in the oxygen-starved waters of heavily polluted lakes, rivers and canals.

Chemical effluent pours from a factory outflow into a river in the north-eastern USA. Such abuse of a natural water-way poses a double threat to the environment. In addition to poisoning local river life the chemicals are swept downstream until eventually they are discharged into the sea.

Innocent victims of a chemical 'war'. Just some of the hundreds of birds, ranging from warblers to goshawks, that perished as a result of a pesticide campaign to eradicate mice from a high-intensity agricultural area in Germany.

Birds as warning lights:
The threat of global pollutants

During the 1960s, scientists were alarmed to discover an ever-increasing number of Peregrine, Sparrowhawk and Golden Eagle nests containing broken or malformed eggs. Further researches then showed that more than 20 bird species across Europe and North America were suffering similar disastrous breeding failures.

The birds were all birds of prey or predatory waterbirds occupying the top levels in their food chains. All showed high levels of DDT contamination, which was causing the hen birds to lay eggs with shells too thin to take the weight of the incubating adult.

Worldwide investigations proved the link beyond argument and strengthened the argument against the use of this most persistent chemical agent. In areas where DDT is no longer used, the affected birds are now, slowly, showing some signs of recovery.

The falcon's warning
The Peregrine Falcon (*Falco peregrinus*) gave a clear warning of the dangers of using persistent pesticides. The species' poor rate of breeding success was found to be due to the birds laying eggs with unusually thin shells. Worldwide investigation showed that the highest levels of shell thinning (*below*) correlated with areas of high DDT use.

Breeding range of
Peregrine Falcon

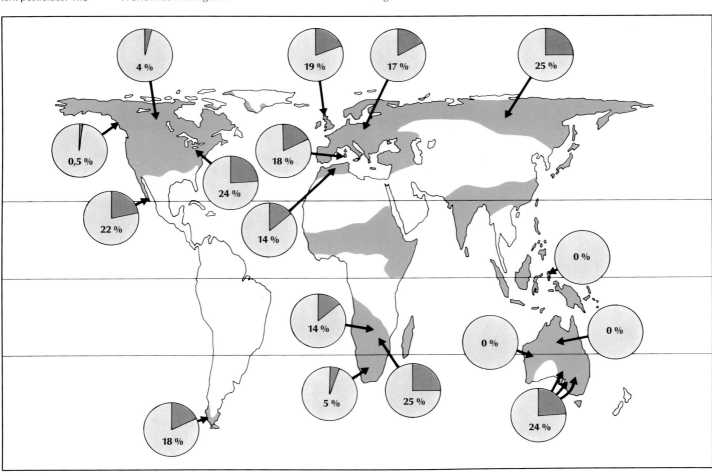

Many of us have had seaside holidays spoiled by having our feet and clothing soiled by tar on the beaches; but it was not until we had to pick our way between the oiled bodies of seabirds that we realized the extent of the damage done to marine and coastal ecosystems by crude oil spilled at sea.

Oil used to be refined at source and was shipped as petrol or kerosene, both of which evaporate quickly if they are spilled. Now most countries refine oil themselves so it is shipped in the crude state which is non-volatile and disperses much more slowly. When spilled at sea it poisons the birds and clogs their feathers, especially those like auks (murres, guillemots and puffins) which dive from the surface for their food. Tens of thousands die each year from oil already in the sea, and hundreds or thousands more are doomed whenever a modern super-tanker goes aground or breaks up at sea. Even more damage is probably done by unscrupulous operators who wash out their ships' tanks at sea in defiance of international law. Sadly, one of the best indicators we have of the level of oil pollution in the world's oceans is the grisly toll of bird bodies counted by routine monitoring of beaches around the world.

The oil tanker *Golar Patricia*, sinking fast with her back broken by an explosion. Accidents like this are a major cause of oil pollution of the oceans.

Heavily oiled seabirds generally have little chance of survival. Their feathers are no longer water-repellent, and their insulation properties are destroyed. The bird usually dies of exposure, or of suffocation. Despite careful cleaning, this Silver Gull (*Larus novaehollandiae*) did not survive its ordeal following an oil-spill off Melbourne, Australia.

In March 1978 the supertanker *Amoco Cadiz* went aground off the coast of Brittany. More than 220,000 tonnes of crude oil spilled into the sea. In the clean-up operation that followed, more than 4500 dead birds were removed from beaches in northwest France and the Channel Islands. At least 33 seabird species were affected, but the highest casualties were suffered by Puffins (*Fratercula arctica*), Razorbills (*Alca torda*) and Guillemots (*Uria aalge*).

Birds as warning lights:
The deadly rain of industry

Perhaps the most serious form of pollution in the world today is acid rain, a noxious brew of toxic chemicals produced by burning fossil fuels in vehicle engines and power stations, and in many industrial processes.

The rain is made acid chiefly by two chemicals. Sulphur dioxide, from power stations burning coal or oil, dissolves in water to make sulphuric acid; and various oxides of nitrogen, released by the same power stations and also from the exhausts of motor vehicles, dissolve in rain to make nitric acid. Between them these two powerful acids have turned the once-refreshing rains of Europe and North America into a deadly spray, killing fish, making lakes uninhabitable for waterbirds, reducing the yields of crops and poisoning vast areas of forest.

In lakes from North America to Scandinavia fish rise gasping to the surface, their gills clogged with a deadly mucus that blocks their ability to absorb oxygen and salts from water. The fish die by drowning and by the breakdown of proteins within the body as the salt level falls. The cause is aluminium, a toxic metal that is normally bound to particles in the soil in an insoluble form that can do no harm. But as the soil becomes more acid, aluminium becomes more soluble, until it is washed out of the soil and into streams and lakes. Fish have almost disappeared from 2000 lakes in southern Norway and from 4000 lakes in Sweden. Many lakes in Canada are now so acid that they no longer support breeding pairs of the Great Northern Diver, or Common Loon, whose haunting call once symbolized the spirit of wilderness for many North Americans.

Acid rain also releases aluminium within the soil itself, where it is just as toxic to trees and other plants as it is to fish in lakes. Where fish die by the lake-full, forests will follow and so will crops, insects, birds and men, for all are linked by their dependence on clean water.

The devastation of huge areas of forest in North America and northern Europe was the first sign of damage. But there is increasing evidence that many species of bird respond to the ecological manifestations of acid rain, and could very well be exploited as sensitive indicators of pollution. Loons on Canadian lakes cannot breed when fish populations decline in acidified lakes, and populations of small forest birds also reflect the extent of contamination by airborne acids. The potential value of birds in monitoring this insidious and devastating pollutant has barely begun to be exploited.

Dust and ash in industrial smoke foul our cities and degrade the quality of life. But far more serious are the long-term effects of the invisible, odourless gases pumped into the atmosphere at the same time. They cause chronic illnesses, erode our buildings, kill plant life and spread toxic compounds throughout the environment.

The Common Loon (*Gavia immer*), one of North America's most striking waterbirds, is now increasingly threatened by acidification of the northern lakes on which it breeds.

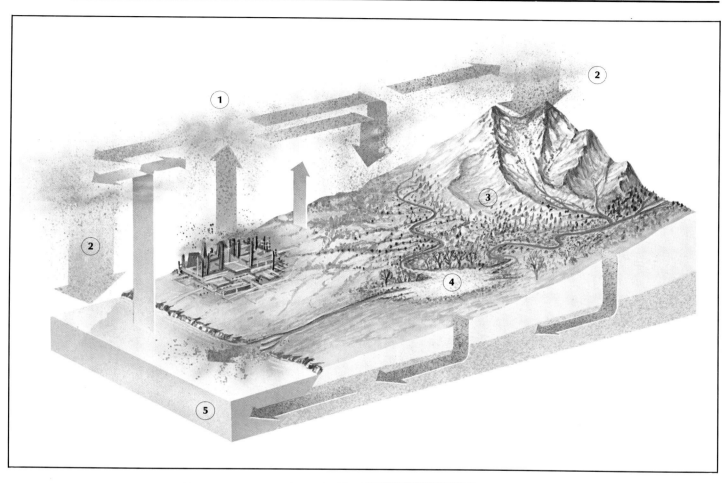

The acid effect
Sulphur dioxide and
oxides of nitrogen
released into the atmo-
sphere from industrial
processes are oxidized
and dissolved in the
water droplets that
make up clouds. The
resulting rain is a com-
bination of dilute acids
which can have a devas-
tating effect on vegeta-
tion, on surface and
ground-water and on
the life they support.

1. Formation of acid
   solutions.
2. Precipitation of acid
   rain.
3. Loss of plant and
   animal life.
4. Concentration of
   pollutants.
5. Pollutants carried
   into the sea.

Dead and dying trees in
the Harz mountains of
north-central Germany
bear witness to the
effects of acid rain.
Some experts predict
that 50% of Germany's
forests could be lost by
the end of the century.

Why are birds in danger?

For as long as animals and plants have lived on earth there have been times when certain species – or even large groups of species – have become extinct. Over the past 600 million years literally hundreds of animal groups have flourished and then died out leaving no living counterparts in the world of today. But while some have succumbed in the fight for survival, others have developed and diversified. Climatic changes and geological processes were responsible for many of these comings and goings, but most important was the onward march of evolution. Many species were forced into extinction because they could not compete for food or living space, or could not adapt to changing conditions, as well as the new species that kept appearing on the scene.

The natural forces that determine the development of new species and the death of others are still at work today. We live in an age totally dominated by one animal species – our own – and with our agriculture and industry, our sprawling settlements, and above all our enormous population growth, we are now the ultimate competitor.

The combination of population growth, environmental pollution and the wholesale destruction of natural habitats has proved too much for many plants and animals: they have vanished forever in the face of overwhelming competition. Since Charles Darwin published his great work *On the Origin of Species by Means of Natural Selection* in 1859, at least 115 bird species have become extinct.

The growth of human populations

In 1970 the world population stood at 3.7 billion people. In 1986 it was about 5.0 billion. By the year 2000 it is estimated that more than 6.0 billion people will be living on earth. In just 30 years the world population will have almost doubled. And where will it end? Even if we assume that there will be a slow reduction in the birth rates of Third World countries, the number of people will still grow to nearly 8.2 billion by the year 2025 and will then slowly stabilize at between 11 and 13 billion over the next 100 years.

The rate at which a population grows is determined by the relationship between birth rate and death rate. The greater the excess of birth rate over death rate, and the greater the probability that children will survive to child-bearing age, the faster will be the growth of the population.

In 1977, the time taken for a population to double in size stood at 693 years for industrialized western Europe; at 173 years for Europe as a whole; at 116 years for North America; 29 years for Southeast Asia; 27 years for Africa and 26 years for Latin America.

In countries with a high standard of living, birth rate and death rate are almost in balance, or death rate may even slightly exceed birth rate. The result is a stable or slightly shrinking population as, for example, in West Germany. But in Third World countries birth rates far exceed death rates, and the decline in infant mortality means that far more children live to child-bearing age. Thus not only are there now twice as many people in Brazil, for example, as there were 30 years ago, but half that country's population is now under 20 years old.

Where the age structure of a population has such a high proportion of young people, the future will bring yet another huge surge in numbers as they in turn produce children. It is a dynamic process that is very hard to control. Change can be brought about only by rigorous family planning programmes – either by intensive public education or by state intervention such as the 'one child family' programme undertaken in China.

But even with such an extreme measure in force it will take until the middle of the next century to balance China's birth rate and death rate and stabilize her population. Until then, China's population will continue to grow, and her people will need ever more food, and more land on which to live.

About 95 per cent of the world's population lives in countries that try to influence their population growth in one way or another. Eastern and southern Asia and Latin America show the first positive results of such policies, with slowly falling birth rates, but particularly in the poorer countries of the world it takes a long time for people to understand that half of their six, eight or ten children are no longer going to die in their first year of life. The poorest and most densely populated countries have growth rates of between two and four per cent a year. A population growing at three per cent will double in size in 23 years, while one growing at four per cent will double in just over 17 years. Add to this the fact that 75 per cent of the world population lives in the less industrialized countries and that 33 per cent are under 15 years of age and the huge scale and geographical distribution of world population growth becomes clear.

The consequences of growth

More people require more food, more living space, more water, more services of all kinds. The demands on the resources of the planet are growing at a staggering rate. Already perhaps one-third of the world's population has too little to eat. Every year about 40 million people die of starvation or from the direct effects of malnutrition. Improved health standards have led to a decline in infant mortality, but more and more children and young people are dying of food shortages. Every increase in the overall population means an even larger increase in the number of starving children. Even now, about 15 million children die of malnutrition every year.

The fate of these children is also the fate of many other creatures whose chances of survival decrease steadily as human populations continue to rise. If we are to change, and develop ways of using the planet's resources more wisely, we must start by tackling the fundamental problems arising from our own overwhelming numbers.

Ninety-five per cent of the world's population live on roughly ten per cent of the non-polar land area. In 1980, the average population density was 36 people per square kilometre. In some areas, population densities are fifteen times the world average, while the migration of rural people to the cities all over the world has produced explosive rates of urban growth, often resulting in sprawling slums and shanty towns.

The people factor
Human populations grow 'exponentially'— that is, by multiplication rather than by addition. The bigger it is, the faster a population will grow, which is why the process, once started, is so difficult to stop. To illustrate the point we will, in the next 12 pages, 'raise' a pictorial population. Starting with a single figure on this page we will double the population on each successive page. Try now to guess how many figures there will be on page 316.

Habitats under attack

About two-thirds of the bird species recognized as endangered are threatened by the loss of their habitat. (This figure does not take into account the long-term threat posed by the loss of most of the world's tropical rainforest, which puts at risk up to 2000 species that are not currently classified as endangered.) Loss of habitat is as fatal to a species as killing all the individuals or preventing them from breeding. Unlike people, birds cannot simply find a new patch of habitat because that is probably already full, nor can they adapt overnight to a new kind of habitat because that will be occupied by other species already adapted to it.

Very few habitats have not been altered by mankind, though the kind of interference to which they are subjected varies from place to place. A forest, for example, may be cut down *en masse*, logged for its commercial trees or for firewood, or burnt to provide grazing land for cattle. Each of these different treatments alters the ecology of the forest and so reduces its suitability for the birds originally adapted to it. And as we have seen, the destruction of one habitat often affects another, sometimes very far away. The greatest danger to the most productive of Sri Lanka's estuaries, Negombe Lagoon, which is an important habitat for fisheries, is deforestation far inland, which loads the rivers with silt which is then swept downstream where it clogs the estuary.

Negombe Lagoon's problems are relatively simple beside those of another of the world's great coastal wetlands, the Waddenzee in northern Europe. This vast complex of coastal habitats supports a great many birds and other wildlife, but it has been extensively reclaimed (that is, drained and filled in) and is polluted by the detritus of several industrialized nations. The Elbe, Ems and Rhine, choked with the discharge of German, Swiss, French and Dutch industry, spew heavy metals and other pollutants into the Waddenzee, poisoning huge numbers of Eider Ducks and Sandwich Terns. Crowds of visitors to the offshore islands erode the sand dunes and marshes and stimulate the construction of new roads and buildings, while other islands are used as military targets in NATO training exercises. So pollution, reclamation and human disturbance inflict a sustained assault on the habitat from many different directions. This is the common pattern in industrialized nations, and is becoming so in countries striving to emulate the worst as well as the best in western civilization.

The Trans-Alaskan oil pipeline may have little direct impact on the tundra ecosystem it crosses, but it does hold many latent dangers and is one more example of man's continuing invasion of one of the world's last great wilderness areas.

In every continent, mountain habitats are being fundamentally altered in the name of energy production. On completion of the Revelstoke Dam on the Columbia River in the Canadian Rockies, the scenery will revert to its former grandeur, but the fast-flowing river in its deep valley will have been replaced, forever, by a huge lake.

Yet it is still possible in some parts of the Waddenzee to look over what appears to be a reasonably undisturbed habitat. The pollution does not always show. Terns still drift above the shore and ducks still bob on the water, and factory chimneys, dockside cranes and roofs of holiday homes barely break the distant hazy skyline. A habitat may be lethally tainted but still appear sound on the surface. Such a habitat is rather like an antique table with advanced woodworm. The surface retains its rich polish and handsome looks, quite unmarked but for a few small holes underneath. But the heart of the piece is already gone, and by the time the damage shows on the surface it is far too late for anything to be saved.

In this book we have treated the major environments of the world separately, each with its own unique communities of birds, its own ecology, and its own set of human resources. Yet we have also seen how they affect and depend upon each other; no ecosystem is insulated from what goes on outside it. The scale of the changes that mankind is now inflicting on the world's habitats is truly global, and affects the very physics and chemistry of the planet by changing the mix of gases in the atmosphere, the balance of radiation between the planet and surrounding space, the distribution of water, and the climate. Most modern habitat destruction is caused ultimately by growth in the human population and its demands. The damage is caused not just by greater numbers, but also by increased aspirations, demanding not only more food and more land for building but also the energy and raw materials with which to make and enjoy the material fruits of modern industrial society.

An extreme example of habitat destruction. The area around this mining settlement in western Tasmania was formerly covered with rainforest. Now, with the forest cleared and the ground poisoned by chemical pollution, the entire area has been reduced to sterile desert, with hardly a trace of plant regeneration.

Networks of shipping canals are part of the record of achievement of the industrial revolution, but many wetland habitats were sacrificed to their construction. The Rhine-Main-Danube Canal in Germany is a major new project. It, too, will have a dramatic impact on the environment – and there are many who contest its economic justification.

The impact of agriculture

Modern methods of farming have a variety of harmful effects on birds, and one of the most important is the reduction of habitat diversity that occurs when mixed farming is replaced by large-scale monoculture. Hedges and small woodlots are removed, and fields are combined to produce a vast homogenous landscape which is often described as 'prairie-like', though it lacks the variety of even the most uniform natural prairie. Few birds can survive in this environment. Not only does the barren landscape lack food and shelter and nest sites, but even those open-country ground-nesting species that are adapted to natural grasslands can rarely cope with the enormous threshing machines which tear through nests, eggs, young chicks and even adult birds as they harvest the crop.

Diminishing returns of pest control

The practice of monoculture needs heavy applications of pesticides and fertilizers to replace the natural predators and soil nutrients that do not survive the conversion from mixed farmland. The pesticides kill what natural insect predators may be left, often making the pest problem worse rather than better. There is a basic biological reason for this. Insects that are crop pests are herbivores, adapted to eating plant tissues. They are the product of millions of years of continuous competition between the insects trying to eat as much plant material as possible and the plants producing natural compounds to discourage or even kill them. A great many plants contain natural insecticides for this reason, and as a result plant-eating insects are used to coping with natural toxic chemicals. When they meet a new one many die, but a few are genetically resistant and these produce a new, resistant

strain. The plant then tries another chemical, the insect adapts again, and so on. Thus the pests at which the farmer's chemicals are aimed treat them as just another poison to which they must adapt. The natural insect predators of those pests, however, are not so adapted and are wiped out – so removing any natural check on the pest's numbers. This is why artificial pesticides very often cause only a temporary decline in the numbers of their target insects, which then increase to greater numbers than before because their natural enemies are dead.

The increasing mechanization of agriculture has had a profound effect on the bird populations of Europe and North America. Once enriched with hedgerows, woodlands and watercourses, the landscape is now dominated by monocultures offering little living space for wild plant and animal life.

Birds, which eat both kinds of insect, are killed or sterilized by the chemicals in the bodies of their prey. The pesticides are extremely persistent – which is one reason why they kill so many insects – and spread throughout the ecosystem. DDT, which has been widely used for over 40 years, has penetrated all the earth's habitats, including the Antarctic, and is even fed to human babies in their mothers' milk. The widespread use of pesticides in modern agriculture is therefore to be deplored not only because it kills birds, contaminates environments and can poison people, but also because in the long run we now know that it simply does not work.

Consequences of 'force feeding' the land

Modern agricultural practices do more harm even than reducing ecological diversity and spreading persistent poisons. The nutrients that modern high-yielding crops suck from the soil are replaced by synthetic fertilizers, which do harm in several ways. They lack the organic matter that gives soil its physical structure and water-retention capability, and their chemicals can actually reduce the remaining natural fertility of the soil by making some nutrients unavailable to plants. Also, much of the fertilizer is washed into

streams and lakes, where it stimulates the growth of algae, reducing the oxygen content and killing much of the original aquatic life. This process of 'eutrophication' can be reversed, but it is a widespread side-effect of modern agriculture found in many aquatic habitats.

We are left with a paradox. As we found when discussing the birds of agricultural land, the rape of natural habitats can be checked only if agriculture becomes more efficient, so that it does not demand more land. Yet efficient farming not only provides a much poorer habitat for birds, but also poisons other environments with pesticides and pollutes them with chemical fertilizers. The fate of many species – and many hungry people – depends on resolving this paradox.

Chemical additives have largely replaced natural fertilizers in order to increase the yield of cultivated land. A potato crop in England, for example, would typically receive three applications in a season (*below*), while a commercial orchard in the southern United States would be sprayed eight or nine times.

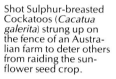

Shot Sulphur-breasted Cockatoos (*Cacatua galerita*) strung up on the fence of an Australian farm to deter others from raiding the sunflower seed crop.

A major cause of habitat loss for forest birds is the replacement of native forests by vast plantations of introduced commercial softwoods. When mature, these Monterey Pines (*Pinus radiata*) in South Australia will form a dark, uniform, closed forest offering hardly any feeding or nesting opportunities for birds.

The toll of the hunter

People kill birds deliberately for a number of reasons. Farmers quite legitimately feel entitled to kill birds that eat their crops, and call this crop protection, not hunting, even if the target ends in the pot. Most birds that are common enough to be treated as pests can withstand considerable hunting, but several species of parrot, especially in the West Indies but also in the Seychelles, were wiped out by such crop protection measures. Until about 60 years ago a great deal of bird hunting was for feathers to supply the plume trade, which itself became extinct only just before many of its victims threatened to do so. Passenger Pigeons in North America were killed by the million for food in the nineteenth century, but the wild population, which was large enough to permit one dealer to handle three million birds in 1878, was extinct 20 to 30 years later. The rapid demise of this bird, which was extremely common only a decade or two before it became extinct, shows that a species' numbers are no guide to its vulnerability to extinction.

Shooting for sport is a common pastime in many countries. In Italy people still shoot small songbirds indiscriminately, as much for fun as for the pot. Waterfowl are particularly popular with sportsmen, and their habit of migrating along well-defined flyways not only makes them easier to shoot but may also give the hunters a false impression of their numbers. Shooting also has the insidious side-effect of dispersing lead shot throughout the birds' habitats. The birds pick this up in their food, and some are poisoned by it.

The hidden menace of 'incidental takes'

As one fishery after another is over-exploited, fishermen turn to new areas and new stocks of fish. Inevitably they come into close contact with seabirds that are also eating the fish. Depending on the fishing methods used, fishermen may either deplete the birds' food supply, causing their breeding success and eventually their numbers to decline, or, if they fish with nets where the birds dive, they may even drown the birds. The largest known mortality from such 'incidental' kills has been off the southwest coast of Greenland, where commercial gill-netting for Atlantic Salmon began in 1965. This area is important to large numbers of Thick-billed Murres, which migrate south through the region at a time when they are moulting their wing-feathers and so are flightless. So many were drowned in the nets that it was impossible to estimate the numbers accurately, but between 200,000 and 1 million were probably killed annually. Huge numbers were also being shot for food and sport on the breeding grounds, and it was estimated that up to 1.5 million birds were being killed each year. Fortunately some controls have been introduced to the fishery, but a great many murres still drown in nets each year.

Thick-billed Murres are one of the most numerous species in the Arctic, but the case of the Passenger Pigeon has warned us not to rely on a species' apparent abundance as a guide to its future.

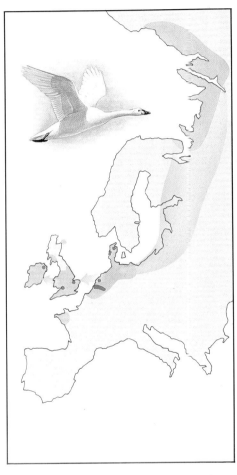

Migration route
◀

Breeding area
▭

Wintering area
•

Main wintering sites

The widely outlawed persecution of migratory song-birds with guns, traps, nets and lime-sticks is a pressing conservation problem in the Mediterranean area. In many countries the birds are sold as food delicacies.

The hidden hazard
Bewick's Swans (*Cygnus columbianus*) are protected against hunting throughout their range, but on migration and in their wintering grounds birds feeding from the muddy beds of rivers and lakes pick up so much lead shot left in the environment by waterfowlers and fishermen that most are contaminated by the deadly substance. Many die as a result.

Accidental entanglement and drowning of seabirds in fishing nets is a serious problem in some areas. Birds particularly at risk are Puffins, Guillemots and others that feed on, or by diving from, the surface of the ocean.

Although often opposed by conservationists, wildfowling is a major recreational industry. Scientific supervision, strict regulation and habitat management are all essential if overexploitation is to be prevented. Here, decoys are being used to attract migrating Canada Geese.

The deadly trade in lives

More than seven million live birds were transported between countries in 1975, and there is no sign that the trade is slackening. The size of this international industry is perhaps the most tragic manifestation of the extent of mankind's love of birds. Small seed-eating songbirds account for about 80 per cent of the trade, with parrots second favourite in terms of numbers but commanding much higher prices. This growing international trade now involves more than one in five of the world's bird species and threatens the survival of about six per cent of our endangered species.

Western countries provide the main market for this trade. Between 1970 and 1975 the USA, Japan and France each imported around one million birds each year, while Italy, Belgium, the United Kingdom, The Netherlands and West Germany each imported half a million or more. In the Far East only Hong Kong (around 700,000) imported as many. It is from the East that most cage-birds originate. India exported nearly two million birds each year over that period, and hundreds of thousands left China, Indonesia, Thailand and Pakistan. Other major exporters are Senegal in Africa, and a number of South American countries led by Paraguay and Bolivia.

The worst aspect of the trade is that these numbers hide an enormous mortality rate. The birds that leave an exporting country alive represent only a fraction of those that were caught. Unknown numbers are killed or maimed during capture, or die before they can be shipped, and many more die in transit. About four per cent of the birds arriving in the quarantine hostel at Heathrow Airport, London, are dead on arrival, and a further five per cent will die during quarantine there. Most quarantine facilities have a very much worse record and it seems likely that losses in quarantine greatly exceed those at any other stage of the journey.

In Europe and America people keep cage-birds mostly for the pleasure they find in their songs and colours, for companionship or, occasionally, for status (why else would anybody pay US$20,000 for a macaw?).

Although nearly 100 countries have signed an international convention regulating the trade in threatened plants and animals, the law is often violated. Here, the crumpled bodies of Ring-necked Parakeets (*Psittacula krameri*) lie beneath the false bottom of an apparently legitimate transit container.

A Rose-breasted Parakeet (*Psittacula alexandri*) with wings clipped. The bird was kept as a pet in an Indian village.

Other cultures keep birds for other reasons. In parts of South America, and in Trinidad, bird-keeping and the attendant skills of trapping achieve considerable cultural status. Bird-keepers hold competitions, and prize birds change hands for hundreds of dollars. Bird-keeping is also rife in parts of the East, where in some cultures it has an added religious significance. A person can gain prestige by releasing a captive bird, so there is a thriving market in birds that are caught solely to be released again.

This kind of trade in birds, and much of that which supplies the domestic market, does not cross national boundaries and so is neither covered by international conventions nor included in the figures for international trade. It is hard to estimate its extent, but in Thailand, for example, in the late 1960s only about one-third of the bird trade involved export. If this figure is similar in other exporting countries then the total number of birds involved in trade – domestic and international combined – must be over 20 million a year. The effects on local populations are poorly documented, but in Trinidad the local trade in small seed-eating songbirds has wiped out almost all of the island's native populations and birds now have to be imported from Venezuela.

Side-effects of the tourist trade

Considerable numbers of live birds, and other wildlife products ranging from seashells to turtle shells, are exported by tourists. The industry also has other, indirect effects on birds, chiefly through the destruction of habitats to provide hotels and other holiday facilities. But tourists can also have serious direct effects. Many beaches in Europe and North America that once held breeding colonies of terns – especially Little or Least Terns – are now so crowded with people during the birds' breeding season that their numbers have been drastically

reduced. Special natural history tours now reach remote seabird colonies in the Arctic, the Antarctic, and on many tropical islands, where the birds are quite unused to people and consequently extremely tame. Such visits have undoubted educational value, but lack of proper controls can all too easily result in serious reduction of the birds' breeding success.

Nestling Grey-headed Parakeets (*Psittacula finschii*) offered for sale in a Bangkok market. The tragedy of such a scene is that during capture the young birds' parents were probably killed and the nesting tree cut down, so causing even greater damage to the species' long-term survival prospects.

In many tropical developing countries, the illegal trapping of wild birds by the local people is a thriving and widely accepted 'cottage industry' driven by demand from industrialized countries.

The innocent invaders

When people colonize new parts of the world, they like to populate their new environments with familiar animals and plants. But this introduction of alien species has probably brought about the extinction of more birds than any other single cause in recent history. This is especially so on islands that lack the rats, cats, dogs and mongooses that are the camp-followers of colonists. Few native birds have any defence against these rapacious intruders.

Some introductions have been made in an attempt to control pests. House Sparrows were introduced to control dropworm in North America, moths in Argentina and mosquitoes in Brazil; Mynahs to control locusts in Australia and the Mascarene Islands; Barn Owls to combat rats in the Seychelles, and Cattle Egrets to control flies in the Seychelles and the Hawaiian Islands. Not one of these has achieved its objective, and in nearly every case the introduced species has itself become a pest.

Birds are among the most commonly introduced aliens, and can be as great a threat to native birds as any exotic mammal. Not only are introductions especially harmful on islands, they are also much more common there than on continents. Of nearly 1200 known introductions of birds, over 70 per cent have been to islands. The Hawaiian Islands (162) and New Zealand (138) have received a disproportionate share: between them they have suffered nearly a quarter of all known introductions of birds.

The New Zealand Weka or Wood Hen (*Gallirallus australis*) may not look particularly threatening, but the bird is a voracious predator on other ground-dwelling species and has totally upset the natural population balance on many islands to which it has been introduced.

314

Since they are better adapted to man-made habitats than most island birds, the introduced species occupy the new habitats that people make when they colonize an island, thus making it much more difficult for native birds to adapt to them. On New Zealand, for example, most of the forests have been greatly changed by browsing mammals introduced by man, and many have been invaded by predatory mammals. The fascinating forest birds of New Zealand did not have time to adapt to these rapid changes, and those that have escaped extinction are now mostly confined to offshore islands, leaving the mainland forests to European Blackbirds, Song Thrushes and Dunnocks.

Exotic birds introduced to Hawaii were immune to a number of bird diseases which the Hawaiian birds had never met and to which they were therefore not immune.

Along with the foreign birds came an insect, the Night Mosquito, which is a carrier of several bird diseases, including avian malaria. It spread rapidly through the low-land forests, infecting the local birds. Many became extinct, and others are now found only above 600 metres, the upper limit of the mosquito's range.

Other island endemics have been hybrid-ized out of existence. The Seychelles Turtle Dove was a distinct race of a Madagascar species, but being only a subspecies it was able to interbreed with the parent form when that was introduced to the Seychelles. The result is that all the Seychelles turtle doves are now either intermediate varieties or of the Madagascar race.

Now that most islands have already suf-fered the most obvious effects of human colonization, the introduction of alien birds which might compete with the native species, bring in diseases, or even interbreed with them, is one of the most potent dangers threatening island birds.

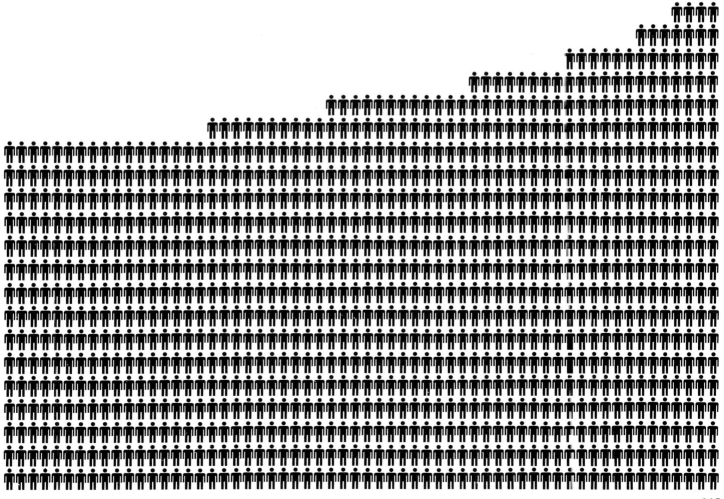

The pressure of population growth

The growth of any human population is influenced by many factors – education, income level, family planning advice and available health services. It is also influenced by social changes such as later marriages, the breakdown of traditional values and social structures caused by the drift to towns and cities, and the rapidly changing role and status of women in many societies. For the rich, children are a luxury that is taken for granted: for the poor in many parts of the world they are a necessity – an essential addition to the family work-force and the best, sometimes the only, insurance against the problems of old age.

Population growth is not just a demographic problem for the countries most concerned. It is a deep-seated social and economic problem lying at the heart of the relationships between industrialized and non-industrialized countries. One individual inhabitant of Britain, France, Canada or the United States consumes, on average, one thousand times as much as someone living in Nepal, Sudan or the highlands of Peru.

A hungry population will have little sympathy or enthusiasm for the conservation of nature and the environment if exploitation of that environment offers their only hope of survival. Nor can the inhabitants of more fortunate parts of the world claim any right to condemn such attitudes. It is estimated that by the year 2000 nearly 1.7 billion people will live in countries where famine is commonplace. Of these countries, 30 will be in Africa, 14 in Latin America and 21 in Asia. It requires little imagination to predict the consequences of such a development: spreading deserts and degraded steppelands, vast areas of sprawling urbanization around the larger cities, and human migration on an immense scale. In addition, the enormous demand for firewood – the only fuel available to roughly half the world's population – will further threaten the forests and woodlands, savannas and steppes of large areas of Africa, Asia and Latin America.

Our human population inhabits two very different worlds. In one, population growth has become minimal or has ceased altogether; hunger is a thing of the past, families are small and incomes large, and consumption of food, goods and services soars year after year. In the other, people die of starvation and malnutrition as they struggle in vain to raise their living standards towards the levels they see in the industrialized countries. The tragic irony is that the worldwide threats to the environment and the increasing numbers of plant and animal extinctions are themselves due to a large extent to the living standards that industrialized countries enjoy – and to which the less fortunate aspire. The exploitation of hardwoods in tropical rainforests, the removal of forests to make way for cattle, and the cultivation of soya to be exported for use as animal feed on European farms, are just some of the consequences of our high standards of living.

The overall effect on the environment will remain negative if we fail to achieve lower rates of population growth and a fairer, sustainable, way of utilizing and sharing the earth's productivity. Plants and animals, and in the end man himself, are threatened not only by the sheer number of human beings but also by the quality of their behaviour towards nature.

The vital question now is whether or not the continued extinction of animals and plants will eventually lead to the collapse of the human population, for we now know beyond doubt that unlimited growth and over-exploitation are eroding the very foundations that made human life possible on earth. There is still hope that birth control, improved education, better health services and improved agricultural methods can contribute to an easing of the pressures on the environment and to the prevention of such an apocalypse. But one thing is certain: we can no longer afford to be unwilling to share.

The twelfth generation
Twelve generations of doubling have given us a population of 2048 figures. Just twelve more generations would carry this figure to a staggering total of 8,388,608, which, if represented by the same small silhouettes, would fill 4096 pages – or nearly 11 books of this size with every page filled with silhouettes.

The rising tide of extinctions

In the last 300 years, species of all kinds have been going extinct between five and fifty times faster than before. And the pace is accelerating. It is expected to reach nearly ten times its present rate by the end of the century, and most of this increase is due to the massive loss of species that will result from the wholesale destruction of tropical forests.

Thousands upon thousands of species are yet to be discovered, even though between 5000 and 10,000 new species are recognized every year. We already have names for around 1.6 million (one-half of them insects and one-fifth plants), and estimates of the total number of species alive today range from three million to ten million. It is even harder to assess how fast they are going extinct than it is to count them, but one well-documented estimate suggests that around one million species will become extinct in the last quarter of this century. That is equivalent to a rate of 100 species *per day,* or about one species every quarter of an hour.

It is even harder to say how many of those species will be birds. About 150 are known to have become extinct in historical times, though many more must have done so without their fate being recorded. If tropical forest species become extinct at the rate at which their habitat is being destroyed, then we can expect to lose at least 400–500 species by the end of the century. That is, in only 15 years we stand to lose three times the number of bird species that have become extinct in the previous 400 years. This estimate does not include all the birds poised on the brink of extinction in other habitats. Yet it predicts that from the continuation of the damage now being done to this one habitat alone, one in twenty of all the species of bird alive in the world today will be extinct in 15 years' time. It is also a fairly optimistic estimate. It does not assume that forest destruction will accelerate, as it well might, and it uses an estimated forest depletion rate of 200,000km^2 per year, although the true figure may easily be 20 to 25 per cent higher.

Cataloguing those in peril

There are no measures of the rates of depletion of the other major bird habitats, but we can be sure that only the deserts are not shrinking. Even the inhospitable polar regions are suffering attrition through various forms of development, especially for oil and minerals. Present methods of keeping track of the endangered status of birds rely largely on worldwide correspondence with local experts to determine which species are becoming rare, and how urgent are the threats to them. These birds are listed in the ICBP *Red Data Book,* the current edition of which contains just over 400 kinds of bird considered to be in danger of extinction. A new edition, in several parts, is currently in preparation: part one, published in 1985, already lists more than 1000 endangered species.

The *Red Data Book* lists relatively few birds from tropical forest – only 80 or so, of which one-quarter are of 'Unknown' status. For this habitat at least, the species-by-species list cannot reflect the true magnitude of the problem. We simply do not know which species are most seriously threatened in tropical forest because we have only the haziest idea of which forests are likely to be destroyed first; but because we have measurements of the proportion of forest area cut down each year we can begin to estimate how many birds are at risk. That is how we arrive at the figure of 400–500 species lost by the year 2000.

A tidal wave of extinctions

We can put this estimate into perspective by comparing it with the speed at which dinosaurs became extinct at the end of the Cretaceous Period. For them the rate was about one species in a thousand years. Many other kinds of animal and plant became extinct around the same time, and the period has been called 'the Great Dying' because it was the fastest period of natural extinctions of which we know. Our estimated future extinction rate of around 30 bird species a year is 30,000 times as fast. It represents a loss of species on a scale the earth has never seen before, and is very largely due to the staggering rate of increase of the world's human population.

This book is about birds and their interaction with mankind and the things we are doing to the planet that birds share with us. The new and unprecedented rates of extinction threaten all forms of life and all ecosystems, and the consequences are quite literally incalculable. Past examples are needed in order to make accurate predictions, and here there are no precedents. We can only sketch, in the most general terms, the losses to genetic diversity, to resources of food, medicines and countless other materials, and the changes in world climate that are almost certain to result. If one-tenth or one-twentieth of all the species in the world go extinct by the end of the century – and the best estimates lie between these two figures – we can be certain that we will have to adapt to a world ecology very different from that which supports us now. And these radical alterations in the living world will be taking place at a time when thousands more human mouths are appearing each day, clamouring for their share of a supply of resources that will be dwindling fast.

Extinct 300 years ago: the bizarre flightless Dodo of Mauritius (*Rhaphus cucullatus*) was a welcome and easy source of food for European seafarers. It did not survive long.

Bird extinctions are therefore important even in a world where several people starve to death each minute. The loss of a species is not only an indication of our misuse of ecological resources; it can, in itself, contribute to further ecological disasters by removing a link that may be vital to the maintenance of an ecosystem. The species in an ecosystem are like the bricks in a building; any one brick can be removed without noticeable effect, but if you go on removing individual bricks the house will eventually fall down. The species whose loss may cause an ecosystem to collapse may be one that an ecologist could identify as a 'keystone' species supporting many others, or it might be one that does not seem important by itself – its subsequent loss contributing to the collapse of the system in the same way that the proverbial 'last straw' will break the camel's back.

The unknown victims

If a bird becomes extinct there is a good chance that we will notice, simply because we now know all the world's birds. But the majority of the lower animals, the plants, and the vital micro-organisms have yet to be properly studied and catalogued. The extinction of such species passes undetected. What we can surmise, however, is that for every bird that becomes extinct, the world has also lost 90 insects, 35 plants and 2 or 3 fish; and that for every two birds lost, one mammal also becomes extinct.

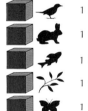

1 bird species

1 mammal species

1 fish species

1 plant species

1 insect species

The vicious circle of mismanagement

People starve, and birds become extinct, because their life-support systems are misused. But why are they misused? In many cases ecosystems founder because they are put to agricultural uses for which they are not suited. People cut down forests or graze their animals in semi-deserts because they need a place to raise their food. In developing countries – where starving people and endangered birds are most densely concentrated – the best farming land is usually devoted to cash crops. These are crops like cotton, sugar, cocoa, rubber, tea and coffee, which do not feed the nation's people but are sold abroad – mainly to developed countries – for foreign exchange, which is then used to buy manufactured goods from the developed world. The industrial nations set the prices for both the crops and the manufactured goods, and of course ensure that the goods cost more than the crops. Small wonder then that rich countries get richer, poor countries sink deeper into debt, and the people of tropical countries are driven deeper into the deserts and forests in search of food. The iniquitous realities of international trade lie at the root of many ecological problems, and affect the ability of people to feed themselves just as much as they influence the fate of wild birds.

In the next few pages we discuss the bird extinctions we know have taken place, and the bird species which we know to be threatened with extinction in the near future. But the extinctions that we can document are those for which we can name the bird and know the place and approximate date of its demise. They represent just a small fraction of the extinctions that mankind has caused. And for every bird that becomes extinct we can expect to lose another 200 named species of other kinds of organism, and between 200 and 1000 others not yet even named. Each bird species lost implies the additional loss of over 90 species of insect, 35 plants and 2 or 3 fish; and for every two bird species lost, one of the world's mammals disappears forever. Frightening though these statistics may be, they represent only the tip of an iceberg of barely imaginable proportions.

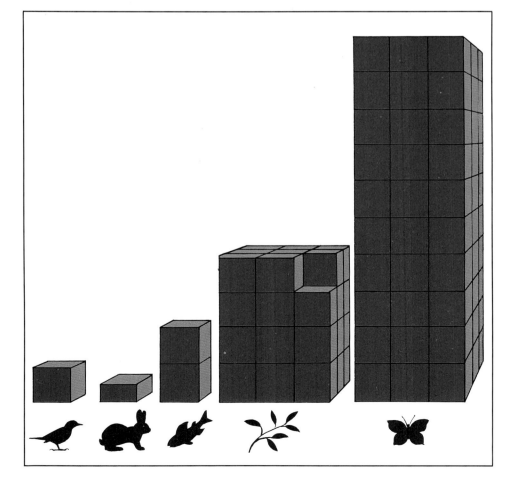

The international 'Red List'

The ICBP *Red Data Book* starkly documents one of the most alarming effects of the economic and social development that has taken place this century. It lists all those bird species that survive only in very restricted ranges and that are threatened with extinction.

The forerunner of the *Red Data Book* was J. C. Greenway's *Extinct and Vanishing Birds of the World,* published in 1958. The book listed 95 internationally threatened bird species. Just eight years later, in 1966, the first edition of the official *Red Data Book* was published jointly by ICBP and IUCN (the International Union for Conservation of Nature). Already the list of threatened birds had swelled to more than twice the original number.

The first part of the latest edition of the *Red Data Book of Birds,* published in 1985, contains more than 1000 species – almost 12 per cent of all existing bird species. This enormous increase is due in part to vastly improved research and data-gathering techniques, but it also reflects the harsh realities of the deteriorating state of the natural environment throughout the world.

Threatened species are not evenly spread over the continents and ecosystems because the natural diversity of species is itself very uneven. Diversity is greatest in tropical forests and least in the polar regions. The high proportion of threatened birds found in the tropical forests – some 43 per cent of the total – simply underlines the enormous importance of this ecosystem on the agenda of international conservation effort.

Where are the world's threatened birds?
The bar graphs here show the proportion of the world's red-listed birds occurring in each major habitat. The high figures for islands and tropical forests partly reflect the great species diversity in those habitats, but more importantly they also indicate just how seriously those habitats are now threatened. The figures total more than 100% because many species are found in more than one ecosystem and will appear in the count for each of those ecosystems.

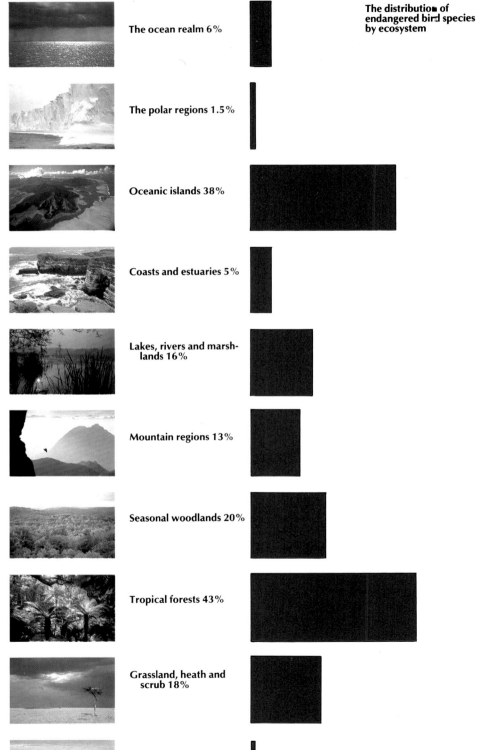

The distribution of endangered bird species by ecosystem

The ocean realm 6%

The polar regions 1.5%

Oceanic islands 38%

Coasts and estuaries 5%

Lakes, rivers and marshlands 16%

Mountain regions 13%

Seasonal woodlands 20%

Tropical forests 43%

Grassland, heath and scrub 18%

Arid regions 1%

The principal threats to birdlife

When the numbers of threatened species are plotted graphically according to the main factors contributing to their decline, a clear picture emerges of the mistakes man has made, and continues to make, in his management of the environment.

The most dangerous threat of all lies in our relentless invasion of natural habitats – the taking over of land for housing, for expanding industries, for the extraction of raw materials and for agriculture and forestry.

In second place comes direct persecution by man in the form of hunting, the collecting of birds and their eggs and the disturbance caused at breeding grounds by sport and leisure activities.

The third major threat comes from the introduction of foreign species. Alien plant introductions can lead to destruction of the original vegetation, alien mammals to habitat loss and high levels of predation, and alien birds to predation, competition and in some cases to hybridization.

Illegal trapping for the cage-bird trade, habitat pollution and alteration, and the incidental takes from fishery operations all add to the toll.

Many birds are not listed in the international *Red Data Book* but are still threatened at regional levels by these principal factors. For this reason, many countries and individual provinces are now compiling their own 'Red Lists' and environmental data-banks.

The principal threats to birdlife

Wetland drainage 4%

Pollution 4%

Habitat destruction 60%

Hunting 29%

Incidental takes by fisheries 1%

International trade in rare birds 9%

Competition from introduced species 20%

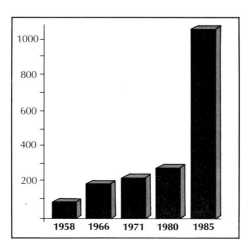

The rising number of threatened species
Over the past 30 years five major surveys have been carried out to determine the number of internationally threatened species. The huge increase from 1980 to 1985 is due partly to improved census methods but is primarily a reflection of the rapid deterioration in the health of the environment.

What are the main causes of decline?
Overall, the destruction and alteration of habitats and the pressure of human hunting are the two major threats to birds, with competition from introduced alien species a close third. As in the case of the species distribution, many birds figure in the statistics for more than one threat so the percentage figures do not total 100.

The world's most threatened birds

The critical areas
The map shows those countries having five or more species listed in the 1980 *Red Data Book*. Brazil heads the list with 34 species, but according to recent research that figure may soon have to be amended to nearer 150.

More than 20
10 to 20
5 to 9

The critical list
Not one of the 25 species illustrated here has a wild population of more than 100 birds.

1. Hawaiian Crow (*Corvus tropicus*)
2. Madagascar Sea Eagle (*Haliaeetus vociferoides*)
3. Chatham Island Black Robin (*Petroica traversi*)
4. Kakapo (*Strigops habroptilus*)
5. Ivory-billed Woodpecker (*Campephilus principalis*)
6. California Condor (*Gymnogyps californianus*)
7. Chatham Island Plover (*Thinornis novaeseelandiae*)
8. White-breasted Silver-eye (*Zosterops albogularis*)
9. Mauritius Kestrel (*Falco punctatus*)
10. Mauritius Parakeet (*Psittacula echo*)
11. Aldabra Brush Warbler (*Nesillas aldabranus*)
12. Puerto Rican Parrot (*Amazona vittata*)
13. Seychelles Black Paradise Flycatcher (*Terpsiphone corvina*)

14. Seychelles Magpie Robin (*Copsychus sechellarum*)
15. Mauritius Pink Pigeon (*Nesoenas mayeri*)
16. Chatham Island Oystercatcher (*Haematopus chathamensis*)
17. Imperial Woodpecker (*Campephilus imperialis*)
18. Lord Howe Island Wood Hen (*Tricholimnas sylvestris*)
19. Okinawa Woodpecker (*Sapheopipo noguchii*)
20. Rodrigues Brush Warbler (*Acrocephalus rodericana*)
21. Noisy Scrub Bird (*Atrichornis clamosus*)
22. Kauai O'o (*Moho braccatus*)
23. Crested Ibis (*Nipponia nippon*)
24. New Zealand Black Stilt (*Himantopus novaezelandiae*)
25. Atitlan Grebe (*Podilymbus gigas*)

T. BOYER

In Memoriam

The roll-call of birds that have become extinct in historical time is a sad testament to the destructive powers of mankind. It is also far from complete. The 150 or so extinct species we know about are those that died out *after* western explorers began to report about such things. We are only just beginning to realize the extent of the extinctions wrought by man *before* recorded history. Many species must also have perished without ever having been recorded by the early travellers to whom we owe our only written records of such birds as the Dodo and Solitaire. Such witnesses naturally wrote mainly of the birds that were large, bizarre or good to eat, or those that ate their crops. Small forest birds were not likely to be noticed, and their demise would therefore frequently have gone unrecorded.

Most of the birds we know have become extinct in the last 350 years lived on islands; many others inhabited parts of continents that had not previously been densely populated. These extinctions reflect the spread of western civilization around the world. The rapid expansion of people across North America caused the extinction of Carolina Parakeets and Passenger Pigeons just as surely as the sudden influx of settlers and the animals they introduced to Mauritius and Rodrigues caused the extinctions of the Dodo and the Solitaire on those islands.

Not all the causes of past extinctions remain as major threats today. Many birds living on newly settled islands, or islands on recently established shipping routes, were killed for food. The Great Auk colony on Funk Island, off Newfoundland, was a vital source of fresh meat to fishermen and others sailing the North Atlantic. The bird's extinction, like that of the Dodo, was due largely to its being large (and therefore meaty) and flightless (and thus unable to escape). Seamen now have refrigerators on their ships and need neither to eat the wildlife of the islands they pass nor to stock the islands with goats to provide meat for future visits.

Later in their sad history, Great Auks were killed as much for their feathers as for their flesh. The trade in bird skins and feathers reached a peak in the late nineteenth century; it has now been replaced by a world trade in live birds, and an illicit but thriving market in the eggs and skins of very rare species. The rampant destruction of natural habitats, which played a large part in past extinctions, is not only still with us but is accelerating alarmingly, supplemented by global contamination of ecosystems.

The world is much poorer for the disappearance of birds such as the Great Auk, Dodo and Solitaire. Would we not be as thrilled by the sight of herds of giant Elephant-birds in Madagascar or Moas in New Zealand as we are now by the elephants and other big game of Africa? Their loss is irreversible; but they were just the vanguard of mass extinctions that threaten to make their loss seem trivial. That great wave of extinctions has yet to happen — but happen it most surely will unless we take effective action to prevent it.

The choice is ours

As they coalesced and developed, primitive cultures the world over had to learn to live in harmony with nature. In different ways, each society discovered the need to protect and maintain the natural balance of its environment, and encoded that knowledge into its own customs and lore. However, as social structures became more complex, and technologies improved, human beings were able increasingly to insulate themselves against nature. Driven by the scriptural command to subdue the wilderness, the spread of West European social and economic influence over the globe, which caused most of the extinctions discussed in the previous chapter, was also a major factor in breaking down traditional conservation attitudes among the societies it engulfed. The dissemination of industrial technologies and the fruits of science and learning have been responsible for many benefits bestowed on the peoples whom Europeans sought to enlighten, but those improved living standards required social adjustments that divorced them from nature. Urban societies have forgotten for the most part the lessons learned by peoples whose existence depended upon a close relationship with their environment.

Modern industrial man has had to rediscover the importance of ecology through scientific research. It has certainly given us a more detailed understanding of the complex web of natural cycles upon which life and a healthy biosphere depend. We now know what we must do to keep it that way, but we have as yet to take the message to heart.

The extinctions of the last 400 years were caused by ignorance. Today, we do not have that excuse. The men and women in government in the countries that consume the lion's share of the world's natural resources – the industrialized nations – have access to enough data to distinguish between policies that are ecologically sound and those that are ecologically destructive. They must act, and where we, as concerned citizens, can do so, we must impress upon them the fact that there can be no higher priority for the future.

Our descendants will never forgive us if, in our lifetime, we fail to conceive a conservation ethic that can be embraced universally. The consequence of failure will be a wave of extinctions that will leave our planet incalculably worse off and will drastically threaten the quality of life for millions of humans.

To succeed, we must turn two human preconceptions around. Instead of seeing our activities as single isolated events, we must learn to think holistically, taking into account far wider implications of our actions, expanding our way of assigning values beyond market-place economics, and considering common good as well as individual gain. And we must learn to look to the long-term future, putting our faith in achievements the benefit of which others will reap after us, and which might even call for some self-sacrifice now. *Save the Birds,* a campaign to promote the conservation of some of our most treasured and important companions in nature, could be a symbolic rallying cry in a revolution as profound as any in history: nothing less than the complete re-evaluation of our relationship with the earth. If we want to guarantee our species' future, we must choose now. There are many possibilities for action.

Our role as teachers and law-makers

Fundamental changes in our lifestyles and attitudes are necessary if ecological disaster is to be averted. But these changes will not happen overnight. They will demand enormous efforts from those who believe in them if their importance is to be communicated to the people who count – the people who are fond of birds, vaguely worried about pollution and the 'greenhouse effect', yet see no connection between those concerns and buying hamburgers and paper tissues.

We need to spread the attitude that we have not inherited the earth from our parents, but borrowed it from our children. We must return it to them in better shape than it is now, and prepare them for their role as planetary stewards. The education of our children in the ecological realities of life is one of the most important tasks facing the parents and teachers of our time. It is not a substitute for other, urgent, actions – reclaiming habitats, rescuing vanishing species, legislating against pollution or educating the general public and decision-makers of our own generations; but if those short-term measures are to last, the next generation must be as thoroughly grounded in conservation as in reading, writing and arithmetic.

It is a curious anomaly that biology – the science of life itself – plays so small a part in education. We all have natural history classes in our early years at school; those pleasant excursions into the park, learning the names and the shapes of the trees, pressing flowers, even learning to recognize the song of a bird or two; but when education begins in earnest, such 'frivolities' are left behind in the kindergarten. Not until some – a very few – decide they want to be doctors, nurses, or even biologists, does biology re-enter the curriculum. The rest of us leave school with a hazy idea of where most of our own important organs are, but with little conception of the part our species plays in the complex mechanisms of the biosphere. It is because so few of us have been taught our place in the living world that our generation continues blindly to inflict such desecrations on the biosphere. Most of us still see 'the environment' as something we ought not to pollute, but something that

also has an awkward habit of getting in the way of development. If our children do not grow up recognizing that 'development' and 'conservation' are *both* best defined as 'wise use of resources', then we shall have failed them as surely as our parents failed us. Our parents had a good excuse; they knew no better. We do.

Taking a lead

One of the best models for a quick, cheap and effective method of conservation education (and one that does not have to wait for the interminable bureaucracy of school-board curriculum development) is demonstrated by the Wildlife Clubs of Kenya. Each school has a branch of the club, which distributes films, slide shows, books and other educational material from a central office with a permanent staff who also organize camps, lectures and field excursions to National Parks. This organization taps the boundless enthusiasm of the young for animals, and makes the most of the limited resources available. In a few years it has produced a generation of young people who not only feel strongly about the future of their land's habitats and wildlife but also know a lot about them and challenge their parents to justify both their own ignorance and their misuse of natural resources. The parents are being educated by their children, always a more effective method than the more traditional relationship – and certainly faster.

Such educational short-cuts must be used more widely. We cannot wait for today's children to become their generation's decision-makers; in another 40 or 50 years too much damage will already have been done. Public education must become a major priority for all who understand how much our children's future depends on how we use their planet.

Where education alone fails to motivate people to conserve nature, it must be backed up by laws. Many countries have legislation that protects wildlife to some extent, but in most parts of the world there is little or no control over the killing or capture of wild birds. Some of the worst offenders are countries with the longest histories of civilization, including China, where birds are shy and hard to find; Italy, where no bird is too small to be shot at in the name of sport; and Belgium, the only northern European nation where government still condones the large-scale trapping of song-birds.

Conservation must start at home. The more we succeed in getting our children interested in nature, the better our chances are of producing a society with respect and understanding for the environment.

Reaching out to the next generation. British naturalist David Bellamy lends his support to national environmental education efforts by leading a young people's field trip in Zambia.

An international responsibility

Bird conservation is much more than a problem for individual nations. Most bird species live in more than one country, and many migrate through several different states. Birds are so mobile that they more than any other kind of animal are an international resource requiring international measures for effective conservation.

The World Heritage Convention is designed to ensure the conservation of cultural and natural sites that are of such international importance that they are part of the heritage of all mankind. To declare a site a World Heritage implies an obligation on the international community to help the nation in which the site occurs to conserve it properly. The Convention has so far been applied to relatively few natural sites. Many more areas can justly be declared to be part of the world's natural heritage. If adequately supported by contributions from the wealthy nations to its World Heritage Fund, the Convention could become an important instrument for redistributing conservation funds from the rich world to the poor, where most such areas are found.

Birds and other animals that migrate across national frontiers are covered by the Convention on the Conservation of Migratory Species of Wild Animals, or Bonn Convention, which came into force in 1983. Parties to this Convention agree to protect endangered migratory species within their borders. The Convention also envisages regional conservation agreements between countries that are range states of particular species, for example, the White Stork. Unfortunately, like any international treaty, it depends for its success on the adherence of the larger nations, and some of these – notably the USA, USSR and Canada – have not yet signed. These countries are reluctant to have their fisheries controlled by international legislation, and since the Convention covers all migrants, including fish, it threatens to founder on this problem.

Of the world's major ecosystems, wetlands are among the most seriously threatened on a global scale. Once drained, they offer large areas of flat, fertile land for agricultural development, and tempting space into which human populations can easily expand. Many birds depend on wetlands in their natural state. The 1971 Convention on Wetlands of International Importance (especially as Waterfowl Habitat) recognizes this fact. The Ramsar Convention, so-called after the town in Iran where the text was adopted, aims to protect the world's remaining wetlands by obliging signatories to include wetland conservation in their national land-use plans. Parties must identify wetlands of international importance in their own countries. As of 1985, over 300 sites had been designated, covering more than 20 million hectares.

The strongest and most widely supported international statute of all is the Convention on International Trade in Endangered Species of Wild Fauna and Flora – 'CITES'. Starting with 10 signatories in 1975, 58 countries had joined CITES by 1980 and over 90 by 1986. It has become a powerful tool for regulating the international wildlife business. It contains provisions not only for regulating trade, through the issue of import and export permits, but also for the scientific monitoring of the status of species within each government's jurisdiction. This is probably the most successful piece of international conservation legislation there has yet been, but it remains widely abused by some member states, and determined traders soon find routes by which to smuggle their cargoes out of CITES countries through non-signatory states.

Laws are respected only when they are understood by citizens, police and judiciary alike. If they are not, only public education can redress the balance. No conservation strategy can succeed without effective legislation supported by an enlightened public.

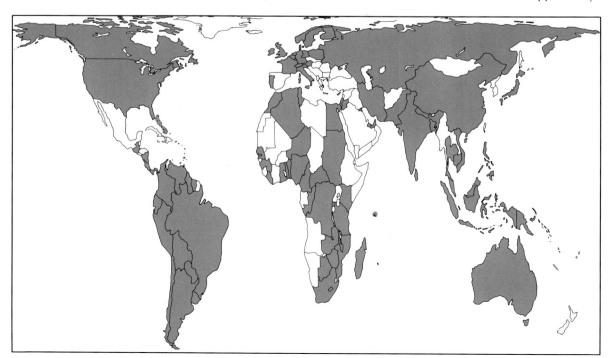

CITES – the Washington Convention
More than 90 countries have signed the Convention on International Trade in Endangered Species of Wild Fauna and Flora (CITES) – the most successful international conservation agreement so far. Since 1975, CITES has banned traffic in endangered wildlife and has placed strict controls on trade in many species judged to be at risk. Parrots and birds of prey have benefited greatly from this important treaty.

Conservation in Action:
Providing physical protection

The measures discussed so far for conserving birds are aimed at the long-term protection of the environment that supports birds and people alike. Economics, education, and legislation all play a vital part in shaping our attitudes to living creatures. This is the preventive side of ecological health-care. But there are ecosystems under such intense pressure, and species declining so fast, that they need immediate attention if they are to have any chance of survival.

Some reserves have an essential role to play in the preservation of individual species. Prime examples are Lake Nakuru and other soda lakes of the African Rift Valley, because these are the main breeding grounds for almost half the total world population of the Lesser Flamingo (*Phoeniconaias minor*).

Protecting habitats

For centuries, societies have recognized their potential for disrupting the natural balance. One solution frequently applied is the concept of closed seasons for hunting; another is the reserve or sanctuary. Today, as population and development press relentlessly against receding natural areas, the designation of protected areas may be the only way to ensure that threatened ecosystems survive. Whether a reserve achieves its goal or remains protected on paper only depends on the resources available for training wardens and for making local people aware of the benefits they gain from it.

One innovative approach to a global system that would protect ecologically viable natural areas has been designed by UNESCO's Man and the Biosphere Programme. Biosphere reserves do not attempt totally to exclude human activities from conservation areas. Rather, they seek to combine the preservation of natural diversity with wise utilization of the ecosystem, based upon scientific study. The archetypal biosphere reserve contains a core area, which is preserved as a natural ecosystem, surrounded by areas that may be used for research or set aside for traditional land uses.

The whole is surrounded by a buffer zone, which might include human settlements. Very few designated biosphere reserves match this ideal set-up, but it is a goal to work towards. The key to the continued protection of the world's remaining natural areas is the co-operation of people at many different levels — locally on the reserve, nationally through the responsible government departments, and internationally through our common concern for the world's natural treasures.

Because the best-known protected areas are National Parks, many people think of reserves as primarily a national asset for which one country has sole responsibility. National Parks, however, have enormous potential as foreign currency earners through tourism. Human tourists are not the only foreign visitors for whom protected areas are important. Wetlands are of special importance for many migrating birds, either as breeding or wintering grounds or as vital stopover places where the birds can rest and refuel on their incredible journeys. They are also very vulnerable to human development pressures. In many industrialized countries, the only major wetlands that still provide natural habitat are those that have been designated as reserves. In North and South America, an ambitious scheme to establish a network of 'shorebird sister reserves' throughout the hemisphere is one approach that recognizes the need for international efforts to establish protected areas for migratory birds — and the key role birds can play in generating public support for such a system. Participation will provide a combination of conservation expertise and political backing that will give additional status to local sites.

Management of reserves

In today's world, very few protected areas are either large enough or sufficiently removed from environmental threat to fulfil their purpose without active management. Where all that remains of an entire coastline is a few hectares of protected land, the 'natural' habitat may even need to be artificially modified if the original diversity of the whole is to be concentrated in just one reserve. The ponds at Minsmere, on the East Anglian coast of England, one of the most famous bird reserves in the world, where thousands of waders congregate during migration, were created by an army excavation team. The habitat on Cousin Island, ICBP's reserve in the Seychelles and the only international nature reserve in the world, required considerable 'human interference' to allow its natural *Pisonia* woodland to regenerate from what had become coconut plantation. ICBP purchased Cousin Island for its amazing seabird colonies, and to save one little bird, the Seychelles Warbler, which lives nowhere else.

Providing better homes

Sites that merit special protection are frequently identified by the presence of rare birds, and Protected Area status can provide a framework for last-ditch attempts to save a particular species like the Seychelles Warbler through intensive care of its environment.

On the island of Bali, Bali Barat National Park is the only home for the remaining wild flock of Bali Starlings. One reason why they are dwindling is that there are simply not enough suitable nest-sites. The birds favour dead *Acacia* trees, and these are collected for fuelwood by the local people, even within the park boundaries. The management plan for the park calls for restoring some areas to native *Acacia* and making the remaining plantations more productive so that they meet local fuel needs. In the meantime, park staff have put up nest-boxes to provide additional nesting sites for the birds.

Birds like the Puerto Rican Parrot, Cahow, Waldrapp, Osprey, Wood Duck and many other species have adopted man-made sites when the supply of natural ones became inadequate. However, in the long term, it is better to modify the way the ecosystem is used so that the supply of natural sites can be increased.

Removing predators and competitors

The control or removal of alien species from islands is one of the most important management techniques in bird conservation. Introduced predators like rats, cats and weasels have turned once-safe havens into death-traps for many birds. Still worse are the herbivorous mammals – goats, rabbits, deer, pigs, sheep and cattle – that have devastated the natural vegetation of thousands of islands around the world and thereby caused even more extinctions.

Fortunately, the same qualities that make islands and their endemics vulnerable to introductions – chiefly their remoteness and small size – can be turned to advantage when it comes to freeing them of exotic predators and competitors. However, of all the management techniques used in bird conservation, this is the most controversial because it may involve killing mammals and sometimes even other birds. The most successful campaigns have always been preceded by extensive public education programmes so that people are fully informed of the reasons for the actions being taken.

The long-term survival prospects of rare seabirds are best served by total protection of both birds and their habitats. Cousin Island in the Seychelles was purchased by CBP in 1968 and has since become internationally recognized as a model for the scientific management of tropical island bird reserves.

Simply establishing a reserve is sometimes not enough. The habitat of the Echo Parakeet (*Psittacula echo*) is heavily modified and invaded by alien plant and animal species. To improve the birds' breeding success their remaining nest sites must also be protected from predatory monkeys.

Conservation in Action:
Feeding and fostering programmes

Some small populations of birds are prevented from increasing by inadequate supplies of food at a critical time of year – usually the winter. Species that habitually flock together at this time to feed – even if they are strictly territorial when breeding – can be helped to increase by giving them extra supplies of food. A classic example of a bird population saved by supplementary feeding is the case of the Trumpeter Swans breeding in the prairie marshes of Montana in central North America. By 1936 this population was reduced to about 15 pairs by habitat destruction, egg-collecting and hunting. The birds fed in winter on aquatic plants in waters kept open by hot springs, and were apparently limited by the area of unfrozen water available in late winter. Grain was scattered for them during particularly cold weather each winter from 1936 onwards and they responded by increasing their numbers to 600 over the next 20 years.

Winter feeding of White-naped, Hooded and Japanese Cranes in Japan has dramatically increased the numbers of all three species in the last 25–30 years. Their feeding stations have become popular attractions for the public, whose knowledge and appreciation of the birds is increased by visitors' centres set up nearby. There are risks inherent in attracting a whole population of endangered birds to one place at one time, and in allowing them to become accustomed to the proximity of people, but so far these risks (chiefly of greater disease transmission and vandalism) have not materialized.

Supplementary feeding has also helped species whose natural food supplies are contaminated. Griffon Vultures in Israel and Spain, and White-tailed Sea Eagles in Sweden, have declined through pesticide contamination of the carcasses on which they feed. In all these cases, putting out uncontaminated food for these scavengers has allowed them to increase their numbers.

Supplementary feeding of endangered birds has been found to be a relatively low cost conservation measure with a high rate of return.

Research on the White-tailed Sea Eagle (*Haliaeetus albicilla*) in Sweden showed that breeding failures were due largely to food shortages and to contamination of the birds' prey species. Feeding programmes (*above*) have already improved the survival rates of young Sea Eagles.

In the case of the Trumpeter Swan (*Cygnus c. buccinator*) in Canada (*left*) the bird was brought from near extinction to a total population of several hundred in just 20 years by this technique.

In Japan (*below*), the winter feeding of Hooded Cranes (*Grus monacha*) and White-naped Cranes (*G. vipio*) has boosted the numbers of both species and has also been a huge success in generating widespread public interest and support.

Fostering programmes

Many endangered species are large, long-lived birds with a low reproductive rate. They may not begin to breed until they are four or five years old, or even more, and produce only one or two eggs a year. Peregrine Falcons, Whooping Cranes, Black Stilts and New Zealand Shore Plovers are among those endangered birds whose breeding rate has been raised well above natural levels by getting the birds to lay more eggs than usual and then fostering them under pairs that have lost their own eggs.

In one variant of the technique, eggs are removed from wild pairs — either immediately after laying or else when the clutch is complete — and are incubated artificially or under a broody hen. The original pair replaces its lost clutch, thus doubling its output of eggs, and depending on how often they can be induced to re-lay like this they may be allowed to keep the replacement clutch or that too may be taken for assisted rearing. Young hatched from these eggs are then put into nests of birds whose own eggs have succumbed to natural mortality. Ospreys in some parts of the USA are heavily contaminated with pesticides and so lay eggs that do not hatch. These can now be replaced by eggs taken from birds in areas that are less contaminated, so allowing birds in polluted regions to continue to rear young.

Cross-fostering is a variant of this technique in which a common species raises the young of an endangered but closely related bird. Sandhill Cranes have raised a number of Whooping Crane chicks in North America in recent years, and not only does this raise the output of the very small remaining population of Whooping Cranes, it also gives the species an opportunity to colonize areas previously occupied only by Sandhill Cranes. Birds tend to return to breed in the place where they were raised, so if young birds can be raised in new sites the species can often be helped to extend its range. The danger that goes with this process of 'imprinting' is that the young birds may imprint sexually on their foster-parents, but in the case of Whooping Cranes this fortunately does not appear to be happening.

Current fostering programmes conducted by the Canadian Wildlife Service are aiding the recovery of the Whooping Crane (*Grus americana*). One egg is removed from the nest of a Whooping Crane in the Wood Buffalo National Park in Canada (*above*) and then flown to Grays Lake National Park in Idaho, where it will be placed in the nest of a Greater Sandhill Crane (*Grus canadensis*). The successfully fostered young crane (*right*), just one week from attaining flight, will with luck return to breed in Idaho — so extending the geographical range of this beautiful bird.

Conservation in Action:
Captive breeding and relocation

When a species runs right out of natural habitat to live in, it is certain to go extinct unless the remaining individuals are taken into captivity. And even that desperate last resort will be pointless unless they can be induced to breed in captivity. In the past, zoos and aviculturists have not been conspicuous in the movement to conserve endangered species, ·and indeed have sometimes increased the dangers to threatened populations by taking precious individuals from the wild. But as more species decline to the point of no return, their only hope of survival may lie in captive breeding, either to be returned to the wild if their habitat can be restored, or to remain perpetually captive.

The conservation movement has so far made far too little investment in the possibilities of captive breeding of endangered species. Not only can populations be held in reserve while efforts are made to ensure their long-term future in the wild by suitable habitat management, but a great deal of valuable information on their biology, vital to their continued management, can be obtained at the same time. The importance of captive specimens to public education has also been neglected. Public feeling about whales, for example, was increased enormously once people could see and enjoy live whales and dolphins in aquaria.

Far more people visit zoos than attend all professional sports combined, so the potential audience for public education in bird conservation is huge, though greatly neglected.

Captive breeding techniques have become vital components of many management programmes for endangered species and are bound to become ever more important as more bird populations dwindle towards extinction.

Captive-bred birds must be carefully monitored in order to ensure the best possible chance of survival. Here a young Sea Eagle chick (*Haliaeetus albicilla*) is weighed in the laboratory of a scientific research station.

The Bald Eagle (*Haliaeetus leucocephalus*), America's national bird, has declined alarmingly in the last 35 years. Though the northern race of the bird is still widespread in Alaska and western Canada, elsewhere its numbers have fallen rapidly due to habitat disturbance and the effects of pes-. ticides. Attempts are being made to breed the eagle in captivity — but so far with very limited success.

Reintroductions and translocations

Birds bred in captivity can be released into the wild to re-establish a wild breeding population. This technique has succeeded extremely well in some cases – notably with Hawaiian Geese, or Nenes, and Mauritian Pink Pigeons – but its success depends ultimately on effective management of the habitat into which the birds are released.

A more daring variant of the technique has been used on several species living on small islands around New Zealand, where a number of birds have been reduced to single-figure populations by introduced predators or vegetation changes. Black Robins, South Island Robins and Saddlebacks have been moved from islands where they appeared doomed to others previously prepared for them by eliminating alien mammals and improving the habitat specifically for them. The practical difficulties are enormous, but these bold and imaginative programmes have succeeded in maintaining populations of birds that would otherwise certainly have died out.

Many conservationists feel uneasy about conservation methods which seem to interfere so much with endangered species and their habitats, especially when these methods involve killing other animals. Yet the hard truth is that species have become endangered through our interference in their environments, and the only way to ensure their survival is to interfere again to undo the damage we have done. The time is not too distant when there will be no truly natural habitats left on earth, and the survival of many species will depend on the management skills we have acquired in manipulating semi-natural or totally man-made habitats. More and more species will come to depend for their survival entirely on our sensitive and skilful 'interference' with them and with their environments.

The Nene or Hawaiian Goose (*Branta sandvicensis*) breeds readily in captivity, and birds bred in controlled environments are now being reintroduced to boost the islands' wild bird population.

The Bearded Vulture or Lammergeier (*Gypaetus barbatus*) is currently being re-established in the Alps, having been extinct there for many decades through direct human persecution.

Several aviaries in France, Austria and Switzerland have embarked on a co-operative breeding programme to produce young birds for reintroduction into the wild.

Economy and ecology: A call for a new world order

RUDOLF L. SCHREIBER

The extinction of bird species all over the world is a clear warning of the extent of habitat destruction and of the scale of the threat to our environment. The causes of the threat are not only very diverse but also closely interrelated. It is not, therefore, simply a case of finding solutions to the problems facing individual birds. In order to tackle the basic causes of these problems we must take action in the fields of world politics and economics at the same time as we implement urgent conservation measures in the field.

Since our world is now dominated by 'Homo oeconomicus', 'management man', it is in the field of economics that we must look for help in the first place. Our economic system is a man-made part of the natural biosphere, and one that depends, like any other, on the proper functioning of natural ecological processes. Where these natural processes are disturbed, man's economic systems too are disrupted. Only systems that are ecologically sound will prove viable in the long term.

Unfortunately, economic progress is seldom linked to nature conservation. Natural warning signs are either ignored, or are seen as signals of isolated problems. They are seldom acknowledged for what they really are — urgent indicators of the need to adjust world economic activities to ecological realities. We are, however, slowly coming to realize that all creatures are part of the system — including, even, man's economic system. Frederic Vester, a German ecologist, has calculated that in its five years of life a single Bluethroat contributes about US$680 to the system, mainly by eating troublesome insects. So if one individual small bird can make a contribution of that magnitude, what then is the economic value of all the birds that share man's environment? And what is the economic value of the rivers and their flora and fauna in providing us with a clean water supply? Or that of the forests in cleansing and replenishing the oxygen in our atmosphere? Every creature has its own unique role to play in the life processes of the planet. If more and more of them are lost, even the greatest economic system will eventually cease to function.

The campaign to save the birds is, then, a campaign to save the biosphere. Its aims are to promote sustained, lasting, long-term conservation through the considerate and informed use of our environment. Last-ditch efforts to save individual species from extinction may always be necessary, but without long-term good management of the biosphere they may be little more than futile gestures.

The need for changed priorities

Continued mismanagement of agricultural land and pastures will, by the end of the century, cause us to lose as much fertile land by soil loss and degradation as we gain by bringing new land into use. Nor is the increased use of artificial fertilizers a viable long-term answer to our need for higher food production. Pouring more and more agrochemicals onto the land creates higher energy consumption, higher levels of pollution in soil and water, higher concentrations of harmful chemicals in the food we eat and a frightening drop in the natural diversity of wildlife.

Our agriculture must become more ecologically orientated, with fewer chemicals and a greater variety of crops grown. Projects in many countries have proved that this is not an unrealistic dream. It is quite possible to make good profits, and achieve good productivity, through agricultural systems more closely adapted to natural conditions. Working with nature can be far more fruitful than the sterile policy of fighting it, especially in difficult or marginal land.

Changes must also be made in our whole approach to foreign aid. Developing countries are best served by the introduction of technologies adapted to their needs. Manufacturers in the industrialized countries may prefer to sell expensive and highly sophisticated machinery, but the recipient country seldom has either the trained personnel needed to man them or the facilities to maintain them. To think of developing countries as new markets for advanced technology products does them a great disservice. If aid is to achieve its goals its techniques and technologies must take account of the habitats and conditions in which they are to be applied. A 'soft' technology would often be much more appropriate, and may even benefit the donating countries by stimulating the creative search for new solutions and techniques. Such research would be a sound investment in what are certain to be the more ecologically minded markets of the future.

The development of agricultural systems not dependent on chemical products is a far better form of aid to developing countries than the export of large quantities of agro-chemicals. In many cases, ecological agriculture — like this freshly planted mixed crop in Rwanda — has proved a highly productive alternative.

There must be evolution rather than revolution in our economic thinking, and a prime precondition of this is the stabilization and eventual reduction of our energy consumption. Industrialized countries must find ways of reducing their energy requirements, and developing countries must resist the temptation to adopt development strategies that will involve huge energy demands.

The 25 per cent of the world's population who live in industrialized countries consume 80 per cent of the world's energy. One American, for example, uses 50 times as much energy as an Indian. An increase in the cost of energy is generally considered to be the only way to redress this imbalance. The introduction of an energy tax, linked to a reduction in other taxes, may be one way by which this could be achieved.

An increase in the cost of energy has a threefold effect; it slows down non-essential use of energy in homes and industries, it favours low-energy industries rather than the big energy users, and it promotes technical and social innovations designed to save energy.

Big increases in energy consumption in the Third World are caused by the massive shift of population from rural areas to the towns. To reverse this trend, agriculture must receive much more support. Pricing structures must be designed to ensure reasonable prices for locally grown food rather than low prices for food sold in city markets. The depopulation of the land can only be stopped, or significantly slowed, if farming really does offer a viable alternative to the young.

The oil crisis of the 1970s showed that the cost of energy from fossil fuels can indeed bring about changes in world economies. Cheap oil never did encourage any thoughts about energy conservation or alternative energy resources, but the oil shortage quickly led to an upsurge in technological research into new energy sources and to a substantial reduction in energy consumption through fuel-saving schemes. Lower energy consumption in turn usually means reduced consumption of raw materials, and this reduces production of wastes and pollutants and degradation of the environment through mineral exploitation. And this is where we come full circle. By using the earth's resources more carefully we begin to take a more responsible attitude not only to our own long-term needs but also to the future viability of the earth's living environments.

We must view the current crisis in the environment in positive terms — as a unique opportunity and a challenge to politicians, scientists and economists to adjust our goals and aspirations to the limitations of nature. Giving up extravagance does not mean abandoning progress: it can mean the beginning of a reconciliation between man and nature, the long-term benefits of which are incalculable.

Solar, wind and wave power offer unlimited resources of energy. We have neglected their potential for too long: only very recently have techniques been developed to harness this type of energy on a large scale. This photograph shows a pilot scheme in California for wind-driven power generation.

The World Conservation Strategy

If we are to save birds from extinction and avert the global threats to the environment, international co-operation of the highest order will be necessary. Without a joint strategy and the co-ordination of national and international efforts, many conservation measures will be little more than temporary repairs to the sinking ark of life on earth.

Nature acknowledges no boundaries. Rivers cross frontiers, the seas embrace all continents and air masses encircle the entire globe. Birds, perhaps more than any other living creatures, symbolize this world without boundaries. Many of them are international travellers whose annual migrations link the peoples of widely separated continents. With their beauty and grace they provide a focus for our concern and a rallying-point for our concerted actions.

ICBP, the International Council for Bird Preservation, is leading the way by appealing for global solidarity — asking the people of all nations to work not only towards the preservation of the world's birds but also towards the effective implementation of the 'World Conservation Strategy', published jointly in 1980 by the three largest conservation organizations in the world — The International Union for Conservation of Nature (IUCN), the United Nations Environment Programme (UNEP) and the World Wildlife Fund (WWF).

These organizations have together compiled a programme of action aimed at conservation of the environment on a global scale. More than 700 scientists and 450 governmental organizations joined with the major conservation movements to pool their professional expertise. The resulting World Conservation Strategy is a wide-ranging plan encompassing shared goals and proposing clear priorities for national and international action.

The Strategy has three main goals. First, to ensure the protection of the basic ecological processes and cycles, by conserving their foundation, the soil; by ensuring the continued recycling of nutrients; and by preserving the cleansing global water cycle.

Second, to preserve the genetic diversity of life on earth. This is essential, not just for moral reasons but also for economic reasons: the breeding of new food crops and domestic animals, and the isolation of valuable medicinal components, can only succeed if we conserve a wide genetic reserve.

Third, to preserve the world's forests and grasslands, fisheries and wild animals, all of which are vital resources for the world's rural and urban populations alike.

The implementation of this strategy is very urgent. Earth's resources continue to be over-exploited while its capacity to support the growing human population diminishes. Hunger and poverty continue to spread, the cost of energy and basic goods continues to rise, and reserves of many important raw materials to dwindle. Yet despite the widespread acceptance of the ideals of the World Conservation Strategy, it is widely ignored in practice. The reasons for this are only too well known. Ecology and economics are still viewed as unrelated disciplines, laws are inadequate and poorly enforced, long-term planning at the highest level is sadly lacking, and the financial support for conservation is inadequate. The seriousness of the situation has yet to be fully appreciated and taken to heart.

This is where the **Save the Birds** campaign really begins. Its two principal aims are to carry the message to the widest possible audience and, at the same time, to raise funds for conservation. ICBP and national conservation agencies can provide the expertise for setting up and managing nature reserves and for designing programmes to rescue critically endangered species. The rest is up to you.

Saving Britain's Birdlife

DAVID ATTENBOROUGH AND IAN PRESTT

Britain today:
Ecological and economic ties

Until about 5000 years ago, the British Isles were physically a part of Europe. At that time, the northern hemisphere was warming in the aftermath of the Ice Ages. The glaciers that had once covered two-thirds of Britain had retreated, and animals and plants from the south and east were slowly reclaiming the land. At the same time, however, the level of the sea was rising, and as the water slowly flooded across the lowlands, it formed a long channel which cut off the British Isles. Many of the land animals that were extending their ranges across Europe were unable to reach Britain. Of the 45 amphibian and reptile species found in continental Europe, only 12 reached Britain and only four penetrated as far west as Ireland. The distribution of mammals shows a similar pattern. Continental Europe has 137 species, but Britain has only 43.

Plants are not so confined by a stretch of water a mere 35 kilometres across. Their seeds are able to cross such a barrier with comparative ease, and once here they are provided with a great variety of habitats. Britain, despite its comparatively small size, is geologically very varied. Calcareous soils lie above its limestone and chalk; acidic soils over its silicious granites. Climatically, too, it is varied. The North Atlantic Drift brings warm Gulf Stream waters to swirl around its coasts, and westerly winds blowing across the Atlantic bring in abundant moisture. As a result the climate of Britain is warmer and wetter than in the same latitudes in central Europe. While survivors from the Ice Age such as Dwarf Birch, Bog Myrtle and Mountain Avens still grow on the mountains of Scotland, down in the Scilly Isles and southwest Ireland, where there is an almost Mediterranean feel to the climate, you can find Strawberry Trees and the very rare Killarney Fern, whose main stronghold is Spain and the Pyrenees.

Even so, Britain's flora is still impoverished compared with that of Europe. Even some of the species that can be claimed to be British, such as Autumn Lady's Tresses, Man Orchid and Marsh Gentian are rarities, whereas they are abundant in Europe. On the other hand, a few species flourish here in a way that Europe cannot match. Bluebells, for example, do grow in Europe, but nowhere do they produce the carpets of blue that are the glory of many a British wood in spring.

For birds, the Channel is even less of a barrier. The prevailing winds put the British Isles on a natural flyway for migrating birds. The Roseate Terns, Pied Flycatchers and Redstarts that travel north in spring from southern Europe and Africa use the islands as a staging post. Other species, such as Barnacle and Brent Geese and Bewick's Swans, come south from northern Europe to spend the winter in Britain. Overall, 160 species of migrants visit these islands at some time each year, while the sea cliffs and estuaries, and varied inland habitats, provide permanent homes for more than 150 full-time residents.

The Mountain Avens (*Dryas octopetala*) is a relict of the Ice Ages — an Arctic and montane plant whose stems and leaves often form dense mats close to the ground.

A sea of Bluebells (*Endymion nonscriptus*) carpets the ground in Darroch Wood in Tayside, Scotland. The plant is widespread in Europe, but nowhere does it grow in such profusion as in the woodlands of Britain.

Britain was the home of the Industrial Revolution, and since that time her economy has been built on importing raw materials and food and exporting manufactured goods to markets overseas. Until the outbreak of World War Two, the bulk of that overseas trade was with her Empire. Today, since the signing of the Treaty of Rome, her major trading partners are within the European Economic Community. She also trades, though to a lesser extent, with other developed countries – those in Europe outside the EEC, the United States, and others elsewhere. But from each of these groups she imports more than she exports. Only with the oil-producing nations, the Communist world and the developing countries does she have a trading credit.

Britain's membership of the EEC requires her to abide by regulations governing trade within the Community. One of these, the Common Agricultural Policy, has brought major changes to the British countryside. Under its rules, farmers are paid premiums which artificially maintain the price of their products; they are given grants to encourage them to improve marginal land; and they are protected from outside competition by the imposition of levies on imports. As a result of all this encouragement, EEC farmers are producing far more than can be consumed within the Community or even sold outside it. So mountains of butter and milk are growing within vast warehouses, and produce that cannot be prevented from rotting often has to be destroyed without ever being put on the market.

The price of this policy is not simply an economic one. It has also been exacted from the British countryside. Artificial fertilizers and insecticides are used to extract the greatest tonnage of crops from each field. Hedgerows are uprooted to exploit every square metre of land. Ponds are filled in, water meadows drained, and land on the very margin of productivity ploughed up. All this is destroying those very elements within the landscape that until now have provided wildlife with its last refuges in the human-dominated landscape of Britain. And all this is being done at a time when the Community is producing more food than it needs or knows what to do with.

Although Britain is producing surpluses of some foods, she still imports others. She buys tea and coffee, for example. These crops represent a major element in the economies of the developing nations that grow them, but they often take up land that could better be used to grow food for local consumption. Britain also buys timber and minerals which she needs for her industries. If the developing countries want to buy goods manufactured in Britain – as Britain would like them to do – then they have to export such commodities in order to earn British currency. And to do that, they must clear more and more of their land. So the industrialization of one part of the globe has major environmental consequences right round the world, wherever the trade routes reach.

Of all the economic developments that have taken place since the last war, only tourism has brought any positive gain to the environment. Its benefits have been felt most markedly in countries such as those of East Africa, where foreign visitors coming to see the wildlife make a major contribution to the economy. But British wildlife, though precious to the British, cannot be reckoned a major earner of foreign currency. So it seems that for as long as the countryside is evaluated in economic terms alone, the pursuit of ever higher levels of agricultural productivity will continue to rob our native wildlife of its living space.

Logs of African Mahogany (*Khaya* spp.) being sorted in the harbour at Lamu in Kenya, in readiness for shipment to ports in Western Europe.

The tragedy of over-production is that while half the world goes hungry, we in the West spend a fortune on storing – and even on destroying – state subsidized 'mountains' of surplus food.

Trade and industry: Impacts at home and abroad

Britain's influence on the ecology of countries overseas is not limited to the direct effects of the demands of trade. It began centuries ago, when British colonists, settling overseas, took their household pets with them. In some places, Australia and New Zealand for example, they even formed societies to import British wild birds so that familiar bird-song might console them in those alien lands. But the effect on the indigenous wildlife was often little short of catastrophic. Introduced birds, if they managed to survive at all, often became so successful that they displaced the native birds. Goats devastated the vegetation. Cats, running wild, hunted the native mammals and birds only too successfully. And rats that had been transported inadvertently in shipping, stole birds' eggs and killed chicks in the nest.

Today, such dangers are well recognized, and for the most part are prevented from recurring. But in many places the damage has already been done. The impact of introduced aliens is particularly severe on those relatively small and isolated islands that over thousands of years of evolution have acquired their own unique species. In the last 25 years alone, 127 such birds have become extinct.

The unbridled and merciless trading in wild creatures and wild products, which in the past has endangered many species, is today being dealt with by legislation. Britain is a signatory of the Convention on International Trade in Endangered Species of Wild Fauna and Flora (CITES). Even so, the trade still continues illegally. In 1982, over 400 living animals and 4000 items of merchandise made from protected species were seized at British ports of entry.

Most industries produce wastes and effluents, many of which are poisonous. Britain, being so heavily industrialized, produces them in great quantity. In the past, they were poured into the rivers and the sea, or blown into the air from tall chimneys, without hesitation, in the belief that somehow they would just disappear. Today, so much pollution is being created by so many nations that even the immensity of the oceans and the atmosphere cannot absorb it or dilute it to a harmless level.

Atmospheric pollution comes from three main sources; from fossil fuels that are burnt to produce gas and electricity, from the exhausts of vehicles, and from gases and dust produced by industry. In 1970, Britain produced over 31 million tonnes of these effluents. Sulphur dioxide and oxides of nitrogen are taken up by the atmosphere and eventually fall as acid rain, often at a great distance from the source. Much of that produced in Britain, for example, is carried north-east by the prevailing winds, and falls in Scandinavia, poisoning lakes and killing trees.

Our waters, too, are becoming increasingly polluted. Britain still discharges 20 per cent of her sewage, untreated, into rivers, estuaries and the sea; and oil is still being swilled out of the holds of tankers at sea in spite of the illegality of this practice. Thus activities within the British Isles have effects that spread far beyond our shores.

No fewer than 30 Asian, South American and African tropical forest birds were discovered packed in wood and canvas boxes hidden in the bodywork of this estate car when it was searched by British customs officers. Five birds were dead; the rest, amazingly, survived. When charges were brought, one defendant was fined £500 with £736 costs; the other was fined £150 and received a suspended prison sentence.

Smoke and dust almost obliterate the pale winter sun over one of the heavily industrialized areas of Cardiff, South Wales.

When man first settled in the British Isles, most of the land was covered with deciduous woodland. Even as recently as the eighteenth century, the country could still be described as largely wooded. But the onset of the Industrial Revolution brought about widespread changes, which have been gathering momentum ever since.

The improvement in techniques of draining and ploughing has brought more and more marginal land into cultivation every year. Today, Dorset has only 15 per cent of the heathland it possessed in 1760. Scotland and Northern Ireland have lost a similar proportion of their bogs. In East Anglia, only one per cent of the original fenland remains, and in the North Kent Marshes, nearly 50 per cent of the area that remained undrained in 1935 has now gone. Such drainage, in recent years, has been speeded by Government grants. In 1940, for example, 10,000 hectares were drained for the first time. By the late 1970s, over 100,000 hectares were being so treated every year.

The use of artificial fertilizers has also escalated during recent decades. Whereas during the 1930s, 100,000 tonnes of nitrogen fertilizer were being used each year, by 1975 that figure had risen to over one million tonnes. Insecticides, too, have been used in vastly greater quantities. In the years 1975–79, 25,000 tonnes were sprayed over 15 million hectares, an increase of 10 per cent over the previous five-year period. Such chemicals have a very damaging effect on many wild species that otherwise manage to coexist with crops. Furthermore, as these substances are washed from the land they cause further problems. Of the 180,000 tonnes of phosphorus used annually, one-third is leached out of the soil. Water draining into the Great Ouse, for example, contains 60 kilograms of phosphorus and up to 23 kilograms of nitrogen from every hectare of land each year. Such major chemical changes in river water seriously alter ecological balances. Food chains are disrupted,

and high concentrations of chemicals produce blooms of algae which deoxygenate the water and kill the fish.

Industry and urban developments occupy over 13 per cent of the land, and every decade a further 3.3 per cent of the country's agricultural land is taken for new industrial developments, building, and the tipping of waste. At the same time, great areas once occupied by industry lie derelict. In 1971, it was estimated that at least 55,000 hectares were wasted in this way. But such land is extremely difficult and expensive to reclaim, and only some 2200 hectares are being brought back into use each year.

Today, the original natural habitats of Britain have been reduced to a few tiny relicts, stranded in a predominantly urban and industrial landscape. The pressure on these last refuges of so many British native species is unremitting.

The hand of man is everywhere in the flat fenland of East Anglia. In Woodwalton Fen, northeast of Huntingdon, isolated patches of fen and woodland survive in a vast expanse of reclaimed fields and pastures.

Even special status is not always a guarantee of protection. Despite being designated a Site of Special Scientific Interest (SSSI), large areas of the ancient Caledonian Pine forest at Abernethy have been clear-cut, ploughed and replanted.

Agro-chemicals can greatly improve farm productivity, but we have been slow to realize the wider implications of their use.

Consequences of change:
Habitats and wildlife under pressure

Man's continuing assault on the natural environment has had a dramatic effect on our native flora and fauna. Many of our rarest plants are now confined to only a handful of sites where conditions still permit their reproduction and growth. The plants associated with our ancient woodlands are probably the best example of this. These woods are remnants of the original woodland that once covered most of Britain, and their plant communities evolved to coexist in the conditions of light, humidity and soil that developed within them. When these ancient woodlands are cleared for agriculture, or replanted with exotic conifers, the new conditions cannot support most of the former woodland plants because of their more specific ecological requirements. Conifers cast a dense shade, produce an acid litter and require very intensive management in order to produce saleable timber. The result is a very simplified ecosystem, often comprising only one or two species of tree, and

with most of the elements of the original woodland ecosystem either reduced or missing. Few of the original flowering plants survive in this changed regime, and consequently many are now extremely rare. Wild Gladioli, for example, are now found only in the New Forest in Hampshire, and the Ghost Orchid is confined to the beechwoods of the Chilterns.

This pattern of change is being repeated in other natural and semi-natural ecosystems throughout the country. Sand dunes, wetlands, estuaries, unimproved grasslands, moorlands and even the high montane ecosystems of the uplands are suffering a similar fate. The causes may be different but the effects are the same, not just for the plants but for all wildlife, which is gradually impoverished and pushed closer and closer to the limits of survival.

Many of the larger mammals have already been lost: the Bear, Wolf, Lynx, Beaver and wild white cattle or Aurochs have long-since gone. The early fragmentation of their natural habitats proved too much, and by the beginning of the eighteenth century all were extinct. Others are still under threat today, and their territories and numbers have been significantly reduced. The Otter and Water

Shrew have suffered seriously from loss of their habitat, as have the Common Dormouse, Harvest Mouse and many species of bat. Amongst the reptiles and amphibians, the Great Crested Newt, Natterjack Toad, Sand Lizard and Smooth Snake are all under threat and have shown serious declines in recent years.

For other groups the story is the same; the Large Blue butterfly is now extinct, several of the hairstreaks are vulnerable and the Heath Fritillary and Black-veined White occur in only a few isolated sites. The overall picture is difficult to quantify. Of the many animal species that occur in these islands only a few have been surveyed systematically; but if these few species are reliable indicators, the outlook is one of continued impoverishment and species loss unless specific action is taken to halt, and where possible to reverse, the current trend.

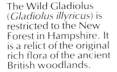

The Wild Gladiolus (*Gladiolus illyricus*) is restricted to the New Forest in Hampshire. It is a relict of the original rich flora of the ancient British woodlands.

A male Natterjack Toad (*Bufo calamita*) joins an evening chorus of loud ratchet-like calls. On a still night, the calls may carry for two kilometres or more.

The reduction or loss of a small and uncommon species of insect may not appear to be a matter for serious public concern, but when seen in the context of *why* this is happening, it is. Through over-use and abuse, the countryside is being impoverished; not catastrophically, but insidiously so that many of the changes go unnoticed. To an increasingly urbanized society this loss is not just an ecological problem but also a social concern. Now, more than ever before, people need to have access to the countryside. Even to those people who do not use such areas regularly, the knowledge that they exist fulfils a deep-rooted psychological need. We are now a far cry from the biblical wilderness of suffering and fasting. Today the wilderness appeal is a priceless freedom; freedom from the man-made environment and its associated pressures. This appeal is as unquantifiable as the effect of its loss, but it undoubtedly exists

— as the growing tide of public interest in environmental problems so clearly demonstrates.

It goes without saying that birds have not escaped the problems associated with habitat loss. Some of the larger species, for example the White-tailed Sea Eagle and Capercaillie, were wiped out in the British Isles during the early periods of agricultural improvement and persecution. Fortunately, the latter was successfully reintroduced in 1837, and attempts to reintroduce the former met with their first success in 1985.

The Great Auk, which became extinct in historic times, is a classic example of how quickly a species can be lost. Through drainage, species like the Marsh Harrier, Black Tern, Bittern, Ruff, Black-tailed Godwit, Black-winged Stilt, and Savi's Warbler now either do not breed at all or breed only in very small numbers. Intensive agriculture in open lowland country has also reduced

species such as the Dartford Warbler, Cirl Bunting and Stone Curlew, whilst the intensive use of uplands for agriculture and forestry now threatens the Golden Eagle, Hen Harrier, Merlin and Black Grouse, the last three all having shown significant declines in recent years.

In some instances the relationship between a particular cause and a species decline are not immediately obvious. Thus it took many years of research before confirmation was obtained that the decline of the Sparrowhawk and the Peregrine Falcon was attributable to the use of certain organochlorine insecticides. With the increased use of chemicals in agriculture and industry, this example provides a good indicator of other possible dangers to the environment and the life it supports. Man, who is the ultimate predator, should take more than a passing interest in these events.

Though widespread and still common over much of Europe, the Heath Fritillary (*Mellicta athalia*) is now found only in a few southern counties of England. The cause of decline is probably the loss of old meadowlands.

The Ruff (*Philomachus pugnax*), pictured above in display at a 'lek' or communal display arena, is one of many species which, through drainage of our wetlands, now breed in Britain only in small numbers. The Black-winged Stilt (*Himantopus himantopus*) has bred here in the past, but in recent years there have been only two confirmed reports. This elegant bird is now very unlikely ever to become a regular breeding species in Britain.

The birdlife of Britain: A heritage at risk

The present avifauna of the British Isles has evolved in response to climatic changes. In Europe, the warming of the climate since the last Ice Age allowed many southern species to expand into northern regions as these became more hospitable. Birds from Africa and the Mediterranean area took advantage of the new habitat available in the summer for breeding, but migrated southwards again for the winter. At the same time many northern species extended their range even further northwards.

Regional changes in bird distribution are still occurring in response to continuing local climatic changes. At the beginning of this century the British climate was one of mild winters and warm, wet summers. These conditions appear not to have suited some species, and a number of previously well-established birds like the Red-backed Shrike and Wryneck have declined to the point of near-extinction. These declines cannot be explained by habitat loss or persecution.

More recently, the occurrence of drier easterly winds has encouraged some northern species to extend their range, with some even reaching the British Isles, where they have re-established a tenuous foothold as breeding species. Scarlet Rosefinch, Lapland Bunting and Purple Sandpiper have all bred in Britain in the last few years, but the success or otherwise of their recolonization will depend on suitable habitat being available for them.

Some 208 species now breed regularly in Britain, and a further 25 have bred here sporadically this century. Three species have become extinct as breeding birds since 1800; the Great Bustard, which suffered both persecution and habitat loss and which is threatened throughout its range; the Great Auk, which became totally extinct due to human persecution; and the White-tailed Sea Eagle, also a victim of persecution and habitat loss but recently successfully reintroduced. A fourth species, the Kentish

Plover, has only attempted to breed a few times since 1956. Its final extinction is thought to be attributable to egg collecting and loss of its coastal breeding sites.

In both European and world terms, the British Isles are of great importance as the breeding home of seabirds. Something like 70 per cent of the world's Gannets breed in Britain — with over half on the island of St Kilda alone. The Razorbill is another species with its main stronghold in Britain — with possibly as much as 50 per cent of the world population. As these and other seabird species breed on remote cliffs and islands they are subject to fewer pressures than many birds, although oil pollution and more recently the use of monofilament fishing nets have caused many deaths.

Fifty-six of our breeding species are summer visitors. Many of our seabirds spend the winter at sea. Terns winter mainly off the coast of West Africa, the Manx Shearwater moves south to an area off the Atlantic coast of South America, and Arctic Skuas winter off the Atlantic coasts of Africa and South America. The bulk of our terrestrial summer visitors migrate to the Mediterranean and Africa, some going right down to South Africa. Population declines in some species can be linked to adverse conditions in their winter quarters. The severe drought in the

The decline of the Red-backed Shrike (*Lanius collurio*) in southern England, from 253 pairs in 1960 to less than 10 in 1986, is probably due to climatic changes both here and in the bird's wintering quarters.

Whitethroats (*Sylvia communis*) are slowly recovering from the disastrous losses they suffered in the late 1960s when droughts hit their wintering grounds in the Sahel.

Almost half the world's population of Razorbills (*Alca torda*) inhabit the cliffs and rocky islands of Britain.

Sahel region of northern Africa resulted in only about 25 per cent of British Whitethroats returning after the winter of 1968, and a drop of over 70 per cent in the Sand Martin population was recorded after the 1983 winter. It remains to be seen if these species recover or whether successive droughts will reduce their numbers even further.

Fifty-two species are primarily winter visitors to Britain, although some of them also breed here in small numbers. Swans, geese, ducks and waders pass the winter along our coasts and in our estuaries and inland wetlands, while divers, grebes and sea ducks winter at sea off our coasts. Britain supports internationally important populations of Pink-footed, Greenland White-fronted and Barnacle geese, and both Bewick's and Whooper swans. Hundreds of thousands of waders winter on our estuaries. In the case of the Knot, something like three-quarters of the European wintering population is found in the British Isles, while a large proportion of Europe's wintering Dunlin, Sanderling and Grey Plover are also found here. Of the passerines, the Scandinavian thrushes – the Fieldfare and Redwing – are probably the most familiar winter visitors.

The major changes to our avifauna, apart from those due to climatic effects, have been caused by loss or deterioration of habitat. Agricultural changes have had the most noticeable impact. The enclosure of pasture contributed to the disappearance of the Great Bustard. The conversion of grassland to arable has caused the decline of the Corncrake and Grey Partridge. Reclamation of open downland has affected the Stone Curlew and the Wheatear. The drainage of wetland areas, with loss of reedbeds, fenland and water meadows, has caused a decline in species like Bittern, Marsh Harrier, Black-tailed Godwit and Ruff, and the removal of heathland and associated scrub and woodland has limited the amount of habitat available to Dartford Warblers, Whinchats, Woodlarks and Nightjars.

Changes in woodland management have also had their effect. Nightingales, which used to benefit from the practice of coppicing, have now contracted their range following its cessation. Much of the alternative woodland habitat is also being destroyed, more often than not to be replaced with a more economic but less suitable uniform habitat of alien conifers. This replacement of native broadleaved woodland with conifer monocultures has greatly reduced the amount of woodland on which species like Redstart, Pied Flycatcher and Wood Warbler rely. However, these newly created conifer forests, if sympathetically managed, can provide a habitat for Tree Pipits, Woodlarks and Nightjars.

The result of these changes is that the availability, variety and diversity of habitats are all reduced. The remaining areas of wetland, ancient woodland, heath, moorland and grassland are thus vitally important as sanctuaries for these species, from which they can recolonize new areas when, hopefully, more nature reserves are established and new areas of suitable habitat are re-created using the ecological knowledge we now possess.

On the credit side, this century has seen the colonization of Britain by two new resident species — the Collared Dove, which first began to breed here in 1955 and is now found over the whole of Britain, and Cetti's Warbler, which spread north from the Continent and was first recorded breeding in southeastern England in 1972.

The coastal mudflats, marshes and fields of north and west Britain are the wintering grounds of thousands of Barnacle Geese (*Branta leucopsis*). Irish and Hebridean populations fly in from breeding grounds in Greenland, while the 10,000 or so birds that winter in the Solway Firth are from Greenland, Norway and Spitzbergen.

The Fieldfare (*Turdus pilaris*) is a familiar winter visitor from Scandinavia to most parts of Britain, but although the species is extending its range westwards it has not yet become a regular breeding bird here.

The Pied Flycatcher (*Ficedula hypoleuca*) is primarily a bird of deciduous woodland, although it has bred successfully in other habitats, including conifer plantations, when nest boxes have been provided.

Britain's endangered birds:
The 'Red List' for the British Isles

The chart at the foot of page 347 lists the main endangered species in Britain today, and indicates the principal factors affecting their status.

Most of the species on the list are classified as 'Vulnerable'. This means that although they may have fairly stable, or in some cases even increasing, populations, their overall small numbers, together with their isolation, mean that their status could easily change and they might then undergo a rapid decline. Good examples of this are the Slavonian and Black-necked Grebes. The number of breeding pairs has fluctuated over the last 10 years, with an average of about 50 pairs of the former and 12 pairs of the latter. The number of sites at which they breed is about 25 and 6 respectively, and the loss of any one of them will result in a significant drop in the British population.

Birds of prey in Britain have, for many years, fared badly from persecution and, more recently, from the effects of certain persistent organochlorine insecticides. The Osprey, through persecution and egg collection, actually became extinct. However, a pair recolonized a site at Loch Garten in 1955, and with protection the total population has now increased to over 30 pairs. The Red Kite, Marsh Harrier and the Goshawk, which also suffered from persecution, have now also increased following better legislation and increased protection. A repetition of the pesticide problem, which wiped out the Peregrine and Sparrowhawk over much of England, Wales and southern Scotland, or an increase in persecution, could, however, quickly reverse the situation.

Waders such as the Black-tailed Godwit and the Avocet are dependent on wetlands for breeding. Both became extinct as British breeding birds, but have recently recolonized. The former is still confined to about a dozen sites, while the latter — although with protection now numbering over 200 pairs — is still restricted to an even smaller number of sites. Their continued survival is thus still tenuous.

'Threatened' species are those that are declining and now exist in such small numbers that unless the decline is halted they will soon become extinct. In some cases habitat loss is the outstanding cause. The Bittern, for example, is dependent on reedbeds, of which only a relatively small number now remain. It also suffers from severe winters.

For some species the cause or causes of decline have not yet been confirmed. The Red-backed Shrike, for example, was once very numerous and widespread in Britain and its decline does not seem to be closely related to either habitat loss or persecution, although these may have contributed. Climate is thought to have affected this species, as it probably has the Wryneck. Both have now reached an extremely low level of population from which they may not recover. The most serious recent addition to our 'Threatened' category is the Roseate Tern, which has suffered through competition from larger gulls at its breeding sites combined with hunting pressures in its winter quarters.

The curious Wryneck (*Jynx torquilla*) is a member of the woodpecker family. It has an extensible sticky tongue, with which it feeds on insects, especially ants, but it lacks the specialized climbing and woodboring abilities of most woodpeckers. Sadly, the species is in decline throughout western Europe, and in Britain, where it is classified 'Threatened', it is close to extinction as a breeding bird.

The Kentish Plover (*Charadrius alexandrinus*) has not bred in Britain since 1956 and is now classed 'Extinct' as a breeding species.

The Avocet (*Recurvirostra avosetta*) is one of the 28 British birds classified as 'Vulnerable'. The bird became extinct in the British Isles in 1842, but new colonies, started in East Anglia in 1947, now have a population of more than 200 pairs.

Some of the species on the list have been 'declining' for some time, but may soon reach such a low level that they will warrant inclusion in one of the previous two categories. Thus, birds like the Merlin and Corncrake have suffered serious declines and have lost a great deal of their breeding habitat. Careful research into ways of helping them is urgently needed if they are not to become 'Threatened' or 'Vulnerable' in the very near future.

The last category – 'extinct' – is the most crucial. In historic times three species have become extinct as breeding birds in Britain. The Great Auk, now extinct worldwide, disappeared because of persecution. The White-tailed Sea Eagle was also persecuted and last bred in Britain at the beginning of this century. Its rarity worldwide meant that it was unlikely to recolonize naturally, and so nestlings from the Norwegian population were brought across to Scotland and introduced into the wild. The first successful breeding was achieved in 1985. The Great Bustard disappeared due to the destruction of its habitat, and given its dwindling numbers in Europe it is unlikely to recolonize. The lack of suitable habitat lessens still further the chances of its reintroduction.

One category of birds not included in the table includes those that only breed here spasmodically because the British Isles lie on the extreme edge of their range. It is possible that in the future some of these may extend their range. Northern species such as Shore Lark, Lapland Bunting, Scarlet Rosefinch, Brambling, Purple Sandpiper and Snowy Owl have all bred in recent years and represent potential colonists. However, the first colonists of any expanding species are particularly at risk, and special measures will be needed to protect them if they are to become established.

Britain's 'Red List'
The current roll-call of British birds in danger contains the names of 46 species. Of these, 5 are in the most critical, or 'Threatened' group; 28 are classified as 'Vulnerable'; 4 are 'Declining' and 5 are considered 'Extinct' as breeding species. Four other species are listed as being of 'Uncertain' status. A major commitment to conservation will be needed from Government and non-governmental organizations alike if this list is not to lengthen in the coming years. The chart below shows the birds, their status and the principal threats affecting them.

Legend:
- Threatened
- Vulnerable
- Declining
- Extinct
- Uncertain

Threat icons:
- Conifer monocultures
- Agricultural monocultures
- Drainage and river management
- Recreation/disturbance
- Hunting/poisoning/collecting
- Poisoning by pesticides
- Destruction of woodlands
- Climatic change

Species	Conifer	Agricultural	Drainage	Recreation	Hunting/poisoning	Poisoning by pesticides	Destruction of woodlands	Climatic change
Black-throated Diver				●	●			
Slavonian Grebe				●	●			
Black-necked Grebe			●	●				
Bittern			●		●			
Garganey			●					
Goshawk					●			
Red Kite	●				●		●	
Honey Buzzard					●		●	
Marsh Harrier			●		●			
Hen Harrier	●				●			
Montagu's Harrier		●		●				
White-tailed Sea Eagle					●			
Golden Eagle	●			●	●			
Osprey					●			
Hobby					●			?
Merlin	●				●	?		
Peregrine					●	●		
Quail		●						?
Spotted Crake			●					
Corncrake		●						
Great Bustard		●			●			
Kentish Plover				●	●			
Dotterel				●	●			

Species	Conifer	Agricultural	Drainage	Recreation	Hunting/poisoning	Poisoning by pesticides	Destruction of woodlands	Climatic change
Whimbrel		●			?			
Black-tailed Godwit			●		?			
Ruff			●		?			
Avocet			●		●			
Red-necked Phalarope					●			●
Stone Curlew	●	●		●	●			
Roseate Tern					?			?
Great Auk					●			
Snowy Owl								●
Wryneck								●
Woodlark	●	●			●			●
Golden Oriole					●			
Chough		●						
Bearded Tit			●		●			●
Savi's Warbler		?						
Marsh Warbler		?	●	?				
Dartford Warbler		●						●
Fieldfare								?
Redwing								?
Red-backed Shrike				●	●			●
Scottish Crossbill	●							
Snow Bunting				●	●			
Cirl Bunting		●						?

Bittern:
Threatened by loss of its reedbed habitat

The secretive and cryptically coloured Bittern (*Botaurus stellaris*) is a resident British species which is joined in winter by a small number of continental birds. It spends most of its time concealed in dense reedbeds and is rarely seen in flight.

The presence of a male in the breeding season is immediately obvious thanks to its distinctive booming call. It is deep and resonant, sounding rather like a distant foghorn. The call advertises the bird's presence to females, and proclaims its territory.

The male establishes a territory in late winter, and occupies it until June or July. The nest is sited amongst dense reeds and is usually well separated from those in adjacent territories. However, males may be polygamous and may have a number of nests within their territories, and in these circumstances the nests may be quite close together. The nest itself is built by the female and consists of a platform of dead reeds, lined with finer material. A single clutch, usually of five or six eggs, is laid from early April to mid-June. The eggs are laid at two- to three-day intervals and incubation, by the female, starts with the first egg. Because of this the eggs hatch sequentially, and in a large clutch the last egg may hatch 12 or 13 days after the first.

Fish, together with amphibians and insects, form the bulk of the Bittern's diet, although worms, molluscs, crustaceans and spiders are also taken. Fish are shaken or bitten to death before being swallowed head first. The bird is generally a solitary feeder, wading slowly through the shallows at the edge of the reedbed during the day or in the evening.

The Bittern's mottled golden-brown plumage provides excellent concealment amongst the reeds, and when disturbed or threatened, rather than fly it will often adopt a characteristic stance with its neck and body stretched vertically upwards. In this position it is wonderfully camouflaged, but is still able to watch any intruder as it has the ability to swivel its eyes downwards. It can remain in this posture for many hours, and will even sway to match the movement of the reeds in the wind.

The species' distribution in Britain is closely related to the availability of its reedbed breeding habitat. Suitable dense reedbeds of *Phragmites* can become established in marshes and fens, along the sides of slow-flowing rivers or near the coast, but the number and extent of suitable sites have been steadily declining, and today it is likely that Bitterns breed in only four counties — one in Wales and three in England.

The Bittern became extinct as a breeding bird in Britain at the end of the nineteenth century. Breeding was not proven again until 1911, although males were heard booming prior to this. By 1919 there were 12 to 13 pairs nesting in Norfolk, mostly in the Norfolk Broads, and by 1928 the number had increased to 23 to 25 pairs. For the next 25 years there was a slow increase and in 1954 the population stood at just over 80 pairs, most of these still in Norfolk.

During the next 15 years the Bittern population spread and increased in most counties, except in Norfolk, where numbers started to go down. By 1970 the bird was more widespread, but the population had declined to about 70 pairs overall. A survey in 1976 revealed that a decline had taken place everywhere except in Suffolk, where an increase of booming birds had occurred even though the number of breeding sites had halved.

The extinction of the Bittern in 1868 was the result of the drainage of wetland habitat for agricultural use, and persecution by hunters and egg collectors. Many factors are thought to be affecting the birds today. Hard weather has always caused a high death rate in Bitterns, as severe frost and snow make feeding difficult or impossible. The hard winter of 1963 probably killed over 25 per cent of the British population. The decline of the Bittern in the Norfolk Broads area is likely

to be largely due to disturbance: the widespread use of motor boats, and an increase in angling, must have reduced the availability of undisturbed feeding sites. Pollution in the Broads may also have had an effect. Increases in nitrates and phosphates have caused a deterioration in the aquatic flora and this may have affected the fish and amphibians on which Bitterns are so dependent. Reed-cutting is unlikely to have an adverse effect in large reedbeds, where areas are left uncut, but it may have caused problems in smaller areas. However, if cutting or burning is undertaken late in the winter it can disturb birds during the crucial stages of territory establishment. Many of the remaining large reedbeds are now reserves and so can be protected from further destruction. They can, however, deteriorate very quickly through drying out, with the resultant encroachment of willow and alder, so careful management is important.

Dense reedbeds near Titchwell in north Norfolk provide a perfect habitat for Bitterns and many other rare birds, including Bearded Tit (*Panurus biarmicus*) and Marsh Harrier (*Circus aeruginosus*).

Great Crested Grebes (*Podiceps cristatus*) are among the many waterbirds for whom reedbeds provide important feeding and breeding habitats.

Four young Bitterns instinctively 'freeze' into the stretched posture which hides them so effectively against the reeds. The young are fed on regurgitated food, mainly by the female. They leave the nest after 15–20 days but remain nearby to be fed. Fledging occurs at 7–8 weeks and the young become independent soon afterwards.

Merlin:
Victim of pesticides and persecution

The Merlin (*Falco columbarius*) is Britain's smallest falcon. Most resident birds remain in Britain throughout the year, and in winter are joined by Icelandic Merlins. Typically, the bird flies with a rapid wingbeat interspersed with short glides, and its prey is pursued in high-speed twisting flight, low over the ground.

Nests are usually on the ground in thick heather or bracken, sometimes on a crag or large rock. Occasionally, the bird will occupy the old nest of a Carrion Crow, but usually it makes a shallow scrape in the ground, containing small pieces of heather or bracken pulled in by the sitting bird. Egg-laying begins towards the end of April, with a few records of clutches as late as the end of June. Three to five eggs are laid, with an interval of about two days between eggs. Normally only one clutch is laid, although a replacement clutch may be laid if the first is lost.

Incubation, which lasts for 28 to 32 days, normally begins with the last egg so that the young all hatch at about the same time. The task is undertaken by both parents, with the female taking the larger share. After hatching, the young are brooded by the female while the male hunts, and she feeds them until they are able to tear up their own food at about 18 days old. At this stage they leave the nest but remain nearby, hidden in the surrounding heather. They fly after 25 to 27 days and gain their independence about three weeks after fledging.

Territories tend to be traditional — used repeatedly by the same individuals, particularly the males, and by successive generations. They are typically spaced about 3.0 to 4.5 kilometres apart, although nests may be closer together. In winter, most birds move off their upland breeding areas and into lowland areas, where sometimes they occupy traditional roosting sites in which they roost singly or communally in thick vegetation or on low branches.

The Merlin feeds mainly on small birds caught by chasing, or less commonly by stooping. Prey can be taken in the air or on the ground. Its main prey are moorland species, caught in a hunting territory of about four kilometres radius, which can include marginal farmland, rough ground with woodland edges and wet areas. The principal prey species are Meadow Pipits, Skylarks, Chaffinches and Wheatears, although the adults and young of small waders, including Dunlin, Redshank, Golden Plover and Snipe, are also taken. Very occasionally, small mammals and insects have been recorded in their diet.

Merlins are still present on Exmoor and thinly distributed throughout most of Scotland, Wales and northern England. Their preferred habitat is open country, with breeding pairs favouring high moorland with extensive heather and blanket bog. Young forestry plantations with thick ground cover are exceptionally used for breeding. Their past status in Britain is not clearly known, but a marked decline has been noted this century, especially since 1950. The total British population is at present estimated to be about 500 pairs. A detailed study by the RSPB between 1982 and 1984 of the Welsh breeding population confirmed a total of about forty pairs, indicating a decline of between 30 and 40 per cent over the previous 10 years. The species has virtually ceased breeding in the Peak District and in southwest England, with the main numbers now occurring from the eastern Pennines northwards to eastern and central Scotland.

Thick heather on the high open moorlands of North Yorkshire provides the perfect nesting habitat for a female Merlin.

High in the Scottish hills a female Hen Harrier (*Circus cyaneus*) swoops back to her young carrying the spoils of a hunting flight.

In common with other birds of prey the Merlin has suffered from the widespread use of organochlorine pesticides in the 1960s. DDE and PCB residues continue to be found in Merlin eggs, and may still be a contributing factor in the present decline. Persecution has also taken its toll in the past, particularly on grouse moors, and continues today from egg collectors and hawk-keepers. Habitat changes must also be having an effect. The conversion of heather moorland to grass, and the afforestation of many upland areas, has deprived birds of both feeding and breeding habitat. In some areas competition with Peregrines and Sparrowhawks may also be having a detrimental effect.

The factors causing declines in Merlin populations are also adversely affecting a number of other species. Thus, the use of pesticides such as DDT and Dieldrin in the 1960s caused Sparrowhawk and Peregrine numbers to fall drastically. The subsequent recovery of these two species has not, however, been paralleled by a recovery in the Merlin. The Hen Harrier, with similar habitat preferences to the Merlin, is still persecuted on grouse moors. A number of other species are dependent on the continuing integrity of upland moorland. The Golden Eagle, now virtually confined to Scotland, has lost important hunting habitat through large-scale conifer afforestation of moorland, while afforestation, together with overgrazing, burning, and conversion to grassland, has reduced the areas suitable for both Red and Black Grouse and upland breeding waders such as Golden Plover, Greenshank and Dunlin.

The speckled plumage of the Golden Plover (*Pluvialis apricaria*) provides excellent camouflage in the bird's moorland summer breeding habitat. In winter, the birds feed in lowland fields and meadows, and on river estuaries and mudflats.

Corncrake:
Seeking refuge from mechanized farming

Like many members of the rail family, the Corncrake or Landrail (*Crex crex*) is a solitary and often secretive bird. It is a summer visitor to Britain, arriving from mid-April to the end of May and departing from August to early October. It winters in Africa, south of the equator. It is mostly active at dawn and dusk, and most of its time is spent hidden in vegetation. Its presence is only betrayed by its characteristic disyllabic call, '*crek crek*', which can be heard over a kilometre away. It is most vocal at the beginning of the breeding season, when it may call for hours at a time, both day and night.

The female Corncrake makes a shallow nest on the ground, concealed in vegetation and lined with dead grasses. Egg-laying commences in mid-May and can continue to late July. Between 6 and 14 eggs are laid and second broods are rare, although replacement clutches are laid if eggs are lost. Incubation by the female lasts for 16 to 19 days. It begins with the last eggs, so that hatching is synchronous, and the young leave the nest soon after hatching. They are fed mainly by the female for the first three to four days and then feed themselves. They begin to fly when they are about five weeks old, and also become independent of their parents about this time.

Corncrake territories may cover several hectares but are only fully occupied while the birds are breeding. They leave soon after their young have hatched, and move out into neighbouring fields. Corncrakes are omnivorous—feeding mainly on small invertebrates, especially insects, but also taking young shoots and seeds.

In Britain the Corncrake is now largely confined to the north and west of Scotland, Orkney and the Hebrides. About 40 per cent of the British population is found on the Outer Hebrides. This distribution is almost certainly explained by their habitat preferences. Corncrakes favour grass fields grown for hay or silage, when they tolerate grass up to a metre high. If occupying denser cover they select shorter vegetation. On the Outer Hebrides they also use damp meadows with iris beds, or marshland edges, moving into more arable areas such as clover, cereal or potato fields after the breeding season.

The Corncrake was once far more widespread in Britain. Its decline was first noticed in the latter half of the nineteenth century, particularly in southeast England. Since then its range has continued to contract westwards to its present-day position. During 1968–72, breeding was confirmed or probable in 528 ten-kilometre squares in Britain. In 1978–79 a survey revealed only 160 such squares occupied, with no more than 750 pairs. This population decline is not limited to Britain. Irish numbers have fallen to 1200 to 1500 pairs, and other Western European countries have all suffered declines. The combined British and Irish populations now form a substantial proportion of the Western European population.

The population crash appears to be directly attributable to changes in agricultural practice. Hay meadows, once cut by hand, are now cropped mechanically. The former method was slow: it allowed nests to be spared, and also allowed adults and young sufficient time to move to safety. Machine cutting is more likely to destroy nests, young and adults, but more significantly it is undertaken earlier, giving the birds less time to breed and disperse.

Hay meadows and crofts on the Isle of Skye. The traditional crofts of Ireland and Scotland are among the last undisturbed breeding grounds for Corncrakes in Britain.

The Corncrake's plight is echoed in lowland Britain by that of the Stone Curlew (*Burhinus oedicnemus*), whose meadowland habitat is also disappearing.

The widespread conversion of grassland areas to arable farming has removed much of the Corncrake's former habitat in England and Wales, although isolated breeding records do occur. The Outer Hebridean population, which inhabits the damp meadows of the machair, is now threatened by the drainage of the meadows followed by agricultural improvement that produces taller and thicker vegetation which is less suitable for the birds.

The Corncrake is not the only species to have suffered from agricultural changes. Another summer visitor to Britain, the Quail, has also suffered a decline which can be largely attributed to the introduction of mechanical grass cutting and pasture improvement. The agricultural improvement of the Hebridean machair will also affect other wet-meadow species such as Dunlin and Golden Plover which breed there in considerable numbers, and the conversion to arable monocultures of meadows in lowland England has had a profound effect on the Partridge and Stone Curlew, while even common species like the Rook have suffered population declines. Considerable effort will be needed in the future to preserve what meadowland has survived, and to provide the opportunity for the continuation of more traditional farming which is sympathetic to wildlife conservation.

With its wings half-raised in a display of aggression, a male Corncrake prepares to defend his territory.

353

Roseate Tern:
Still in decline – for reasons unclear

The Roseate Tern (*Sterna dougallii*) is the rarest British seabird, and like all terns it is a summer visitor to Britain, arriving in late April or May and leaving from mid-July to mid-September. It spends the winter off the west coast of Africa.

It is a gregarious species, nesting in colonies sometimes containing several hundred pairs, although these larger colonies are often divided into smaller sub-colonies. Pairs are often faithful to a particular colony, but like other terns they may suddenly move to

another site for no apparent reason. The birds roost communally on beaches and mudflats, and during the breeding season the roosting area will be near the colony. On arrival some birds may already be paired. Both ground and aerial displays take place,

Roseate Terns wheel in flight over a colony on Jackdaw Island, in Strangford Lough, County Down, Northern Ireland.

with most of the ground courtship being undertaken at the roost outside the colony before a small nesting territory has been established.

The nest is a shallow scrape on the ground, usually in the cover of vegetation or sheltered in a depression or rock crevice. Rabbit burrows are sometimes used. The scrape is made by both sexes and this activity forms an important part of the courtship. One or two eggs are laid from mid-June to mid-July, and normally only one clutch is laid, although a replacement clutch may follow if the first is lost early in the season. Incubation is undertaken mainly by the female, with some assistance from the male. It usually lasts about 23 days but can be prolonged if the parents are kept away from the nest by predators or other disturbance. It starts with the first egg laid, and in clutches of two eggs the second hatches two to five days after the first. The young remain by the nest for 15 to 20 days, during which time they are fed and protected by both parents. Fledging occurs after about four weeks, with the young apparently remaining dependent on their parents for a further eight weeks.

The birds feed mainly on small marine fish, caught by plunge-diving from the air.

In northwestern Europe the Roseate Tern now breeds only in Britain, Ireland and Brittany. The breeding distribution in the Brtitish Isles is extremely local, with only one major colony remaining in Britain and five in Ireland. Rocky or sandy offshore islands with vegetation such as marram grass are favoured for breeding, although occasionally pairs will breed amongst coastal colonies of other tern species. Roseate Terns are highly maritime, and after breeding the adults and young move south to their wintering area off the coast of West Africa, particularly off the coast of Ghana.

The decline of the Roseate Tern began in the first half of the nineteenth century when the species was persecuted for eggs and for the millinery trade. At the beginning of this century an increase in numbers occurred, particularly in Ireland, and by the early 1960s about 3500 pairs were breeding in Britain and Ireland. In 1969 there were 648 pairs at the main sites in Britain and a further 1828 in Ireland. However, by 1974 this had fallen to 443 pairs and 991 pairs respectively, and by 1984 it was down to 212 pairs in Britain and 268 in Ireland.

The factors responsible for this present decline are not altogether clear. The birds are vulnerable to disturbance at their breeding sites, which probably explains their restriction to less accessible islands, but nearly all colonies are now on nature reserves so disturbance can be kept to a minimum. Lack of breeding sites does not in itself seem to be a serious limiting factor, however, as there is room for expansion at many colonies. The breeding success seems to be stable and shows no obvious decline, although losses do occur in years when exceptional high tides flood across sites and cause desertions. Predators and egg collectors still account for some losses, but it is not known whether this affects the total population. Given the world distribution of the species, with large populations still present in tropical seas, it may be that climatic changes are affecting the European birds.

There is little competition for nest sites between the Roseate and other terns, but increasing gull populations have been a cause for concern. Herring and Lesser Black-backed gulls have been occupying new sites as their existing colonies become full, and this has included some of the offshore islands particularly favoured by Roseate Terns. The gulls establish their territories before the terns arrive, and defend them against the terns when they try to breed.

There has been growing concern recently for the welfare of the species on its wintering grounds. Most ringing returns come from Ghana, and in most cases these birds have been trapped or shot. Given that the European population is now so small, it may be that this persecution is a contributing or even major cause of the decline. A joint ICBP and RSPB project has now been agreed with the Government of Ghana, which it is hoped will benefit the Roseate Tern and other coastal birds that winter there. The project includes providing education in Ghana to make local people more aware of their natural environment and the effects that hunting can have on birds. Studies will also pinpoint the important roosting and feeding areas for seashore birds, which can then be given protection. In this way it is hoped to ensure that suitable conditions for Roseate Terns are provided throughout the year.

A breeding pair of Roseate Terns on the nest at the Strangford Lough colony. Of all British terns, only the Roseate has suffered such serious decline in recent years. A similar decline in the Little Tern (*Sterna albifrons*) appears to have been reversed since steps were taken to protect its main breeding sites.

Dartford Warbler: Survivor of the lowland heaths

The Dartford Warbler (*Sylvia undata*) is a resident species, and before the recent colonization of the Cetti's Warbler it was Britain's only truly resident warbler. It is a small long-tailed bird, very secretive and usually found skulking in thick cover. During the breeding season it becomes more conspicuous, perching on the top of bushes and scrub to sing. Its song is like a rapid and metallic version of a Whitethroat's warble and may be given in a dancing display flight. It also has two distinctive call notes which are heard throughout the year; a harsh, grating '*tchurr*' and a hard '*tuc*' given when the bird is excited or alarmed.

Nest building begins in April, and both birds share the work. The nest is usually built in heather or gorse — about 25 centimetres from the ground in heather and generally higher in gorse — and is made of heather and grass with a lining of fine grass, rootlets, spiders' webs and a few feathers. The eggs are laid from the end of April through to the end of June, or occasionally even later. The usual clutch size is four, with some clutches of three or five. Smaller clutches tend to be laid early in the season with those of five being laid later.

The Dartford Warbler's strong preference for habitat with extensive gorse cover is well illustrated by the population densities found in recent surveys. In the New Forest, for example, areas with more than 50 per cent gorse cover (*above*) could support 14.2 pairs/km²; areas of open heather, without gorse, could support only 1.3 pairs/km².

Burning (*left*) is a natural part of the ecological life-cycle of grasslands and heaths, but it must be carefully controlled and managed if the Dartford Warbler's very specific habitat requirements are to be met and maintained.

Incubation, which lasts from 12 to 14 days, begins when the last egg is laid and is shared by both birds, although the female contributes the larger share. Brooding of the young is also shared by both parents, but again is mostly undertaken by the female. For the first four days brooding is almost continuous, but during the next four days it becomes less important as feeding intensity increases. Both parents bring food, with the male bringing more than the female. Fledging occurs after 10 to 14 days, although if disturbed, the young may leave the nest earlier. Feeding of the young by the parents continues for 10–15 days after they leave the nest. Once independent the young disperse, sometimes settling several kilometres away from the nest site.

The fragmentation of the species' lowland heath habitat makes an assessment of territory size difficult, but the highest densities of birds are found in sites with a high proportion (over 50 per cent) of gorse cover; the lowest on open heather without gorse. Pine plantations with a ground cover of heather also provide suitable habitat until they become too mature.

Dartford Warblers are insectivorous throughout the year, feeding mainly on beetles, spiders, bugs, flies and caterpillars. Gorse bushes provide most of these food items, although they are a minor constituent of the vegetation of most heaths.

The Dartford Warbler is restricted to southern England, with its main populations in Hampshire, Dorset and Surrey and a few pairs in Devon and Cornwall. Its scarcity is due to the limited area of southern lowland heath now remaining. The main breeding area is in the New Forest, which contains a total of about 1700 hectares of suitable dry heather and gorse habitat holding nearly 50 per cent of the British population. The heaths of Dorset, which have less gorse, hold about 30 per cent of the population on about 2200 hectares of dry heathland.

In the nineteenth century, when dry heathland commons were more extensive, the Dartford Warbler was found over most of southern England, north into Suffolk and also in Shropshire and Staffordshire. Its populations have always suffered during severe winters, when insect food is scarce and difficult to find, and the succession of bad winters that occurred during the 1940s must have caused a large population drop. In 1961 there were about 460 pairs, but after the severe winters of 1961–62 and 1962–

63, only 11 known pairs remained. Milder winters then followed, and the population recovered to 70 pairs in 1970 and to 560 in 1974. However, further hard winters in the late 1970s have reduced the total now to around 400 pairs. A detailed study of this species, from 1974 to 1976, confirmed that the main reasons for its decline were the succession of severe winters combined with the destruction and fragmentation of its heathland habitat. The area of Dorset heathland, for example, has declined from 10,000 hectares in 1960 to 5512 hectares in 1984.

The steady increase over the last 20 years has allowed the return of Dartford Warblers to Cornwall for the first time in 40 years, and one pair in Surrey has now increased to 69 in just ten years. The future is still precarious, however. Loss of habitat is still occurring. In addition to its actual destruction, excessive burning of heathland removes mature gorse and allows invasion by grasses and bracken, while an absence of controlled burning and grazing can lead to invasion by birch and pine. In either case, the habitat becomes less suitable for the birds; thus, in order to maintain or increase our Dartford Warbler numbers, heathland habitats should not simply be protected but must be managed to provide a suitable mix of heather and gorse.

The European Nightjar (*Caprimulgus europaeus*) (*below*) and the Woodlark (*Lullula arborea*) (*right*) are among several bird species associated with lowland heath. But the importance of this much-reduced and fragmented habitat goes much further. As well as an unusual avifauna, it supports a unique assemblage of British plants and animals, including the Smooth Snake, Sand Lizard, Adder and Natterjack Toad. The survival of our lowland heaths is thus the key to the survival of a whole community of increasingly rare species.

Nature under siege:
The main threats to British birds

The threats to birds in Britain over the last few centuries have been many and varied. Some are less significant today; others more so; and some are only just beginning to make themselves known. The most outstanding threat today is undoubtedly the loss of habitat, particularly as a result of the extension and intensification of forestry and agriculture and the increased efficiency and mechanization associated with it.

Conifer afforestation

Large-scale commercial timber growing using alien coniferous trees is now common throughout Britain and even competes with agriculture in marginal areas. In particular, large tracts of heather moor, blanket bog and rough grassland fell are disappearing under a carpet of conifers. Birds that depend on these habitats for feeding and breeding territories, such as the Golden Eagle, Merlin, Hen Harrier, Golden Plover, Curlew, Greenshank and Dunlin, are lost as a result.

Areas of ancient and semi-natural woodland have also been disappearing at an alarming rate. Almost half the remaining ancient woodland in Britain has been lost in the last 30 years, most of it replaced by conifers or exotic broadleaf species. Those birds which depend upon a well-established and diverse woodland structure, like the Pied Flycatcher, Wood Warbler and Redstart, fare badly in these sterile commercial plantations.

Agricultural practices

The small and diverse field systems of earlier farming practices have today given way to huge monocultures of cereals and other crops. Once-common species like the Corncrake and Stone Curlew have been eliminated or greatly reduced in numbers, while the removal of small patches of scrub, and hedgerows, has deprived species like the Grey Partridge of shelter and food. The extension of agriculture has also been responsible for the loss of marshes, farm ponds, farm woods, heaths and chalk grasslands, and the increased use of pesticides has caused huge reductions in the numbers of insects and wild flowers.

Drainage and river management

The drainage of wetland areas has been responsible for the decline of many species. Areas such as the Ouse and Nene Washes in Cambridgeshire are all that remain of the once-extensive East Anglian Fens and are one of the few areas where the rare Black-tailed Godwit breeds, but even commoner species like Lapwing, Curlew, Redshank and Snipe have lost their marshland breeding areas. Reedbeds have been destroyed and with them birds like the Bittern. The modification of habitats can affect birds almost as much as their destruction. The stripping of bankside vegetation as part of river management removes valuable habitat. River banks used by Kingfishers and Sand Martins can be destroyed by the canalization of rivers and streams, and pollution can cause harmful algal blooms and general degradation of an aquatic ecosystem.

Even relatively minor changes to habitats, such as the thinning or partial removal of riverbank vegetation, can have major adverse effects on resident wildlife communities.

The inexorable spread of softwood plantations over the uplands of mid-Wales, northern England and Scotland has greatly reduced the range of habitats available to wildlife.

Recreation and disturbance

Many species are sensitive to disturbance and this can be particularly harmful for those that are already vulnerable. Areas of the country which were once remote and undisturbed are now readily accessible, and even the remotest upland areas of northern Scotland, home of great rarities like the Dotterel and Snow Bunting, are now in danger from increased numbers of visitors. Rock climbing can cause disturbance to breeding Peregrines and Golden Eagles; the increase in boating on waterways like the Norfolk Broads has brought disturbance and pollution to the detriment of wetland birds; and coastlines where Little Terns breed attract thousands of holidaymakers who unwittingly cause desertion of nests. Even thoughtless birdwatching has at times caused harmful disturbance.

Despite its protected status, the Sparrowhawk (*Accipiter nisus*) is still subject to persecution, and along with other birds of prey, especially owls, is a common victim of illegal pole-traps.

Persecution

Many species have suffered directly at the hands of man. In the nineteenth century egg collecting, slaughter of species for their plumes, and the deliberate destruction of birds of prey caused serious declines in many species. Regrettably, egg collecting is still a problem today. In 1985 six pairs of Red Kites out of a total British breeding population of 40 pairs, lost their eggs to collectors. Peregrines, Golden Eagles and Goshawks all have eggs or young taken – some for egg collections, others for sale to hawk-keepers.

Concern over possible predation on pheasants, grouse and lambs still leads to the destruction of birds of prey, and although illegal, traps and poison are still used to kill eagles, hawks and falcons. While the laws now exist to protect our birds, legislation is only as good as its enforcement.

Pesticides

The danger of pesticides to wild birds was not fully appreciated until the 1960s, when an alarmingly rapid decline in Sparrowhawk and Peregrine populations was linked to the use of certain persistent organochlorine insecticides, principally DDT and Dieldrin. Voluntary restrictions have now reversed the decline, but large numbers of pesticides are still in regular use and there is need for continuous vigilance. Just a few years ago, an organophosphorus seed-dressing caused the deaths of wild geese and swans feeding on winter wheat.

Herbicides indirectly affect birds by reducing the weeds on which seedeaters like finches depend. Fungicides, used widely on cereals, also have a powerful insecticidal property and appear to be reducing the food supply of warblers and flycatchers in woodland adjacent to farmland. A more detailed assessment of the total effect of pesticides on the environment is still urgently needed.

One section of a tray of raptor eggs – part of a confiscated egg collection now in the safe-keeping of the RSPB. It is estimated that more than half a million eggs are held in private collections in Britain, and that 10 per cent of these are from protected rare breeding birds such as Golden Eagles (*Aquila chrysaetos*) and Avocets (*Recurvirostra avosetta*).

Woodland destruction

The character of the British countryside has been drastically altered by man, and one of the greatest losses has been that of our natural woodlands. Some woodland species have managed to adapt to marginal habitats and gardens, but many are now confined to the fragments of original forest.

The Honey Buzzard, once widespread, is now a comparative rarity, while the Red Kite, once a familiar raptor, has declined through persecution and is now found only in mature oakwoods in Wales. The survival of both these species depends on the continued protection of their woodland habitat.

Environmental pollution

Industrial waste discharged into rivers or the air can cause severe local problems, but may also be responsible for more widespread environmental damage. Many of our rivers are now showing changes in their acidity linked with conifer plantations and 'acid rain', and recent research has linked a reduction in the numbers of Dippers on some rivers with an increase in water acidity.

Oil pollution kills a large number of seabirds each year, but so far does not seem to have caused any long-term decline. A serious spill near a major seabird colony during the breeding season could, however, have serious consequences for the local populations; and with the increased oil exploration off our coastline, and continued oil tanker traffic close to island seabird colonies, it may be just a matter of time.

What can we do?
Mobilizing people for conservation

The public interest in natural history in Britain today is huge. Television programmes on the subject can attract audiences of over eleven million, and are regularly among the 10 most popular programmes on each of the four television channels. The *Field Guide to the Birds of Britain and Europe* by Mountfort, Hollom and Peterson, first published in 1954 and now in its fourth edition, has sold over a million copies.

These figures indicate the extent of the interest in the environment that is felt by town-dwellers at least as much as by those who live in the countryside. In the last century that interest manifested itself in the making of collections. Butterflies and birds' eggs, beetles, and pressed flowers were all once gathered in huge numbers by an army of passionate enthusiasts, young and old. Today, the sheer size of the human population and the great reduction in the numbers of many animal and plant species has meant that such activities cannot continue unabated without seriously endangering the survival of many of them. So legislation has had to be introduced, making it an offence to engage in such activities. Now people collect, not eggs, but sightings. Rare migrant birds that are blown off course and happen to land exhausted on British shores are likely, within hours, to find themselves surrounded

by several hundred enthusiasts staring at them through binoculars, telescopes and cameras.

There are plenty of organizations to encourage and direct this interest. The British Trust for Conservation Volunteers organizes parties of young people who set about removing rubbish from ponds, cleaning ditches and tackling any other tasks that concerned land-owners or environmental organizations may put to them.

Those who have a particular interest in birds may join the Royal Society for the Protection of Birds. This organization not only arranges meetings for its members all over the country but also gives instruction in practical ornithology and, on occasion, organizes its members on countrywide assignments to count birds, either individual species or parties of migrants, so that an overall picture of the avifauna of the country can be obtained. In this way it has created a body of knowledge that cannot be paralleled for birds in any other country or in Britain for any other group of animals.

In 1926, one group of ardent naturalists in Norfolk got together to form a Naturalists' Trust as a means of creating a nature reserve where birds and other animals might find food and sanctuary. It was the first County Trust for Nature Conservation. Today they

number 44 and cover the entire country. Their members are active not only in the reserves but throughout the countryside, acting as watchdogs for environmental damage. They raise substantial funds for purchasing more reserves, for engaging staff to care for them, and for building information centres for the benefit of visitors. The support of their members or those of the RSPB is not, however, limited to money. Like all such charitable enterprises they need, and gratefully deploy, the varied specialist skills of their members, such as accountants, lawyers, journalists and builders.

In addition to those organizations specifically concerned with conservation, there are others, such as the National Trust, the Ramblers' Association, the Council for the Preservation of Rural England, the British Field Sports Society, the Pony Club, the National Federation of Anglers and many more, whose members find their recreation in the countryside and who are also concerned about its protection and conservation. Together they number over one and a half million people and constitute the most highly developed voluntary conservation movement in the whole of Europe.

Members of a local Conservation Corps in Sussex set about the restoration of an overgrown and heavily silted-up dewpond.

Young or old, novice or professional, bird-watchers everywhere share the pleasures and rewards that come from observing wild creatures in their natural surroundings.

The County Trusts for Nature Conservation are all members of a single federal organization, the Royal Society for Nature Conservation, which represents their interests nationally. The RSNC gives evidence at inquiries, and seeks funds that might not be available on a more parochial basis. It serves as a central source of expertise on legal matters, in land management and in techniques of fund raising. It supplies catalogues and goods for the Trusts to sell, and it produces a magazine, *Natural World*, which is distributed by each Trust alongside its own locally produced literature. The 115,000 members of the individual Trusts thus have a national and increasingly powerful voice.

The Royal Society for the Protection of Birds has more than 520,000 members. It has been conspicuously successful in fundraising and has purchased and manages over 100,000 hectares of land in 101 reserves. It mounts protection over the nest sites of especially rare and uncommon species, and its officers are active in ensuring that the legal protection given to birds is not flouted. On average, 20 to 25 legal actions are taken each year against egg collectors and dealers in illegally captured birds. It, too, publishes its own magazine, *Birds*.

Both the RSNC and the RSPB, together with other interested non-governmental bodies like Friends of the Earth and the Fauna and Flora Preservation Society, are active in arguing the case for conservation. To focus attention on issues and co-ordinate action, the voluntary groups liaise through Wildlife Link, which acts as an umbrella organization through which approaches can be made to Government and governmental agencies. When the 1981 Wildlife and Countryside Bill was debated, a record number of 2300 amendments were moved, the majority of which were stimulated in some way by these societies. Both also maintain a close connection with the Nature Conservancy Council, the main governmental organization concerned with nature conservation.

The RSPB is one of several organizations concerned with the welfare and study of birds in Britain. The British Trust for Ornithology collects data on bird numbers and distribution as well as promoting and undertaking research. It has over 7000 members and a budget of over a quarter of a million pounds. The Wildfowl Trust specializes in the study and protection of ducks, geese and swans, both nationally and internationally. It maintains three establishments, mainly for migratory and overwintering birds, but in addition to these free-flying wild stocks it also has large collections of captive breeding birds. As a result of its great specialist expertise, it has been instrumental in saving from extinction such rarities as the Nene, or Hawaiian Goose.

Conservation in Britain today is also promoted by many smaller, more specialized, and in many cases highly scientific bodies with largely academic memberships. Their publications include the *Journal of Ecology, Journal of Applied Ecology* and *Journal of Animal Ecology*, produced by the British Ecological Society; *Ibis*, the journal of the British Ornithologists' Union; and *Ecos*, produced by the British Association of Nature Conservationists. The research findings published in such learned journals provide a firm scientific foundation for the policies adopted by the larger governmental and non-governmental organizations.

Ducks, herons and a rich variety of plantlife are among the many attractions at Leighton Moss – one of more than 120 reserves run by the RSPB.

The visitors' centre at the Wildfowl Trust's Arundel reserve. The Trust runs three major reserves, at Slimbridge in Gloucestershire, Welney in Norfolk and Caerlaverock on the Solway Firth, and five smaller parks all of which hold large collections of waterbirds.

The role of government: National and international agencies

Although 80 per cent of the inhabitants of the British Isles live in urban surroundings, their interest in nature conservation is considerable. Books and television programmes on nature continue to grow in popularity, and more than half a million adults and children are subscribing members of the long-established Royal Society for the Protection of Birds. Much of this public concern stems from a strong environmental element in education at all levels, but this element must continue to grow if conservation legislation in Britain is to be successful.

In schools, most of the impetus comes from voluntary organizations. In 1984, some 4000 teachers attended courses run by the RSPB, and this organization, the County Trusts for Nature Conservation and many of our larger industries all provide information materials for schools. Government support for conservation in school curricula, however, has been slow to appear, and training in higher education is sadly limited to a few specialized courses.

Agriculture and forestry together use up more than 85 per cent of the country's land surface, and almost all bird habitats are affected by them in some way. In general, the trends have been towards high-intensity productivity, with enormous consequent losses of natural habitats such as wetlands and moorland. This has often had dramatic effects on wildlife populations. While groups like the Farming and Wildlife Advisory Group have made some concessions to conservation, a much more fundamental revision of land-use policies is now urgently required. Agriculture, through the European Common Agricultural Policy (CAP), and forestry, through a system of tax incentives, have long enjoyed a substantial level of financial subsidy. However, the strategic argument for large-scale planting of alien conifers, which began in wartime, no longer applies, and British agriculture has now largely succeeded in its aim of producing 75 per cent of the country's temperate foodstuff requirements. There is, therefore, little justification for continuing to subsidize overproduction, much of which is wasted.

Without grants, subsidies and other incentives, many agricultural and forestry practices which destroy natural habitats would not be economically viable. However, the withdrawal of such support, or the bringing of these activities under a system of planning controls similar to that operating in the urban environment, is strongly opposed by rural communities. What is required is a shift of emphasis from the paramount precedence of food and timber production on to a more balanced view that recognizes the social functions of the countryside and the importance of conservation. The British Government has recently made a number of moves in this direction, but it remains to be seen whether these are sustained in the face of powerful opposition from farmers and from some other European states.

A significant problem is the division of responsibility for land-use planning between different Government departments, for where their aims conflict there is a danger that they will end up spending public funds competing against each other. Integration is, however, improving in some areas – as, for example, in the water industry. Regional Water Authorities now have a duty in law to 'further conservation' in the course of their river engineering and other works. Putting this obligation into practice, however, can still cause difficulties, and here, too, it is often the voluntary bodies that have made the greatest contribution through their provision of practical advice.

The progress we all expect and demand can not be achieved without some impact on the environment. It is the responsibility of governments and major industries to ensure that negative effects are minimized. The two photographs show what can be done. They illustrate two stages in the laying of a 91.5 cm Shell pipeline to carry crude oil from Anglesey, across North Wales to Stanlow Refinery in Cheshire. In the second photograph (*above*), reinstatement of the land is almost complete. In another year all sign of the buried pipeline will have disappeared.

Over most of the British countryside, major developments, which often involve the investment of public funds, can proceed without public scrutiny or any statutory requirement for cost-benefit or environmental impact assessments. Conservation legislation, embodied in the 1981 Wildlife and Countryside Act, relies heavily on the voluntary co-operation of the land-owner or occupier – a responsibility which, while respected by many, has been seriously abused by others. There are mechanisms for holding planning enquiries, withholding grant-aid on conservation grounds, and for imposing conditions on developments; but apart from a few areas carrying special designations, these procedures are discretionary and are applied inconsistently. The Council of European Ministers has been considering a proposal for a Directive that would make formal environmental impact assessments a requirement for certain types of development. The application of this measure to agriculture and forestry, however, is not fully supported by the British Government, and while it might perhaps increase accountability, it would otherwise be of little value in resolving countryside conflicts. In Scotland, a useful contribution has been made by a series of national planning guidelines which take into account the overall demands made on environmental resources.

The Wildlife and Countryside Act includes provisions for the protection of species, conservation of wildlife habitats and access to the countryside. Part of the reason for this great improvement and consolidation of earlier measures was the requirement of the British Government to comply with international bird conservation obligations, notably the European Directive on the Conservation of Wild Birds, and the Ramsar Convention on Wetlands of International Importance as Waterfowl Habitats.

The 'Birds Directive' requires certain areas important to uncommon or migratory species to be protected by law, but while the Wildlife and Countryside Act has established the mechanisms for some measure of protection (though even this is by no means guaranteed) the British Government's Department of the Environment has been notably slow to apply the appropriate legal designations to the sites concerned. Out of a preliminary list of 197 sites, only 7 have so far been notified. The rest remain unprotected, even from other Government departments. In 1984, for example, the Scottish Office gave its permission for development on one site of international importance for wintering Greenland White-fronted Geese. Similarly, out of 129 sites that qualify for protection under the Ramsar Convention, only 19 have been notified.

However, in spite of these and some other failures to meet international agreements, Great Britain's Wildlife and Countryside Act has in general been a great advance on earlier legislation. Northern Ireland's separate legislation has also recently been revised along similar lines. Many of the current difficulties relate less to the legal framework of the Act than to the slowness of Government in ensuring that it is properly applied. The Nature Conservancy Council's

budget is small and chronically overstretched, and much of the running is left to the voluntary organizations. There are signs of improvement, but for a country that likes to think itself in the forefront of bird conservation, a great deal remains to be done.

Jim Hall, an organic farmer from Burray, South Ronaldsay, uses up to 40 tonnes of seaweed per hectare to fertilize his land. With other committed environmentalists he spoke out against proposals to build new nuclear reprocessing facilities at Dounreay on Scotland's north coast. Such enquiries are essential if people are to exercise any control over events that profoundly affect the environment.

Greenland White-fronted Geese (*Anser albifrons*) came under threat in 1984 when the Scottish Office approved the exploitation of peat mosses (bogs) used by the birds in winter.

The Ouse Washes:
Winter refuge for visiting wildfowl

Britain has many bird reserves of national and international importance. Some harbour vast seabird colonies, some provide wintering areas for Brent and Barnacle geese, while others are remnants of specialized habitats such as the lowland heath so vital to the Dartford Warbler. Some reserves were selected just to protect one or two species, while others are important because of the large number of different species they hold.

A reserve may represent a natural habitat such as mountain plateau, ancient woodland, marsh or fen, or an artificial site like a reservoir, a chalk grassland or a grouse moor, which with time has evolved its own rich and distinctive birdlife. For all areas, management — whether by simply limiting access to the public or by positive action such as grazing, burning or flooding — is essential if the reserve is to maintain a rich and diverse habitat and hopefully increase its wildlife interest.

The Ouse Washes are one of the principal wintering grounds in Britain for visiting Bewick's Swans (*Cygnus bewickii*) and Whooper Swans (*C. cygnus*).

The drainage ditches of the Ouse Washes Reserve represent a botanical treasure-house containing more than 40 per cent of all aquatic plants found in Britain.

The rare Black-tailed Godwit (*Limosa limosa*) returned to breed in Britain in 1952 after an absence of more than half a century.

The 850 hectares of the Ouse Washes in Cambridgeshire represent the largest area of regularly flooded grazing marsh left in Britain. They comprise a diverse, largely artificial, habitat of flood meadows, drainage channels and ditches, some of which have small patches of willow trees along the banks. The system has been extensively modified by man over the centuries but the form of management has proved favourable to wildlife and is an excellent example of the integration of flood control, farming and conservation.

For the optimum bird breeding and feeding conditions, a range of grass swards of varying lengths is required. This is provided by grazing animals which are moved from field to field as required. Numerous areas of shallow water have been created by flooding lower field bottoms, digging new ponds, and creating gently shelving islands. Even the drainage ditches are maintained, and they hold a great diversity of aquatic plants: over 40 per cent of all aquatic species found in Britain are now present in the Ouse Washes Reserve. Even some of the willow trees are managed as osier beds, to provide stems for basket making, and the different ages and sizes of the beds in turn provide a variety of nest sites. The larger willows are regularly pollarded, thus providing nest sites in their crowns for Barn Owls.

The site is of international importance for both the breeding birds and overwintering wildfowl. Of the breeding birds, the once extinct Black-tailed Godwit returned to breed in 1952, and the site remains its national stronghold with an annual total of about 50 pairs. Ruff started breeding in the 1960s, and other waders such as Snipe, Lapwing and Redshank breed in large numbers. Black Terns have also bred here.

In winter, the Bewick's Swans arrive, with peak populations of 3000 to 4000 birds, representing a high percentage of the total world population. And of the other overwintering wildfowl, Wigeon have been recorded in numbers of up to 40,000 at the reserve at one time.

Loch Garten:
Return of the Osprey

Loch Garten Reserve forms part of the larger Abernethy Forest in the heart of the Scottish Highlands. This is one of the few remaining ancient Caledonian pine forests which are now restricted to this part of Scotland. The reserve extends to 615 hectares and includes several different habitats – Scots Pine woodland, moorland, peat bog, loch and farmland. The terrain has been extensively moulded by glacial activity.

The reserve is important as a representative of an endangered and uncommon habitat, which contains many species of plants and animals. Roe Deer and Red Squirrels are the commonest large mammals. Foxes, rabbits and hares are also present along with the occasional Red Deer. Badgers, Wild Cats and Otters are present in the area. The plant communities include three species of wintergreen and several species of orchid, including Lesser Twayblade and Creeping Lady's Tresses. Overall, 240 plant species have been recorded on the reserve, along with a wide variety of insects, including 19 species of butterfly and over 60 species of moth.

Loch Garten has large populations of some of the more unusual migrants like the Redstart, Spotted Flycatcher and Siskin, and although best known for its breeding Ospreys, the reserve also has large populations of Crested Tits (one of Britain's rarest birds), Scottish Crossbills, Black Grouse and Capercaillie. The loch is also used by wildfowl in passage, including Pinkfoot and Greylag geese.

Management of the reserve is designed to maintain its distinctive habitats and, wherever possible, extend or enhance them. For example, in the woodlands a more diverse age structure is being promoted by felling selected groups of trees and allowing natural regeneration, whilst on the open moorland the spread of trees is controlled to maintain a balance of open ground and woodland. The richness of the open heather areas is maintained by controlled burning, thereby providing nesting and feeding areas for species such as Meadow Pipit, Wheatear, Red and Black Grouse and Short-eared Owl. Because of its location and considerable wildlife interest, this reserve has proved to be a popular tourist attraction and is an excellent example of how people can enjoy its special wildlife interests with a minimum of disturbance.

Loch Garten in the Scottish Highlands: home of the Osprey (*Pandion haliaetus*), the most spectacular of our breeding birds.

The Osprey's nest is a massive structure built of sticks, grass and heather, right at the top of an old pine or spruce.

The Crested Tit (*Parus cristatus*) is now very localized in Scotland due to the removal of the old pine forests that are its preferred habitat.

Loch Garten Reserve contains a large population of Scottish Crossbills (*Loxia scotica*). The birds' highly specialized bills enable them to extract the seeds from spruce, larch and pine cones.

Grassholm:
Island of Gannets

The island of Grassholm off the coast of Wales is one of Britain's most important seabird colonies. The island covers only 9.5 hectares, yet holds the third largest gannetry in the world. Only 20 pairs nested in 1860, but the numbers had risen to 20,000 pairs by 1980. Other breeding birds include Kittiwake, Razorbill, Guillemot, Shag, Herring Gull and Great Black-backed Gull. Grey Seals are common around the shores.

As with most sea-cliff and island reserves holding seabird colonies, the steepness and height of the cliffs and the isolation of the site are the birds' main safeguards. Usually the reserves require little management except where livestock grazing may be a convenient and useful way to maintain suitable short vegetation. It is important to minimize disturbance by visitors, or by recreational activities such as rock climbing. Because of its location, Grassholm remains relatively undisturbed, as special arrangements must be made for boat parties to visit the island. Also, just before the start of the breeding season, conservationists visit the reserve to check the gannetry and to clear away pieces of plastic fishing nets from the nests. These fragments are picked up by Gannets as nesting material along with seaweed, and can be lethally dangerous to both young and adults if they become entangled in them.

The main concern for this and other seabird colonies is the danger of a serious oil spill during the breeding season. Twice in recent years, tankers have run aground on rocks near Grassholm. Most recently, in July 1985, 5000 seabirds were killed in the area when the *Bridgeness* went aground, and while the Gannets were relatively unaffected on Grassholm, the 300 pairs of Guillemots there were reduced to 50 pairs. The only way to prevent this type of incident is by establishing exclusion zones around seabird islands at risk.

The wonderful sheen on the plumage of the Shag (*Phalacrocorax aristotelis*) has given rise to the alternative name 'Green Cormorant'. Like other fishing birds, the Shag is vulnerable to oil spills and other forms of marine pollution.

Hundreds of Gannets (*Sula bassana*) soar and wheel over the island of Grassholm, site of the world's third largest gannetry.

Both parents share the task of feeding the single offspring, and of protecting it from the dagger-like bills of their neighbours. When the chick leaves the nest after 15 weeks it weighs more than an adult.

Loch Gruinart: Haven for rare geese

Islay is the third largest island in the Inner Hebrides, situated off the northwest coast of Scotland. A major feature of the island is Loch Gruinart, which is about 6.5 kilometres long and nearly dissects the eastern third of the island, creating a long, broad estuary. Around the head of the loch, the RSPB has purchased 1215 hectares of farmland and created one of its newest bird reserves.

The reserve includes grass fields with heather on the higher ground. The shores of the loch itself are close-cropped seawashed saltings, broken up by numerous small creeks and gullies. For many years the land has been managed for dairying, but it still maintains a high conservation interest. For over half the year, during the winter, up to 20,000 geese use the island for feeding and roosting. This total is largely made up of two endangered species – the Barnacle Goose and the Greenland White-fronted Goose. It includes almost three-quarters of the Barnacle Geese that breed in Greenland and almost a third of the world population of the Greenland White-front. The latter favour the small hill fields or poorer rushy fields, whereas the former are found mainly on the improved grassland. In addition to the geese, a host of other birds are recorded regularly, with Golden Eagle, Merlin, Peregrine, Buzzard and Hen Harrier being frequent visitors, and waders like Lapwing, Curlew, Golden Plover and Redshank present in large numbers.

But without doubt the geese are the 'stars', and the area is managed primarily to ensure optimum conditions for their large overwintering populations. This entails retention of the reserve as grazing pasture to provide nutritious grass swards for the geese. The objective is to create such favourable conditions on the reserve that the geese will concentrate there, so easing the pressure on the surrounding farmland and removing the need for goose control.

Thousands of Barnacle Geese (*Branta leucopsis*) winter at Loch Gruinart, feeding off the short rich grasses of the managed grazing land. The birds feed during the day and return at dusk to their roosts on the tidal flats.

The Peregrine (*Falco peregrinus*) is one of several birds of prey regularly seen on the Loch Gruinart Reserve. This adult has just killed and started to feed on a Golden Plover (*Pluvialis apricaria*).

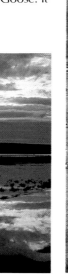

Evening sunlight reflected off the saltings at Loch Gruinart on the island of Islay.

Barnacle Geese on migration. The Loch Gruinart population includes almost three-quarters of the birds that breed in Greenland.

Royal Society for the Protection of Birds

In recent years the Royal Society for the Protection of Birds (RSPB) has greatly expanded its international activity, and the greater part of this new work has been in response to the urgent need to protect migrant birds both here in Europe and in Africa.

A large proportion of our breeding birds are migrants, and almost without exception they suffer from shooting and trapping outside the British Isles and from the large-scale destruction of their habitats, especially in developing countries. The RSPB has been one of the organizations campaigning against this slaughter, which is particularly severe in the Mediterranean countries. Hundreds of millions of birds are killed every year; mainly for 'sport', but sometimes also for sale, for food, or to prevent damage to crops. Robins, thrushes, flycatchers, warblers, larks and birds of prey all fall foul of this deadly barrier of shotguns, traps, nets and bird-lime.

In 1976 the British Committee for the Prevention of Mass Destruction of Migratory Birds was set up by ICBP as part of a European campaign, and a 'Stop The Massacre' fund was established. The money raised by this appeal has gone towards the creation of nature reserves, to support public awareness campaigns in Mediterranean countries, to help bird protection societies in southern Europe and to publicize the need for international co-operation to solve the problems of the persecuted migrants.

The importance of education as a means of furthering conservation has long been recognized, and as part of its overall strategy the RSPB has co-operated with ICBP to produce a series of beginners' birdwatching guides. *My First Bird Book* has now been published in Portugal, Morocco, Greece, Turkey and Lebanon, and further translations are planned in other Mediterranean countries.

RSPB has also been working with the Ghanaian Government to help protect the Roseate Tern and other seashore birds that spend the winter along the coast of Ghana. The 'Save the Seashore Birds Project – Ghana' was set up in conjunction with ICBP and the Ghana Game and Wildlife Department. Fully equipped survey teams, with Land-Rovers, have gone out to Ghana to work with Ghanaian wildlife officials on ways of conserving the terns and other seashore birds. Training and education is an important element of the project. Ghanaian staff have spent time training in Britain through courses organized by the RSPB, and a major educational programme, including the launch of Wildlife Clubs, is under way in coastal areas. In due course it is hoped that the RSPB will be able to establish projects with other African countries where similar problems exist.

The RSPB has always made visitors from other bird protection organizations very welcome, and is ready to share its expertise with them, particularly as many of these countries are struggling to develop a greater public awareness of the need for conservation, often against heavy odds. Recent visitors have come from India, China and Vietnam. The Indian visitors, from the Bombay Natural History Society, signed a special agreement with the RSPB and the Nature Conservancy Council, who will be working together on a series of projects for the next three years. These will include research into the environmental impact of afforestation, pesticides and industrial developments.

1987 will witness a unique co-operative venture between European bird protection organizations. 'Birdwatch Europe '87' has been organized as part of the European Year of the Environment, and the 12 member countries of the European Community will be taking part. This event is a co-ordinated public awareness campaign aimed at showing people more about birds, birdwatching and bird protection in Europe.

In the last two years, the RSPB has been involved in specific international conservation projects in more than 20 countries, and has also participated in the many more general aspects of international conservation. Most of the Society's activities, however, are concentrated on Europe and Africa, and recent projects aided or funded by the RSPB include an education centre in Malta, a survey of coastal birds and habitats in Liberia, and a high-level intervention in France aimed at bringing to an end the shooting of Turtle Doves.

A brilliantly coloured European Bee-eater (*Merops apiaster*) lies shot in a field in Malta – a grim reminder of the huge task that lies ahead for RSPB, ICBP and other conservation organizations attempting to end this slaughter.

RSPB and Ghanaian ornithologists surveying a stretch of coastal wetland as part of the 'Save the Seashore Birds' project.

International Council for Bird Preservation

CHRISTOPH IMBODEN

'. . . But we must win hearts as well as minds if we are to reach the universal audience that we seek, and if conservation ideals are to take hold at the grassroots. Birds have a unique power to stir the emotions of men, women and children the world over. ICBP harnesses that power so as to save not only birds but the world's ecosystems as well.'

Prince of the Netherlands

In many countries, especially industrialized ones, public concern for wild birds and for the environment has grown rapidly in recent years. The ever-increasing number of local clubs and nationwide societies demonstrates a solid base of support for conservation at the national level. But there is only one world organization devoted entirely to the protection of birds and their habitats, especially in developing countries: the International Council for Bird Preservation. ICBP is the world's oldest international conservation group and represents the interests of some ten million individuals. ICBP derives its strength from the inspiration birds provide for people everywhere. The international conservation movement was born of the need to protect migratory birds all along their flyways. ICBP was the first to tackle such conservation problems on a global scale, and has been a pioneer ever since.

One of the early milestones in international conservation legislation was the Convention on Migratory Birds, signed by the United States and Great Britain (on behalf of the Dominion of Canada) in 1916.

T. Gilbert Pearson was President of the National Association of Audubon Societies at the time. He was an indefatigable campaigner for the protection of migratory birds, and toured Europe at the end of the First World War to promote international co-operation on conservation issues. His efforts culminated in the setting up of the International Committee for the Protection of Birds in June 1922.

ICBP's evolving role

Since those early days, ICBP's mission has evolved to encompass concern about environmental hazards like persistent toxic chemicals and acid rain which the original Committee could not have imagined. Scientific research by conservation organizations like ICBP has enormously increased our understanding of the ways in which complex ecological processes work, and how they can be unbalanced, and even destroyed, by pollution, population pressures and other human impacts.

With greater understanding, broad support for conservation has developed in the industrialized world. We now know that everything is tied to everything else. We are all – animals, plants, humans – inextricably bound together on one beautiful but fragile planet. It is, as far as we know, the only one of its kind. What kind of a world would it be if so much beauty and fascination were lost? Birds are an essential part of the quality of our lives. We ignore their warnings of impending environmental ills at our peril. By saving the birds, ICBP is working for a better environment for everyone.

ICBP's global network
The International Council for Bird Preservation (ICBP) is a confederation of bird conservation societies and representatives covering more than 100 countries worldwide. Through this global network, ICBP promotes international co-operation on a wide range of conservation issues.

National Sections

Representatives

Saving the world's birds . . .

How does it operate?

ICBP gets results by harnessing the human and financial resources of its most powerful member organizations to the cause of international conservation. Our main task is to spread the conservation word to developing countries in the tropics and on islands where conservation is almost unknown. That is where 75 per cent of the world's threatened birds are found. In such countries, the efforts of a handful of people are all that stand between many forms of wildlife and extinction. They need help.

An international network of scientists alerts us to specific conservation dangers all over the world. Specialist groups of leading experts have all the latest information on whole families of birds such as herons, birds of prey, storks and ibises. ICBP has Sections and Representatives in over 100 countries, and they, too, play an important role in identifying issues, verifying facts and undertaking special investigations.

At ICBP headquarters, in Cambridge, England, conservation experts evaluate the specific needs of threatened birds and habitats and design projects that meet those needs practically and cost-effectively.

Our mission has four interrelated goals; conservation action, data-gathering, education, and conservation counselling.

Conservation action

Threatened birds are our top priority. Field researchers study the little-known habits and ecology of birds like Audouin's Gull (*Larus audouinii*) and Lear's Macaw (*Anodorhynchus leari*). Conservationists need accurate information if they are to design sound conservation plans; development agencies also need such data if they are to avoid unnecessary environmental damage.

ICBP carries out field projects all over the world, and nearly all involve a mixture of scientific research, educational work and the development of management plans for bird reserves.

Here, an ICBP field scientist checks a Maleo egg at one of the protected hatcheries established on Sulawesi.

ICBP has also launched a number of successful last-ditch efforts to bring back birds from the brink of extinction. On Mauritius, a joint captive breeding effort with the Jersey Wildlife Preservation Trust has saved the Mauritius Kestrel (*Falco punctatus*) and Pink Pigeon (*Nesoenas mayeri*), both found only on the island. On Cousin Island, ICBP's nature reserve in the Seychelles, the world population of the threatened Seychelles Warbler (*Acrocephalus sechellarum*) has increased tenfold under ICBP's care.

Habitat conservation is the key to the preservation of birds and also of entire ecosystems. ICBP undertakes surveys of critical areas for wildlife in close conjunction with other national and international conservation groups. Inventories of birdlife can be used as an index of the importance of habitats like wetlands for conservation; recommendations that would protect ecosystems and their genetic diversity are the results of field studies and surveys.

ICBP's management plan for the Maleo reserve is designed to improve the birds' breeding success and secure their future while also enabling the local people to benefit from the Maleo's potential as a food resource and tourist attraction.

Data-gathering

ICBP compiles up-to-date information on threatened birds and publishes it jointly with IUCN as the *Bird Red Data Book* — recognized internationally as the most authoritative reference source available on the status of the world's threatened species.

Thanks to the international network, ICBP generates detailed information on many other conservation issues; for example, islands, migratory birds, and important sites for birds. Expeditions and surveys also produce data and recommendations which must be accessible to specialists as well as other organizations if they are to be followed

Detailed information about the status of endangered species and their habitats is collected by ICBP and collated and stored in computer data-banks.

up successfully. All such information is electronically stored and analysed on a computerized data-base at ICBP headquarters. Special reports using this information help planners make crucial decisions on the conservation of fragile ecosystems.

Education

Birds make ideal symbols with which to stimulate popular awareness and concern for the environment, and ICBP's conservation activities always include a strong educational thrust. Colourful posters on migration or unique birdlife bring home the conservation message in communities where it is otherwise unknown. ICBP also produces popular books and pamphlets in many countries and languages, designed to arouse an interest in the beauty of birds and through them an appreciation of the value of conservation as well.

The involvement of local people is an essential part of all ICBP activities in the field.

High-level contacts with governments and institutions in Third World countries are important prerequisites for effective conservation work. Here, HRH Prince Philip, President of WWF, and Paul Goriup, ICBP Programme Director, present the ICBP/IUCN 'Red Book' of Africa's threatened birds to Barthélémi Vaohita, ICBP's representative in Madagascar.

Local experts are included in expeditions wherever possible to ensure that conservation benefits endure after the end of a project. Conservation research can lead to the formation of local bird clubs, which can then blossom into a grassroots commitment to conservation.

Conservation counselling

Government support for conservation is essential if birds and wildlife are to be protected. An ever-growing number of Third World nations have signed the major international conservation treaties; CITES, the Ramsar, Bonn and Bern Conventions, and the United Nations Charter for Nature. Promoting accession to these treaties is an important part of ICBP's mission.

Legislation is half the battle; but implementation and enforcement is even more important. Where government agencies fail to fulfil their legal obligations towards conservation, ICBP uses its international influence to make high-level representations on behalf of birds and wildlife. Such interventions also draw international attention to the problem and are always based on reliable reports from ICBP's contacts in the countries concerned. ICBP endorses the World Conservation Strategy and promotes policies that benefit local people as well as wildlife.

A Partnership for the future

Wildlife and humans are dependent upon each other if either is to face a viable future. All of us share the responsibility for undertaking the immense environmental task that lies ahead. Together we can preserve a beautiful and living earth. By ensuring that no more birds follow the Dodo, ICBP is working to guarantee your future. That is what the *Save the Birds* Campaign is all about.

Already, through the purchase of this book, you are supporting three of ICBP's high-priority conservation projects:

Project 'Wetland'

The immense Okavango delta in Botswana, the largest wetland in southern Africa, is home to millions of birds. It is also under threat from agricultural development. ICBP is developing management strategies that will enable men and birds to exist side by side in harmony.

Project 'Forest'

Hundreds of unique plants and animals are confined to the vanishing Atlantic forests of Brazil. These remarkable remnant forests and their inhabitants must be saved: they are an irreplaceable part of the world's genetic resource.

Project 'Island'

The flightless Kagu lives only on the island of New Caledonia, where it has been forced to the brink of extinction by feral animals and forest destruction. By saving the Kagu, ICBP is preserving a unique natural heritage.

You can give further support to these and many other ICBP projects around the world by making a donation to —
Save the Birds World Account
Account number 30509000
Barclays Bank PLC
Bene't Street, Cambridge CB2 3PZ

A challenge to save the wetlands

Every autumn, birds by the million leave their breeding areas and head for safer wintering grounds. Their annual journeys cover thousands of kilometres, across oceans, deserts and national frontiers. Where land and water meet — along coasts, around lakes, in flood-plains and estuaries — the flying visitors gather to feed and rest. Wetlands are especially important for huge flocks of migratory waterfowl and waders. To protect migratory birds, ICBP is committed to wetland conservation.

Wetlands are vital for humans, too. In their natural state they could offer us a never-ending supply of food to feed our growing populations. Wetlands also provide essential services like flood and pollution control. But all these advantages are destroyed when we 'improve' the land by draining and filling marshes and lakes.

Most important, wetlands are a major source of one of life's basic requirements — water. We need unpolluted wetlands to fill our reservoirs with fresh, clean water. Birds can tell us a lot about the quality of wetlands and the water we drink. If we want a guaranteed supply of pure water for ourselves and future generations, we must protect our lakes and swamps. Saving the birds is a good place to begin.

A challenge to save the forests

Tropical forests contain the greatest biological variety in the world. Complex relationships have evolved between myriad plants, animals and insects, each making a unique contribution to the health of the whole system. Some of the world's rarest birds live here. At the phenomenal rate at which tropical forests are being destroyed, they could easily become extinct.

Many ICBP research studies are aimed at important forest areas in Africa, South America, and Southeast Asia. Although ICBP's special interest is in the birds, all sorts of other wildlife have been protected as a result of its actions. Sometimes spectacular birds can become symbols for saving ecosystems.

The whole biosphere depends on the tropical forests that girdle our planet. They pump out vast quantities of oxygen and water vapour, influencing climates thousands of kilometres away. Without them, global climatic patterns could change, resulting in catastrophic effects on the food-producing zones of the earth and threatening the livelihood of a large proportion of mankind. Protecting our tropical forests will save more than just birds — we all need them.

A challenge to save nature

A Galapagos Buzzard alights on a Giant Turtle. Both are found only on the Galapagos Islands; since Darwin's visit, the symbol of evolution. Isolated over long periods of time on islands like the Galapagos, unique species of wildlife evolved together into highly specialized communities in perfect equilibrium. Over the last thousand years, man's intrusion has invariably unbalanced sensitive island ecosystems, and in numerous cases has devastated the endemic flora and fauna.

Islands are ICBP's top priority. An holistic approach aimed at saving ecosystems, not just species, can succeed on islands because of their limited area. Island resources must be managed so that they will continue to benefit humans and all other wildlife forever. Birds tell us about the state of an island's environment and which islands should be protected first.

Islands surrounded by ocean are a microcosm of our planet. We live on an island in the universe, highly specialized according to chemical and biological conditions found nowhere else. Viewed from space, our earth floats alone in a void — beautiful and fragile, the ultimate island of life.

Index

JILL C. HALLIDAY

Throughout the index, page numbers in normal type (57) refer to the main text; page numbers in bold type (**57**) refer to illustrations and to information in the captions to illustrations.

379

Index

Acknowledgements

PRO NATUR, ICBP and the publisher would like to express their sincere thanks to the many photographers and illustrators whose creative skills and dedication have contributed so much to this book.

Photographers

Photographers are credited by descending order of the base line of each photograph. Where two or more photographs lie on the same base line, credits read left to right. Photographers' agents and other sources are abbreviated as follows:

Ardea/AR; Bruce Coleman/BC; Frank Lane/FL; Natural Science Photos/NSP; Australasian Nature Transparencies/ANT; Eric and David Hosking/H; Aquila/AQ; Oxford Scientific Films/OSF; Biofoto/ BO; Biofotos/BS; Planet Earth Pictures/PE; Nature Photographers/N; Photobank/PH; Jacana/J; Rex Features/RF; Press-Tige Pictures/PT; Swift Picture Library/SPL; Robert Harding Picture Library/RH; Photri/P; Stockphotos/S; The Image Bank/IB; US Fish & Wildlife Service/FW; Vireo/VI; Visum/V; Magnum/M; Rapho/RA; *Stern* magazine/ST; Mauritius/MS; World Wildlife Fund/WWF.

Cover photograph by Hans Reinhard

2–3 M. Wiechmann 4–5 R. König 6–7 F. Lanting 8–9 G. Ziesler 10–11 F. Pölking 12 B. Kerber 14 H. Hagen 16 U. Walz, Air France, W. Hockenjos 17 F. Mayer/M, Anders/ST 18 G. Gerster 19 T. Mayer, D. Smiths 20 Höpker/ST, H. Sund 21 K. Schubert, M. Friedel 22 E. Hartman/M 23 NASA, Krämer/ST 24–25 G. Ziesler 26 T. Thomas 28 R. & D. Keller/ANT, B. Bingel/RF, J. D. Mikkelsen/ BO, B. & C. Calhoun/BC 30 W. Möller/AR, E. Hosking, P. Davey/BC, H. Silvester/RA 33 H. Reinhard/BC, R. van Nostrand/FL, M. Price/ANT, R. Austing/FL 34 J. Hawkins/H, J. Hancock/AQ 35 P. Krauss/ANT, G. Moon/FL 36 N. Fain/NSP, Photri, R. Crane/N, Champlong-Arepi/RF 37 K. Carlson/N, S. Werner, R. Lockyer/S, E. Jones/ AQ, I. Miles/IB, J. Mackinnon 38–39 M. Withers/ FL 40 G. Le Grande 42 K. Schubert, C. Walker/ NSP, H. Landvogt 44 H. Dossenbach 45 H. Hagen 46 J. Resch, Photri 47 J. Resch 48 NASA 49 H. Landvogt 52 P. Steyn/AR 56 Thomann/ST, J. Fünfstück, A. Burnhauser 57 H. Hagen, J-P. Ferrero/AR, P. Jones 58 H. Landvogt, H. Landvogt 59 D. Hadden, D. & M. Plage/OSF, K. Schubert, H. Landvogt 62 Astrophoto Laboratories 64–65 NASA 68–69 K. Schubert 70 B. Osborne, D. Wilson/H 73 J. De Korte, H. Dossenbach/AR 75 S. Bainbridge, P. Farrell, D. Hadden 77 K. Fink/AR, S. Gooders/AR 79 T. Ennis/N, E. & D. Hosking, J. Varela 80 H. Hasegawa, H. Hasegawa 81 H. Hasegawa 83 Fievet/J, W. Suter, S. Broni, P. Steyn/AR 85 B. Nelson, D. Merton, D. Merton 86 Greenpeace, Ducatez/MS, W. Steche/V 87 E. Hosking, D. & K. Urry/AR 88–89 C. Carvalho/FL 90 E. & D. Hosking 91 C. Buxton & A. Price/OSF 93 J. & D. Bartlett/OSF, C. Walker/NSP 95 M. Hill/N 96 M. Soper 97 S. Krasemann/BC, S. McCutcheon/FL 98–99 N. Devore/BC 100 Menuhin/PE 102 J. Hoogesteger/BS, R. Crane/N 103 M. Harris/N 104 J. Watson 105 J. Watson, M. England/AR 106 J. Watson, A. & E. Diamond, D. Houston/BC 107 A. Cheke 108 D. Scott/N 109 F. Robiller, J. Brunet/J., C. Veitch/PH, J. Blossom/OSF 111 N. Snyder, N. Snyder 112 P. Evans 113 C. Kepler 114 C. Kepler 115 C. Kepler, C. Kepler 116 W. Townsend/BC 119 A. Diamond, M. Soper/ANT, P. Steyn/AR 121 J. Watson 122 A. Diamond, St. Vidler/MS 123 C. Veitch/PH, H. Watkins/PT, D.

Merton 124–125 G. Doré/SPL 126 R. & D. Keller/ ANT, J. Mason/AR 127 G. Ziesler, P. Ward/ NSP, M. Chinnery/NSP 129 J. Fennell/BC, M. Soper 130 AD. SF 131 A. Lindau/AR, R. Matthews/PE 133 Y. Suzuki, A. & E. Diamond 134 G. Behrens 135 G. Cubitt/BC 136 R. Bunge/AR 137 K. Schubert, J. & G. Harrison/AQ 138 S. Fraser, K. Wüstenberg, A. Cheke 139 A. Maywald, W. Steche/V, Rex Features 140–141 C. Imboden 143 N. Callow/N, S. Gooders/AR, P. Davey, R. Kemp/NSP 144 G. Ziesler 145 C. Walker/NSP, B. Kerber, J. Mackinnon 147 M. Fogden/BC 148 M. Harris 149 M. Harris 150 F. Erize/BC 151 F. Gohier/AR 153 R. Müller, A. Fatras/AR 154 E. Bezzel, D. Botting/BC, R. Müller 155 U. Hirsch/BC 157 E. & D. Hosking, M. Soper/BC, C. Veitch/PH 158 D. Hadden, H. Axell 160 J. Archibald, J. Archibald 161 T. Komiya, T. Komiya 162 R. Douthwaite 163 M. Western, P. Davey/BC, J. Hancock/BC 164 B. Gibbs/NSP, L. Norström 165 J. & G. Harrison/ AQ, G. & H. Denzau, S. Gooders/AR 166 W. Steche/V 167 R. Kemp/NSP, D. & R. Sullivan/BC, F. Sunquist 168–169 D. Stock/M 170 E. Bezzel, S. Fraser 171 H. Dossenbach, G. Ziesler, A. Deane/BC 172 C. Imboden, L. Goldman/FW 173 S. Wilbur/FW, C. Imboden 175 M. Ridley, R. van Nostrand 176 S. Fraser, J. & D. Bartlett/BC 177 J. van Wormer/BC 179 T. Tilford/PT, C. Imboden, E. & D. Hosking 180 J-P. Ledant 181 G. Gerster, G. Mangold 182–183 B. Sage/AQ 184 A. Maywald, H. Landvogt, H. Landvogt, H. Landvogt 185 A. Edgar 187 H. Clark/N, H. Angel, D. McCaskill/NSP, P. Trötschel 188 P. Goriup 189 R. Vaughan/AR, P. Goriup 191 D. Roby/VI, W. Lankinen/BC, N. Tucker 192 M. Ridley, M. Ridley 195 A. Brewer/AR 196 A. Sugden, T. Tilford/PT 197 T. Tilford/PT 199 C. Veitch/PH 200 G. Moon/FL, D. Merton, C. Veitch/PH, D. Merton 201 C. Imboden, D. Merton 202 C. Imboden, N. Cattlin/FL 203 P. Davey, L. Brown/N, K. Wüstenberg 204 C. Meffert, J. Dubois/J 205 V. Kramer, G. Le Grande/BC, I. de Boroviczeny 206–207 J-P. Ferrero/AR 208 K. Bishop 209 S. Dalton/OSF, E. Lindgren/AR 210 B. Rogers/BS, J. Dunning/AR, P. Morris/AR 211 A. Greensmith/AR, C. Banks/NSP, H. Angel 212 B. Coates/BC 213 D. Cam/RF, D. Hadden 215 B. Coates/BC, A. Compost/BC 217 D. Watling, D. Watling, D. Watling 218 F. Futil/BC, D. Bishop, W. Weisser/AR 220 D. Hadden 221 C. Frith/BC 223 N. Tomalin/BC, CNRS/J 224 ICBP, S. Stuart 225 D. Richards, A. Lévêque 226 M. Fogden/BC 227 D. Dickins 228 C. König 229 B. Burbidge/N 230 K. Fink/AR, Photri 232 G. Ziesler 233 L. McIntyre 234 A. Eddy/NSP 235 D.

Dickins, S. Bisserot/N 236 P. Steele, F. Sunquist 237 H. Sylvester/RA 238–239 G. Ziesler 240 T. Tilford/PT 241 J. Shaw/BC, E. Bezzel, M. England/AR 243 P. Goriup, P. Goriup, F. Goriup 244 U. Hirsch/BC, E. Bezzel, U. Hirsch 247 D. Merton, D. Merton 248 D. Houston, A. Cheke 249 D. Kinzler/FL, H. Axell 250–251 J- P. Ferrero/AR 252 E. Bezzel 253 L. Marigo/BC, A. Weaving/AR, J. & D. Bartlett/OSF, 255 P. Goriup, H. Axell, E. Hosking 256 E. Lindgren/AR 257 L. Robinson/FL, L. Robinson/FL 259 H. Dossenbach 261 C. Kepler 262 A. & E. Diamond, P. Jones 263 S. Fraser, E. Bezzel 264–265 D. Dickins, 266 M. Kahl/BC, S. Robert /AR 267 F. Labhardt, S. Fraser, J. Gooders/AR 269 M. Sallaberry, A. Glade 270 T. & P. Gardner/ANT, P. Ward/NSP 271 E. Hosking 272 J-P. Ferrero/AR 273 G. Chapman/AR, R. & D. Keller/ANT 274 J. & S. Bottomly/AR 275 E. & D. Hosking 276 Thomann/ST, K. Schubert 277 K. Schubert, R. Schreiber, W. Rawlings/RH 278–279 J. Mason/ AR 280 H. Schmitt/ST, J. Launois/RA, Thomann/ ST 281 E. Liebermann, E. Liebermann 282 M. Hamblin/FL 283 R. Mills/AQ, S. Meyers 284 C. Langsbury/BC 285 A. Saunier, H. Reinhard 286 S. Werner, Jacana 287 M. Leach/N, M. Scott 288–289 H. & G. Denzau 291 L. Schack-Nielsen/BO, G. Ziesler 292 J. Weber, B. & C. Alexander 293 B. & C. Alexander, Wild Nature/ ANT, S. Jonasson/FL 294 J. Free, J. Daniels/AR, P. Davey/FL 295 B. Sage/AQ, M. Harris, J. & D. Bartlett/OSF 296 Art Directors 297 J. Simon/BC, L. Norström 298 Photri, D. Smith/N, S. Bisserot/ N 299 J. Swedberg/AR, J. Reichholf, J. Resch 300 AGW 301 W. Rawlings/RH, R. & D. Keller/ ANT, L. & T. Bomford/OSF 302 C. Ott/BC, B. Wiklund/BO 303 K. Wüstenberg 305 M. Freeman/BC 306 S. McCutcheon/FL, S. Roberts/ AR 307 J-P. Ferrero/AR, A. Schliack 308 H. Sund 309 T. & P. Gardner/ANT, R. & D. Keller/ANT, N. Cattlin/FL 310 I. Beames/AR 311 F. Lanting, C. Fear 312 T. Inskipp, F. Sunquist 313 C. Frith/ BC, A. & E. Diamond 314 E. & D. Hosking 317 NASA 318 Smithsonian Institution 320 K. Schubert, C. Carvalho/FL, N. Devore/BC, G. Doré/SPL, C. Imboden, D. Stock/M, B. Sage/AQ, J-P. Ferrero/AR, G. Ziesler, J-P. Ferrero/AR 321 W. Steche/V, J. Swedberg/AR, H. Sund, J-P. Ferrero/AR, C. Fear, C. Frith/BC, E. & D. Hosking 324 R. Müller 325 D. Klees 326 K. Schubert, H. Angel 328 H. Reinhard 329 D. Houston, A. Cheke 330 B. Helander, J. Foott/BC, N. Yoshio 331 E. Kuyt, E. Kuyt 332 C. von Treuenfels, J. Foott/BC 333 B. Sage/AQ, WWF-H. Jungius/BC 334 I. Neumann 335 W. Volz 336 G. Ziesler 337 B Turner/FL 338 G. Doré/BC, M. Read/SPL

339 Hincjosa/RF, H. Mante/ZEFA 340 C. Howes/ PE, (Composite) RSPCA 341 RSPB, J. Mason/AR, S. Bisserot 342 B. Gibbons/AR, J. Mason/AR 343 G. Ziesler/BC, G. Ziesler/BC, G. Hyde/H 344 D. Avon/AR D. Curl/OSF, D. Saunders/OSF 345 K. Scholey/PE, G. Langsbury/BC, M. Read/SPL 346 M. Read/SPL, R. Vaughan/AR, E. Hosking 349 J. & G. Harrison/AQ, D. Whitaker/AQ, G. Ziesler/ BC 351 R. Vaughan/AR, D. MacCaskill/NSP, E. & D. Hosking 352 P. Skerry/N, J. Hawkins/H 353 R. Mills/AQ 354 L. Brown/AR 355 T. Ennis/N 356 J. Burton/BC, M. Read/SPL 357 K. Wothe/ BC, J. & S. Bottomly/AR 358 F. Blackburn/N, C. Molyneux/BC 359 A. Cleave/N, C. Gomersall/ RSPB 360 H. Frawley/NSP, C. Imboden 361 H. Angel, M. Hill/N 362 Shell Photographic Library, Shell Photographic Library 363 M. Smith/RF, G. Langsbury/BC 364 H. Angel, A. Shay/OSF, T. Andrewartha/N 365 G. Langsbury/BC, P. Helo/ BC, D. Whitaker/AQ, B. Turner/FL 366 A. Cleave/N, P. Hunnam/PE, D. Hosking 367 G. Langsbury/BC, E. & D. Hosking, R. Beecroft/ NSP, J. Hawkins/H 368 A. Baldacchino/RSPB, C. Gomersall/RSPB 370 ICBP, A. Compost 371 ICBP 372–373 K. Schubert, U. Walz 374–375 K. Schubert, L. McIntyre 376–377 Jacobi/ST, F. Pölking 378 K. Schüle 380 H. Hagen 382 S. Meyers 383 U. Walz 384 K. Schubert.

PRO NATUR, ICBP and the publisher wish to express their sincere thanks to Wella AG for their sponsorship of worldwide photographic reproduction rights.

Special thanks are also due to the paper manufacturer Carliere del Garda, Riva, Italy, for their support for the world campaign and for the supply of their acid-free paper.

Artists

Portraits of endangered birds featured in **Earth's Great Ecosystems** (66–287) were painted by Alistair Robertson.

Portraits of rare and endangered British birds in **Saving Britain's Birdlife** (337–368) were painted by Robert Gillmor.

Maps throughout were prepared by Eugene Fleury.

Diagrams, technical illustrations, composite illustrations and additional bird portraits were painted by the following artists:

26–27 Trevor Boyer/Linden Artists 29 (Aerofoil) Mike Saunders, (bird) Trevor Boyer/Linden Artists 31 Trevor Boyer/Linden Artists 32 Trevor Boyer/ Linden Artists 35 John Rignall/Linden Artists 41 Mike Saunders 43 Mike Saunders 45 Mike Saunders 47 Trevor Boyer/Linden Artists 50–51 (upper) Mike Saunders, (lower) Trevor Boyer/Linden Artists 52 (Birds) Mick Loates/Linden Artists, (flowers) John Rignall/Linden Artists 53 Trevor Boyer/Linden Artists 54–55 (Landscapes) Mike Saunders, (inset birds) Trevor Boyer/Linden Artists 56–57 Trevor Boyer/Linden Artists 60–61 Mike Saunders 63 Mike Saunders 72 Trevor Boyer/Linden Artists 90–91 Trevor Boyer/Linden Artists 101 Mike Saunders 112 John Rignall/Linden Artists 115 John Rignall/Linden Artists 117 Maurice Pledger/Linden Artists 120 John Rignall/ Linden Artists 149 John Rignall/Linden Artists 186 John Rignall/Linden Artists 214 John Rignall/Linden Artists 216 John Rignall/Linden Artists 224 Original painting by Norman Arlott for ICBP 231 John Rignall/Linden Artists 274 (Map) Eugene Fleury, (inset bird) Trevor Boyer/Linden Artists 303 Mike Saunders 305–316 (Silhouettes) Stefan Werner 310 (Map) Eugene Fleury, (inset bird) Trevor Boyer/Linden Artists 319 Mike Saunders 320–321 Stefan Werner 322–323 Trevor Boyer/ Linden Artists 347 Hayward Art Group.

Personal thanks: Rudolf Schreiber

No project of this complexity can succeed without the help, support and encouragement of a great many people.

First of all I would like to thank my colleagues: Christoph Imboden, for his confidence and unwavering support; Martyn Bramwell, who has guided the project and been at my side through countless presentations; Tony Diamond, for his patience and his major contribution to this work, and our 'national authors' for their special contributions to the various international co-productions.

My special thanks are due to my closest colleagues Helga Schaer, Siglinde Böllmann, Nikolaus Dahl and Stefan Werner for their loyalty and hard work, and to Gerd Müller for his design direction.

I owe a particular debt of gratitude to my friends Ludwig Darmstädter and Paul Greinader for the contribution of their management expertise, and to Peter Winters and Johannes Zindel for their legal advice.

My thanks go also to many old and new friends for their advice and encouragement; especially to Bo Streiffert, Christian Strasser, Malte Bischoff, Klaus Richter, Rüdiger Ruoss, Friedrich Sandmann and Wolfgang Schröder.

Thanks are also due to the publishers of *GEO* and *Stern* magazines, who have given valuable assistance in photo-acquisitions; to several regional breweries of the German Federal Republic who contributed towards the research and development costs; and to Wella AG who sponsored the international photographic reproduction rights.

Finally I wish to join with Tony Diamond in expressing sincere thanks to all the scientists and conservationists around the world who have given freely of their time and expertise to answer queries, check facts and verify and update our species accounts. Our thanks are due in particular to the following:

George Archibald, Brian Bell, David Bishop, Anthony Cheke, John Cooper, Bob Dowsett, Peter Evans, Sylvia Fitzgerald, Anthony Gaston, Derek Goodwin, James Hancock, Mike Harris, Björn Helander, Hiroshi Hasegawa, Carl Jones, Alan Kemp, Cam and Kay Kepler, Stephen Kress, Ernie Kuyt, Anne LaBastille, Mark Leighton, Andrew MacFarlane, Phil Moors, Norman Myers, Bryan Nelson, John Ogden, David Peakall. Christopher Perrins, Iola Price, Hugh Robertson, Ralph Schreiber, Derek Scott, David Snow, Ron Summers, Noel Snyder, Simon Stuart, Mike Swales, Dick Watling, Evelyn Weinstein, David Wells, Jim Wiley, Michael Wilson and David Wingate.

SAVE THE BIRDS is the first worldwide campaign created by PRO NATUR. It was developed in collaboration with the International Council for Bird Preservation (ICBP) and will be implemented in close association with national and local nature conservation organizations in each country of publication.

Behind this initiative lies the concept of promoting a worldwide alliance in defence of our threatened environment, not only because global problems demand a global response but also because each and every one of us is bound to be more highly motivated and more optimistic about the outcome if we know that like-minded people throughout the world are dedicated to the same ideal.

That there is indeed such a worldwide desire for co-operation beyond the boundaries of individual countries and continents has already been demonstrated by the SAVE THE BIRDS team — the authors, illustrators, scientists and publishers who have committed their time, effort and skills to this project.

The global campaign, however, can only realize its full potential through local action and the commitment of many, both now and in the future.

Looking to the future, PRO NATUR is already planning further campaigns to follow SAVE THE BIRDS. The PRO NATUR team develops not only books but also many other products; it provides advice to businesses and industries on the development of ecologically sound products, and it co-ordinates publicity and public information campaigns — all with the aim of protecting our environment and creating a society that understands and respects ecological principles and demands that the resources of our world are used wisely and with thought for the future.

Our aim is to encourage an awareness of the importance of a healthy environment, so that in all countries of the world, conservation will become an integral and natural part of our whole approach to life.

PRO NATUR GmbH, Frankfurt/Main, West Germany.